The Turnaround Experience

Real-World Lessons in Revitalizing Corporations

Frederick M. Zimmerman
University of St. Thomas
St. Paul, Minnesota

McGraw-Hill, Inc.

New York   St. Louis   San Francisco   Auckland   Bogotá
Caracas   Hamburg   Lisbon   London   Madrid
Mexico   Milan   Montreal   New Delhi   Paris
San Juan   São Paulo   Singapore
Sydney   Tokyo   Toronto

HD
58.8
.Z55
1991

Library of Congress Cataloging-in-Publication Data

Zimmerman, Frederick Michael.
    The turnaround experience : real-world lessons in revitalizing
corporations / Frederick M. Zimmerman.
        p.   cm.
    Includes bibliographical references and index.
    ISBN 0-07-072899-2 :
    1. Corporate turnarounds.   2. Industrial management.   3. Quality
of products.   I. Title.
HD58.8.Z55   1991
658.1'6 – dc20   91-3509
                                                                           CIP

1 2 3 4 5 6 7 8 9 0   DOC/DOC   9 8 7 6 5 4 3 2 1

ISBN 0-07-072899-2

*The sponsoring editor for this book was Betsy N. Brown, the editing supervisor
was Olive H. Collen, and the production supervisor was Suzanne W. Babeuf.
It was set in Baskerville by McGraw-Hill's Professional Book Group composition
unit.*

Printed and bound by R. R. Donnelley & Sons Company.

To
Joanell Eleanor Felker Zimmerman
Frederick Josef Zimmerman
Carita Michelle Zimmerman
Christina Joanell Zimmerman
Brigitte Aimee Zimmerman
Hans Anthony Zimmerman
and
all the people who have tried
to do their best,
including

Charles Nash, Walter Chrysler, Lew Veraldi, Henry Leland,
George Romney, Fred Zeder, Hans Mathias, Douglas Fraser,
Dr. John Cich, Rudy Jones, Charles Wiman, Ray Kline,
Bill Laughlin, Jim Russel, Karl Hohlmaier, John Povolny,
Tom Rowe, Jim Boaz, Bud Trisko, Paul Moor,
Lillian Gilbreth, Bud Ruvelson, Frank Gilbreth, Larry Horsch,
Mary Parker Follett, Dwight Jereczek, Denny Earley,
Jim Boice, Dr. Stacy Roback, Harold Steele, Rick Passek,
Dan Carroll, John Kraemer, Tom Perry, John Kokesh,
Steve Helmueller, John Kreiner, Robert L. Nichols,
Bob Brattland, Bill Iacoe, Ron Bennett, John Walker,
Jim Benson, Glen Thommes, Don Stolz, Clarence Shallbetter,
Franz Mueller, Bruce Erickson, Ray Willis, Marty Swerin,
John Adams, Francis W. How, Lee Radermacher,
Mary Ann Savage, Judith Adams, Ronaldo Custodio,
Gary King, Rahn Worcuff, Reverend Jerome Kern,
Jean-Luc LaHouze, Joseph Baglio, Barbara Shallbetter,
Lee Lucas, Mel Hazelwood, Dan Stenoien, Tom Glisczinski,
George Gleeson, Fred Wagner, Luke Radtke,
Lillian Zimmerman, Frederick Otto Zimmerman,
Ruth N. Zimmerman,

and all the nurses and staff at
Minneapolis Children's Hospital

Contents

Part 2. The Strategic Advantage of Low-Cost Operation 37

Part 3. The Value of Product Differentiation 115

Preface

The Turnaround Experience is an account of a longitudinal study of 16 business turnaround endeavors—successful and unsuccessful. The strategies employed in successful turnarounds and the managerial skills and character traits present among successful turnaround agents are compared and contrasted with those of unsuccessful turnaround efforts.

The proposition examined here is that the successful business strategy for turnarounds focuses on improving a firm's effectiveness as a low-cost producer of increasingly differentiated quality products. A corollary to this is that successful turnarounds involve leaders who focus on operations, possess strong ethical values, have good personal reputations, and follow the principles of fair play in dealing with employees, creditors, suppliers, and customers.

Sixteen attempted turnarounds were examined in this study. The cases were drawn from occurrences during the period from 1902 to 1988 in the automobile and agricultural equipment industries. Data covering many years—usually 20 years—were examined for each case. Specific criteria and measurement procedures were used to select the cases for study and to classify the cases as successful or unsuccessful. Quantitative and narrative information, business histories, and interviews were used to examine strategies and key functional operations, including marketing, manufacturing, product development, and finance.

There were several key findings: Successful turnarounds often experienced more dramatic initial declines in revenue and deeper loss rates than unsuccessful turnarounds did. Unsuccessful firms were less severely affected by dramatic downturns but declined gradually over many years. Successful turnarounds were much more proficient in both manufacturing efficiency and production development than were unsuccessful cases. Most successful turnaround agents were product people or engineers and had extensive experience in the industry in question. Unsuccessful turnarounds were more likely to be headed by marketing or finance people who had comparatively little experience in the industry. Successful turnarounds usually involved a constant process of incremental improvement and focused on operational issues. Unsuccessful turnarounds often involved major dramatic shifts in products, businesses, or markets served. Successful turnaround agents were able to instill values, they reduced their own compensation during the period of crisis, and they shared credit for accomplishments with others. Unsuccessful turnaround agents generally did not exhibit these characteristics.

Frederick M. Zimmerman

Acknowledgments

Many people played roles in the creation of this book. The process began with my father, Frederick Otto Zimmerman, who was obliged to leave engineering school during the Great Depression to become an automobile mechanic. Later, he became an industrial arts teacher and then a quality assurance specialist. His deep understanding of product quality, coupled with his technical knowledge of the cars he repaired, instilled in me an interest in the link between manufacturing methods and economic survival.

My early years with IBM—in three branch offices, a large manufacturing plant, and the headquarters in New York—exposed me to the excellent leadership of a highly capable management team that was dedicated to differentiated products, low cost of operations, organizational professionalism, and fair play on the part of both managers and workers. I am particularly indebted to C. P. Trisco, Ralph Pickard, Luke Radtke, Denny Early, Lee Lucas, Ray Kline, and Jim Boaz for their constant guidance and exemplary leadership.

The difficult recession of the early 1980s, when I was serving as CEO of an industrial automation company, impressed upon me the need to understand more about the process of industrial survival. We did manage to sell some systems, and the company continued. But the experience left me convinced that we needed a more scientific understanding of the survival process. In this regard, I am indebted to two of our investors, Larry Horsch and Bud Ruvelson, whose sound advice, constant wisdom, and ethical standards encouraged the firm to make considerable progress during the most difficult economic times since the 1930s.

In 1982, I returned to the University of Minnesota to complete graduate work I had started earlier. By chance, the doctoral program office assigned Professor Andrew H. Van de Ven as my adviser. I cannot fully express my gratitude. As an older graduate student with mainly industrial experience, I was ill-equipped to effectively handle the assignments before me. Professor Van de Ven not only was patient, he was inspirational. His deep insights into organizational behavior, along with his thorough knowledge of the literature in the field and his observations as a corporate board member, provided a source of new information to complement my own observations of the industrial world. In industry or in academe, I have met few people I respect more. I also wish to extend my thanks to my other advisers, Professors W. Bruce Erickson, Raymond Willis, Jim Simler, and George Green (who really had the idea for this manuscript), and to A. K. Wickesberg (who instilled in all of us an appreciation for historical study of the process of management). I am also indebted to my old friends John Adams and Clarence Shallbetter for sharing their perceptions of economic processes and the role that values and character traits play in the unfolding of key events.

I also wish to thank my colleagues at the University of St. Thomas, particularly John Povolny, for his added insights stemming from his years of experience as a vice president of 3M, and Marlene Houliston and Steve Helmueller, for handling so many of the departmental responsibilities during the preparation of the manuscript. Special thanks are in order for Marilyn Magee-Powell, editor of the *Journal of Applied Manufacturing Systems*, for her professional assistance. Special appreciation is also in order for Olive Collen and Betsy Brown of McGraw-Hill for their patient editing of this manuscript.

Most of all, I wish to thank my wife, Joanell, who endured many responsibilities associated with an extended illness in our family and still remained cheerful and supportive while her husband completed this work. As the mother of five wonderful children, a professional social worker, and foster mother to over twenty other children, Joanell is a master of organization in her own right.

Introduction

Over the past decade, U.S. trade deficits have run at record levels, sometimes $18 billion in a single month. Bank failures have reached near-depression levels. The agricultural sector has experienced severe decline. Several key industries continue to operate in a depressed state and are now joined by some of the previously glamorous high-tech industries. Trade deficits have improved only marginally in spite of a shrinking dollar while capital markets have become increasingly volatile. Unprecedented consumer debt, government deficits several times the amounts formerly regarded as astronomical, the quick transition of the United States from the world's largest creditor to its largest debtor, volatile capital markets, monumental trade deficits, and a plethora of unfriendly and underanalyzed corporate takeovers, all provide testimony that our world economy, though prosperous, lacks equilibrium.

Manufacturing Still Matters

As with many other sociotechnical system problems, questions surface regarding the cause of economic difficulties. Is it the lagging character of production capability? Or, is it the increasing burden it must bear? Should production be increased? Or, is it necessary to reduce the expenditures of the nonproducing part of the system? Perhaps most important, is the present situation largely a matter for public policy or are the remedies best left to individual managers and companies?

Those sharing the practical view of economics argue that the performance of the entire economy is highly influenced by the performance of individual firms. To improve the U.S. balance of payments, U.S. products have to be better and must be produced at lower cost. These are the practicalities that guide firms. The key action variables are indi-

1

vidual characteristics of specific firms and they include such basics as product quality, production efficiency, organization, and leadership. Advocates of this perspective contend that there have been few across-the-board improvements in the U.S. economy. What has been accomplished is due to the competitive effectiveness of individual firms.

The deteriorating U.S. balance of payments during recent years has drawn particular attention to tangible production as the functional area of the economy most crucial for survival. Manufacturing and other forms of tangible production, along with essential maintenance services, provide the real economic wealth of the nation. Cohen and Zysman suggest that 40 to 60 percent of all jobs in the United States depend upon manufacturing alone. The following conclusions reflect their analysis:*

> The choices we make as a nation, the policies and priorities we choose, will determine whether the transition marks the end of a half century of American power and industrial leadership.... The argument of this book is straightforward. It can be summed up as follows:
>
> 1. There is no such thing as a postindustrial economy. Manufacturing matters. The wealth and power of the United States depends upon maintaining mastery and control of production.
>
> 2. Changes in the extent and forms of international competition coupled with the mass application of microelectronics-based technologies are revolutionizing production. The United States is not doing very well in this new international competition....
>
> 3. A flight offshore for cheap labor will not provide a winning long-term strategy; after a few rounds of product and process innovation, it will just compound the problem. A strategy of trying to hold onto the high value-added activities while subcontracting production to foreign producers who have a manufacturing edge defines the fast track to disaster. Over time American firms will not be able to control what they cannot produce.... (Cohen and Zysman 1987)

Some people suggest that the United States is so distinctive in the provision of services that it can build a viable comparative advantage based on financial, accounting, and other professional services. This question has to be dealt with factually. The stresses placed on the industrial economy of the Unites States soon permeate the service economy—some-

*Adapted from *Manufacturing Matters: The Myth of the Postindustrial Economy* by Stephen S. Cohen and John Zysman. Copyright © 1987 by Basic Books, Inc. Reprinted by permission of Basic Books, a division of HarperCollins Publishers Inc.

times with even greater ferocity. Only four of the world's fifty largest banks are American. They do not compare well with those in other major industrial countries as they are generally smaller and often lose money. The banking and finance industry is, in general, becoming the object of grave concern and the security industry is retrenching. Accounting firms are facing greater fee sensitivity as the shrinking number of separate corporations shop for greater value in accounting services. Major insurance firms are worrisome because of their heavy investments in junk bonds and overpriced office real estate. Highly leveraged consolidation continues to take place in the transportation industries. Even the nation's colleges and universities request ever-increasing allocations from government as they simultaneously attempt to pass on record tuition increases to the customers.

The future of the economy of the United States is inescapably tied to the efficiency and quality of its tangible production. In the interest of economic stability, a more favorable balance between production and consumption must be developed.

Improving the U.S. Economy...One Company at a Time

If the service economy is not a meaningful substitute for a strong basic economy, then the United States must ensure that those industries engaged in tangible production (agriculture, construction, extraction, and manufacturing) are well positioned for the future. The variation in performance of individual firms is so extensive that it is meaningless to talk about national programs when so many individual industrial companies produce low-quality goods at too high a cost. No single macropolicy can renew America's competitive strength—though some policies may be helpful. The most sensible economic policy is to gear for international competition by improving one company at a time.

Yet, because of differing perspectives, public policies have not always focused on improving the effectiveness of present industries. In response to the strains on local economies, many industrial communities have adopted vigorous programs to attract new industry to replace industrial jobs lost through plant closings or staff reductions. These programs are rarely helpful. Not enough industrial movement occurs to be significant, the approach does not build upon the strengths of the community, and it takes too long. In order to survive, steps must be taken that will ensure the competitiveness of present industries. To achieve economic stability, we must develop the industrial infrastructure of our respective countries one company at a time.

The development of industrial infrastructure one company at a time should be a primary objective of corrective efforts. The U.S. trade deficit will not be improved simply by changing the dollar's value. During the past decade, the United States' position in such critical products as machine tools has declined substantially. In 1976, approximately 96 percent of the machine tools sold in the United States were made here. Recently the U.S. position in computerized precision machine tools declined to a small fraction of the total market. Similarly, as American steel manufacturers shaved capacity, they also reduced the variety and sizes of steels and alloys provided. The American producer wishing to obtain specialty steels often must obtain them from overseas suppliers and at prices likely to increase in the future. For an increasing number of crucial industrial components, only a few suppliers (and in some cases, only one supplier) remain in the United States. Unfortunately, the U.S. negative trade balance has persisted so long that the infrastructures have shifted. Other countries now control production technology and expertise. It took considerable time for us to lose this production expertise. It will take some time for us to regain it. The recent "improvement" to an annualized deficit of over $100 billion, even when the dollar has severely depreciated, is hardly a favorable indicator.

Competition in a Global Economy

Improvement in the U.S. balance of payments depends on the ability to improve the competitive positions of the individual firms participating in strategically important industries. These influential strategic industries employ large numbers of people in activities related to the tangible production of goods (and services) most integral to the development of a strong industrial infrastructure. It is not practical to regain prosperity by diversifying into new areas where we have little experience. Instead, world economies must cultivate the skills necessary to restore the competitive edge of particular companies.

Improving the competitive position of the individual firm in strategic industries is the key remedy to the faltering economies of developed countries. As evidence for this proposition, we can observe which products are imported and which are made in the United States. One can hardly find an American TV set or an American videocassette recorder, but imported electric tools are quite rare. We are well aware of the penetration of the Japanese automobile, yet almost all U.S. major appliances are made here. The United States imports large quantities of textiles but not much carpet. When we examine the production processes employed in the manufacture of these various products, we see similarities between both imported and domestically produced goods. The same sorts of stampings, die castings, wires, switches, transmissions, actuators, and finishings used in the manufacture of major appliances, where the United States has almost no imports, are also used in automobiles where competition from imports is extensive. Small electric tools are made of some of the same materials and employ some of the same processes as do consumer electronics. Yet the United States makes most of its electric tools and imports almost all its small appliances. Clearly, the United States has the engineering and scientific capability to produce products at favorable costs in markets where the country is not doing well.

When we examine the characteristics of the markets where the United States has not done well, we quite often find that even before imports, inefficient or untrustworthy producers of mediocre products dominated the market. In contrast, the markets that have resisted imports are often populated by well-trained, efficient producers of high-quality products who maintain good relations with employees, suppliers, creditors, and customers. We must ask the question: Do foreign producers target intriguing markets or ineffective companies? Why should major industrial competitors from overseas tangle with efficient producers such as Maytag Corporation, Whirlpool Corporation, 3M Company, Loctite Corporation, or the Boeing Company, when less capable competitors inhabit other markets?

Conditioning individual companies for global competition is crucial to industrial survival. The threat to the viability of the company is a problem of social as well as economic concern. Few events destroy the dignity and self-confidence of people more than the loss of permanent employment. As the prospects for continued employment diminish, personal problems such as drinking or family difficulties emerge where they had not existed previously. Unfortunately, as this investigation will show, business failures often have a disproportionate effect on people who have served their company for many years, are above 40 in age, and, ironically, are the ones that the companies tried to keep until the very end because they were the best employees.

Turnarounds Are Multifaceted

The effect of business failure is widespread. Many other supplier and dealer organizations are also affected, as are financial and service institutions. The general community is affected in that when major companies close, the affordability of essential community services is inevitably reduced. Home prices decline, thus limiting mobility and making it difficult for even the most talented individuals to seek employment opportunities in new locations. The special skills developed by individuals, often in response to company needs, are frequently of limited value to other employers. Even those who have good work habits and valid training often have limited geographical or occupational alternatives.

Companies rarely fail because of any one single cause. Inept company management is certainly a factor in some situations. Though many variables are involved in turnaround success or failure, competent management can impact most of them. Management is the principal catalyst and the root of ultimate responsibility in the revival of troubled firms. But the workers, financial intermediaries, government, and the community also have their responsibilities. Characteristics of the economy, the quality and personal traits of the people hired by the company, the degree of support from the community, and many other factors help determine turnaround success.

Our understanding of turnarounds may involve unlearning some managerial concepts as well as assimilating new ideas. For much of the period following World War II, American industry experienced an enviable competitive situation. The rest of the industrial world was recovering from the destruction of its physical plant and the maiming of its work force while American industry, less affected by the war, survived and prospered. The managerial practices and conventions that were utilized during this artificial period of prosperity are seldom useful during turnaround attempts. Any analysis of turnarounds must therefore include a review of those managerial practices that were relevant during periods of less affluence (before 1940 and after 1980). Fortunately, some of the richest and most applicable managerial concepts were developed during these periods, and many of these were uniquely American.

How Do Firms Turn Around?

Not all firms are in trouble. Some are doing well, even after experiencing severe economic hardship. Yet, we have to respect the fact that the pace of economic change is rapid. International Harvester went from 103,000 employees to under 16,000 in less than 4 years. Computervision fell from having record earnings and being the industry leader in one of America's most emerging industries to a weak competitor with record losses in under 5 years. Control Data's employment dropped approximately 40 percent in 4 years. Several major industrial companies have become unwilling acquisition targets in part because it has been difficult for them to face global competition on their own. Many companies have been impacted by the economic stresses of the 1980s and before. Some have come back from disaster to become strong and viable world-class competitors, in some cases much stronger than before. Others have failed. There are many questions regarding the causes of decline of individual firms and the turnaround process. How does it happen? What kind of people achieve it? How many people are involved? What skills are necessary? What character traits are present? What resources are employed? How long does it take?

To the benefit of this inquiry, considerable research on turnaround management has already been conducted, and this research can be used as a foundation for further examination of the turnaround process. In addition, there have been many successful and unsuccessful attempts at rescuing companies facing economic stress, and much can be learned by studying previous attempts. A more detailed comparison of both successful and unsuccessful turnaround attempts over longer periods of time should allow us to gather some insights into how individual companies either failed or recovered.

The history of turnarounds is an encouraging one. All 16 companies examined here were in severe financial difficulty during critical periods of their history. Yet, one of these companies is now the largest in its industry, with nearly a 60 percent market share, and is known as one of the most advanced producers in the world. Another is the flagship line of one of the world's largest automobile producers. A third firm, after two narrow escapes from total disaster, became the most rapidly growing U.S. producer in its industry and operated at record profit levels for several years.

Other turnarounds were not successful. One failed turnaround attempt was experienced by a huge company that at one time was the fourth-largest firm in the country. Another firm survived two turnarounds and at one time emerged as perhaps the most efficient producer in its industry but later succumbed to ineffective management practices 70 years after the first turnaround and 30 years after the second. Sometimes, the turnarounds showed initial promise but did not last—usually because the practices that enabled the company to turn around were forsaken at a later stage under different management. The history of successful turnarounds provides many lessons for those involved in management generally. The practice of management can well benefit from a systematic review of past practices.

This analysis focuses on turnaround attempts in two manufacturing industries: automobiles and agricultural equipment. There are some historical reasons for choosing these two industries. The industries have some common traits in that they involve similar manufacturing skills, are reasonably capital intensive, and were at similar stages of growth during the periods examined. However, a more powerful reason is because a great deal more information was available on the personal characteristics and abilities of the people involved in turnaround efforts in these two industries. Both the automotive and agricultural equipment industries employ vast numbers of people, play major roles in the U.S. economy, and are currently faced with intense global competition.

While these automobile and agricultural equipment industries may be significantly different from some other types of industries such as service industries, during a period of crisis all industries have common concerns. These concerns usually involve questions about productivity, quality, integrity, and managerial training and experience. It is our hope that the lessons learned by the companies presented here will be of use to firms in other industries as well, so that they, too, are well positioned for continued growth. Because turnarounds take some time to unfold, we chose to look at these companies over a period of 20 years to fully understand the reasons behind success or failure. What we found was that three key factors were evident in each of the success stories: (1) a low-cost operation, (2) differentiated products, and (3) quality of leadership.

PART 1

The Individual Firm and the Turnaround Process

Companies do not have to fail. Even the most distressed companies can resurface to again become strong world-class competitors in their industries. If the survival of individual firms can be achieved, financial systems will be more stable, workers will have greater security, shareholders will receive a yield on their life savings, governments can afford to operate, and managers will achieve dignity commensurate with their performance. If the individual firm does fail, everyone is affected—it is merely a question of degree.

Survival, however, is an active process involving new skills blended with historical expertise, new strategies based on previous successes, and new products to serve more competitive markets. Survival is virtually impossible if nobody wants to change. Yet, too much change becomes traumatic and dysfunctional. Survival requires innovation, stamina, integrity, discipline, prudence, and sacrifice.

Too often, companies attempt to survive without modifying their behavior—an approach which most always ends in tragedy. Sometimes, companies delay too long waiting for a clearer picture of what should be done—another disaster. Occasionally, too much change is introduced too soon—a tactic which brings more confusion than progress. Other companies approach the turnaround process more systematically and achieve better results. Superior methods can save the firm. Inferior methods, employed at critical times, can destroy it.

Although the lessons relating to turnarounds have been learned before and are consistent with established theories of management, a troubled situation also carries with it some uniqueness and particular requirements. The skills to manage adversity are not entirely commonplace. The sharp contrasts between successful and unsuccessful turnaround experiences, coupled with the enormous social and political realities of a declining industrial infrastructure, provide evidence that remedial management is a skill worthy of cultivation, a skill needed not only for companies, but also for societies.

Part 1 examines the process of turnaround within a practical framework. Chapter 1 briefly introduces three key factors to a successful turnaround which should be of interest to managers, executives, board members, and employees. Chapter 2 discusses some common characteristics of troubled firms and suggests ways to recognize turnaround situations during earlier stages when actions have a greater potential for success. Chapter 3 examines the profit patterns of successful and unsuccessful firms in the automobile and agricultural equipment industries with the hope that the analysis will be helpful in other situations.

1

Three Key Factors in Successful Turnarounds

The practicing manager will be primarily interested in two basic questions: Is it possible for troubled companies to come back from difficulty to become strong economic contributors once again? How do they do it? The evidence gathered in this inquiry, along with the evidence gathered by others, suggests that it is possible for troubled companies to turn around. The successful companies studied here had no special advantages which were unavailable to the unsuccessful companies. Successes and failures emerged during the same economic times. The successful and unsuccessful companies were serving the same industries, and, in several cases, the unsuccessful firms were more established. All experienced adversity. Yet, some companies found a way to successfully emerge from adversity and others failed.

What the successful companies did to survive was a process of organizational learning involving an intricate combination of strategy, thrift, technical expertise and industrial experience superimposed on a framework of traditional morality, personal integrity, and clearly articulated, focused ideals. *The general proposition advanced here is that a successful business turnaround involves improving the company's position as a low-cost provider of increasingly differentiated products and services, along with the nurturing of an appropriate turnaround organization which is competent, possesses industry-oriented technical expertise, and employs a general sense of fair play in dealing with employees, creditors, suppliers, shareholders, and customers.* Successful turnarounds involve this very special form of leadership. A more detailed description of the model being described is that successful turnarounds are a function of three principal factors:

1. A strategy that focuses primarily on improving the firm's effectiveness as a *low-cost operator*. Low-cost operation implies the design of products and services for low-cost delivery, the attainment of high rates of efficiency, and the containment of overhead costs to below industry levels.

2. A strategy that focuses at a later stage on improving the firm's effectiveness as a provider of increasingly *differentiated products*. Producing differentiated products implies products with distinguishing features, high reliability, and significant performance, exceptional product quality, and the development of long-term continuity with the markets being served so that product differentiation can be recognized by potential buyers.

3. *Leadership* involves turnaround agents who have significant experience in the industry being served and in some technical function such as manufacturing or engineering, and who have a major propensity to focus on operational issues such as manufacturing, product development, and sales. Successful turnaround agents tend to have longer-term associations with the company and make incremental changes based on information which is appropriate to the decisions being made. Successful turnaround agents enjoy generally favorable personal reputations; employ a sense of fair play in dealing with employees, creditors, suppliers, and customers; and focus intensely on the important operational questions that are pertinent to the business the firm is in at the time.

Figure 1-1 provides a very brief outline of the turnaround process, including some of the subcomponents of the three principal factors listed above.

Many successful turnarounds possess all the subelements for a particular major factor such as low-cost operation or product differentiation, but some employ different combinations of subelements to achieve turnaround success. Again, it must be emphasized that even the best executed turnarounds are seldom effective in every respect. Similarly, unsuccessful turnarounds rarely fail in every respect. Turnarounds are a mixture of hundreds of partially developed successes and failures with the successful firms being more thorough and consistent.

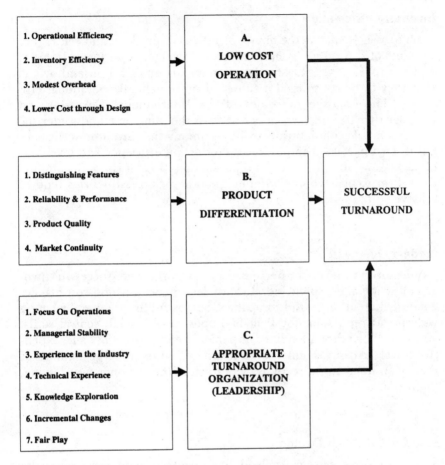

Figure 1-1. Framework of a successful turnaround process.

Tactics of Low-Cost Operation

Operational Efficiency

Operational efficiency refers to the amount of work that gets done in a day. General efficiency is required in all aspects of the organization, not just production. But, production efficiency relates keenly to the competitive edge of the firm and delineates the importance of well-organized factories. Operational efficiency implies up-to-date equipment, the systematic layout of production space, well-trained managers and workers, and other factors that relate to general efficiency.

Inventory Efficiency

Inventory efficiency is the ability of a firm to produce and sell higher amounts of a product, generating more revenue from lower levels of on-hand inventory. It has too large an impact on cash flow and overall efficiency to be considered a subset of more general operational efficiency. The opposite outcomes of the International Harvester and Chrysler turnarounds, which occurred at the same time and under the same economic conditions, provide testimony that inventory efficiency has its own particular importance. Production efficiency and inventory efficiency are often pursued as separate objectives; it is not uncommon for a firm to achieve one without the other. Successful firms tend to achieve both, however.

Modest Overhead

As measured in terms of percent expense to revenue, successful turn-around companies spend significantly less money on non-cost-of-sales expense than unsuccessful companies. Successful firms generally have a widespread reputation for frugality, operate with small central staffs, and spurn excessive spending on personal embellishments and expensive travel. In contrast, unsuccessful firms often spend large amounts of money on items not directly related to what the customer was buying, the product.

Low Cost through Design

Successful firms systematically design products (and services) to be produced (and delivered) at low cost. Proactive efforts aimed at the re-duction of cost through design is an essential tactic if profits are to be improved. Effective turnaround managers understand production pro-cesses well and insist that product design and production capability in-teract with one another to achieve an enhanced competitive position. In contrast, management of unsuccessful turnarounds treats manufactur-ing (or services) more as an afterthought and less as a proactive com-petitive force. Difficulties with the manufacturability of specific prod-ucts or the design of services have contributed to the demise of some of the largest industrial firms in the United States.

The commonality of component parts is a meaningful factor in achieving low-cost operation, and successful firms often have programs to utilize common component parts in the manufacture of several prod-ucts—after the products themselves are designed for lower cost.

Tactics of Product Differentiation

Distinguishing Features

In order for customers to be attracted, the product must possess distinguishing features. Successful companies field products customers need, products often created through a blend of competent technical research and ongoing familiarity with customers. Unsuccessful companies offer products that can be sold, but unfortunately, they cannot always be sold with sufficient margin during all economic periods. Successful turnaround companies offer innovative well-tested features which are introduced to the market in sync with or slightly ahead of emerging market trends. In contrast, unsuccessful companies offer "me too" products or, in some cases, products with substantial negative features.

Reliability and Performance

Some products do not do enough for the customer, for periods that are long enough, to secure repeat business. Successful companies ensure that their products perform at levels beyond what the customer is expecting and that the products are reliable enough to continue performing for long periods of time. The products of unsuccessful companies either do not meet customer expectations or do so for short periods and then wear out.

Product Quality

Many companies fail simply because their products are not good enough to effectively compete in world markets. They are able to sell a few products in good times but suffer acutely when times are bad. At successful companies, product quality is actively managed and constantly improved even if it is already the best in the industry. At unsuccessful companies, product quality is assumed to be good, but nobody checks for sure.

Market Continuity

Market continuity can be briefly described as the predisposition of the firm to focus on providing products for one very familiar market before expanding into any new markets or into other new activities. Successful firms work very hard to remain familiar to their historical customers and they avoid making changes that are confusing to customers. Unsuccessful firms often jump from one market niche to another or into altogether new markets, all without much success, while neglecting their mainline businesses. They allow competitors to exploit their historical markets.

Tactics of Leadership

Focus on Operations

Focus on operations can be described as the propensity to focus on operational problems such as production cost, product quality, customer satisfaction and short-term sales. Unsuccessful firms stray away from day-to-day operational issues to acquisitions, divestitures, poorly thought-out expansion, politics, entertainment, or other matters which are either less immediate or else totally unrelated to the firms' present business.

Managerial Stability

Because of the long-drawn-out nature of the turnaround process, managerial stability is often present among successful turnaround cases while instability and internal political turmoil often characterize failure. Most successful turnarounds involve a top-management team that is essentially constant for at least 7 or 8 years following the period of crisis. Unsuccessful firms have frequent managerial changes, sometimes even when progress is being made.

Experience in the Industry Being Served

The evidence is quite strong that those who head successful turnaround efforts have vast experience in the industry being served while those who head unsuccessful attempts commonly do not. One reason why experience may be powerful as a determinant of success is because so much of what needs to be known is unique to particular processes, competitors, suppliers, customers, or individual people within an industry. Broad managerial concepts are rarely sufficient for the short time available for a turnaround. Detailed, industry-specific knowledge is almost always required.

Technical Experience

It is a mistake to assume that all problems can be solved with the application of management principles. Some problems are technical problems. Technical experience is common in the backgrounds of successful turnaround agents and is often lacking in those who fail. Empirically, successful turnaround agents frequently have technical backgrounds either by education or by virtue of many years of experience in manufacturing or engineering positions. Unsuccessful turnaround agents are more likely to have backgrounds in finance or marketing. Perhaps more accurately, successful turnaround agents understand how to make money in physical, people, process, and customer terms, rather than in general terms. They understand more about the inner workings of their companies.

Knowledge Exploration

Knowledge exploration is a concept difficult to measure, but meaningful to turnaround success. Decision making in unsuccessful turnarounds is frequently too intuitive, often lacking an essential knowledge base, and insufficiently grounded in fact. Successful firms are more studious about obtaining the information necessary for good decisions; they do not simply rely on information that is available. Successful companies arrange to gather, or to know, the information critical to making key strategic decisions. Unsuccessful firms frequently have significant gaps in their information and are disinclined to seek external information that is needed. Suboptimal decisions made on the basis of inaccurate, but available, information were very costly and contributed to the ultimate demise of very large firms. Successful firms overtly seek information necessary for appropriate decisions.

Incremental Changes

Gradual and consistent incremental improvement is the managerial style of successful turnarounds. Improvements are made one day at a time by improving one thing at a time. Great changes in corporate strategy are discussed only rarely at the meetings of successful companies. What is discussed are letters of complaint from dealers or customers, ideas presented by employees as to how products or quality can be improved. Gradual and constant incremental improvements, interspersed by occasional major improvements, provide the framework for successful companies to constantly progress. The rate of change is not linear. Periods of relative stabilization and consolidation follow periods of major innovation. Successful companies "do common things uncommonly well," and once in a while, they do something that is wonderful.

Incremental change extends far beyond product changes to the process of organizational learning as old values are used as a foundation for new values and beliefs. The subtle mechanisms of change resistance are well understood by successful turnaround agents who show more appreciation for the positive contributions of people who may have been with the organization at the time problems developed. In contrast, unsuccessful firms make abrupt, drastic changes in plant location, markets served, products, and the makeup of management teams.

Fair Play

Though fair play is a very difficult concept to measure, proxy indicators show that successful turnaround agents are generally perceived as dealing fairly with employees, creditors, suppliers, and customers. Successful turnaround agents commonly know many employees on a first-name basis and tend to nurture long and mutually beneficial relationships with them. Often, the executive corps at successful companies take substantial compensation reductions during periods of economic difficulty as the first step in programs or retrenchment. As a counter example, unsuccessful turnaround executives often extract too much compensation at times when employees are being asked for greater personal sacrifice. Equity theory, commitment theory, and historical writings in the field of management provide some theoretical basis for the relevance of fair play as a variable in organizational performance. In addition to the internal considerations, fair play by successful companies often extends outside the firm to suppliers and other members of the general community.

2
Recognizing a Turnaround Situation

A crisis serious enough to necessitate turnaround is a feature event for any company, an experience that can be catastrophic or a healthy and positive force of strengthening and renewal. A turnaround attempt can draw together the people of the organization or it can tear them apart. It can foster innovation or stop it completely. A turnaround event is different from other periods of economic reversal because of the uncommon severity of the situation. A turnaround event occurs when the very existence of the company is threatened.

Yet, turnaround situations frequently go unrecognized. Company managers often fail to differentiate routine business situations requiring less spectacular change from more serious situations where extraordinary action is required for the firm's survival. Occasionally, gradual drift takes place until the threatened firm deteriorates beyond the point where reasonable action can save it. These are the most serious cases because they represent situations in which the firm could have been saved but was not. The resulting catastrophe takes a cruel toll on employees, creditors, suppliers, stockholders, customers, and members of the local community. For both business and societal reasons, it is worthwhile to understand the early signs of decline.

Signs of Decline

The signs of decline indicate slippage in the company's financial and competitive performance.* The warning signals present during the onset of decline frequently occur in one or more of seven basic families of problems which are easy to detect:

- *Liquidity problems* including frequent cash shortages, borrowing levels up to collateral limits, or cash-on-demand status with many vendors

- *Collection problems* including an unusually large number of disputed balances or frequent sales to a customer base which is not equipped to pay

- *Profit problems* such as ongoing losses in the general business or chronic losses in a main segment

- *Quality problems* and other product problems resulting in low levels of customer acceptance

- *Employee problems* including attrition of high-caliber people, low morale, high rates of absenteeism, or low productivity

- *Organizational problems* including a confusing organizational structure, dispersed responsibility, or inappropriate staffing for key positions

- *Ethical problems* including the falsification of financial statements, excessive executive compensation, unreasonable perquisites, theft, chemical dependency, or improper supplier-purchaser relationships

John Argenti (1976) lists 12 major causes of corporate demise in *Corporate Collapse*. He sees failure as a sequential process involving a progression of steps toward the ultimate demise of the firm.

1. Poor management, including one-man rule, a nonparticipative board of directors, an unbalanced top team, and lack of management depth.

2. Defective accounting information, including erroneous cash flow forecasts, costing systems, and asset valuations.

3. Exposure to change, including competitive, economic, social, and technological change.

---

*Signs of decline have been described by John Argenti, Donald Hambrick, Peter Lorange and Robert Nelson, Danny Miller, Stanley Goodman, and others, all excellent references.

4. Externally induced constraints, including governmental, union, public opinion, and consumer constraints.

5. Overtrading, involving expansion that is faster than cash flow or profits will permit.

6. The big project, in which cost and time are underestimated and revenue is overstated.

7. Excessive gearing up, in which the company borrows more money than the volume of business can reasonably support.

8. Bad financial ratios, which, with traditional financial analysis, indicate slippage in the firm's competitive position.

9. Creative accounting, involving the delayed publication of financial information, capitalized research and development costs, payment of dividends from borrowed money, reduction of maintenance on capital equipment, treatment of extraordinary income as ordinary income, and incorrect valuation of assets.

10. Normal business hazards, involving strikes by suppliers and fires or other disasters for which the firm is unprepared.

11. Nonfinancial symbols of decline, including low morale, poor maintenance, poor housekeeping, and slippage in quality of service.

12. "Last few months" indicators, including low stock prices, management's denial of circumstance, and callous disregard for customers.

Lorange and Nelson (1987) add that organizational decline is commonly preceded by early warning signals including:

- *Replacement of substance with form* and a scarcity of clear goals and decision benchmarks

Goodman (1982) focuses on the troubled firm's organizational characteristics including:

- *Operating the same way as in the past,* independent of the operating environment
- *No firm plans for corrective action*

Any one or more of these disorders may plague the company in trouble, and it is surprising how often problem situations fester and worsen before responsible members of management or the board of directors initiate corrective action. The unusual managerial practices of Allegheny International went on for years and finally made the cover of *Business*

Week before changes were made in the firm's management. The sorry state of some savings and loan institutions was well understood by distant observers but apparently not by the regulators, managers, or directors most directly involved. Lengthy periods replete with early warning signals occurred at Allis-Chalmers, Control Data, Lone Star Industries, CPT, LTV, and many other troubled firms, yet insufficient action was forthcoming. The results were diminishing business prospects, shrinking employment, and worsening community well-being.

However, it is not always true that managerial incompetencies are rampant throughout the troubled organization. Economic and market conditions also stress corporate resources and cause revenues, cash flows, and profits to decline. These misfortunes affect capable as well as incapable firms, and it cannot be assumed that because a company is in trouble it has no sound management and no distinctive competencies. Organizations, like people, get sick, but some recover—in part because they may not be sick all over.

This distinction between illness and failure is an important one that is too often lost on the casual observer of the company in trouble. Often, failure is the result of extreme behavior, too few or too many controls, an overly powerful chief executive or a mere figurehead, or too few or too many markets or products (Miller 1977). Bank officials, directors, and newly recruited managers often make the assumption that everything needs to be changed to restore a troubled company to health. Most companies in trouble are doing at least some things very well. Well-trained, dedicated, competent people are interspersed with people of limited training and dedication. Turnaround management is a specific science which requires the ability to nurture, encourage, and reinforce what is good as well as root out what is unsatisfactory. The turnaround practitioner is well advised to proceed cautiously. Many potentially successful turnarounds have been ruined by newly appointed top managers operating with the assumption that everything needed changing when everything did not. Turnaround managers must be quick but not cavalier and must appreciate the limitations of the information supplied.

Recognizing a Turnaround Situation

Some terms might be helpful to the recognition of problem situations. Some situations referred to as *turnarounds* may not be turnarounds under all definitions because the company did not actually survive as an active participant in its major business. Occasionally, corporate names survive when customers are lost, plants are closed, employees lose their lifetime employment, and the company's market influence is severely damaged. Also, the endurance of the recovery should also be considered in determining whether success or failure has been achieved. A turnaround of a year or so is not much of a turnaround. We must also integrate our discussion of the turnaround process with other lessons we have learned in management.

The Turnaround Candidate

For a company to be considered a turnaround candidate, the situation must be serious. Survival as a major participant in the industry needs to be at stake. That doesn't mean that the company will survive completely intact. Some unsuccessful turnarounds unfold with a skeleton of the initial company surviving in a formal sense, but with the company's market position greatly weakened and employment severely reduced. A turnaround candidate could be defined as a company or business entity faced with a period of crisis sufficiently serious to require a radical improvement in order to remain a significant participant in its major industry.

The requirements for the radical improvement may have been imposed by a variety of causes including the state of the economy, mistakes made by management, distress to key customers, a physical disaster, crime, or even sporadic unpredictable events. We should understand the causes of decline because of their relationship to the ultimate remedies applied; however, the main objective is to examine the state the company was in and how it got out of it. The following criteria are offered as conditions necessary to establish a company as a turnaround candidate as distinguished from other, more usual, business situations.

1. *Profitability has declined* from the previous 4-year average for a period of at least 1 year and profitability should not only be low but slipping.
2. *Profitability is either negative or significantly below the industry average* and there are instances when other competitors are clearly able to achieve higher profit rates selling similar products.
3. *Real revenue levels (revenue levels adjusted for inflation) have declined.*
4. *Market position is deteriorating* as represented by a loss in market share, a decline in the number of key distributors or dealers, or price erosion in the company's products.
5. Investors, board members, or managers express concerns regarding

the condition of the company, and initiate actions in response to these concerns. These concerns commonly coincide with a deterioration in the company's cash position to the point that satisfaction of cash obligations is difficult.

The above criteria, along with other subjective information about the individual case, can help us make a judgment about whether we are dealing with a true turnaround situation or a more routine business fluctuation.

The Stages of the Turnaround Process

Most corporate crises start slowly and then accelerate and become critical. As Hofer (1980) and others have observed, the greatest opportunity for turnaround success is in the early stage of the crisis, before resources are fully spent and when enough time remains for corrective actions to work. Yet, it is also during this early stage of the crisis when there exists the least consensus among organization members about the degree of difficulty, its fundamental causes, and what should be done. As circumstances worsen, consensus is often easier to achieve, but there is less time available and less maneuvering room to implement strategies. Time, by itself, influences turnaround outcome, and it is useful to examine turnaround events in three distinct stages: the preturnaround situation, the period of crisis, and the period of recovery. Each of these three stages has distinct characteristics which can impact failure or success. Figure 2-1 provides a visual example of revenue and cost histories during an actual turnaround of an authentic company. Each stage is identifiable and possesses it own unique operational characteristics and organizational dynamics.

The Preturnaround Situation

The preturnaround situation is that period of time before profitability begins to decline severely or, if profitability has declined, before the point when the general health of the firm becomes an appreciable concern to investors, employees, or other stakeholders. This could include the early life of a firm when it is getting established.

During the preturnaround situation, gradual drift may be taking place. The competitive position of the firm may indeed be weakening, but the condition may be rationalized by managers and stakeholders as

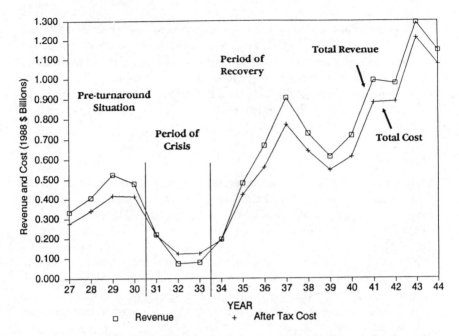

Figure 2-1. The stages of the turnaround process. The situation with Deere & Co. during the 1920s and 1930s illustrates the dramatic patterns of revenue and cost during the preturnaround situation, the period of crisis, and the period of recovery.

a temporary misfortune due solely to external events, such as the general state of the economy, temporary abnormalities in world trade, an uncooperative banker, or other factors. A preturnaround situation may also be quite robust. Decline can sometimes occur quickly as in the case of International Harvester, which went from its best year ever in 1979 to devastating losses in the next few years. The chief characteristic of the preturnaround situation is that the emergence of a crisis is not broadly perceived. Key stakeholders do not usually accept the compelling need for change during the preturnaround situation.

The Period of Crisis

During the period of crisis, concern for the need to change is more pronounced. Profitability has declined or is negative, market share is falling or is negligible, and the company's cash situation is of concern to investors, creditors, and/or employees.

The existence of these conditions during the period of crisis does not necessarily mean that the managers of the company see themselves as major contributors to the problem. The fact that a crisis exists is acknowledged, but responsibility for addressing the crisis may be diffused. Company managers may view people from the bank, the union, or the Federal Reserve Board as the ones most in need of behavior modification. In some cases, managers do seek changes in their own behavior and occasionally bravely shoulder the responsibility. In the period of crisis it is broadly perceived that something must be done.

The Period of Recovery

During the period of attempted recovery, specific actions are put in motion to improve the health of the firm. The actions taken can be appropriate or inappropriate—effective or ineffective. The actions can be proactive specific steps, or they can be thinly veiled rationalized abdications. The turnaround itself may be either successful or unsuccessful. But, concern is expressed and attempts are made to restore the financial health and market position of the firm. The period of successful recovery occurs when the firm experiences a return to profitability, substantial improvement in its balance sheet, and a restoration of its competitive position.

The Nature of Recovery

The recovery of a turnaround firm is more than the restoration of book profits. It matters how the profits are restored. Recovery has to be accomplished by actual improved performance on the part of the firm itself, without the benefit of legal restructuring, such as bankruptcy. Formal restructuring procedures such as bankruptcy occasionally permit the company to become better off by exporting problems to other parties (unsecured creditors, lenders, governments, investors, or employees) who must involuntarily assume the debts the firm is obliged to pay but cannot. In a scientific sense, these situations are not turnarounds, they are restructurings. What societies need are turnarounds that operate in a positive sum game rather than the shifting of obligations within a zero sum game—recoveries that make the firm better off without making someone else worse off.

Furthermore, the term *recovery* must be interpreted as a lasting event—covering at least several years and resulting in a measurably better situation for the company in terms of profits, market position, technical contribution, and general contribution to the economy. Key necessary conditions for recovery are a return to profitability and a substantial improvement in the balance sheet and in market position (increased market share or increased sales through a more secure market share in a smaller market). After a valid recovery has been accomplished, the firm should operate without a serious threat to its viability for at least several years.

Individual Turnaround Events

Most companies will experience severe adversity at some time during their history. Individual turnaround events can occur during severe recessions, unfavorable industry market conditions, or internally induced misfortune. Usually, these events span several years, perhaps 15 years for the three stages to unfold. So, the proper investigation of turnarounds involves the close monitoring of company affairs over very long periods. In order to identify a turnaround event, the preturnaround situation, the period of crisis, and the period of recovery should all be identifiable and quantifiable and should be totally supported by qualitative as well as quantitative information.

Turnaround Agents

Turnaround agents are those individuals or groups of individuals most involved in directing the turnaround attempt during the period of recovery. In most cases, the chief turnaround agent is the firm's chief executive. However, many people are involved in leadership roles in the most successful turnaround cases. One person may receive the bulk of the publicity but a more thorough examination will reveal that team efforts, rather than singular leadership, are really responsible for the restoration of company health. We, therefore, must distinguish between the chief turnaround agent, such as Lee Iacocca in the case of Chrysler, and the other very important additional turnaround agents, such as Hans Matthias of manufacturing, Hal Sperlich of product development, Douglas Fraser of the United Auto Workers, or Gerald Greenwald of finance who played crucial roles in restoring the competitive strength of the firm. The turnaround process involves many essential steps, and seldom can total success or failure be attributed to any single individual.

The Turnaround Process

The turnaround process is that amalgam of managerial skills, systems, and procedures used; the value systems and individual character traits exhibited; and the actions taken during the turnaround event to achieve a recovery. The turnaround process is a multifaceted process of organizational learning. Many people throughout the company learn to do things in a new, usually less costly, way. A broadly based learning experience of this magnitude is not easy to describe because it involves so many people and so many parts of the organization. Serious examination of the process involves consideration of a great many variables — some are managerial, some are technical. Some lend themselves to quantitative analysis, and some are more organic. The entire process is holistic, and every variable impacts every other variable.

3
Profit Patterns in Successful and Unsuccessful Turnarounds

Turnarounds take time. Little can be learned by examining turnaround situations for short periods such as 2 or 3 years. Because of the amount of time that passes when a firm first becomes weaker, then attempts to become stronger, and finally either recovers or fails, long observation periods are necessary to capture the intricacies of the turnaround process, especially since successful firms often look worse during the early stages of the turnaround and operate unprofitably for longer periods than do the unsuccessful firms. (Successful firms average 3 years in the red before profitability is restored.) Long periods of observation are also necessary because so many things change, especially management, within unsuccessful companies. Each new wave of management usually brings with it a new strategy and a new operational focus. Understandably, all these activities must be followed over long periods to distinguish successful from unsuccessful efforts.

Selection of Turnaround Cases

The selection of turnaround cases covered here was based on a specially prepared database of information on most of the significant firms operating in the automotive and agricultural industries since the turn of the century. The initial industry database contained sales, financial, and operational data on the key firms in these industries for the period from 1900 to 1985. Obtaining a full set of data for the entire time period for all firms was not possible. But, it was possible to gather a fairly complete set for most of the significant firms.

The second step was the identification of companies suitable for the study using the criteria explained in Chapter 2 (revenue and profit declines and concerns among stakeholders). This selection process involved the examination of sales and financial and operating results of the firms to determine when a falloff in business occurred, and the use of industrial business histories to determine when and if turnaround attempts took place.

The 16 turnaround cases were then examined over a 20-year period, in most instances. The most severe period of crisis was considered to be year 0. Usually, this was the year when the most money was lost. Data were then collected for the 5 preceding years, year 0, and 14 succeeding years for a total of 20 years. Financial records, product specifications, actual component parts, manuscripts, histories, interviews, and other data were examined to provide information for the full analysis.

In order to facilitate comparisons among the various stages of the turnaround process, data were collected separately for the full period (up to 20 years) and for each of the following stages:

1. *The preturnaround situation* (year −5 through year −2)
2. *The period of crisis* (year −1 through year +1)
3. *The period of recovery* (year +2 through year 11)
4. *Additional periods* (year 12 through year 14 and in one case through year 17)

The actual stages did vary somewhat from one case to another, and when the individual cases were analyzed, each year of every case was examined separately. The conclusions reached were based on that level of analysis. Some groupings by virtual time periods were employed to facilitate comparisons.*

Criteria for Success: Lasting Performance

The method used for determining whether the turnaround was successful centered around three necessary conditions: a return to profitabil-

---

*The appendix discusses the research procedures in more detail.

ity, a substantial improvement in profitability, and an overall improvement in market position—all lasting at least several years and resulting in a measurably better situation for the company with respect to these criteria. More specifically, a turnaround was classed as successful if the following were achieved:

1. *Profitability improved* from the levels of the period of crisis for a period of at least several years.
2. *Profitability was positive.*
3. *Market position was significantly strengthened* either by increasing market share or by successfully concentrating on an important subset of the market.

The measures employed in evaluating turnaround success included:

Units of production

Units of production as a percent of the industry total

Revenue in current dollars

Revenue as a percent of estimated industry revenue

Revenue in constant dollars (1988 dollars)

Revenue as a percent of the U.S. gross national product

After-tax earnings in current dollars

After-tax profit rate (as a percent of revenue)

Because of the lack of standardization in accounting systems over the span of time examined, and the differing requirements of financial reporting, a few data points were either unavailable or unusable for at least some years of the earliest cases. Narrative information supplemented the quantitative information in classifying a case as a success or failure. Table 3-1 notes the final placement of the individual cases into the successful and unsuccessful categories based on the measures and narrative information listed above. You will note that a number of these cases are not from recent years. The reader should not be put off by this. These cases are included because of their relevancy. Indeed, one of the most exciting aspects of putting this book together was to discover how applicable these earlier experiences were to the very problems facing U.S. companies today.

Table 3-1. Cases in the Turnaround Sample

Case 1	Buick, 1906–1925	Successful
Case 2	International Harvester, 1966–1985	Unsuccessful
Case 3	Jeffery Motors, 1911–1930	Successful
Case 4	Willys-Overland, 1916–1935	Unsuccessful
Case 5	American Motors Corporation, 1951–1970	Successful
Case 6	Ford Motor Company, 1975–1988	Successful
Case 7	Kaiser-Frazer, 1944–1956	Unsuccessful
Case 8	Cadillac, 1897–1916	Successful
Case 9	Hudson Motor Company, 1927–1946	Unsuccessful
Case 10	Chrysler Corporation, 1975–1988	Successful
Case 11	AMC/Renault, 1971–1987	Unsuccessful
Case 12	Maxwell-Chalmers, 1916–1935	Successful
Case 13	Allis-Chalmers, 1963–1986	Unsuccessful
Case 14	Packard, 1929–1948	Successful
Case 15	Studebaker-Packard, 1949–1966	Unsuccessful
Case 16	Deere & Company, 1927–1946	Successful

Profit Patterns in Successful and Unsuccessful Turnarounds

Companies that ultimately succeed in turnarounds are quite often more severely affected initially. Successful companies experience more pronounced downturns and respond more quickly. Unsuccessful companies tolerate conditions lethal to their survival long before actions are taken. The Schendel and Patton (1976) landmark study of turnarounds hypothesized that rapid decline promotes action and gradual drift does not, a hypothesis reinforced by several of the cases studied here. Success was preceded by more serious declines in revenue and profit. Revenue falloff was more substantial. Loss rates were more severe. Costs had to be reduced much more in order to survive. Failing companies experienced less severity. Figure 3-1 displays the profit patterns of successful and unsuccessful firms during their turnaround attempts.

The decline in revenue experienced by both the successful and unsuccessful firms was substantial, but the declines were especially severe among the successful cases, as Table 3-2 makes clear. From year −3 to year 0, constant dollar revenue declined 46 percent in the case of Packard, 86 percent in the case of Deere, 43 percent for American Motors in the 1950s, and 57 percent for Chrysler in the 1980s. Other firms experienced similar declines in physical units of production. Buick's shipments declined from 30,525 in 1910 to 13,389 in 1911. Though some production capacity was diverted to trucks, Jeffery automobile shipments declined from 10,417 in 1914 to 4608 in 1916. Shipments totaled only three units during year 0 of the Cadillac case. Maxwell-Chalmers' production declined by 46 percent from year −3 to year 0.

Unsuccessful firms also experienced revenue and profit declines but,

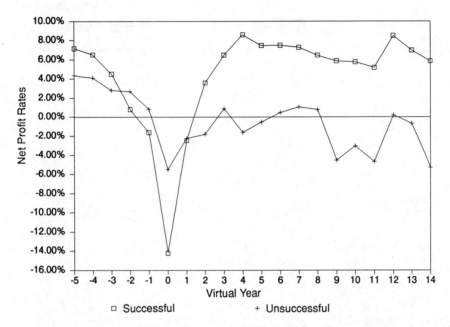

Figure 3-1. Net profit rates: Successful and unsuccessful turnarounds. During periods of crisis, successful companies experience more dramatic declines and deeper loss rates than unsuccessful companies. These sharp declines appear to prompt dramatic action which restores the company to health and profitability. Unsuccessful companies gradually drift toward oblivion when little action is taken.

with the exception of Hudson and Willys-Overland, they were not as pronounced. Hudson's revenue did decline 86 percent from 1929 to 1932, and Willys-Overland's production declined by 46 percent from 1918 to 1921. The other five unsuccessful firms either experienced relatively small revenue declines or had revenue increases (Table 3-2).

One of the unsuccessful companies, International Harvester Corporation (IHC), was at one time the fourth-largest firm in the country. At other times in its history, IHC was the largest firm in its industry by a factor of 8. Three of the unsuccessful firms (Hudson, Willys-Overland, and Allis-Chalmers) were at one time the third- or fourth-largest in their industries. Most of the unsuccessful turnarounds involved companies which were comfortably among a very few leading companies in their industries. In contrast, three of the most successful cases, Cadillac, Jeffery, and Maxwell-Chalmers, were quite small firms when the turnarounds were attempted, and two of these, Cadillac and Maxwell-Chalmers, were near liquidation. This study did not yield evidence that either firm size or economies of scale were substantial factors in turnaround success.

AMC/Renault and Chrysler Corporation provide an interesting con-

Table 3-2. Change in Revenue and Units Produced between Year −3 and Year 0

	Change in revenue (1988 $000), %	Change in units produced, %
Successful cases		
Cadillac		*
Buick		†
Jeffery		‡
Maxwell-Chalmers		−46.2
Packard	−44.6	−54.2
Deere	−86.0	
American Motors I	−43.0	−51.3
Chrysler	−56.7	−48.3
Ford	−23.1	−48.9
Unsuccessful cases		
Willys-Overland		−45.9
Hudson	−82.7	−80.9
Studebaker-Packard	−15.6	−56.1
International Harvester	−0.8	
Allis-Chalmers	−3.2	
Kaiser-Frazer-Willys§	+186.9	+75.9
American Motors II	+6.4	−14.5

*Units produced at the predecessor to Cadillac, the Henry Ford Motor Company, increased from no units in 1899 to three units in 1902.

†Although Buick sales in year 0 were actually greater than the sales for year −3, the company did experience a 57 percent decline from 30,525 units in 1910 to 13,389 units in 1911.

‡Jeffery automobile sales had declined from 10,417 in 1914 to 4608 in 1916.

§Kaiser-Frazer-Willys revenue declined from $2,419,606 in 1948 to $1,166,223 in 1949 (1988 dollars). Kaiser's unit sales declined from 317,963 in 1948 to 141,309 in 1949.

trast between the profit patterns of successful and unsuccessful turn-around firms. Both firms were adversely affected by the oil crisis of the 1970s and the recession of the early 1980s, although AMC should have been less affected because the recession was moving buyers toward AMC's traditional market. Chrysler experienced a 57 percent decline in real revenue from year −3 to year 0. AMC experienced a 6.4 percent increase. Chrysler's loss rate reached 18.5 percent of revenue during the low point of its crisis. AMC's loss rate was 2.0 percent of revenue. After its crisis in 1976, AMC's real revenue increased to record levels in 1978 and 1979, while Chrysler's revenue had declined to $18 billion (1988 dollars) from $29.6 billion 2 years earlier. Yet, as AMC revenue climbed to record levels, so did cost. During its last year of significant profit, AMC's 1979 earnings were 2.7 percent of revenue. When revenue declined in 1980 and 1981, the company did not reduce cost, and huge losses began to accumulate. In 1987, AMC was absorbed into Chrysler after losing $683 million in 5 years.

In contrast, Chrysler Corporation, although affected much more severely, chose to bring costs down to the levels of then current real revenues, which reached slightly more than $12.0 billion in 1982. Chrysler's real costs, which had reached nearly $30 billion in 1977 (1988 dollars), were reduced to less than $12 billion 5 years later (Appendix Table A-3). Chrysler's systematic reduction of the firm's breakeven point produced record profits in subsequent years and a solid position in the industry (Table 3-2). American Motors succumbed to inefficiency, and the firm that at one time was one of the most efficient and systematic producers of cars in the world disappeared as an independent company.

Practical Lessons on Profit Patterns

- Large dominant firms, as well as smaller producers, fail. Size does not seem to be a factor in turnaround success.

- During the early years of a turnaround, successful turnarounds often experience more pronounced business declines and deeper loss rates than firms that ultimately fail.

- Improved performance on the part of successful turnarounds is frequently not apparent for about 2 years. From year 2 forward, the successful companies begin to emerge as much more consistent and much more profitable.

- Successful and unsuccessful firms experience loss periods of similar length, 3 years for successful companies versus 2.71 years for unsuccessful companies, before profitability is restored.

- Successful firms accept economic conditions for what they are and reduce cost to existing revenue levels. Unsuccessful firms commonly attempt to sell more to cover existing costs and put less emphasis on cost reduction.

- During the period of recovery, successful firms averaged after-tax profitability of 6.5 percent while the unsuccessful firms operated at an average loss rate of 1 percent.

PART 2

The Strategic Advantage of Low-Cost Operation

Low-cost operation provides a strategic advantage far more enriching than the simple preservation of needed cash. Low-cost operation enables the funding of better product quality, more differentiated products, and better customer service. Low-cost operation disciplines and conditions the organization for international competition and forms a bond that brings members of the troubled company together and promotes commitment. Low-cost operation is absolutely essential to the survival of the troubled firm.

In contrast, higher costs produce three principal side effects far more significant than the mere reduction of profits. All operate independently but have a similar effect on the probability of turnaround success:

1. *Excess or unnecessary costs reduce profit, cash flow, and the availability of resources.* To persevere under unfavorable business conditions, the troubled firm must develop high levels of efficiency in its main operations so that it can satisfy financial obligations and

fund product differentiating activities. Perhaps the most damaging aspect of inefficiency is the opportunity cost—the cost of not being able to adequately fund essential activities such as product development, effective marketing, and customer service. This is the economic consideration, the most well known of the three side effects.

2. *Unnecessary costs result in operational inefficiency.* The things that cost money—extra people, extra facilities, extra programs, and extra managers—get in the way of efficient operation, just as excess inventory impedes operational efficiency. This is the operational consideration.

3. *Unnecessary costs reduce commitment.* Organization members are skeptical when they are asked to reduce costs while the firm continues to make acquisitions, pay executive bonuses, or offer elaborate executive perquisites. Workers are seldom motivated to save money when management is still spending it. The reduction of manager-induced costs affects organizational behavior by providing organization members with important evidence that the company is serious in its collective resolve to improve its situation. This is the organizational behavior consideration.

Cost efficiencies are dynamic ingredients in the internal culture of successful firms, and effective turnaround agents understand the difficulty of turning a company around when too much money is being spent. Reducible cost must be avoided, and successful turnaround efforts require a high degree of well-placed frugality. However, successful turnaround agents also understand the operational and organizational aspects of cost, and they actively work to reduce costs for reasons beyond the simple preserving of cash.

The cost efficiencies necessary for a successful turnaround extend beyond production alone and involve general internal efficiencies. Production cost, or operation cost in the case of a service company, is especially consequential because it represents such a significant percentage of total cost for most firms. However, in equally important ways, nonproduction costs such as overhead, administration, and interest also reduce the firm's ability to survive as a viable competitor.

Successful turnarounds differ from unsuccessful turnarounds in one very important and consistent respect: for at least several years, the company becomes established as a low-cost provider in its industry. Unsuccessful firms concentrate on other matters and do not attain status as low-cost providers. The relationship between low-cost operation and turnaround success among the 16 cases examined can be summarized as follows:

1. The successful companies were *noticeably more efficient in manufacturing* than the unsuccessful firms. Gross profit rates and inventory turn ratios were significantly higher. Narrative information corroborated the statistical indications of greater efficiency. The differences in manufacturing efficiency accounted for more than 70 percent of the differences in profitability between successful and unsuccessful firms.

2. Successful companies stayed with their cost-reduction programs longer and made deeper cuts. *Successful firms brought the costs down to the then current levels of revenue.* Unsuccessful firms attempted to increase the level of revenue to cover existing costs, either by selling into new markets or by making acquisitions.

3. *Cost-reduction programs* during the successful turnarounds were *pragmatic, disciplined, and even-handed.* Management often played an exemplary role in the cost-reduction programs of successful firms by accepting less pay and by eliminating unnecessary perquisites.

4. Successful companies *handled money conservatively* on an ongoing basis with cost consciousness more likely to be a cultural trait than was the case with the unsuccessful firms. Successful firms spent money primarily to improve current operations rather than for expansion into new business areas or for corporate image.

5. The *successful companies spent less on selling, general and administrative expense, and other non-cost-of-sales-expense.* Dramatic increases in operational efficiency were sought in all departments (sales, finance, operations, product development, and others) of the successful organizations. The efficient management of the organization was viewed as crucial to turnaround success.

An encouraging finding is that attainment of low-cost operation among the companies examined was achieved independent of scale. Some people suggest that larger companies have an advantage in economies of scale because they can amortize their fixed costs over a larger number of units and thus have higher profits per unit sale. It is also argued that they can invest these profits in better operational methods that will further increase their cost advantage. This logic often contends that smaller firms are at an almost impregnable disadvantage to larger-scale competitors. To some extent, this perspective is implicit in the theory that profitability is correlated to market share (Schoeffler et al. 1974). However, economists have maintained for a very long time that at some point, economies of scale fall prey to the law of diminishing returns. The 16 cases examined here indicate that diminishing returns may be present in some circumstances because larger firms often did worse than smaller firms. In the industries discussed here, as well as some others we have studied, an interesting historical pattern emerges. Dominant producers, first Ford during the 1920s, then International Harvester during the 1970s, and later General Motors during the 1980s, were all relegated to much weaker positions over time—a truly surprising phenomenon considering their vast size and enormous resources. In these industries, the most efficient producers gained ground on larger, less efficient firms, and then surpassed them. The important lesson is that successful firms are efficient first and large second. It does not work the other way around. Efficiency is a necessary condition of market leadership. Firms that become market dominant develop manufacturing efficiencies and general operating efficiencies before attaining market leadership.

Evidence also suggests that it makes no sense to discuss firmwide scale economies. Scale economies have to be analyzed vis-à-vis the particular operational process, an assembly line, a particular machine tool, an individual plant, or perhaps even the abilities and characteristics of a single worker. The people active in successful turnarounds spent much of their time in pursuit of microefficiencies and small-scale improvements.

One of the most important questions is whether cost reduction or revenue expansion (or both) is the preferred strategy in a turnaround situation. The practical real-world question is how easily can a company sell its way out of a problem. For reasons that are both economic and inherent in the time constraints facing the turnaround agent, revenue expansion is a risky strategy that may result in little profit improvement. The all-too-frequent pattern of expenses growing faster than revenue makes the revenue expansion strategy impractical for many turnaround situations unless it is preceded by major improvements in efficiency.

Part 2 examines the linkages between operational efficiency and turnaround success. Chapter 4 discusses the breakeven profile of the typical firm in trouble and then describes the practical improvements in operational efficiency needed to restore health to an industrial firm. Chapter 5 reviews steps successfully taken to achieve and sustain modest overhead. Chapter 6 examines the linkages between product (or service) design and operational efficiency.

4

Achieving Operational Efficiency

During the early life of General Motors, the company's largest operation, Buick, experienced a decline in automobile production of 55 percent from 1910 to 1911 and a loss of market share from 17 to 7 percent. Buick had abruptly dropped its most popular car, the Model 10, because the company was not competing successfully in the low end of its market. But, over the next 6 years, as the prices of Buick products were gradually reduced, Buick revenue quadrupled while net profits increased sevenfold. The dramatic reversal of Buick's fortunes was not achieved with a breakthrough new product, marketing wizardry, or a timely divestiture. It was achieved with many small, painstaking improvements in operational efficiency. The sum of these improvements established Buick as a low-cost producer, a key to survival for companies in trouble.

From 1980 to 1982, the Ford Motor Company lost $3.3 billion as yearly car shipments dropped to under half of the levels of the late 1970s. Physical-unit market share dropped from 20 percent in 1977 to 16 percent in 1980. Yet by 1987, Ford had emerged as one of the world's most profitable automobile companies with an after-tax profit rate of 6.5 percent of sales. As was the case with Buick in 1915, Ford in the 1980s achieved a turnaround by making thousands of incremental improvements to become a low-cost producer of differentiated products.

Companies able to implement successful turnarounds achieve and maintain operational efficiency. They exhibit much better statistical performance on the traditional measures of manufacturing efficiency, and they achieve efficiency in other matters as well. Production efficiencies and other internal efficiencies combine to provide the successful firm with a competitive cost advantage that enables further improvement in products and services.

The differences between successful and unsuccessful turnarounds in the gross profit rate (the residual profit on revenue after production costs have been deducted) are particularly striking. During the period of recovery (years 2 through 11), the gross profit rate averaged 19.56 percent among successful firms versus 13.29 percent among unsuccessful firms, a rate nearly 50 percent higher among successful firms.

All the successful firms in our sample enjoyed gross profit rates above 15 percent during the most critical stages of their recovery periods. Of the seven unsuccessful cases, only Allis-Chalmers' gross profit rates exceeded 15 percent, and this advantage was offset by higher expenses in other categories. As evidenced by better performance on manufacturing measures and narrative reports on the procedures employed, operational efficiency was a primary factor in every successful turnaround case and was absent in almost every unsuccessful case (Table 4-1).

This observed difference in gross profit rates accounted for about 70 percent of the difference in after-tax net profit rates (10 percentage points) between successful and unsuccessful turnaround firms. If these higher gross profit rates had been experienced by the unsuccessful firms, most of them would have operated at respectable levels of net profit during the critical years of attempted turnaround and probably would have survived.

If more complete cost-of-sales figures could be included for the very early Cadillac and Buick cases, and if the gross profits of Packard had not been artificially lowered by the company's role as a defense contractor in World War II, the observed difference in gross profit rates between successful and unsuccessful companies would have been several points higher.

The higher gross profit rates among successful firms was widespread and pronounced, even when similar products were produced. During the mid-1930s, Deere's gross profit rates averaged 36 percent. International Harvester operated in the same industry making the same sort of products on a much larger scale during the same economic period, yet had gross profit rates between 19 and 28 percent. International Harvester was from five to eight times the size of Deere at the time, but IHC's vast size did not generate higher rates of operational efficiency. Oliver, Minneapolis-Moline, and Allis-Chalmers had gross profit rates similar to those of International Harvester and all ultimately failed.

Table 4-1. Gross Profit Rates during Periods of Attempted Recovery

	Successful	
Case 1	Buick, 1906–1925	Very high
Case 3	Nash Motors, 1911–1930	23.90%
Case 5	American Motors Corporation, 1951–1970*	14.92%
Case 6	Ford Motor Company, 1975–1988	16.53%
Case 8	Cadillac, 1897–1916	Very high
Case 10	Chrysler Corporation, 1975–1988	17.48%
Case 12	Maxwell-Chalmers, 1916–1935	15.73%
Case 14	Packard, 1929–1948†	11.55%
Case 16	Deere & Co., 1927–1946	36.88%
Mean of successful cases		19.56%
	Unsuccessful	
Case 2	International Harvester, 1966–1985	14.37%
Case 4	Willys-Overland, 1916–1935	11.23%
Case 7	Kaiser-Frazer, 1944–1956	5.74%
Case 9	Hudson Motor Co., 1927–1946	8.09%
Case 11	AMC/Renault, 1971–1987	12.50%
Case 13	Allis-Chalmers, 1963–1986	22.80%
Case 15	Studebaker-Packard, 1949–1966	11.63%
Mean of unsuccessful cases		13.296%

*The gross profit rates of American Motors ranged from 14.48% to 20.09% during the period from 1958 through 1964 but declined during the late 1960s under different management.

†Packard's statistical gross profit rates were lower because of the company's role as a prominent defense contractor in World War II. Packard's gross profit rates averaged 21.99% from 1936 to 1939.

NOTE: The gross profit rates were computed on the basis that each year of each case is taken as one observation. Some cases were followed for more years than others, because of the termination of a business or other circumstances.

Massey-Harris experienced even lower gross profit rates (about 17 percent) and was restructured at a later time. Only Deere and J. I. Case had gross profit rates in excess of 35 percent. Although these companies have passed through many changes in the 50 years since, these are the two major long-line agricultural equipment companies that survive in the United States today.

A similar situation has existed in the U.S. automobile industry at various times in its history. During the late 1940s, two operators, Nash and General Motors, experienced gross profit rates that were approximately 50 percent greater than the rest of the industry. General Motors continued with solid performance, but Nash experienced a sales decline in the mid-1950s that could have been lethal had it not been for the firm's operational efficiency. Nash did survive the crisis under the name

American Motors. However, the reconstructed Ford Motor Corporation began to emerge as the second most efficient operator in the industry. Chrysler Corporation ranked behind the others. Chrysler had lower gross profit rates than Ford, GM, and AMC from 1958 through 1960 and lagged behind Ford and GM in gross profit rates from 1961 through the mid-1980s. The problems experienced by Chrysler Corporation during the late 1970s began shortly after World War II and were related to problems of operational efficiency.

These substantial differences in operational efficiency impacted the health and survivability of each firm and the outcome of the turnaround attempts examined. Table 4-1 displays the differing gross profit rates among successful and unsuccessful companies during their period of attempted recovery. The high correlation between operational efficiency and turnaround success is understandable because manufacturing costs represent a large fraction of total costs for industrial companies. However, managers of both successful and unsuccessful companies were in positions to observe these important cost relationships. The difference between successful and unsuccessful firms was that the managers at the successful firms knew what to do and did it. Managers at the unsuccessful firms apparently did not know what to do to improve the efficiency of factory or other operations.

Companies successful in turnaround situations prevail because the turnaround agents possess analytical, managerial, and technical expertise. Successful turnaround agents like Walter Chrysler, Charles Nash, or Donald Petersen do tend to manage people well and exhibit strong leadership traits. However, they also understand more about the economics of breaking even in physical terms and in process terms, for instance, how products can be designed for quicker assembly, how fit and finish can be improved by redesigning stamping dies, and what product characteristics are of most interest to customers.

Lewis C. Veraldi served as Ford's vice president of car program management during the development of the highly successful Taurus/Sable project, which was chartered when Ford was losing over $1 billion per year. People who had the opportunity to speak with Lew Veraldi will remember the endless array of specifics he committed to memory. He could recall at will almost every dimension on the car. He knew the weight of each part, what materials were used, why they were used, and how many fasteners were used in assembly. Perhaps more important, Veraldi could remember which Ford employee or supplier suggested the improvements which led to greater operational efficiency. To a very large extent, Ford's consistently improving profits are due to executives like Don Petersen, Lew Veraldi, and John Manoogian, who understand the technical and managerial aspects of *breaking even* in physical as well in financial terms.

Successful turnaround agents apply both technical and managerial expertise to restore the firm to health. Their understanding of the economics of breaking even is characteristically internal to the firm. This internal focus often leads to remedies that are polar opposites of the actions taken by unsuccessful firms. Unsuccessful firms often spend more time on acquisitions, new markets, and new ventures, and less time on internal efficiencies.

The Economics of Breaking Even

Managers of companies in difficulty often believe that the mere restoration of sales is sufficient to restore profits. The success of this approach is contingent upon the efficiency achieved by the firm in obtaining additional revenue. If the firm has to spend an additional 99.5 cents to bring in an additional $1.00 in revenue, it doesn't matter much whether more is sold or not. For instance, from 1983 to 1987, General Motors' revenue increased from $75 billion to $102 billion while profits declined by $180 million. It is quite difficult for a company to work its way out of a hole if each additional dollar of revenue costs nearly a dollar to obtain. Under some circumstances, the true revenue and variable cost lines on the breakeven chart can be parallel or even divergent. Variable cost can exceed variable revenue, thus necessitating an improvement in efficiency.

Donald Hambrick and C. Schecter (1980) have suggested that most short-term turnaround attempts by industrial companies employed efficiency-oriented rather than entrepreneurial (revenue-expansion) moves. One explanation for this finding may be that the relationship between variable costs and revenue was such that revenue-expansion moves did not improve profits enough to meet the demands of the turnaround situation. The value of additional revenue in a turnaround situation depends on the nature of the firm's cost structure. If variable costs are low, additional revenue has value. If variable costs are high, additional revenue will not solve the firm's financial difficulties. In these cases, the reduction of cost emerges as the appropriate short-term strategy, and internal efficiency should be emphasized more than selling.

Short-run costs are often divided into two groups: fixed costs, which remain fixed over wide ranges of output levels, and variable costs, which vary with the number of units produced. The manner in which costs change as revenues change can by very crudely illustrated by the breakeven chart in Figure 4-1.

Commonly, the firm operating in a reasonably competitive environment has available three possible ways to improve profits: reduce fixed cost, reduce variable cost, or sell more. In this sense, the successful and unsuccessful firms clearly differed in their approaches. Successful firms developed internal efficiencies that reduced both fixed and variable costs, while unsuccessful firms attempted to remedy their situations by selling more or by acquiring additional business segments.

Although revenue expansion is subject to pitfalls, quite often turnaround agents pursue it as their primary strategy to improve profit performance. One possible explanation may be that selling is perceived as less painful than reducing costs. Very few managers enjoy reducing costs, especially if people are involved. It is often more comfortable to launch new programs aimed at generating new business than to institute broad programs of internal efficiency. In addition, turnaround agents may not possess the skills necessary to implement efficiencies (organizational skills, technical skills, motivational skills). Also, most business downturns since World War II have been mild and short and often managers are not expecting and are not prepared for more serious downturns of longer duration. Whatever the reasons, managers often procrastinate in improving efficiency and opt instead for revenue expansion. Yet, we should look closely at the economics of breaking even

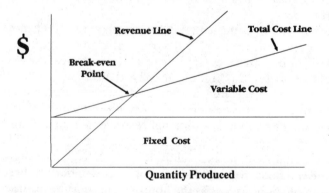

Figure 4-1. Although this breakeven chart illustrates some theoretical concepts useful to the turnaround manager, the concepts are overly simplistic and perhaps do not match real-world patterns of cost and revenue relationships. Two improper assumptions are often responsible for its misuse: variable costs are low with respect to revenue, and variable costs are constant over wide ranges in output. Neither assumption seems to be supported by evidence in the cases examined here.

to determine under what conditions revenue expansion and cost reduction will work.

As a practical matter, the relationship between revenue changes and cost changes is quite intricate and seldom can it be suitably described by a simple diagram. Still, it is useful to explore the revenue and cost relationship as an ingredient in strategy formulation for the troubled firm. We should be particularly interested in small incremental changes in the position from which the firm is presently operating. We can begin by examining the changes that take place in both revenue and cost when there are changes in unit volume. As more (or fewer) units are sold, revenue changes, yielding the incremental revenue per unit.

$$\text{Incremental revenue} = \frac{\text{change in revenue}}{\text{change in units of output}}$$

Costs also change as more (or fewer) units are produced, yielding incremental cost per unit.

$$\text{Incremental cost} = \frac{\text{change in cost}}{\text{change in units of output}}$$

Although it makes intuitive sense to examine costs as a function of the number of units produced, most companies produce such a wide variety of products in different price categories that analysis of costs in relation to the number of units produced has practical limitations. For these reasons, it is more practical to examine costs in relation to revenue. This is not a serious limitation if we are dealing with firms that have extensive competition, which is certainly the case with most firms in turnaround situations. One way of looking at incremental cost is to express it as a ratio of the change in cost divided by the change in revenue. For instance, if cost changes by $85,000 when revenue changes by $100,000, then incremental costs are 0.85 or 85 percent of incremental revenue.

$$\text{Incremental cost rate} = \frac{\text{change in cost}}{\text{change in revenue}} = \frac{\$85,000}{\$100,000} = 0.85$$

We could also look at the matter from the perspective of incremental profit. In our example, the incremental profit would be 0.15, or 15 percent of incremental revenue.

$$\text{Incremental profit rate} = \frac{\text{change in revenue} - \text{change in cost}}{\text{change in revenue}}$$

$$= \frac{\$15,000}{\$100,000} = 0.15$$

In the United States, accurate data on incremental revenue and incremental cost are not commonly available in the conventional accounting records, so the turnaround manager is left to deal with some cost problems intuitively. Our understanding of the economics of breaking even could be improved if the fixed costs and variable costs were neatly divided into identifiable categories on the accounting statement, but they are not. The accounting concepts of direct and indirect costs are helpful, and sometimes they are interpreted to have meanings similar to "variable" and "fixed costs." However, real-world conventions impede the use of this information. Often, variable selling or customer service expenses are included as indirect cost, and the standard costs used to describe the costs of production include overhead costs, which in reality are quite fixed. As Oskar Morgenstern (1954, 1959) has observed, traditional accounting practice does not correspond closely with economic theory.

An additional problem arises because of the lack of uniformity among individual companies and sometimes even within the same company. This lack of uniformity in accounting treatment, though less of a problem now than earlier and less of a problem here than in some other countries, is still appreciable enough so that comparisons between companies are difficult. The most scrupulous company-to-company comparisons of product cost figures and breakeven points can provide only rough approximations. Even day-to-day conventions such as how time cards are charged can affect intracompany comparisons. For those interested in business history as a form of analysis, we have the added complexity of accounting conventions changing over time.

Still, we do have information that provides some insights into changing cost patterns during the turnaround process. In this investigation, incremental cost changes were compared with incremental revenue changes for 16 companies over several decades. The time periods for the individual companies ranged from 20 to 50 years. Business cycles spanned both good times and bad. Two important questions about cost grew out of this analysis and both are relevant to turnaround situations:

1. *Are variable costs sometimes much greater as a percentage of revenue than we may have suspected?* The data in some of the cases examined suggest that variable costs can run from 90 to 110 percent of revenue. Several companies spent more money getting additional business than they received by getting it. Incremental costs advanced faster than incremental revenue. This finding implies that severe limitations apply to revenue expansion strategy as a remedy for turnaround situations unless expansion is preceded by efficiency.

2. *Are variable cost rates constant over short-range changes in revenue, or are they higher when revenue is increasing than when revenue is falling off?* The information collected in the cases we examined suggests that if revenue is increasing, costs commonly increase by a high percentage (for example, 95 percent of revenue). However, if revenue drops it is likely that a lower percentage will be saved (for example, 70 percent of revenue). With respect to revenue movements away from a particular point, variable costs (as a percent of revenue) are usually higher going up and lower going down.

The notion of marginal cost generally implies that costs of small changes in output are bidirectional. An increase in revenue should increase cost. Reductions in revenue should provide some cost relief. However, long ago economists observed the stickiness of cost during periods of declining revenue. More recently, Jeffrey Ford (1980) referred to the lack of bidirectionality in cost movements as "structural hysteresis," a well-developed concept describing how decreases in structure during periods of decline do not follow the same path as increases in structure during periods of growth.

This resistance to cost reductions during periods of declining revenue was confirmed in Ford's analysis of companies in distress. Costs do decline when revenues decline, but not by nearly as much as they increase when revenue increases. A check valve seems present in the system. Firms often add sizable costs when revenue increases and cut back slightly when revenue retreats. The difference ranges greatly from firm to firm, but the magnitude of this difference can be around 25 percent. If revenue goes up by $1.00, perhaps $0.90 or $0.95 will be added to costs. If revenue drops by $1.00, costs will be reduced by only about $0.70 or $0.80 and sometimes far less.

Upside and downside efficiency refers to the degree cost varies as revenue fluctuates. When revenue is *increasing* and incremental cost increases are low as a percentage of incremental revenue, and the resulting incremental profit is correspondingly high, this condition is referred to as upside efficiency. When revenue is *decreasing* and incremental cost reductions are high as a percentage of incremental revenue, and the resulting incremental profit erosion resulting from declining revenues is reduced, this condition is referred to as downside efficiency.

In order to illustrate this point further, let us examine the changes in revenue and costs in the automobile industry after World War II. Generally, most producers saw their revenue increase during this period, but so did cost. There were, however, periodic reversals, some quite severe. In order to gather more definitive information about the performance of cost during different economic periods, these were roughly divided into economically identifiable periods such as the postwar buyers market and the auto slump of the early 1980s.

The U.S. Auto Industry: The Postwar Boom

During the years immediately following World War II, the U.S. automobile industry was very healthy. Revenue grew for almost all firms in the industry. From 1946 to 1953, Chrysler Corporation's revenue, for example, increased every year and General Motors experienced only one slight decline. During these years of robust revenue increases, costs for most U.S. producers increased only modestly. General Motors experienced incremental cost increases that were less than 80 percent of incremental revenue, and GM's after-tax profits generally exceeded 9 percent of revenue. Ford was beginning to challenge Chrysler as the nation's second-largest domestic producer, and differences between these two companies are evident in the cost patterns of the two firms. Because of internal efficiencies, Ford's costs rose only 88 percent as fast as revenue while Chrysler's incremental costs rose by 97 percent. Although Chrysler's revenue almost tripled from 1947 to 1953, after-tax earnings increased by less than 20 percent.

Comparison of Incremental Cost Changes, 1946–1953

	Number of years		Average percent change in cost	
Cars	Revenue up	Revenue down	Revenue up	Revenue down
GM	6	0	79.37	
Ford	5	2	88.38	72.88
Nash	5	2	93.75	71.56
Chrysler	7	0	97.24	

Concentration and Stabilization

The interval from 1954 to 1963 was a time of economic concentration and market stabilization in the U.S. auto industry. During this period some of the most familiar companies left the industry, while the remaining firms converged toward similar degrees of efficiencies. Studebaker, Packard, Hudson, Willys-Overland, and Kaiser all ceased operations as domestic auto producers. Forced by competition among themselves, and not yet affected by foreign competition, the four remaining domestic producers all kept incremental cost in a range from 89.4 to 91.6 percent of incremental revenue when revenue increased. Chrysler's profits remained thin during this period, but did improve modestly. American Motors, under the leadership of cost-conscious George Romney, emerged as a respected and profitable U.S. auto producer.

However, a phenomenon unfamiliar since the 1930s developed between 1954 and 1963. For all producers, periods of revenue increase were interspersed with periods of revenue decline, and when revenue did decline, costs dropped by a lower percentage than did revenue.

Comparison of Incremental Cost Changes 1954–1963

	Number of years		Average percent change in cost	
	Revenue up	Revenue down	Revenue up	Revenue down
Chrysler	6	3	89.40	92.16
AMC	6	3	90.35	88.26
GM	6	3	90.50	86.66
Ford	6	3	91.61	82.56

From Prosperity to Tension

During the mid-1960s most domestic auto producers enjoyed some of the best years in the history of the U.S. industry. General Motors' profits exceeded $2 billion and 10 percent of revenue in 1965. Chrysler's profit rate in 1963 was the best it would be for the next 19 years. Ford also enjoyed record profits in 1965. As the high growth period of the 1960s drew to a close, however, several domestic producers began to experience problems. Markets shrank with the recession of 1970. Competition from foreign auto producers became significant for the first time, and the oil crisis of the early 1970s brought volatility to markets and changed consumer tastes for automobiles. In spite of generally increasing sales, the fortunes of U.S. auto producers began to decline.

For Chrysler Corporation, revenue increased during 7 out of 9 years during this period, but incremental cost rates crept up to nearly 97 percent of incremental revenue. Ford's revenue increased 8 of 9 years, but incremental cost rose to over 99 percent of incremental revenue. While Ford's revenues doubled from 1965 to 1972, profits increased only 23 percent. Revenue for General Motors increased only 6 of the 9 years, but incremental costs remained at 89 percent. Although AMC had only 3 years during which revenue increased, incremental costs remained low as a percent of revenue.

However, downward trends in revenue continued for several U.S.

auto producers from 1964 to 1972. Business, in general, was becoming more volatile. In addition to the volatility, an important phenomenon developed: the industry had significantly lower rates of decline in incremental cost during the years when revenue fell. For GM, costs declined only 43 percent of revenue during down years. For Ford and AMC, the figures were 68 percent and 55 percent respectively. Chrysler's costs declined by 51 percent of revenue declines in 1969 and then increased during 1970, another down year. A common situation with uncompetitive firms was taking place in the U.S. auto industry. When revenue increased, costs increased nearly as much; when revenue declined, not much money was saved. This is the folly of the revenue-expansion strategy for inefficient firms.

Comparison of Incremental Cost Changes, 1964–1972

	Number of years		Average percent change in cost	
	Revenue up	Revenue down	Revenue up	Revenue down
AMC	3	5	86.59	54.69
GM	6	3	89.05	43.41
Chrysler	7	2	96.66	−25.70*
Ford	8	1	99.24	68.60

*Chrysler Corporation's incremental costs increased 26 percent when revenue declined.

Loss of Control

By the mid-1970s, the cost situation of U.S. auto producers had become critical. Even during the better years, when revenue was increasing, costs were generally increasing faster. U.S. products were becoming harder to sell. Consumers, now faced with viable alternatives from other countries, were no longer willing to accept cost increases routinely passed along by the major U.S. auto producers. Inefficiencies caused costs to rise at rates the market would not absorb. Only GM managed to keep average incremental costs under 100 percent of revenue, but even at GM, profit margins shrank. The company that had after-tax profit rates of more than 10 percent in 1964 and 1965 was earning 4 percent in 1979 and operating at a slight loss in 1980.

The combination of higher incremental costs during up years, lower incremental costs during down years, and increasing numbers of down years resulted in disaster for the U.S. auto industry. In the late seventies, U.S. auto producers lost billions of dollars and Ford, Chrysler, and AMC teetered on the brink of insolvency. Survival required major changes in product differentiation and improved internal efficiencies.

The dire situations at Ford and Chrysler prompted readaptation to the environment. AMC did not adapt sufficiently and ceased operations as a separate company.

Comparison of Incremental Cost Changes 1973–1980

	Number of years		Average percent change in cost	
	Revenue up	Revenue down	Revenue up	Revenue down
GM	6	2	97.70	61.67
Chrysler	4	4	107.80	68.18
AMC	6	2	101.28	102.24
Ford	7	1	119.49	57.80

Adaptation and Rebuilding

By the early 1980s, it became clear that the U.S. automotive industry would have to change radically in order to survive. Massive readaptation programs were instituted at Chrysler and Ford in particular. Fixed costs and variable costs were trimmed, and giant steps were taken to improve the internal efficiencies of both firms. Quality became an essential ingredient to sales, and end-product quality became a high priority at both firms. To improve end-product quality, in-process quality was also improved. With in-process improvements came an important fringe benefit: operational efficiency greatly improved because of fewer internal stoppages and reruns as a result of bad parts. Other steps to improve efficiency were also taken, and the U.S. auto industry was able to produce more new models, each with more advanced engineering features, and bring them to market more quickly and at lower cost. All these tasks were accomplished with smaller staffs.

The recession of the early 1980s did not affect GM as severely, and GM did not make as many fundamental changes to improve efficiency. This may have been the company's undoing. By the late 1980s, GM's profit margins shrank further and it lost significant market share.

Comparison of Incremental Cost Changes 1981–1987

	Number of years		Average percent change in cost	
	Revenue up	Revenue down	Revenue up	Revenue down
Ford	4	3	79.3%	100.3%
AMC	2	4	89.0%	87.0%
GM	4	3	107.5%	172.3%
Chrysler	4	2	125.3%	654.0%

How Efficiency Changes over Time

The preceding analysis of incremental revenue and costs shows how efficiency can change over time and how it can be influenced by external factors such as foreign competition and the availability of natural resources—and accompanying changes in consumer tastes. The analysis suggests some refinements in our thinking about what should be done in turnaround situations.

The ratio of cost increase to revenue increase is one rough measure of efficiency, and over a prolonged period GM had the better record at generating additional revenue at a reasonable cost. However, this comparative advantage changed markedly over the years. In the 1940s, GM spent only $0.79 to obtain an additional $1.00 in revenue. By the 1970s, this ratio rose to $0.98. Although GM's profit margins still ranked as the best among American producers at the time, the 1970s was a period of decline vis-à-vis GM's previous performance. From 1981 to 1987, GM's performance had improved but less than either Chrysler or Ford in terms of this measure of efficiency.

Chrysler and Ford had similar performances from 1947 to 1980 with one distinction: Ford's efficiency in generating new revenue worsened considerably from 1950 to 1980, going from roughly 88 to 119 percent. However, the company actively reduced costs when revenue declined; on the other hand, Chrysler and GM lagged Ford by 8 to 10 percent in this regard.

American Motors was threatened more by mediocre downside efficiency coupled with too many down years than by its weakness in upside efficiency. During American Motors' turnaround from 1954 to 1963, its performance was very respectable. Upside efficiency was roughly equal to that of GM and Ford and downside efficiency was better. From 1964 to 1972, after the departure of George Romney, American Motors' upside efficiency performance was again acceptable. American Motors handled revenue increases well, and the firm did a better-than-average job with revenue declines, but, since declines are less efficient than advances, American Motors gradually lost ground and the firm ultimately ceased operations as a separate company. The experience of American Motors reinforces the interdependence of low-cost operation and product differentiation.

Chrysler's improvement in upside efficiency since 1980 is only part of the story. Some of the Chrysler turnaround was due to the downside efficiency achieved in the years prior to 1981. It should be noted that the substantial cost reductions of almost $6 billion which were initiated from 1978 to 1980 were crucial in the Chrysler turnaround of the 1980s.

The Strategic Advantage of Upside and Downside Efficiencies

Both upside and downside efficiencies are important in turnaround situations in several ways. Turnaround progress is very slow if each additional dollar of revenue costs close to or more than a dollar to obtain. This was often the case with International Harvester in the 1960s and 1970s, Studebaker in the 1950s, and Hudson in the late 1920s. There continues to be evidence today that, in several industries, firms are spending incrementally more to attract and conduct business than they are receiving in incremental revenue, a condition indicating a fundamentally weak competitive position.

Comparing Deere and International Harvester offers another example of radical differences in internal efficiencies. The relative performances of Deere and International Harvester ebbed and flowed over the years, and there were times when IHC did better. However, Deere gradually gained ground on IHC because of more internal efficiencies. For most of the past 50 years, Deere captured additional revenue at significantly lower costs than International Harvester. Deere's gross profits were about 70 percent higher than IHC's, and incremental profit rates were roughly double. This pattern of achieving greater internal efficiency began in the 1930s, when Deere was one-eighth the size of IHC. The pattern continued through the 1970s and 1980s, when Deere overtook International Harvester in both revenues and profits up to the point in 1985 when International Harvester exited the industry in which at one time it had held a 70 percent market share among longline producers.

Figure 4-2 may be representative of the true breakeven situation of the industrial firm that lacks upside and downside efficiency. Being able to capture additional revenue at a reasonable cost is an especially key ingredient to the successful turnaround. This capability reduces the demand on resources, increases profits once they are obtained, and moves the firm's breakeven point to the left.

The economics of breaking even is a subtle ingredient in turnaround success, and some managers never fully understand the intricate relationships between costs and revenue. Consequently, the revenue expansion strategy is often pursued as the major remedy while efficiency moves are neglected. Unsurprisingly, profits are seldom fully restored. Revenue restoration is of immense consequence to the troubled firm, but successful exploitation of the revenue expansion strategy depends upon attaining both upside efficiency and product differentiation.

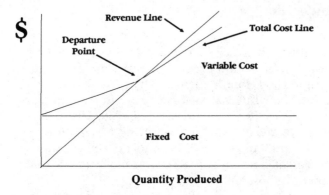

Figure 4-2. Possible breakeven chart for a troubled firm. How profitability changes as revenue changes is wholly dependent upon the behavior of variable cost and the presence or absence of upside and downside efficiency. The typical dilemma of the inefficient firm is that when revenue increases, costs increase by nearly as much, thus limiting the effectiveness of the revenue expansion strategy. Correspondingly, when revenue falls, expenses are not proportionately reduced. For profitability to be improved, efficiency moves must precede strategic moves.

Low-Cost Operation and Product Differentiation Are Interrelated

For turnaround situations, the important variables of low-cost operation and product differentiation are interrelated. Low-cost operation affects product differentiation by providing resources that enable the company to more adequately differentiate its products. Product differentiation also impacts low-cost operation by reducing the frequency of revenue decline, when costs may be reduced by a lower percentage than the falloff in revenue. Profits inevitably shrink if product differentiation is not continuously enhanced, and this crucial relationship between product differentiation and low-cost operation is one reason why "cash cow" or "harvest" strategies seldom work in the real world. The harvest strategy produces an inherently unstable condition in which some managers mistakenly assume that market position can be held without investment.

Successful turnaround agents understand the imperative to improve organizational performance and reduce cost simultaneously, and they possess the managerial skills to accomplish more with fewer resources. Some of these attributes will be discussed in later chapters. Successful turnaround agents understand that any attempt to sell an undifferentiated or low-quality product by employing greater resources will most likely result in greater expenditures and greater losses. The appropriate strategy is efficiency first, then differentiate the product, and sell later. This sequence of actions has proved to be the most effective in achieving turnarounds that last.

Because low-cost operation and product differentiation interact positively to reinforce competitive strength, efficiency must be asserted in every aspect of the organization in order to effect recovery. The turnaround agents observed in this analysis understood the importance of efficiency and allocated significant portions of their own time to ensure that efficiency was improved. Following this step, product differentiation was improved so that sales could be obtained with fewer resources.

The matter of operational efficiency must be examined in excruciating detail. Mere conceptual knowledge that efficiency must be improved is not sufficient in implementing a turnaround. Specific managerial and technical steps must be taken to restore the operational efficiency of the troubled firm. This means that managers must commit their time and be present on the factory floor or at those locations where the firm's chief value-added activities take place. Achievement of low-cost operation also involves extensive technical knowledge of company products and of operational processes. The achievement of low-cost operation is an outgrowth of specific knowledge rather than general conceptual knowledge. The process involves knowing what the product is like, how it can be changed, what production equipment can do, what people can do, and how to integrate all these important variables into a cohesive, effective, goal-integrated system which will last.

Practical Lessons on Operational Efficiency

- Successful firms concentrate on efficiency first, products second, and then on marketing and sales. Revenue expansion based upon inefficient operations results in severe operating losses.

- Successful companies reduce cost to present revenue levels. Unsuccessful companies attempt to increase revenue to cover existing costs.

- Successful companies implement proven efficiencies immediately — but work through people.

- Successful firms achieve scale economies at the component or process level and not at the level of the overall business unit.

- Top managers who know how to achieve efficiencies in the particular industry being served.

- Successful companies work productively with suppliers to reduce product cost.

- Successful managers make investments to sustain and improve efficiency — but understand processes well enough to know what really pays off.

Case Histories

In 1910, the fledgling Buick Motor Company and its younger parent, the General Motors Company, experienced a problem common to many expansion-minded firms. Expansion and acquisitions caused cash to run short, and for a brief period, General Motors was in jeopardy. Buick and GM emerged from the crisis to continue much stronger than before, benefiting from the forethought that preceded the crisis and the corrective measures that were taken during it. Nearly 70 years later, as the venerable International Harvester Corporation completed the most profitable year in its history, the company was moving into a period of decline which would ultimately cause it to exit from its major business. The early history of Buick and the recent history of International Harvester provide useful illustrations of the practical steps that must be taken to restore companies as low-cost operators.

Case 1

Masters of Production at Buick

In Flint, Michigan, in 1899, David Dunbar Buick organized the Buick Auto-Vim and Power Company for the purpose of building engines for marine and agricultural use. In 1902, the company was reorganized as the Buick Manufacturing Company. From the very beginning, Buick engines utilized overhead valves, an engine design principle that David Buick thought would ultimately become the standard for the industry. But Buick was less a promoter than an engineer and soon found it necessary to seek financial backing from some local businesspeople. Among those who expressed an interest in David Buick's work was William Crapo Durant, who headed one of Flint's most successful businesses, the Durant-Dort Carriage Company, and had other business interests. As the grandson of a prominent lumberman and governor of Michigan, the nephew of a congressman, and a prominent business executive in his own right, Durant had many associations with the financial community in that part of Michigan. His own financial backers included most of the prominent people in Flint (Dunham and Gustin 1985, 10–61).

Within a few months, Billy Durant infused money into the Buick Motor Company and took control. Under Durant, the Buick Motor Company increased promotional activities, established an extensive distribution system, developed several new models, and set up manufacturing processes for all of them. Buick soon became one of the nation's leading producers of automobiles. Buick's unit sales increased from 37 in 1904 to 8820 in 1908, making Buick the largest single producer of automobiles. Its production total exceeded the combined total of the two next-largest producers, Ford and Cadillac.

Durant was seldom satisfied with the status quo, and he began to lay plans for building Buick into the largest automotive complex in the world. Durant, personally, could promote the company and raise capital, but he did not possess the necessary technical skills and he was not interested in handling important day-to-day matters. To achieve his goals, Durant needed technical and managerial talent to augment his own entrepreneurial skills. David Buick left the company in 1908, and Durant never recruited experienced manufacturing personnel. Even though the Buick Motor Company was first in unit sales, it produced so many models that its breakeven point kept rising.

Durant's strategy was to build an automotive empire through acquisition under the umbrella of the newly formed General Motors Company, with the Buick operation in Flint as its backbone. By mid-1910, Durant had either purchased or negotiated cooperative arrangements with 30 companies involved in the production of automobiles and parts. Some of these, such as Cadillac and Champion Ignition, turned out to be excellent acquisitions, but many of the remaining operations such as Elmore, Welch, and Heany Lamp had severe problems. Losses incurred by Heany Lamp alone were estimated at $12 million (Dunham and Gustin 1985, 74–75). In these early years of GM, only Cadillac, Buick, and a few component divisions made substantial profits. Most of the other operations lost money, sometimes lots of money. Since many of Durant's acquisitions were financed on the back of the Buick balance sheet, the company was heavily in debt. Buick's debt alone was estimated at $7 million.

Meanwhile, both technical and sales problems surfaced at Buick. An internal debate had developed over the future of the division's leading car, the Model 10, as some Buick directors felt the company could not effectively compete building a low-priced car. Given Buick's high breakeven point at the time, the concern may have been well placed. Ultimately, the Model 10 was dropped from the 1911 Buick line, and sales for 1911 fell by·55 percent. Buick's market share declined from 17 percent in 1910 to less than 7 percent in 1911 (Table 4-2).

By 1910, GM was in financial trouble. An interim loan was negotiated during the summer of 1910, only after a persuasive speech by Wilfred Leland of profitable Cadillac. But cash needs remained high and Buick sales continued to slip. By November of that year, the company again needed cash. A syndicate led by the Seligman and Lee Higginson firms agreed to underwrite a loan of $15 million, with many strings attached. Durant was relegated to a background position. The board of directors and the important finance and executive committees were all reorganized, and James J. Storrow of Lee Higginson was named president of GM. Two months later he was succeeded by another member of the banking fraternity, Thomas Neal. However, during this period, James Storrow's influence remained very high.

The new regime began to take action to improve production by

Table 4-2. Buick Production, 1904–1921

Year	Number of models	Price range	Units produced
1904	1	$ 750	37
1905	1	750 to 1200	750
1906	2	1150 to 1250	1,400
1907	5	1150 to 2525	4,641
1908	4	900 to 2500	8,820
1909	5	900 to 2750	14,606
1910	6	950 to 2750	30,525
1911	8	800 to 2750	13,389
1912	5	900 to 1725	19,812
1913	4	950 to 1650	26,666
1914	3	950 to 1985	32,889
1915	4	900 to 1635	43,946
1916	3	985 to 1875	124,834
1917	2	660 to 1835	115,267
1918	4	790 to 1845	77,691
1919	2	1595 to 2585	119,310
1920	2	1495 to 2695	115,176
1921	2	1795 to 3295	82,930

drawing upon the established production expertise of Cadillac. Cadillac, Champion Ignition, and Weston-Mott were operating quite well, but severe problems existed at Oldsmobile, Oakland (later to become Pontiac), and at several other GM operations. Meanwhile, with the onslaught of problems at Buick, it became apparent that more professional technical management was needed. At about the time of the banking crisis, Charles Nash, an experienced production manager with Durant's old Durant-Dort Carriage Company, was asked to join the Buick organization. When Storrow's influence rose in GM, he quickly sought a more lasting solution to the management problems of GM's largest operation, and Nash was appointed head of Buick after being recommended by Durant. In 1911, with the help of James Storrow, Nash hired another technical man to assist in Buick's turnaround, Walter Chrysler. Chrysler was a former locomotive mechanic who became the Pittsburgh plant manager of American Locomotive Company. Chrysler was anxious to enter the automotive business and took the position at Buick at a substantial reduction in pay (Chrysler 1937).

Chrysler and Nash were different as people but shared some common interests and traits. Both were from modest backgrounds. Chrysler was a farm boy from Kansas, Nash an orphan born in Illinois and raised in Michigan. Neither had a college education. Both worked hard and demanded results. Nash was a bit more reserved than Chrysler, but they worked well together. While Walter Chrysler was implementing improvements to make the shop moreproductive, Nash was organizing the company and reducing the inventory. Chrysler and Nash

were friends with Henry and Wilfred Leland of Cadillac, and both were
occasional visitors to the Leland country home in Wilchester, where there
was an opportunity to discuss alternative approaches to manufacturing
(Leland 1966, 114).

During the time Chrysler and Nash worked together at Buick, they took
many steps to improve the effectiveness of Buick operations: they reduced
inventory, improved financial controls, developed a new six-cylinder Buick,
and made painting and assembly operations substantially more efficient. They
also reduced the number of major models offered from eight to two with the
resulting improvement in parts commonality. They oversaw other
improvements in the production processes that resulted in Buick's output
increasing from 45 cars per day in 1911 to 200 per day in 1915. Walter
Chrysler described some of the activities in his *Life of an American
Workman:*

> We evolved a better working method merely by supporting the roof
> on stouter trusses and taking out the posts that were in every
> workman's way.
> We were doing our painting before we started to assemble; in
> that way we could have a stock of parts painted and ready without
> holding [up] other workmen. Then we developed a way to squirt
> paint, using air pressure; it was the old principle of the atomizer.
> We went on with one improvement after another until, in that same
> room, instead of merely forty-five cars we were making 200 cars
> each day.
> When you had figured out a way to speed the crankshaft flow,
> some other kink would be revealed. Starting with the assembly line,
> we worked backward through the plant until everything was tied in.
> Every new thing was an invention....The motors began to get their
> shapes riding on a conveyer line; then the axles, crankshafts,
> camshafts; until now it would be difficult to find an operation
> which requires men to exert their muscles like they used to. The
> workmen have machines to do their bidding....Out of our insistent
> needs, machine tools were developed. A machine tool salesman
> would no [sooner] show his head inside my office than we'd be after
> him: "We have to have a machine that can do———." Then he'd
> take his pencil out and write down what we needed....We were
> making the first machine of considerable size in the history of the
> world for which every human being was a potential customer.
> Henry Ford, after we developed our line, went to work and
> figured out a chain conveyer; his was the first. After that, we all
> used them. Instead of pushing the cars along the line by hand, they
> rode on an endless-chain conveyer operated by a motor. (Chrysler
> 1937, 135–137)

In 1912, Nash became president of General Motors and continued
to work with James Storrow to improve its effectiveness. In a formal
sense, Nash remained head of Buick while he was also president of GM.
However, Walter Chrysler was heavily involved in the day-to-day
responsibility for Buick.

During the Nash-Storrow regime, many inefficient manufacturing operations were eliminated. Buick, Cadillac, Oakland, Oldsmobile, and General Motors Truck became the surviving end-product manufacturing divisions. Many product improvements were made, and a program of testing and product evaluation was initiated. Significant progress was made in attracting competent administrative and technical talent. Some progress, although it was far from complete, was even made in getting the sprawling GM empire to work together. GM emerged from the banking crisis intact, with its competitive position greatly strengthened (Fink 1975, 64).

One of the most notable aspects of the Buick turnaround was the systematic concentration on a smaller number of more thoroughly tested and more efficiently produced production models. In 1911, Buick produced 13,389 cars divided among eight basic models for an average of 1673 units per model. In 1917, Buick produced 115,267 cars divided among two models. Average production per model had increased from 1673 to 57,633.

Many engineering improvements were introduced during the Nash-Chrysler era at Buick, including improved lubrication and braking systems, more efficient transmissions, and easier access to frequently replaced parts. In 1914, the company completed development of a new overhead valve six-cylinder engine. Consistent with the efficiency and standardization programs instituted by Nash and Chrysler, all Buick engines now standardized on a 3.75-inch bore, thus creating the opportunity for further sharing of component parts.

Product quality and in-process quality also received the attention of Buick managers. They added centrifugal water pumps and dual ignitions to the Buick product line along with diagonal struts to stabilize suspension characteristics. The firm adopted a slogan which reflected the program of constant improvement. The slogan served the division well for the next 50 years. "When better automobiles are built, Buick will build them" (Dunham and Gustin 1985).

The sound management practices of Nash, Chrysler, and other members of the General Motors team, from 1911 to 1915, allowed the firm to grow and prosper. From 1911 to 1916, General Motors' sales increased 3.7 times while profits grew 7 times. By 1915, GM was making more than 15 percent net profit and reinvesting most of the earnings in the business (Table 4-3).

Meanwhile, Billy Durant was busily forming a new venture called Chevrolet. Durant raised a huge sum for those days, $80 million. However, instead of using all the money to build Chevrolet automobiles, Durant used much of it to buy GM stock with the objective of regaining control of GM. Storrow and Nash unwittingly played into Durant's hands by holding down dividends in favor of reinvesting the proceeds in improving the company's operations. Many stockholders interested in short-term gains were therefore attracted to the Durant camp. In January 1916, the fledgling Chevrolet Motor Company became the controlling owner of the General Motors Company. Durant had regained control.

Table 4-3. General Motors Company
Sales, Profits, and Reinvested Earnings, 1911–1915

Year	Sales	Net profits	Profit rate, %	Reinvested earnings
1911	$ 42,733,303	$ 4,066,251	9.5	$ 2,474,177
1912	64,744,496	4,746,756	7.3	2,856,082
1913	85,603,920	8,184,053	9.6	6,410,937
1914	85,373,303	7,819,968	9.2	6,201,055
1915	94,424,841	14,794,191	15.7	13,408,839
1916	156,900,296	28,789,560	18.4	17,010,437

SOURCE: Lawrence Seltzer, *The Financial History of the North American Automobile Industry*, Houghton Mifflin, Boston, 1928, pp. 230–231.

The regaining of control by the Durant interests caused some of General Motors' most experienced managers to depart (Chandler 1962). In June 1916, Nash resigned to take over, with Storrow's backing, the Thomas B. Jeffery Company in Kenosha, Wisconsin, the enterprise that eventually became American Motors. Chrysler remained head of Buick, and Buick continued to prosper. By 1919, Buick was making half of GM's total profit (Fink 1975, 120). Yet, in spite of the warm feeling that existed between Durant and Chrysler, Durant continued to interfere. In 1919, a final argument ensued over the manufacture of auto frames—Durant wanted to build them, Chrysler wanted to buy them from A. O. Smith, an innovator in frame-making processes and one of GM's most trusted vendors. Chrysler retired in 1919.

From 1917 to 1921, Buick continued to be a strong contributor to the progress of GM, accounting for roughly 60 percent of its unit sales and many innovations. But Buick could not contribute enough to overcome Durant's ambitious acquisition and spending plans. In 1921, GM faced another crisis owing to a slowdown following World War I, and Durant was removed permanently. In the meantime, Chrysler, Nash, the Lelands, and several other key people left to pursue other opportunities. But they left behind them a legacy of operational efficiency along with a cadre of trusted associates that served GM well for many years.

The Buick turnaround of 1911 to 1920 was one that focused on business basics, primarily production basics. Chrysler and Nash worked hard, studied hard, instilled values, taught other people, and enjoyed favorable personal reputations. Most important, both were masters of production. They knew a great deal about how to produce quality products at a lower cost. Nash's approach to finance was quite basic: he didn't spend much. When he did, it was to improve the company rather than to enhance executive perquisites or to acquire silly external signs of company prosperity. Chrysler saw the need to cultivate a strong productive working relationship with suppliers, a belief that finally contributed to his departure from GM.

The primary strategy behind the Buick turnaround was to become a low-cost producer by dramatically improving operational efficiency through incremental improvement, better product design, and a smaller number of production models. Financial resources were deployed to provide for the long-term development of the company, a policy that left the firm somewhat vulnerable to the 1916 equivalent of a hostile takeover.

Buick Survived Because...

- Operational efficiency was vastly improved.
- Top management understood the strategic advantage of good manufacturing.
- Parts were made more common.
- Run sizes were increased by focusing on fewer models.
- Quality was improved.
- Earnings were reinvested to further improve operational efficiency.
- Process improvements were researched and implemented.

Case 2

The Harvesting of International Harvester

In 1979, the International Harvester Company (IHC) reported record revenues of more than $8 billion and record earnings of $370 million. The company had enjoyed a long and noble history as one of the most significant industrial firms in the United States. Yet 3 years later, this huge, prestigious company was losing more than a billion dollars per year and was teetering on the brink of insolvency. In 1985, International Harvester was forced by economic circumstance to divest itself of what was, for most of its history, its major business, agricultural equipment—an enormous business in which IHC had been by far the dominant producer. International Harvester's failure was not due to lack of size, product recognition, market position, or experienced financial managers. It had all of these. International Harvester failed because it combined several characteristics that almost always lead to disaster— rampant inefficiency, lack of focus on the day-to-day aspects of the business, managerial arrogance, and industrial inexperience on the part of top management.

International Harvester was formed in 1902 as an outgrowth of the merger activities of J. P. Morgan. Many companies were merged into what became International Harvester, among them McCormick Harvesting Machine Company (which dated back to the activities of Cyrus McCormick in 1831), the Deering Harvester Co., Warder-Bushnell, Plano Harvester, and Milwaukee Harvester. By the start of World War I, International Harvester was the fourth-largest firm in the country.

IHC continued as the market leader in agricultural equipment for well over a half century. During the early 1930s, the company was eight times the size of its nearest competitor, Deere & Co. Revenues came from agricultural equipment, trucks, steel, and other products. It emerged from World War II in excellent financial condition, with after-tax profits at 7.1 percent of sales. Revenues from both the farm and the truck business segments were high. The shortages caused by World War II and the Korean War produced a seller's market. But, as the seller's market subsided in the late 1950s, some of IHC's long-established competitors, such as Minneapolis Moline and Oliver, were beginning to weaken.

International Harvester continued as the industry's largest firm well into the 1970s (though Deere did take over first position in agricultural machinery in 1958). Still, IHC's total revenues remained about 2½ times larger than those of Deere & Co. The company was a leading supplier of farm equipment, trucks, construction equipment, appliances, and many other products. By 1963, the company employed 103,000 people, and the corporation's individual revenues, apart from those of related suppliers and dealers, equaled one-third of 1 percent of the nation's entire gross national product.

International Harvester, however, was a huge complex of many different businesses, very few of which were in strong competitive positions:

> Harvester's hefty dividends only exacerbated the strategic syndrome of nurturing more businesses than it could afford.... Instead of husbanding its resources, Harvester drifted, propagating more businesses, ultimately starving them all, and, inevitably, losing market share in its three main heavy equipment businesses. A former Harvester executive draws an old horticultural analogy: "You water all of the plants but you've got limited water, so none of your plants really blossom and produce the kinds of flowers that you want them to produce. (Marsh 1985, 123–124)

In 1962, an executive from the company's aging Wisconsin Steel Division, Harry Bercher, became president of the company. Wisconsin Steel produced steel solely for International Harvester, and its profitability was difficult to determine. Bercher continued to make investments in the steel business

but did not seem to fully understand the mainstream businesses of the
company (Christiansen et al. 1982). By 1971, after-tax earnings had dropped
to 1.5 percent of sales, and Brooks McCormick, a great-grandnephew of
Cyrus McCormick, took over to rejuvenate the company and execute a
turnaround. International Harvester did improve under Brooks McCormick.
From 1971 to 1976, the following changes took place (Christiansen et al.
1982):

- Capital spending increased from $62.7 million to $168.4 million.
- Earnings rose from $45.2 million to $174.1 million.
- Return on sales rose from 1.5 to 3.2 percent.
- Agricultural equipment revenue increased to $2.3 billion.
- Total revenues grew from $2.9 billion to $5.5 billion.

In spite of the improvements made during the early 1970s, the company
was still less efficient than several of its smaller competitors. Although
International Harvester was larger than Deere, Caterpillar, or Paccar,
profit rates were substantially lower, a disparity that would have been even
greater had International Harvester invested as heavily in research and
the development of new products. Value added per employee was
two-thirds what it was at Deere and Caterpillar and three-quarters of what
it was at Paccar (Christiansen et al. 1982, 771).

Over several decades, International Harvester had slipped behind its
competitors in product differentiation as well as in operational efficiency.
Although the company was huge, revenues came as a result of offering
practically every available product to the principle markets being served.
Only a few individual product lines were market leaders. In most markets,
IHC had major, stronger competitors. IHC enjoyed a solid position in very
large trucks but lagged both Ford and GM in medium-sized trucks and
almost everyone in small trucks. In the worldwide truck market, IHC had
to contend with many, very able foreign competitors including Benz,
Saab-Volvo, Iveco, Hino, Mitsubishi, Renault, and Nissan. A similar
situation existed in agricultural equipment. Deere had taken over first
place in farm equipment as the result of decades of superior operational
efficiency, lower-cost product design, greater investment in plant
modernization, and better product development. The J. I. Case Division of
Tenneco, Ford, and others, including some short-line producers, were all
eating away at IHC's market share.

In many respects, Brooks McCormick was a product of the environment
he was trying to change. The company was regarded as "staid, old
fashioned, conservative, inbred and having little sense of direction"
(Christiansen et al. 1982, 762). McCormick set about to reorganize the
company and instill new vigor. Two consulting firms were brought in to
address the company's organizational structure and to assess

manufacturing personnel utilization. The resulting organization exhibited a fairly traditional group-division market-oriented structure of the type often employed to address overseas markets. This contrasted with the more functional organization that IHC had been using for many years. Most of the leaders in the new organization were also top-level managers in the old organization, but many had changed positions. Unfortunately, the new organizational changes did not directly address the company's inadequacy in manufacturing efficiency, nor did it explicitly provide for stronger product offerings. Instead, the changes were oriented to IHC's main strength—marketing.

As a part of the general reorganizing at IHC in the mid-1970s, the company also recruited a new chief executive officer. This choice also reflected interests in areas other than those which troubled the company most. The company went outside for a new CEO and recruited Archie McCardell from Xerox, who had a functional background primarily in finance. Before joining IHC, he had served on the board of directors of American Express, General Foods, and Blue Cross and had spent some years in financial positions with Ford. McCardell then hired Warren Hayford of Continental Group as the company president. Soon, more and more of the key executives at Harvester were replaced by individuals with little experience in Harvester's main industries. Barbara Marsh describes what transpired:

> By 1980, early retirements of veteran executives had robbed Harvester of an invaluable store of market wisdom it would sorely miss as the recessions in its markets gained ferocity that year. Executive recruits from other companies and other industries streamed into Harvester's top ranks in the McCardell era frequently lacked the intimate knowledge of its business necessary for reading and reacting to the ominous signs in the company's marketplace. One former long time executive who left for another company in 1981 says: "It was horrible working there in the last three or four years. There was so much change with top management being replaced from the outside that we lost all executive knowledge of products and markets." (Marsh 1985, 226)

Under McCardell and Hayford, International Harvester exhibited a tendency to deal only globally, and not specifically, with the company's slipping competitive position. Costs were too high, and the answer to this rather general conclusion was an attempt to persuade union workers to accept lower pay rather than address product design, production processes, and managerial expertise for their impact on profitability. International Harvester workers were asked for $100 million in labor concessions along with significant changes in work rules. Labor relations stalled, as they often do when traditional avenues of improvement are not explored before help is requested of the union. A prolonged strike in 1979 and 1980 worsened employee relations as the company sought concessions from its manufacturing workers at a time when executives were being awarded large salaries and extensive bonuses (Marsh 1985, 235). The strategy to reduce labor costs backfired, and after a costly strike lasting 170 days, the longest in the history of the industry, the company was forced to drop most of its demands.

The aftermath of the strike created additional problems for International Harvester. A high-cost producer, the firm had difficulty operating profitably on anything less than very high volume. Following settlement of the strike, the company began a massive effort to catch up on lost production. Unfortunately, the United States was entering its worst economic downturn since the 1930s. IHC's new management team was out of touch with trends in the marketplace, and the high production levels were continued long after there were sales to support them. Dealers had been neglected by the new breed of outsiders. Plant updating had lagged. Incremental product improvement and quality programs were set aside in pursuit of more flamboyant, all-encompassing "grand slam" efforts that lacked specificity.

The absence of specificity at International Harvester was evident in the caliber of its forecasting. On March 21, 1981, *The Wall Street Journal* reported that International Harvester officials had projected a $90 million loss for the fiscal year ending October 31 and that the firm would be profitable during its fourth quarter and in 1982. Seven months later, when the results were announced, the actual loss for the quarter was $393 million, *helped* by a $243 million tax credit. The actual loss for 1982 became nearly $1.3 billion. International Harvester was in a serious profit tailspin that was not being reversed by the recipes being applied. From 1980 to 1985, the company lost over $3 billion and flirted with formal bankruptcy on several occasions (Table 4-4).

Table 4-4. International Harvester Profitability and Inventory Efficiency

	Revenue	Profit	Profit, %	Ratio of revenue to inventory
1979	$8,035,650,000	$ 369,572,000	4.6	3.43
1980	5,968,414,000	(374,798,000)	(6.3)	2.56
1981	7,040,920,000	(635,684,000)	(9.0)	4.31
1982	4,292,000,000	(1,266,000,000)	(29.5)	5.66
1983	3,601,000,000	(533,000,000)	(14.8)	5.82
1984	4,802,000,000	(61,000,000)	(1.3)	6.93
1985	3,507,000,000	(363,636,000)	(10.4)	10.50

SOURCE: *Moody's Industrial Manual,* 1981, 1983, 1985, and 1986.

The historical contrast between the operations at Deere and International Harvester was striking. At IHC, commonality of parts was not a priority. For approximately 40 years, from about 1920 to 1960, John Deere tractors had 1400 fewer parts than comparably powered International Harvester products. During the 1970s, IHC's huge inventory turned only at a ratio of around 3. At Deere, the ratio was usually around 6, and perhaps would have been higher had Deere not placed so much of its inventory with dealers. While Deere executives made concerted attempts to remain in touch with customers and dealers, IHC management was less attentive. During the 1930s, the people at Deere hand-addressed much of their correspondence to customers. During the farm crisis of the early 1980s, Archie McCardell sporadically visited distraught IHC dealers in a posh limousine. Most important, Deere led International Harvester in gross profit rates every year from 1955.

McCardell was replaced during the downtrend by board member Louis Menk, a retired chairman of Burlington-Northern railroad, who in turn was replaced by manufacturing executive Donald Lennox. Lennox proceeded to concentrate on the reduction of corporate costs and focused the company on selected markets. Many operations were closed. Eight company limousines were sold. Greater stress was placed on the commonality of parts and the efficient utilization of inventories. Costs were reduced in other important ways. Finally, in January 1985, the company divested itself of the business that at one time had made it one of the largest firms in the country. The agricultural equipment business was sold to the J. I. Case Division of Tenneco.

During its unsuccessful turnaround attempt, International Harvester applied the wrong remedies, cajoled the wrong people, and spiraled downward until it nearly went out of business. Ultimately IHC management was forced to reduce the size of the company dramatically in order to survive at all, and then with only a weakened portion of its business intact. The magnitude of the dramatic decline in International Harvester is seldom completely understood. A few facts describe the changes from the mid-1970s to 1986 (Figure 4-3):

- Employment was reduced from more than 100,000 workers to 16,836.
- The number of plants was reduced from 47 to 8.
- Plant square footage was reduced from 38 million square feet to 7.5 million square feet.
- Net worth before the obligations on preferred stock declined from $2.196 billion to $41.7 million.
- Net worth after preferred stock obligations declined from a positive $2.246 billion to a negative $871 million.

Whether the efforts of future IHC managers will be sufficient to allow such a weak company to prevail in what is increasingly becoming a global market

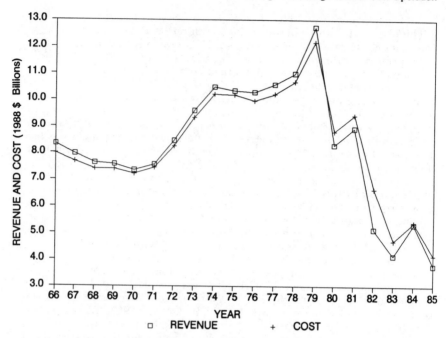

Figure 4-3. Revenue and cost at International Harvester. International Harvester's revenue and earnings peaked in 1979, but the company lacked the efficiency that would have enabled it to adjust to the lower revenue levels of the next 4 years. When revenue did increase, costs increased by nearly as much. When revenue fell, not much money was saved. Within 6 years of record earnings and record profits, the company exited what, for most of its history, had been its major business.

remains to be seen. Perhaps what is left of International Harvester can survive as a revitalized Navistar International. That can be the subject of another longitudinal study at another time.

In the meantime, it is worthwhile for us to ponder both the causes of the decline and its cost. The cost to the country, families, creditors, communities, banks, and government institutions of International Harvester's mismanagement was staggering and it may never be accurately assessed. It did not need to happen. The company surely had a sufficiently comfortable position from which to stage a successful turnaround at many points during its long history. But, company management failed to initiate the basic requirement of becoming a low-cost producer of differentiated products and, in the view of some observers, to play fair with employees, creditors, suppliers, and customers. The company lacked discipline and failed to maintain a basic expertise in operational efficiency.

International Harvester Failed Because...

- Operational efficiency lagged that of competitors.
- Workers were pressed for concessions before management did its own job.
- Forecasting systems were defective.
- Appreciation was not shown for old values as a foundation for new beliefs.
- Top management lacked experience in the industry being served.
- Major businesses were victimized by ill-managed diversification.

5
Achieving and Sustaining Modest Overhead

During the 1920s, two companies emerged from crises to become high-volume producers of automobiles. One became the industry's third-largest producer and failed. On less than half the volume, the other attained the highest profit rate of any firm in the industry and operated independently for another 60 years before merging with another successful company. The first firm, Willys-Overland, loudly focused its energies on promotion, publicity, and sales. The firm's chief executive became famous as a business entrepreneur and later as an ambassador. The second firm, Nash Motors, which later became American Motors, focused on product quality, inventory efficiency, and the minimization of overhead. While John North Willys was busily promoting both cars and his public image, Charles Nash was eating lunch with the factory hands at the Kenosha plant and getting their ideas on how costs could be reduced.

> Every brain in the plant, from foreman to president, meets every Monday afternoon at 5 o'clock to offer and hear suggestions for improving this process or that, to consider communications from owners and dealers offering comments or constructive criticism, to discuss conditions, sales plans, etc. Always when at home Mr. Nash presides over these sessions. (Forbes 1972, 217)

Expenses Unrelated to What the Customer Is Buying

As unrefined as the concept may seem, some companies are in financial trouble because they spend too much money. In particular, they spend too much on items unrelated to what the customer is buying—the product or service provided. The well-managed company prudently and carefully spends money designing, building, and nurturing the products and services it provides to customers. All these expenditures benefit customers. Unsuccessful companies spend money on overhead, offices, promotion, and executive compensation, and none of these benefit customers. This simple difference is often a crucial factor in turnaround success.

Beyond the fact that successful and unsuccessful companies spend money on different things, they also spend different amounts. Though some variation exists, the unsuccessful companies examined here spent a higher fraction of their revenue on general and administrative expenses, selling expenses, and other non-cost-of-sales expenses (14.0 percent versus 13.2 percent) during the period of recovery. This figure includes income taxes, however. Since the successful firms were far more profitable during their recovery periods, the after-tax measure presents a bias in favor of the unsuccessful companies. When non-cost-of-sales expenses excluding income taxes are compared, the actual difference is almost 4 percentage points (9.5 percent versus 13.2 percent), a significant fraction of usual corporate profit rates. As a percentage of revenue, the successful companies spent about 28 percent less money on overhead.

The reputations of the chief turnaround agents corroborate the statistical evidence. Charles Nash, who had a widespread reputation for frugality, conducted the company affairs from a modest office with no carpet and a pedestrian desk. He was intensely interested in the day-to-day management of the business and generally spurned social activities. Yet, Nash Motors was still able to produce milestone products and greatly increase market share while spending very little money for product development, selling, and general and administrative expense.

> Mr. Nash's office on the second floor of the administration building in Kenosha is typical of the man himself; it is well furnished but extremely modest; no rug adorns the floor, but the chairs are comfortable and the broad flat desk at which Mr. Nash works costs less, perhaps than the desk of many a chief clerk or office manager. And, as any man in the Nash organization will testify, the door to that office is always open. (Forbes 1972, 224)

The Packard Motor Car Company of the 1930s also operated with a small central staff while it simultaneously developed a whole new line of automobiles, revamped its dealer network, maintained first place in prestige auto sales, and became established as a respected defense contractor. At American Motors during the 1950s George Romney avoided excessive spending on personal embellishments and expensive styles of travel. Officer compensation was substantially reduced at Packard, Deere, Chrysler, Nash Motors, and American Motors during the 1950s, when business turned downward.

In contrast, Allis-Chalmers, Studebaker-Packard of later years, International Harvester, and Willys-Overland made substantial expenditures on items unrelated to the production of products. Allis-Chalmers averaged 20.2 percent of revenue for non-cost-of-sales expenses. From 1979 to 1982, revenue at Allis-Chalmers declined by 46.5 percent, but non-cost-of-sales expenses were reduced by only 21 percent. Willys-Overland also spent more than 15 percent of revenue on non-cost-of-sales items. One successful firm, Deere, spent heavily on non-cost-of-sales items, mostly because of the heavy product development program, but in the main, successful companies were much less inclined to spend higher percentages of their revenue on items unrelated to production (Table 5-1).

Achieving and sustaining modest overhead did not adversely affect the ability of the successful firms to compete. During the Chrysler turnaround of the 1980s, the number of salaried staff members was reduced from 44,000 to 23,000. Yet, even with this very substantial staff reduction, the company entered one of its most prolific periods in terms of

Table 5-1. Non-Cost-of-Sales Expense as a Percent of Revenue
During the Period of Recovery

	Excluding tax expense, %	Including tax expense, %	Turnaround outcome
Jeffery (Nash)	4.44	7.56	Successful
Packard	6.83	9.23	Successful
Hudson	7.56	8.09	Unsuccessful
Kaiser-Frazer	8.04	9.03	Unsuccessful
Chrysler	8.43	11.52	Successful
Ford	9.04	11.71	Successful
Maxwell-Chalmers	9.56	10.34	Successful
American Motors	10.45	12.82	Successful
Studebaker-Packard	12.94	14.99	Unsuccessful
International Harvester	13.86	14.66	Unsuccessful
Willys-Overland	15.24	15.50	Unsuccessful
AMC/Renault	15.37	14.70	Unsuccessful
Deere	17.71	25.70	Successful
Allis-Chalmers	18.20	20.24	Unsuccessful

new-vehicle development, marketing, and service. Ford Motor Company also operated with smaller staffs. After losing billions of dollars in the early 1980s, Ford responded with the award-winning Taurus/Sable project that came in under budget and with a smaller staff. The Taurus/Sable project and other Ford projects were so successful that the firm came back from disaster to become the industry's profit leader and to accumulate over $10 billion in cash. Major technical and marketing accomplishments were implemented during periods of expense reduction at American Motors (during the 1950s), Deere, and Packard. There does not seem to be evidence that vast resources are crucial to either product differentiation or corporate development.

The Packard Motor Car Company of the 1930s illustrates what can be done with a small central staff. Packard spent little money on advertising and promotion, reduced executive compensation, and still maintained high-quality products. Statistically, Packard had the lowest non-cost-of-sales expense of any firm in the sample except Nash. Yet the company produced one of the longest lists of prestigious automobiles in the history of the world. Sixty-seven Packard models produced in the 1930s are recognized as full classics by the Classic Car Club of America, all produced by a company with very low expenditures on research and development.

Maintaining modest overhead was a learned behavior rather than an inherent trait. The successful companies learned to keep expenses low as a part of the turnaround process. Successful firms generally had higher overhead expenses during their preturnaround periods, but they learned to reduce these expenses to below industry levels. Unsuccessful firms actually permitted overhead expenses to grow as a percent of revenue. Table 5-2 shows this progression.

The Vigilance of Cost-Reduction Programs

Most successful and unsuccessful companies reduced costs as revenue declined. But the successful companies stayed with their cost-reduction

Table 5-2. Non-Cost-of-Sales Expense as a Percent of Revenue
Excluding Tax Expense

	Preturnaround period, %	Period of crisis, %	Period of recovery, %
Successful cases	10.03	15.21	9.53
Unsuccessful cases	7.76	11.24	14.01

programs longer, until costs were more comfortably below revenue levels. Unsuccessful companies permitted expenses to stabilize or increase when profits were still very low or even negative. These patterns reflected different operating philosophies. Successful firms gracefully accepted lower revenue levels during times of adversity and brought expenses down to match revenue. Unsuccessful firms put less emphasis on cost reduction and tended to pursue revenue expansion as the principal remedial strategy.

Two excellent examples of ongoing vigilance in the reduction of cost occurred with the Deere & Co. and Chrysler turnarounds. From 1929 to 1932, Deere reduced constant dollar costs by more than 70 percent. From 1977 to 1980, Chrysler reduced constant dollar costs by 48 percent and then followed with further reductions in the next 2 years. Figures 5-1 and 5-2 illustrate the cost-reduction programs of Deere and Chrysler over the several years of their turnaround periods. Table 5-3 shows the cost reductions of successful and unsuccessful firms in constant dollars.

Chrysler actually reduced constant dollar costs from $29 billion in 1977 to $12 billion in 1982, a reduction of 57 percent. Ford reduced

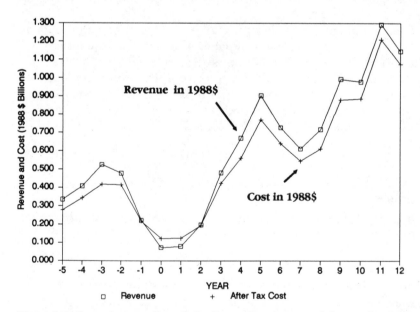

Figure 5-1. Cost reduction at Deere & Co. Deere reduced constant dollar costs by more than 70 percent from 1929 to 1932, starting with the amounts paid to managers and owners. These dramatic cost reductions strengthened the firm's efficiency and prepared it to capitalize on the revenue expansion which was to occur during the later 1930s and the 1940s.

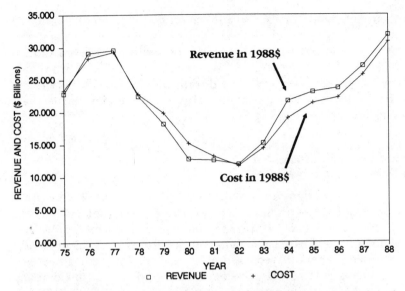

Figure 5-2. Cost reduction at Chrysler Corporation. Chrysler was not saved by federal bank guarantees but by massive cost-reduction programs, dramatic increases in internal efficiencies, and improved product engineering. From 1977 to 1978, Chrysler reduced constant dollar costs by 48 percent and then followed with further reductions during the next 2 years.

Table 5-3. Total Company Constant Dollar Cost (1988 dollars)

	Year −3 total cost ($000)	Year Zero total cost ($000)	Percent change year −3 to year 0	Year 0 profit as percent of revenue
	Successful Cases			
Packard	280,544	212,492	−24.3	−49.9
Deere	417,972	122,462	−70.7	−66.8
American Motors	2,815,744	1,691,053	−39.9	−4.8
Chrysler	29,297,999	15,199,417	−48.1	−18.5
Ford	64,047,395	53,693,209	−16.2	−4.2
	Unsuccessful Cases			
Hudson	1,334,578	297,087	−77.4	−21.0
Studebaker- Packard	2,881,214	2,607,761	−9.5	−4.4
International Harvester	7,404,984	7,451,420	+0.6	−1.5
Allis-Chalmers	2,308,905	2,469,493	+7.0	−7.1
Kaiser-Frazer	1,885,185*	1,296,276	−34.8	−11.2
AMC/Renault	3,876,654	4,425,940	+14.7	−2.0

*Year −3 for Kaiser-Frazer was 1946, an atypical year in the U.S. auto industry because of the end of World War II. Year −2 (1947) is used instead.

costs from $68 billion in 1978 to $45 billion in 1982, a reduction of 34 percent. Yet, for three of the unsuccessful cases, expenses during year 0 (the low point) actually grew during the period of crisis even though profits had worsened considerably. Among the unsuccessful firms, only Hudson substantially reduced cost during periods of adversity. Even then, the reductions were not enough. Hudson lost money 7 of 10 years during its attempted recovery.

Pragmatic and Even-Handed Cost-Reduction Programs

Cost-reduction programs during the successful turnarounds were pragmatic, disciplined, and even-handed with respect to rank. Often, top management set the course for cost reductions by reducing its own pay and eliminating unnecessary expenses in its offices. Several successful turnaround managers played exemplary roles in cost reductions. For instance, during the Great Depression, the Packard Motor Car Company reduced total officer compensation from $748,000 in 1929 to $152,000 in 1933, resulting in an average yearly compensation of about $16,000 per officer. Nash Motors reduced the total compensation of its officer group from $802,000 in 1928 to $96,547 in 1937 resulting in an average yearly compensation of $16,091 per officer. Substantial reductions in officer pay also took place at Deere. Iacocca's salary at Chrysler was reduced to one dollar per year during the crucial stages of the Chrysler turnaround. During the 1950s, George Romney and the management team at American Motors voluntarily took substantial pay cuts as the first element of cost-reduction programs.

The management teams of unsuccessful turnarounds did not usually play exemplary roles in cost reductions and occasionally continued to consume corporate resources when the organizations needed to reduce cost. In contrast to the behavior of Romney at American Motors, during the same period and under similar economic conditions, James Nance, president of Studebaker-Packard, collected $150,000 (about $700,000 in 1988 dollars) per year during 5 straight years of substantial losses. In addition, Mr. Nance had a $600,000 consulting agreement if he left the company (Dawes 1975). Archie McCardell's salary at International Harvester made him one of highest-paid executives in the country in 1977 (Marsh 1985). McCardell did reduce his salary by 20 percent during the severe difficulties of International Harvester, but the award of $2.7 million in loan forgiveness to himself and the company's president during the period of the company's longest strike exacerbated relations with company workers. Recently, the heavy compensation to General Motors' executives, when the company's market share has been contracting and plants have been closing, has diminished the rapport between GM management and other members of the organization. Control Data, Firestone, Midwest Federal, and other companies are examples of where heavy executive compensation continued when the firms' main businesses were in severe decline.

The conservative handling of costs was more of an ongoing process at the companies which experienced successful turnarounds. Most of them avoided lavish expenditures in both good times and bad. The money they spent was directed toward improving the effectiveness of existing operations. Walter Chrysler and Charles Nash refocused the resources of the Buick and GM organizations away from dividends and acquisitions to improving product quality and manufacturing efficiency. Henry and Wilfred Leland did the same at Cadillac. George Romney spurned frivolous spending when he was chief executive of American Motors, but he spent substantial funds to keep AMC plants upgraded and efficient.

Unsuccessful companies were more sporadic in their spending and occasionally wasted large sums of money on poorly thought-out plans for expansion. Studebaker-Packard spent over $41 million on just one of several misguided acquisitions during a time when the company was severely pressed for cash. Kaiser constructed two plants which were never used. Studebaker-Packard did the same. Hudson bought a steel company. International Harvester invested heavily in capacity expansion at a time when it was already experiencing severely declining sales, an erosion of market share, and the initial stages of a serious recession.

Both successful and unsuccessful companies showed progress in reducing their losses, but the progress made by the successful companies was more pronounced, more internally focused, more technical, and less oriented to financial juggling, and it tended to be much longer lasting. Acquisitions, mergers, or divestitures were sought much more by the unsuccessful companies. Acquisitions, mergers, or divestitures played almost no role in the recovery of any of the successful companies.

The Systematic Withdrawal of Resources Improves Performance

An important operating principle which applies to all business situations but fits particularly well with turnaround situations is that it is usually possible to do more with less. Sandor Brent (1978) discussed the concept of accomplishing more with less by describing the work of a European scientist, Ilya Prigogine, who was awarded the Nobel prize for his observations on the development and entropy (increasing amounts of disorder) of complex systems. Using the laws of thermodynamics as a basis for his study of complex systems, Prigogine addressed the conditions under which complexity and disorder expand within a system to curtail progress and increase costs. Unfortunately, some of these same entropic conditions tend to occur almost naturally with a firm in trouble. The struggling company is often viewed by investors, bankers, creditors, or other stakeholders as being out of control. Various mechanisms are then instituted to restore the health of the firm, actions sometimes viewed as restoring control. In a practical sense, when a control mechanism or another function is added to a complex system like a machine or an organization, energy is consumed. The governor on an engine requires some energy to operate, and though the engine is better controlled, it is less efficient. Entropy can exist in organizations as well as in machinery. It takes time for people to communicate with the coordinators and the managers at various levels and even with other members of the organization. Under some circumstances, the organization itself becomes an enormous consumer of its own resources.

Chester Barnard also observed entropy in organizations and commented on unproductive communication paths in *Functions of the Executive* (1938). He noted that the number of communication paths increases geometrically with the number of people in the organization. These additional communications, resources, and control mechanisms pose severe burdens, which the already stressed turnaround organization can seldom afford. The result is an inhibition of the organization's effectiveness. Paul Lawrence and Davis Dyer make similar observations in their book *Renewing American Industry* (1983), wherein they suggest that the companies most likely to progress toward readaptation are those that fall in the intermediate ranges in both resource scarcity and information complexity. Resource surplus retards readaptation.

No single person turns a company around. Turnarounds progress because the entire organization learns new tasks and how to do old tasks better. Too many resources interfere with organizational learning. Few people will take the trouble to learn a task or accept full responsibility if they feel it is somebody else's job. The presence of many specialized organizational elements reduces overall effectiveness. Conversely, if fewer people are involved in a function, a renewed sense of responsibility often surfaces on the part of those who remain. An important holistic advantage emerges in operating with fewer resources. Giving responsibility to one person or to small units improves effectiveness because participants can see the entire problem, thus reducing the need for special technical groups. Organizational learning permits the company to get more done while it systematically withdraws resources. If a company promotes broadly based organizational learning, it can improve performance while using fewer resources.

Broadly based organizational learning does not take place at unsuccessful companies. Willys-Overland, for example, never really learned to produce better cars at lower cost. Except for a brief period under the stewardship of Walter Chrysler, the company did not progress toward either modest overhead or operational efficiency. Nor did the company learn to produce cars of distinction. Perhaps it was for these reasons that Walter Chrysler chose not to take a permanent position in the company when he had the opportunity.

At Willys-Overland, the perquisites and rewards of management became disconnected from responsibilities. Public notoriety was achieved at the expense of detailed involvement in the day-to-day problems of the business. The results were enormous losses to investors, creditors, and dealers along with layoffs and ultimately the loss of employment for the company's employees. At one time, close to 1 percent of the nation's GNP was related directly or indirectly to the activities of the Willys-Overland Company. Production reached 315,000 units in 1928, and employment reached 21,000, with many more people employed by dealers and suppliers. Management became comfortable, and the firm's leader retired to become an ambassador after selling his stock shortly before the market crash in 1929. Five years later, the firm declared bankruptcy. Meanwhile, the officers and owners of surviving companies were developing technically appropriate improvements, cutting their own compensation, and pledging their personal assets to keep their firms in business.

Attaining Inventory Efficiency

The principle of modest overhead extends well beyond the executive office and permeates the production process as well, particularly regarding the handling of inventory. During the late 1920s, Willys-Overland consistently tied up between $20 and $35 million in inventories. Nash had $6 million to $7 million. Willys-Overland's ratio of sales to inventory (inventory turn ratio, sometimes called inventory turns per year) was about 7, while Nash's was 19. Nash operated at 4 times the dollar profits on one-half the market share. In terms of inventory efficiency and other measures as well, Nash was clearly the superior company. Yet, this was not always so. In 1916, the Willys-Overland Company produced 140,111 units, approximately 1 of every 10 American cars, while Nash Motors' predecessor, the Thomas B. Jeffery Company, produced 4608 units, a market share of well under 1 percent. The steps taken during the successful Jeffery/Nash turnaround provide important lessons about inventory efficiency as an ingredient to turnaround success.

Inventories represent unutilized resources and indicate inefficient production. The successful turnaround firm will rigorously manage its inventories, but in some very special ways. Cash is absolutely critical to a firm in trouble, and inventory efficiency can make available huge amounts of cash. Assume two companies with annual sales of $1 billion find themselves in trouble. The unsuccessful firm could have an inventory turn ratio of about 6.4 and inventories of about $156 million, while the successful firm could have an inventory turn ratio of about 9.7 and inventories of about $104 million. The difference is $52 million and, for a company in trouble, that is a precious amount.

A good historical illustration of the importance of inventory efficiency can be developed by comparing Chrysler Corporation to International Harvester. Both these firms were hit hard by the recession of the early 1980s. Chrysler's turnaround was successful, at least for a decade. International Harvester was unsuccessful, and it was forced to exit the industry in which it was once so dominant. These two firms exhibited great differences in inventory efficiency. International Harvester had revenues of $8 billion and record profits in 1979. Inventory turns per year, however, were typically around 3, resulting in a huge inventory of $2.342 billion. Chrysler Corporation gradually worked on inventory efficiency until it achieved an inventory turn ratio of more than 13 in 1986. During the entire period of recovery, Chrysler's inventory turn ratio averaged 11.02. Had this same level of inventory efficiency been achieved by International Harvester in 1979, the firm would have entered the downturn with an additional $1.6 billion in cash. At one point International Harvester had an inventory of over $2.3 billion, turning at a rate of only 2.56 times per year. This immense inventory amounted to about $1000 for every farm in the United States. International Harvester actually had in its possession, in the form of excess inventory, a reserve of hidden cash greater than the face value of the bank guarantees received by Chrysler Corporation. Conversely, if Chrysler Corporation had operated during its turnaround with the same level of inventory efficiency as International Harvester, the firm's turnaround would have required an additional $3.2 billion in cash. Considering Chrysler's financial position at the time, raising this amount of money would have been very difficult. The outcomes of these two turnarounds, involving so much money and so many people, were in part determined by the specific matter of inventory efficiency.

Inventory Efficiency and Turnaround Success

Inventory is much more than a reserve of potential cash. Inventory acts as a negative index of operating efficiency. Charles Nash was against inventory, not because Nash Motors couldn't afford inventories, but because inventory got in the way of efficient production. His concept of production imposed the discipline that every operation produce quality parts all of the time. The utilization of inventory as a buffer against production failures was not permitted. In this sense, the experience at Nash Motors preceded by 50 years some of the modern concepts of just-in-time inventory management.

In the book *Japanese Manufacturing Techniques* (1982), Richard Schonberger contrasts American production methods with those in use in Japan, and then formulates his observations into nine lessons. Three of these lessons are particularly relevant to the impact of inventory efficiency on operations:*

> Lesson #2: Just-in-time production exposes problems otherwise hidden by excess inventories and staff. Just-in-time (Kanban) production forces a stern discipline'into component quality, product design, workmanship, scheduling, space utilization and the preventive maintenance of production equipment.

> Lesson #7: Travel light. Make numerous trips like the water beetle. Japanese production systems depend upon an exceedingly close relationship with highly trusted nearby suppliers. Because pipelines are so short, defects are detected before many component parts are produced.

> Lesson #9: Simplicity is the natural state. Japanese production systems attempt to get by with less—less inventory, fewer specialized machines, fewer staff specialists and fewer departments.

Schonberger compares Japanese and Western production systems, pointing out that Western production systems use inventory buffers to cushion the effects of equipment failure, whereas Japanese systems employ maximum preventive maintenance to keep equipment from breaking down. His explanation provides a helpful commentary on the fact that excess cost often negatively affects production. The things that do cost money (extra inventory, extra space, extra information, extra people, and extra communications) get in the way of operational efficiency. Charles Nash's 1920 concept of just-in-time inventory was a key element in keeping his plants efficient.

With respect to the actual turnaround experience of the 16 firms examined, inventory turn ratios averaged 8.52 for successful firms versus 6.15 for unsuccessful firms during the period of recovery (Table 5-4). The difference in inventory performance consumed the current equivalent of about $2 billion among seven struggling companies.

*Reprinted with permission of Free Press, New York.

Table 5-4. Inventory Turn Ratio by Turnaround Stage

	Preturnaround situation	Period of crisis	Period of recovery
Successful cases	6.43	5.09	8.52
Unsuccessful cases	7.08	6.63	6.15

The successful firms learned an important lesson as they progressed through the turnaround process: They learned to handle inventory more efficiently. Before and during the period of crisis, unsuccessful firms had high inventory turn ratios, while successful firms substantially improved their inventory efficiency as their turnarounds progressed. Ford's inventory turn ratio rose from 7.4 in 1979 to 12.4 in 1988, as the firm made progress toward full recovery. Chrysler's rose from 6.4 in 1979 to 13.4 in 1986. The inventory turn ratio of American Motors under Romney progressed from 5.1 in 1953 to 11.0 in 1962. The unsuccessful firms did not improve their inventory efficiency. International Harvester, for example, had inventory turn ratios of below 3.5 for the first 9 years of its attempted turnaround (Figure 5-3).

The strategy of using common component parts was frequently employed to achieve inventory efficiency. However, this requires further clarification. Several successful firms (Buick from 1911 to 1919, American Motors in the 1950s and 1960s, and Chrysler Corporation in the 1980s) did utilize well-organized programs to utilize common component parts in the manufacture of several products. Hudson and Kaiser both used common parts extensively also, but their turnarounds were still unsuccessful. In the Hudson and Kaiser cases, although the firms used common parts, the products themselves were not designed for manufacturability and many were quite expensive to produce. Hudson used the same piston and valve assemblies in both six-cylinder and eight-cylinder engines, but the engines were antiquated in design and expensive to manufacture. The successful companies employed standardized parts within a framework of design for manufacturability, which includes producibility, value engineering, and installation requirements, and these qualities permitted higher levels of inventory efficiency. Chapter 6 discusses the achievement of lower cost through design in more detail.

Inventory efficiency is not always coincident with manufacturing efficiency. Companies often pursued operational efficiency and inventory efficiency as separate objectives and occasionally managed to achieve one without the other. Deere, for instance, achieved exceptionally high operational efficiency but not such high inventory efficiency, in part be-

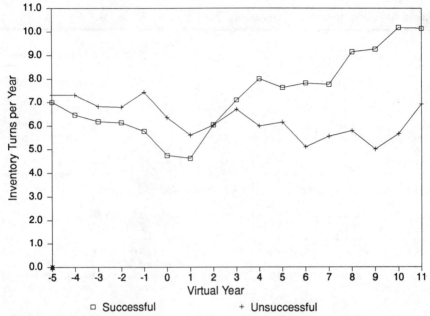

Figure 5-3. Inventory efficiency: successful and unsuccessful turnarounds. Successful firms learned to handle inventory more efficiently as a condition necessary for survival. After experiencing lower rates of inventory efficiency during the preturnaround and crisis periods, the successful firms met and surpassed the unsuccessful firms in what is one of the most important sources of cash.

cause of the company's benevolent relationship with its dealers. Successful firms tended to achieve both, however, and the pursuit of both strategies increased the probability of turnaround success. Table 5-5 displays the inventory turns per year of a sample of companies during the 1920s and 1930s. Substantial differences existed among the major producers.

During the 1920s, Nash Motors, the Hudson Motor Car Company, and Chrysler Corporation had relatively high inventory turns per year, perhaps indicating greater attention to the operational considerations of inventory. Other companies, such as Studebaker, Willys-Overland, and Reo, had high sales during this period without attaining either high levels of manufacturing or inventory efficiency. During the depression, sales fell off, and without efficient manufacturing, these companies were in serious trouble and all ultimately failed.

When industry began to emerge from the depression during the 1930s, companies varied widely in their inventory efficiency. Packard and Hudson improved theirs while International Harvester continued with low inventory turns per year in spite of very high sales. Chrysler became the industry leader. During the late 1950s and early 1960s

Table 5-5. Comparison of Inventory Turn Ratios.

Year	GM	Chrysler	Nash	Hudson	Pack-ard	Stude-baker	IHC	Reo	Willys	Deere
1924	...	...	13.55							
1925	...	...	12.93							
1926	6.77	9.95	19.56	...	6.77					
1927	7.35	9.66	16.91	13.38	7.56	...	...	4.55	7.46	
1928	7.60	7.01	20.79	14.11	7.25	...	...	3.92	6.90	2.99
1929	7.98	9.84	19.74	14.93	8.12	5.57	...	4.78	8.84	3.18
1930	7.21	7.98	18.74	11.41	5.20	4.86	...	4.45	5.53	3.01
1931	7.60	8.32	26.65	8.54	3.81	3.97	...	3.28	6.77	1.91
1932	5.73	7.43	14.99	7.15	2.69	...	...	2.63	6.88	0.68
1933	4.92	6.91	4.33	5.24	3.53	...	...	3.10	...	0.74
1934	6.09	9.65	9.20	11.52	3.06	...	...	3.54	...	1.52
1935	5.89	10.60	10.18	12.91	6.16	...	2.57	3.70	...	3.04
1936	6.38	11.02	5.51	9.64	7.33	...	2.58	3.13	...	3.95

SOURCE: Data are from *Moody's Industrial Manual* and Lawrence Seltzer, *The Financial History of the North American Automobile Industry,* Houghton Mifflin, Boston, 1928. Gaps in the data on inventory turn ratios exist because of variations in the financial reporting of the companies.

American Motors, under George Romney, emerged from crisis to again become the industry leader in inventory efficiency.

Although it is difficult to isolate a single cause of turnaround success, modest overhead and high rates of inventory efficiency are commonly present among successful companies. These well-managed firms spend less money on general and administrative expenses, office buildings, purposeless travel, unnecessary selling expenses, and other items not related to products or customers. They employ frugality as an ongoing mode of operation. In addition, cost-reduction programs at the successful firms are longer lasting and more even-handed with respect to rank. When expenses must be cut, managers lead the way by cutting their own salaries first before implementing cost reductions elsewhere in the organization. When expenses need to be reduced, they are reduced. Unsuccessful firms apply token cost reductions and then permit expenses to rise before the firm's health is restored. Excessive costs impede efficient operations.

Practical Lessons on Modest Overhead

- Successful companies spend money on important things that relate to what it is the customer is buying.

- Unsuccessful companies spend money on things unrelated to what the customer is buying.

- Successful companies systematically withdraw resources to improve operational performance.

- Successful companies keep inventory efficiency high to preserve cash and to improve operational efficiency.

- Employees view cash preservation and modest overhead as indices of competence and trustworthiness on the part of management.

- Employees are anxious to help save money—if management is too.

Case Histories

Willys-Overland and Nash Motors exhibited radically different corporate priorities as they progressed during the 1920s. As John North Willys sought sales volume and personal prestige, Charles Nash was nurturing new programs to reduce expenses, improve relations with dealers, and build better products. In particular, the two firms contrasted in their treatment of overhead expenses. Willys tolerated them with minimal scrutiny. Nash actively sought to reduce them in every possible way. As the depression deepened during the 1930s, the frugality employed at Nash Motors enabled the firm to survive while Willys-Overland, a firm that at one time shipped 80 percent as many cars as General Motors, filed for bankruptcy—a common outcome when too much money is spent.

Case 3

Professional Frugality at Nash

In Chicago, before the turn of the twentieth century, Thomas Jeffery and Philip Gormully founded and developed the second-largest bicycle factory in the country by producing a bicycle named the "Rambler." The two men also manufactured tires in another operation which ultimately became part of U.S. Rubber. By the mid-1890s, Jeffery and his son, Charles, had developed a keen interest in building automobiles. Thomas Jeffery produced his first car in 1897; it was followed 1 year later by a more advanced design by Charles. By 1900, a car known alternatively as the "G & J" and the "Rambler" was exhibited at a few of the automotive shows. But, Philip Gormully died suddenly in 1900, prompting the two Jefferys to reassess the business. The bicycle business was sold to the Pope interests, and the Jefferys headed north to Kenosha, Wisconsin, to purchase a large factory for the purpose of building automobiles.

In selling their bicycle business, the Jefferys retained the rights to the

Rambler name, and the earliest Rambler automobile appeared in 1902. It was a well-built, high-quality, inexpensive, one-cylinder car that sold for $750. Production during the first year totaled 1500, a production level exceeded only by Oldsmobile. Although the Jeffery company produced a wide variety of good cars, sales did not keep pace with the rest of the industry. Thomas Jeffery was comfortable with production of 3000 to 3500 units. Production volume of the Rambler peaked in 1913 at 4435 units. From 1905 to 1913, the company's market share declined from over 10 percent to 1 percent. After Thomas Jeffery died suddenly in 1910, his son, Charles, took over and made several changes, one of which was to affect the name recognition of the product in the market. In an apparent burst of sentimentality, Charles named the new car after his deceased father. By 1914, one of the respected names in the industry had passed from the scene. The new car was called the "Jeffery."

Several new models of Jefferys were produced in 1914, including the company's first six-cylinder car. Two four-cylinder models were offered in addition to the new six. Furthermore, the conservative company offered the more common left-hand drive for the first time. The combination of three new models, a more conventional configuration, and a six-cylinder engine temporarily boosted sales. Unit sales for 1914 were 10,417, more than twice the 1913 shipments. But, the higher sales levels did not last. In 1915, sales slipped back to 3100 units (Table 5-6). In contrast, sales for Buick, which shipped half as many cars as the Jeffery company in 1906, increased to 124,000 units in 1916.

Meanwhile, World War I had begun in Europe, and the Jeffery Company became a substantial producer of army trucks. By 1915, truck shipments were outpacing automobile shipments by 2 to 1. The name change to Jeffery, an inconsistent and confusing assortment of cars, and a partial withdrawal from the automobile market in favor of trucks discouraged potential buyers. By 1915, the manufacturer that at one time had been in second place in the industry was selling approximately 3 percent of the volume of Willys-

Table 5-6. Rambler and Jeffery Product Offerings

Production year	Name	Cylinders	Price range	Units produced
1902	Rambler	1	$ 750	1,500
1904	Rambler	1&2	650 to 1350	2,342
1905	Rambler	1&2	750 to 3000	3,807
1906	Rambler	2&4	800 to 3000	2,765
1907	Rambler	2&4	950 to 2500	3,201
1908	Rambler	2&4	1400 to 2250	3,597
1909	Rambler	2&4	1150 to 2500	1,692
1910	Rambler	4	1800 to 3350	2,273
1911	Rambler	4	2175 to 4150	3,000
1912	Rambler	4	1650 to 4200	3,550
1913	Rambler	4	1650 to 2750	4,435
1914	Jeffery	4&6	1550 to 3700	10,417
1915	Jeffery	4&6	1450 to 2900	3,100
1916	Jeffery	4&6	1035 to 1350	4,608

Overland. The company's market share dropped to one-third of 1 percent in 1915.

In May of 1915, Charles Jeffery set sail on the *Lusitania,* which was sunk by the Germans during the voyage. Charles was among the 761 survivors, but the long hours spent in the cold water before being rescued helped him to reassess his priorities. The next year, at the age of 40, he decided to retire. Jeffery's retirement would open his company to new leadership that would ultimately orchestrate the Jeffery Company's transition from a small family-owned concern into a major producer and alter the course of U.S. automotive history.

Meanwhile, the Durant interests had repurchased control of General Motors, prompting the gradual withdrawal of several GM executives. James J. Storrow, an investment banker from Boston, was called upon to provide money and managerial leadership during the GM problems of 1911. Storrow then recruited Charles Nash to help unscramble the manufacturing problems of GM during the period between the two regimes of William C. Durant. Later, Nash served as president of GM, and Storrow was chairman of the board of directors. In spite of strong personal ties between Nash and Durant, it became clear that Durant's repurchase of GM would mean a reemphasis of acquisitions, financial dealings, and external expansion as opposed to the emphasis on efficiency and internal investment, which characterized the Nash-Storrow regime. In 1916, Nash and Storrow left GM in search of new opportunities.

Storrow, Nash, and Walter Chrysler initially tried to purchase the Packard Motor Car Company. When that deal fell through, Storrow and Nash purchased the Thomas B. Jeffery Company. Chrysler declined to join them, reportedly because he did not want to put his family to the trouble of another move. GM's future chairman, Alfred B. Sloan, Jr., was impressed enough with Nash to buy stock in the new company when Nash left GM, and he remained on excellent terms with him. Sloan remarked in his autobiography that the investment was "highly profitable" (Sloan 1964). What Nash was able to accomplish with the Jeffery Company was summarized by James Storrow in an interview at the New York office of the Lee Higginson Co. in 1925.

> Charlie Nash had been a good wagon manufacturer, and then a fine Buick factory man. I picked him to be head of General Motors. In five years, he turned a wreck into a concern having $25,000,000 in the bank. When Durant took control of General Motors away from us, I wired Nash to come here, and I said: "Charlie, you did a fine job of G.M.; if you could do that once, you can do it again; look around for another wreck; I'll back you." He picked the Jeffery outfit, which we bought for less than $5,000,000. Nash made a hundred million dollars for us out of it in seven years. There was nothing to the Jeffery outfit. Nash was everything. He could do the same thing with a railroad. (Seltzer 1928)

What Nash did, of course, was to organize production. He believed that sales performance was an outgrowth of efficient production. If the company's cost of production was low, it could afford to add differentiating quality features that would enable further penetration of the market. This happened with

Nash products. The products were efficiently produced at low cost. Part of the production savings were then reinvested in differentiating features such as higher-quality engines with more main bearings and overhead valves, better brakes, and dual ignition. For a company of modest size, Nash Motors contributed a significant number of engineering features. But, the facility to do this originated with efficient production. In the words of Charles Nash, "Sales is ninety percent a production problem" (Forbes 1972, 212).

During the recovery period, Nash Motors experienced dramatic growth, not only in revenue and physical units but in market share as well. Physical units increased by a factor of 12. Revenue grew by a factor of 10. Profits grew enormously and market share increased four times (Table 5-7).

The steps Charles Nash took to restore the vitality of the newly constituted Nash Motors, to achieve turnaround, and to become one of the most significant producers in the industry were very specific operational steps. Nash was a strong believer in collecting valuable information which was external to the firm. "We don't pretend to know it all here at the factory," he would say. "The Nash product is a result of cooperation, extended by our partners in the business, the Nash dealers." Nash placed a very high value on communications from dealers and customers. Nash products were innovative, and the customer received good value. He emphasized efficiency, distinguishing product features, and product quality. Company management believed in using the money saved by efficient production to increase the quality and value of the products produced.

Nash spent a great deal of time walking around the plant looking for ways to improve the production process. He understood the production process very well and worked cooperatively with managers and the rest of the work force to eliminate wasted motions and material. Nash Motors had a policy that, whenever possible, employees would be paid according to results. Inventories were systematically handled in a just-in-time fashion. Only small quantities of inventories were kept on hand, and the flow of inventory through the plant was highly efficient.

Table 5-7. Nash Motors, 1917–1927

Year	Output	Revenue	Profits	Unit market share, %
1917	12,027	$ 16,761	$ 2,027	1.00
1918	10,283	41,072	1,474	1.09
1919	27,081	41,754	5,089	1.63
1920	35,084	57,186	7,007	1.84
1921	20,850	25,428	2,226	1.37
1922	41,652	40,238	7,613	1.76
1923	56,677	58,590	9,280	1.51
1924	53,626	57,284	9,281	1.62
1925	85,428	97,821	16,256	2.21
1926	135,520	131,175	23,346	3.43
1927	122,606	113,441	24,089	3.98

Employees, whether union or nonunion, were treated alike. Interest was shown in the welfare of the workers. The company maintained an athletic field, a tennis court, and a baseball field with a seating capacity of 6000. The company provided free legal advice, free title examination for those interested in buying homes, temporary loans in the case of emergency, as well as assistance in arranging home loans. The company employees' club maintained a band, an orchestra, and a motion picture theater. By the mid-1920s, Nash Motors had emerged as one of the most efficient and consistently profitable firms in the industry. Table 5-8 displays some key ratios among major producers of the time.

One operational area where Nash Motors clearly excelled was in the efficient management of inventories. During the 1920s, the inventory turns per year at Nash Motors were superb when compared to those of other manufacturers. Nash's inventory turns per year climbed above 9 to 1 in 1921, reached 12 to 1 in 1923, and were nearly 20 to 1 in 1926. All of this was accomplished without the benefit of computerized material-requirements planning systems, computerized process planning, or large professional staffs. Yet, the Nash inventory turn ratios in the 1920s are not dissimilar from those achieved by some of the most efficient manufacturers in the world in the 1980s (Figure 5-4).

Nash Motors based its operating procedures on the principle that too many resources can get in the way of efficient production. Charles Nash did not want extra inventory, not only because it was expensive but because it sat in the middle of the factory floor. Total quality control was another modern concept anticipated at Nash. Nash products were carefully made, and quality achieved during the production process was emphasized as the key ingredient to end-product quality. With procedures similar to those employed by his friend Henry Leland of Cadillac, Nash understood that the highest cost of bad quality was disruption of the product process itself. He wanted superb in-process quality, not only to satisfy customers but also to keep production from being interrupted because of bad parts.

Table 5-8. Nash Operational Performance versus Other Manufacturers

Manufacturer	1926 profits per car	1926 profits of sales, %	1929 sales-to-inventory ratio
Nash	170	17.8	19.74
Packard	400*	17.1	8.12
General Motors	143	16.7	7.98
Ford	55*	12.8*	?
Chrysler	90	10.5	9.84
Studebaker	119*	8.8*	5.57
Hudson	52	3.3	14.93
Willys-Overland			8.84

*Approximations.

SOURCE: *Moody's Industrial Manual* 1928 and 1930.

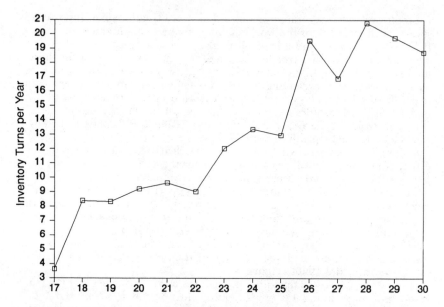

Figure 5-4. Nash Motors' inventory turns per year. Through a combination of frugality, scientific observation, and keen attention to operational practicalities, Nash Motors was able to achieve inventory turns per year which were far above the norms for the industry at the time. The very modern production system which resulted established Nash as the industry's leader in profit rates and overall efficiency.

   Efficient production and modest overhead provided funding for additional features and benefits which were above industry standards at the time. Nash automobiles had four-wheel brakes as standard equipment a full 6 years before some higher-priced General Motors models did. Nash eight-cylinder engines had nine main bearings and overhead valves at a time when competitive engines usually had five main bearings and an L-head configuration. Nash introduced rubber engine mounts in 1922, and turning signals in 1932. The first practical heating and ventilation system appeared on Nash automobiles during the 1930s, as did reclining seats and unibody construction.

   Nash Motors continued to show operational performance far better than the industry average well into the depression. General Motors, Chrysler, and Nash all fared relatively better during at least the early part of the depression. Through a combination of frugality and clever positioning in the market, Nash managed to operate with continuous profitability from 1917 through 1932. Ford lost money in 1927, 1928, 1932, 1933, and 1934. Chrysler lost money in 1932 and 1933. Hudson lost money from 1930 to 1934 and from 1938 to 1940. Packard lost money in 1931, 1932, and 1934. Studebaker,

Franklin, Willys, and several others entered receivership or ceased operations. But Nash operated profitably until 1933, when some modifications to the Nash product line necessitated greater investments to revitalize sales. This was accomplished in a few years, and by 1940 Nash emerged as an efficient producer of higher-quality and innovative, lighter cars. By 1941, the company was operating again at an acceptable rate of profit and at a gross profit that was the second highest in the industry.

What type of leadership style did Nash employ to achieve these combinations of product quality and organizational efficiency? He was distinctly frugal himself. He was a tough but well-respected, value-oriented working manager who had a particular strength in organizing production. He was rather conventional in his personal life. The following quotations from Alfred P. Sloan, Walter Chrysler, and others provide us with a brief sketch of Charles Nash.

> A bit paternalistic by today's standards, what with his practice of personally distributing $10 bills to his factory workers at Christmas time, Nash nevertheless enjoyed a uniquely cordial relationship with his employees. Oftentimes at noon he would be found in the company cafeteria, eating his lunch side by side with the factory hands. He could call hundreds of them by name, and he rejoiced when they responded by calling him "Charlie." (Brown 1981. Copyright © 1981 by *Special Interest Autos*. Reprinted with permission.)

> He [Charles Nash] was as steady and careful as Mr. Durant was brilliant and daring—or reckless as you may choose to call it. In 1910, Mr. Nash had little experience in automobiles, but he demonstrated talent in the art of manufacturing and administration....The great automotive producers in General Motors had been Mr. Durant, Mr. Nash and Mr. Chrysler. (Sloan 1964, 8–55)

> Mr. Nash gets more satisfaction from his association with "the boys" in the organization than from "society." (Forbes 1972, 223)

> But, if you would watch this manufacturer of motor cars enjoying the recreation which he likes best, you would not have to travel further than his home in Kenosha and see him in action with his four little grandchildren. He is an even greater success as a granddaddy than as a motor manufacturer. (Forbes 1972, 224)

> The resignation of Charley Nash left a big hole in the General Motors organization. He had been a vital factor in the success of the corporation and I hated to see him go away. Not only was he a loyal friend and a grand man but I knew him to be one of the country's greatest industrialists. The tremendous success that he has made at Racine with the Nash Motor Company is something any of the friends he left behind him at General Motors would have predicted from the day he left Michigan to go to Wisconsin. (Chrysler 1937, 144)

Charles Nash compiled an impressive record by emphasizing efficiency, frugality, and returning to the customer part of that savings in the form of higher-quality, market-appropriate products. He fully understood the importance of being a low-cost producer, and he also understood how this cost leadership could be transformed to provide greater product differentiation. The Jeffery turnaround was based on efficient production and modest overhead. These efficiencies permitted the company to invest in product-differentiating features and higher product quality. The personal traits of the leader were basic. He was quiet, honest, frugal, and focused on managing the business the firm was in at the time. He liked building things, he liked the people who built them, and he liked the customers who bought them. As an innovator, he skillfully judged his product offerings to accommodate what he thought the society would need in the future—more fuel-efficient, lower-cost, well-built smaller cars employing unibody construction. The company, known later as American Motors, survived as a separate company until 1987—as one of four remaining U.S. auto producers. It now operates as the Jeep/Eagle Division of Chrysler Corporation.

Nash Survived Because...

- Operational efficiency was among the highest in the world.
- Inventory efficiency was the highest.
- Management focused on operational matters.
- Employees were individually known and respected by top officers.
- Frugality prevailed in all matters.
- Money that was spent pertained to what the customer was buying.
- Quality problems were brought to the attention of the entire organization and suggestions were sought.

Case 4

Majestic Laxity at Willys-Overland

Prior to 1920, the Willys-Overland Company was one of the largest automobile producers in the country. The company began as the Overland Company, but after a troubled start, one of the Overland dealers, John North Willys, made a trip to the factory to register his concerns regarding the tardy deliveries of Overland products. Willys ended up taking over control of the company in 1907 and began pouring his energies into improving the company's offerings and building a stronger sales organization. Sales greatly improved—from 4860 cars in 1909 to over 140,000 cars in 1916. Market share moved from negligible levels before the arrival of Willys to more than 10 percent by 1915.

By 1915, Willys-Overland was the industry's third-largest producer with production volume nearly equal to that of General Motors, which produced only 102,000 cars in 1915. Willys-Overland was not only an enormous producer of automobiles but also a substantial component supplier to other automobile companies, because of its ownership of Auto-Lite Electric Company and other component manufacturers. In contrast to the 91,000 cars produced by Willys-Overland in 1915, Hudson produced 12,684, Jeffery produced 3100, and Maxwell produced 44,000. Chevrolet, then a separate company, produced 13,292 cars in 1915.

John North Willys achieved both prominence and personal wealth, and he began to travel and diversify his interests. By 1916, the dual problems of neglect and overexpansion began to surface in the Willys organization. The company had acquired several related and unrelated businesses, and some of them were not successful. In addition, the costly development of the sleeve-valve engine had begun. The sleeve-valve engine employed a series of precision sleeves to accomplish the intake and exhaust valving from the combustion chamber. The purpose was to alleviate some of the wear and performance problems of the poppet-valve engines used by other manufacturers. However, when other manufacturers solved some of these same problems by improving metallurgical processes, the few advantages of the sleeve-valve engine could not outweigh its additional cost and its other operational disadvantages of excessive oil consumption and limited revolutions per minute. Willys-Overland was faced with cost and product disadvantages after a substantial capital investment.

As Willys withdrew from day-to-day involvement in the company, he left the business in the hands of individuals who built a comfortable life for themselves but neglected day-to-day operations and wasted company resources. Sales declined from 140,000 units in 1916 to 48,000 in 1921. Willys-Overland finances, already stretched thin from the acquisitions, were stretched further. Financial backers exhibited concern, and in 1919 they actively sought an outside manager to bring the affairs of the company back into order. Meanwhile, Walter Chrysler had left General Motors in 1919, perhaps intending to retire or perhaps because of dissatisfaction with the Durant financial interests, after Durant had gained control of GM. In 1920, the backers of Willys-Overland were able to convince Chrysler to undertake the task of revitalizing Willys-Overland for a fee of $1 million per year.

Walter Chrysler was not an admirer of Willys products and did not manifest a strong interest in becoming personally involved in the company, but he did his job as a turnaround agent. He significantly reduced overhead expenses, increased operational efficiencies, got the company refinanced, and worked with an outside consulting firm to develop a new automobile for the company. Through a combination of frugality, better production management, improved handling of inventories, and the restructuring of the operations, Chrysler was able to reduce the company's bank loans from $46

million to $18 million (Forbes 1972, 35). Production and sales improved, as
seen in Table 5-9.

Willys remained president during the period but operated with instructions
from his financial backers to cooperate with Chrysler. This he did. He even
willingly accepted the reduction in his own salary imposed by Chrysler and
worked diligently to sell the merits of Chrysler's involvement to the concerned
dealer organization.

However, Willys was far more comfortable in a sales mode than in a
retrenchment mode, and he had long considered Willys-Overland to be his
own personal company. In 1923, he arranged with some financial backers in
Toledo to take the company into bankruptcy and regain control through this
means. Chrysler had already become involved in the troubled Maxwell-
Chalmers Company, and Willys again took control of Willys-Overland. The
new model car developed during the Chrysler era was later sold with the
plant to Durant Motors to raise cash.

Willys then poured his energies into selling cars and restoring the
confidence of the dealer network. What was to follow, of course, was the

Table 5-9. Willys-Overland Production and Market Share

Year	Production	Market share, %
1909	4,860	3.8
1910	15,598	8.6
1911	18,745	9.4
1912	28,572	8.0
1913	37,422	8.7
1914	48,461	8.9
1915	91,904	10.3
1916	140,111	9.2
1917	130,988	7.5
1918	88,753	9.4
1919	80,853	4.9
1920	105,025	5.5
1921	48,016	3.2
1922	95,410	4.0
1923	196,038	5.2
1924	163,000	4.9
1925	215,000	5.6
1926	182,000	4.6
1927	188,000	6.1
1928	315,000	7.8
1929	242,000	5.1
1930	69,000	2.4
1931	74,750	3.7
1932	26,710	2.3
1933	29,918	1.8
1934	7,916	0.4

most robust automobile market for the next 30 years. He enthusiastically barked the merits of Willys-Overland products, copied elements of the respected styling of Packard, and effectively marketed his way back into third place in the industry.

The turnaround of Willys-Overland after the departure of Chrysler was marked by extreme response to the marketplace. Under Willys, relations with dealers were cooperative and cordial. Even more important, they were continuous. Willys was on the road constantly, recruiting, encouraging, and listening to dealers. The company manifested no particular operational or technological strengths, but it did display a limited closeness to the customer.

This willingness to respond aggressively to customer's interests enlarged the Willys-Overland product line beyond what would be expected for the share of the market the firm possessed. Production increased from 48,016 in 1921 to 315,000 in 1928. However, the number of basic Willys-Overland models proliferated greatly to achieve greater sales. Table 5-10 compares Willys-Overland and Nash Motors for the years 1927 to 1928 and reflects the differing emphases of the two firms.

With a much lower market share, Nash Motors had been able to make almost four times the profit of Willys-Overland. Even during its best sales year in 1928, Willys-Overland achieved a gross profit rate of only 11.4 percent as compared to 20 to 30 percent by GM, Chrysler, Nash, and Packard. Though the company did well in sales all through the 1920s and gained significant market penetration, it had not cultivated the skill to manufacture cars efficiently. One sage observer of the industry remarked that

Table 5-10. A Comparison of Profits for Nash and Willys-Overland

		Nash		
Year	Units	Revenue	Profits	Unit market share, %
1923	56,677	$ 58,590	$ 9,280	1.51
1924	53,626	57,284	9,281	1.62
1925	85,428	97,821	16,256	2.21
1926	135,520	131,175	23,346	3.43
1927	122,606	113,441	22,671	3.98
1928	138,137	120,746	21,342	3.44
		Willys-Overland		
Year	Units	Revenue	Profits	Unit market share, %
1923	196,038	...	13,034	5.22
1924	163,000	...	2,087	4.92
1925	215,000	...	11,423	5.56
1926	182,000	...	1,820	4.60
1927	188,000	153,120	6,342	6.10
1928	315,000	187,233	6,382	7.85

John North Willys could build more cars and make less money doing it than anyone in the industry (Kennedy 1941).

The Willys-Overland problem of manufacturing inefficiency was exacerbated by management's decision to enter the low-priced field as a high-cost producer. The Whippet automobile was announced in 1926. The car was similar in size and price to a Chevrolet, but the engine was smaller and lacked the styling and durability of the Chevrolet. However, the car sold well, and 197,000 Whippets were produced in 1928. Manufacturing costs remained high, and the incremental revenue achieved in 1928 was actually less than the additional costs incurred in obtaining the revenue. The expenses of Willys-Overland were too high for the low-priced field.

When the Great Depression arrived, Willys' strategy of a car for every taste was inappropriate. For one model after another, car sales fell below their breakeven points. Total unit sales fell from 315,000 units in 1928 to 242,000 in 1929. Sales fell again to 69,000 units in 1930, then to 26,710 in 1932, and 7916 in 1934. From 1928 to 1934, unit sales declined by 97.5 percent. In 1935, the company entered receivership. John North Willys had sold his stock in 1929 before the crash.

After the company emerged from receivership with a plan of reorganization in August of 1936, operations were centered around a small, low-cost, four-cylinder automobile which utilized the old Whippet engine. The engine, although not initially known for its durability, was refined during the 1930s by Barney Roos, an engineer who had had successful experiences with Pierce-Arrow, Marmon, and Studebaker. This engine's performance allowed the company to predominate in the manufacturer of Jeeps during World War II and provided it with some life even after the war. After two bankruptcies, significant losses in the 1950s, a 15-year stretch as part of Kaiser Industries, and 17 years as a part of American Motors, the operation survives today as part of Chrysler Corporation.

The Willys-Overland turnaround of 1920 to 1928 was primarily a sales-based turnaround that was made possible by some quick operational and financial measures taken during the 2-year stay of Walter Chrysler. But, the turnaround was not successful in the long term. Inefficiencies in production and excessively high overhead ultimately consumed the resources necessary to create product differentiation. In less favorable economic times, the company's products were insufficiently differentiated, and the company failed to develop new ones. The efficiencies of Willys-Overland were such that only during boom periods could the firm operate profitably against competitors who had plenty of business.

The Willys-Overland turnaround is interesting because of its emphasis. Sales-based turnarounds can work for short periods but do not necessarily provide the company with the operational expertise to survive over longer periods under differing conditions. In the final analysis, Willys-Overland resurfaced only after restructuring on the strength of the product capabilities of one of its engines, and then only with the help of two court restructurings. The turnaround did not fail because of the Great Depression. Other, smaller firms did survive. Nor did it lack sufficient sales. Other survivors sold substantially fewer units. The turnaround ultimately failed because the desires and the skills necessary to achieve operational efficiencies and modest overhead were not nurtured and sustained over prolonged periods. The company did not develop the organizational infrastructure that fostered efficiency and proficiency in product development. The turnaround also failed because the company spent too much money and time on things unrelated to what the customer was buying.

Willys-Overland Failed Because...

- Variable costs exceeded variable revenue.

- Operational efficiency was lacking.

- Management lacked technical experience.

- Inventory efficiency was poor.

- Top management became diverted and did not focus on operational matters.

- Too much money was spent.

- Expenditures were unrelated to what the customer was buying.

6
Lowering Cost through Design

From 1980 to 1982, Ford Motor Company experienced devastating losses totaling more than $3 billion that threatened the existence of the 80-year-old company. Market share slipped from 23 percent in 1977 to less than 14 percent in 1982. Over the years, Ford had always been able to produce interesting new products, but from 1970 to 1982, the company found it difficult to produce those interesting new products at less than the selling price. Incremental costs had substantially outpaced incremental revenue, and during the early 1980s, Ford losses exceeded $3 billion. Yet years later, in 1987, 1988, and 1989, the Ford Motor Company emerged as one of the most profitable automobile companies in the world. Integral to Ford's turnaround was its ongoing commitment to the lowering of costs through product design.

A quarter of a century earlier, American Motors had been faced with extreme competition when unit sales plummeted from 333,829 units in 1950 to 113,571 in 1954, a domestic market share of under 2 percent. At the time, American Motors manufactured two lines of full-sized automobiles and two lines of compacts including seven complete engines. Forced by the pressures of losing $60 million from 1954 to 1957, American Motors' astute management chose to concentrate its efforts on one highly manufacturable make called the "Rambler." By 1960, sales moved up to 485,000 units, and American Motors regained a 7.25 percent market share, while profits rebounded to healthy levels. What enabled American Motors to move from disaster to vitality in the fiercely competitive low-priced market was intense focus on the manufacturability of its products.

At the close of World War II, one of the country's most reputable and efficient industrialists teamed with an experienced automobile marketeer to enter the automobile business. Within 3 years, Kaiser-Frazer had surpassed, in unit sales, all other independent producers, including such highly regarded marques as Packard, Nash, Hudson, Studebaker, and Willys-Overland. Eight years later, the firm suspended all operations in North America. What led to the demise of Kaiser-Frazer was not product styling or ineffective marketing but limited experience in designing products for low-cost production.

The design of products (and services) for manufacturability (and deliverability) is a favorable strategic attribute with application across industries. Service providers, material suppliers, utilities, retailers, and wholesalers must also be concerned with the design of their products and delivery systems. Design of delivery systems for service companies is as important as the design of the products of manufacturing companies. It is difficult for a firm to make money if products and services are expensive to deliver.

The process of turning around a company is only partly managerial; it is also technical. There are limits to what managerial concepts can accomplish in reducing the cost of difficult-to-build products. Successful companies have clear-cut programs to design products and services for manufacturability and low-cost delivery. Successful manufacturability programs include highly intricate processes involving broad consensus among team players and clear understanding of technical detail on the part of management.

Many firms have greatly improved their competitive position by improving the design of their products. IBM, Black and Decker, Deere, Maytag, Lincoln Electric, and Chrysler all endured competitive pressure to design products for low-cost delivery. The manufacturability features incorporated into the Ford Taurus and the Mercury Sable product design were instrumental in the resurgence of Ford Motor Company from billion dollar losses in the early 1980s to the industry's leading profit position in 1986 and 1987. From 1981 to 1987, Ford's market share increased from 16.4 to 20.2 percent, while GM's market share slipped from 45.8 to 36.3 percent. During both 1986 and 1987, at much lower revenue levels, Ford earned greater profits than GM. What is perhaps most significant is the 1983 to 1987 differences in before-tax profit rates. Ford's before-tax profit rate rose from 4.87 to 10.30 percent, while GM's before-tax profit rate shrank from 7.98 to 1.97 percent.

Ford and GM employed different strategies in pursuing profitability following the recession of the early 1980s. GM launched an all-out program of factory automation designed to reduce per-unit manufacturing cost. Ford chose to incrementally improve the efficiency of internal operations and improve the manufacturability of its products. The result is clear. Ford did much better, at least for several years.

Automation versus Designing for Manufacturability

The manager wishing to improve profitability must achieve a delicate balance between efficiency in the manufacture and design of products so that they can be effectively produced. Both strategies are necessary, and competence with one strategy usually improves the odds of being successful with the other. IBM has product costs among the lowest in its industry and has long been a leader in factory automation. However, the manufacturability of the IBM ProPrinter was such that heavy assembly automation was not required. The unit snapped together with minimal assistance from either tools or fixturing. The design of the IBM ProPrinter allowed IBM to continue as an active competitor in a highly competitive market dominated by foreign producers.

During the highly competitive decade of the 1980s, much has been written regarding the need to apply computer technology to U.S. manufacturing as a defense against low-cost foreign competition. Situations do exist in which automation is the appropriate solution, while in other instances changes in materials, in product characteristics, or product design will have a greater impact on cost, particularly short-term cost, which is of most immediate interest to the turnaround agent. Unfortunately, some of the late-arriving text material on manufacturing is appropriate for very large-scale activities such as those carried on in Chevrolet plants, yet the average size of American plants is shrinking. Automation can help a producer attain greater economies on a smaller scale, but like any other turnaround factor, it does not lend itself to simple, block-diagram interpretations. By itself, automation is not an especially useful turnaround strategy because it takes a long time to install good automation, even with the help of a solid and experienced support staff. Until automation becomes easier to install, more cost-effective, and more sophisticated, the lowering of costs through product design will remain a highly practical turnaround strategy.

Bold new design initiatives such as the Ford Taurus often require new automation systems, of course. However, many companies such as Harley-Davidson have been able to significantly increase profits by coupling design changes with the intelligent use of existing machinery. This was indeed the case during the troubled times of Maxwell-Chalmers, when product designs were modified to make most effective use of equipment in the Chalmers factory. The same methodologies were employed at Dahlman Equipment in 1983 and in other instances since. Product designs and production methodologies must work together and not be treated as separate unconnected activities, as is still the case with many companies.

Designing for Manufacturability

Successful companies routinely address product manufacturability as a main priority. Product manufacturability programs were present at Deere, Buick, Cadillac, Nash, Chrysler, Packard, and American Motors during the late 1950s and early 1960s. The managers of these successful turnarounds understood production processes well and insisted that product design and production efficiency interact to improve competitive position. The successful firms actively reduced their number of component parts by designing parts usable in several applications with only minor modifications. American Motors made five engines, three sixes and two V8s from nearly identical sets of pistons and valves. Deere's two-cylinder tractor contained 1400 fewer parts than the comparably powered International Harvester models. Chrysler Corporation built several passenger cars and several series of minivans from the same basic platform. Many other examples in the case materials provide additional evidence that successful turnaround companies achieve low-cost operation through the effective design of products and services. They accomplish manufacturability not only by employing more capable designers but also through the assistance of key suppliers, maintenance people, and company employees.

In contrast, management of the unsuccessful turnarounds treated manufacturing more as an afterthought rather than as a proactive competitive force. Product manufacturing difficulties with specific products contributed to the unsuccessful turnaround performance of Willys-Overland (with the sleeve-valve engine), International Harvester (with crawler tractors and some trucks), Hudson (with the Monobilt body and frame), Kaiser (with its sculptured styling), and AMC/Renault during the later years with the Pacer. Unsuccessful firms more commonly employed only short-term cost-reduction programs and neglected manufacturability and parts commonality in product design.

Attention to detail is the key to reducing manufacturing cost through product design. Each individual part must be properly designed to meet competitive cost requirements. An expensive part, an expensive procedure, or an additional service requirement can plague a company through the entire life of a product. For example, the Hudson valve lifter was installed in all Hudson engines from the 1920s through 1947 and in all eight-cylinder engines from 1948 to 1952. In contrast to other valve lifters in use at the time, Hudson's was much more expensive to produce—probably about $2 more per unit in today's cost. While most valve lifters required machining on one or two basic machines, the Hudson part required complex operations on several different machines. Further, the design of the part produced early wear, which altered the critical valve clearance, thus affecting engine performance, and it also made the engine very noisy (Figure 6-1). The significance of this one bad part in the history of the Hudson Motor Car Company becomes clear when we reflect on the fact that the company made approximately 35 million of them. A poorly designed, expensive, unreliable part with a run size of 35 million is not the way to implement a turnaround. Hudson's practice of pinning piston rings also added extra cost to the product, increased the probability of ring breakage during both assembly and repair, and probably did not improve product performance in any material way. Hudson did have some product designs that employed the same nominal parts. However, the machining tolerances were such that a great many parts designed to be the same were identified with different part numbers reflecting various sizes over and under the nominal dimensions of the part. This variety further complicated manufacturing efficiency at Hudson.

Willys-Overland also neglected manufacturing cost, as did International Harvester and AMC/Renault. Willys-Overland's profit margin eroded for many years because of the expensive sleeve-valve engine. Initially the engine had some advantages over the conventional poppet-valve engine, but improvements in the metallurgy and design of poppet-valve components soon erased any appreciable difference in performance. Willys-Overland was left with an expensive design that burned too much oil. International Harvester had too many basic components for both its trucks and its farm equipment. The AMC Pacer had 500 pounds of additional weight as compared to cars in the same price class. Though the car handled well, this additional weight raised manufacturing cost and reduced gas mileage during a major oil shortage. AMC/Renault's after-tax profit margins ranged from −5.8 percent to 2.7 percent during the years when the Pacer was a significant seller. The design of product for manufacturability did not emerge as an important part of the turnaround strategies employed by the unsuccessful companies.

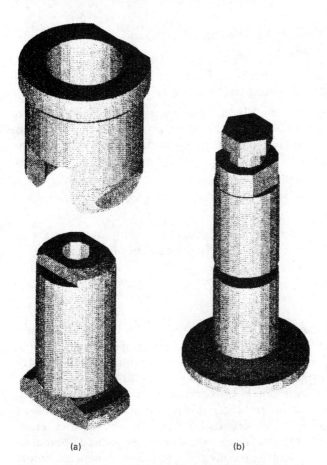

(a)   (b)

Figure 6-1. Success and failure, influenced by a single part. The two valve lifters shown here appear to be similar, and both fulfill the same functional role in engine operation. However, they are dramatically different in terms of both reliability and manufacturing cost. (*a*) This valve lifter is a complicated part requiring several machine setups, along with the grinding of complex surfaces. It was not a reliable part because its inability to rotate with cam shaft movement caused a groove to be worn in the valve lifter, thus disturbing the critical valve lash adjustment. The Hudson Motor Car Company produced about 35 million of the unreliable and expensive parts. (*b*) This valve lifter is easily made on conventional turning and grinding equipment, requiring a minimum of setups and few machines in the process. When operating in the engine, the part rotates with the operation of the cam shaft, thus reducing wear.

Practical Lessons on Lowering Cost through Design

- Successful companies routinely address design as a main priority in lowering the cost of the products and/or services provided.

- Successful companies critically examine most offered services and most utilized parts to ensure that the costs for these items are below industry standards while quality is maintained. Unsuccessful companies do not sufficiently scrutinize the quality and delivery cost of most frequently used components.

- Commonality of parts is an appropriate strategy only if the parts are easy to produce.

- Well-orchestrated programs of lowering cost through design have at least as much cost impact potential as automation programs.

Case History

American Motors Corporation's recent acquisition by Chrysler Corporation is ironic because 25 years earlier, AMC had developed what was probably the most advanced manufacturability designs existing in the industry at the time. Low-cost product designs helped the Nash Motors Company, reconstituted as American Motors Corporation, surface as the lone survivor among the independent producers during the falloff of the seller's market and fierce competition between Ford and General Motors. From 1955 to 1963, five out of the six independent producers ceased operations but, under dire financial and competitive circumstances, American Motors found ways to survive. The chief prescriptions were simple: spend less money than is taken in and design easily produced products. The company not only survived, but for a brief period of time, the American Motors Rambler became the third best selling car in the world. In many respects, American Motors' performance of the late 1950s anticipated by 30 years the demands that U.S. producers must face in surviving against low-cost global competition today.

Case 5

Making the Most of American Motors

For more than 20 years, under the stewardship of Charles Nash, Nash Motors Company was an especially well-run automobile company. Production was efficient, costs were low, innovation was high, and a good rapport existed between the company and its work force. The depression affected Nash Motors, but the firm successfully weathered this period because of its low production costs and a strong balance sheet. Charles Nash, however, was growing older. As he entered his mid-seventies, the company merged with the Kelvinator Co., a manufacturer of home appliances. This merger provided the company with some diversification and a knowledgeable successor to Nash in Kelvinator CEO, George Mason, an understudy of Nash's friend Walter Chrysler.

Mason was a capable, personable, and innovative chief executive officer, well respected in the industry. During his regime, Nash-Kelvinator built high-quality, innovative products, including automobiles with unibody construction, reclining seats, and the first truly good heating and ventilating system, the Nash Weather Eye. A joint venture with a British firm produced the Nash Healey sports car, which brought further traffic to Nash showrooms. One of Mason's most significant accomplishments was the authorization to build a high-quality, well-designed, compact car. To name the car, the designers reached well back into Nash/Jeffery history and picked the name Rambler.

The 1950 Rambler represented a marked departure from contemporary attempts to build a lower-cost automobile because the car was of very high quality. Ramblers came complete with radios, rustproofing, attractive bright metal trim, reclining seats, and thoroughly proven running-gear components. Two body styles were offered, a safety-oriented convertible with a reinforced steel top and an all-steel station wagon. Considered a niche car at the time, the car sold well, with sales reaching 57,000 units in its second year.

Meanwhile, the fierce price competition between Ford and Chevrolet had produced a decline in the sale of medium-priced cars produced by the independents. Kaiser-Frazer sales fell from 166,000 in 1948 to 23,000 in 1953. Packard unit sales declined from 98,000 in 1949 to 71,000 in 1953. Studebaker sales fell from 268,000 in 1950 to 161,000 in 1953. Full-size Nash model sales dropped from 169,000 to 94,000 during the same period, while full-size Hudson sales plummeted from 144,000 to 57,000. Improved engine, drive train, and model offerings from higher-volume manufacturers intensified the competitive pressure on independent automobile producers. A wider variety of cars was being produced, more efficiently and in greater volumes by the major producers, thus putting pressure not only on the independent producers but also on their dealers, and many dealers were switching to the major brands.

Mason understood well the practical problems facing smaller manufacturers, and to buffet his firm from the increasing competition, he initiated the formation of American Motors via a merger between Hudson and Nash in 1954. Initially, Mason wanted to merge with Packard. He felt that Packard was stronger financially and enjoyed more prestige in the marketplace. The higher-priced Packards would line up well with the medium- and low-priced products offered by Nash, but the Packard deal fell through primarily because of resistance on the part of Packard's new president, James Nance. Mason then turned to Hudson.

Theoretically, the opportunity for synergy existed between Hudson and Nash. Both companies offered conservative, medium-priced cars that often competed with one another. Both firms employed unibody construction. Both emphasized six-cylinder rather than eight-cylinder engines. Both used some of the same electrical components and other parts. Both dealer networks needed strengthening, but the merger was one of near desperation on the part of Hudson and perceived opportunity on the part of Nash. By the mid-1950s, the independents were caught in a cost squeeze between Ford, Chrysler, and GM. The market share of the independents had decreased from 19.2 percent in 1948 to 4.1 percent in 1954 (Edwards 1965, 14). Hudson sales had been hit particularly hard. By 1954, both Nash-Kelvinator and, to a much greater extent, Hudson were incurring substantial operating deficits (Table 6-1).

The merger did not work immediately. Production was concentrated in the more efficient Nash plant at Kenosha, Wisconsin, and the slow-selling Hudson Jet was dropped in favor of the Rambler. But the early days of the newly created American Motors Corporation were fraught with confusion because Mason's new responsibilities forced him to leave some important details unattended. In late 1954, Mason died and the title of CEO passed to his able lieutenant, George Romney. Romney took immediate action to correct many of the company's problems. The results were not immediate; in 1955 and 1956 American Motors showed greater and deeper losses.

George Romney had gained considerable experience in the automobile business as the coordinator of the production capabilities of the U.S. auto companies in support of the war effort in World War II. In his previous American Motors positions of vice president and executive vice president, he spent considerable time in efforts to improve AMC's manufacturing efficiency. Born of Mormon missionary parents when they were residing in Mexico to escape religious persecution, Romney was educated in the obligations of the Mormon religion. His feelings of responsibility and proper behavior were well cultivated — and these attributes which served him well as AMC's crisis deepened.

Romney quickly took several important steps to turn the operations of the company around. He effected austerity measures beginning with the chairman's own comforts and compensation. George Romney cut his own salary by 26 percent, insisted on staying in single rooms at modest motels, spurned fancy offices and expensive dinners, and frequently carried his own lunch. Other managers followed suit. Twenty-four executives took voluntary

Table 6-1. Hudson and Nash Shipments, 1949–1954

Marque	1949	1950	1951	1952	1953	1954
Nash (full-size)	143,268	169,466	105,499	100,005	93,694	25,232
Rambler	0	20,782	57,555	53,055	41,885	37,779
Total Nash	143,268	190,248	162,154	153,060	135,579	62,911
Hudson (full-size)	144,685	143,581	92,586	79,117	57,040	36,436
Jet					21,143	14,224
Total Hudson	144,685	143,581	92,586	79,117	78,183	50,660
Combined total	287,953	333,829	254,730	232,777	213,762	113,571

pay cuts. Overhead expenses were trimmed $38 million in 1955 to $28 million in 1958. Following the expense reductions at higher levels, he respectfully confronted the company's bargaining unit with the objective of improving productivity. Productivity did improve. He initiated high-profile programs to improve manufacturing productivity by standardizing components, by improving rapport with workers, and by developing products that were explicitly designed for higher rates of operational efficiency (Mahoney 1960).

Still, the sales of American Motors' midsized cars (Hudson and Nash) continued to languish. By 1956, unit sales of the midsized cars had declined to 25,000 units, less than one-tenth of Hudson/Nash's total for the 1950 model year. Romney's strategy was to concentrate the full efforts of AMC's dwindling resources and energies on one main model, the Rambler. Hudson's smaller car, the Jet, had been dropped under Mason.

Romney also took steps to develop a more broadly based decision-making system within the company and to improve and cultivate the management team. With missionary zeal, he instituted an intensive program to mend relations with the company's dealers. The theme of this program was America's emerging interest in a high-quality compact car as opposed to the opulent gargantuan automobiles of the late 1950s, which Romney titled the "dinosaur in the driveway."

Perhaps the most important contribution of all during the Romney era was development of the American Motors' manufacturing strategy. He was particularly interested in having American Motors be competitive in manufacturing cost. During this period, American Motors developed a philosophy that Romney articulated before the U.S. Senate Subcommittee on Antitrust and Monopoly in 1958:

> Our studies, based on our own experience and that of our competitors, [show] that optimum manufacturing conditions are achieved with a production rate of 62.5 cars per hour per assembly line. To absorb the desired machine-line and press-line rate, two final assembly lines would be required. Of course, your press line and your machine line are the principle lines on which you depend for work leading up to subassemblies and the ultimate production of the car itself on the assembly line. This would result in production of 1,000 cars per shift.
>
> A company that can build between 180,000 and 220,000 cars a year on a one shift basis can make a very good profit and not take a back seat to anyone in the industry in production efficiency. On a two shift basis, annual production of 360,000 to 440,000 cars will achieve additional small economies but beyond this volume, only theoretical and insignificant reductions in manufacturing costs are possible. It is possible to be the best without being the biggest (Edwards 1965, 155).

The strategy emphasized commonality of parts, operational efficiency, design for manufacturability, effective purchasing, and product design for the minimization of tooling expense. Aluminum extrusions replaced the expensively tooled metal stampings for window frames, a change which made the rest of the door easier to produce and made production of a common component for hardtop, convertible, and two-door sedan models possible. The doors and door frames for the prior year's senior Rambler became the door and door-frame assembly for the Rambler American. Running gear parts were largely standardized among product lines. Wherever possible, parts were designed so that right and left versions of the part were interchangeable.

Both Nash and Hudson had pioneered the development of unibody automobile construction (integrated body and frame of all welded components), the same system that had become the standard for small-car production throughout the world by the 1970s. The unibody design of the Rambler allowed the company to produce a lightweight car which was very strong and yet employed fewer component parts. The design of the Rambler body and frame unit was a key element in manufacturing efficiency. Components such as the dashboard and the rear storage shelf, which had previously been bolted to other structural components, became welded structural components themselves. The results were better products, lighter products that consumed less fuel, and lower manufacturing cost.

The American Motors' penchant for designing products for manufacturability was reflected in engine design as well. Larger engines differed from smaller engines only in terms of stroke. Bores, pistons, valves, and most other engine parts were the same except for occasional minor modifications. The company was able to produce five separate engines (three sixes and two V8s) from nearly identical sets of pistons and valves.

The programs of constant improvement in design for manufacturability developed a competitive edge for American Motors. By 1958, the firm's amortization of tooling was the lowest of any U.S. producer, an edge it was to hold for most of the next decade (Table 6-2).

Table 6-2. Amortization of Tools, Dies, and Equipment

	Per car				
Year	AMC	Stud/Pack	Ford	GM	Chrysler
1956	138	118	77	132	59
1957	112	82	111	152	104
1958	62	85	177	205	119
1959	32	35	108	166	110
1960	23	61	76	175	163
1961	47	72	109	171	139
1962	44	76	88	141	94
1963	40	...	96	148	90

SOURCE: Charles E. Edwards, *Dynamics of the United States Automobile Industry*, University of South Carolina Press, Columbia, SC, 1965, p. 206.

The savings resulting from product manufacturability and manufacturing efficiency provided funding for further increases in product quality. Rambler bodies were fully dipped in rustproofing, and extensive use of galvanized steel was introduced on the 1963 model. Mufflers and tail pipes were ceramic-coated to reduce corrosion. The sturdy Rambler six-cylinder engine had seven main bearings, a strong block, hydraulic lifters, and a heavy-duty timing chain. Competing engines in the same price class often had three or four main bearings, rubber timing belts, and thinwall castings. The company pioneered in low-cost sound insulation and individually adjustable reclining seats. In 1961, American Motors introduced separate independent front and rear braking systems and the collapsible steering column to promote safety. AMC was also the first U.S. firm to install seat belts (Table 6-3).

By conserving resources and concentrating on a particular niche in the automotive market and by emphasizing product quality and value, the

Table 6-3. American Motors Innovations, 1953–1970

Year	Innovation
1953	Concealed gas filler
1954	Air conditioner mounted under hood
1957	Full-body dip method of prime painting
1957	Fuel injection
1958	Variable-speed engine fan
1959	Individually adjustable seats
1960	Side-hinged rear station wagon door
1961	Ceramic-coated muffler and tail pipe
1961	One-piece fiberglass headliner
1961	Six-cylinder aluminum engine
1962	E-stick automatic clutch transmission
1962	Factory front and rear seat belts
1962	Dual brakes
1963	Transistorized voltage regulator
1967	Collapsible steering column
1968	Headlight warning buzzer
1969	Fiberglass bias-belted tires
1969	Translucent battery case
1970	Granulating safety windshield
1970	High-back seats with integral head rest

SOURCE: William J. Abernathy, Kim B. Clark, and Alan M. Kantrow, *Industrial Renaissance: Producing A Competitive Future for America,* Basic Books, New York, 1983, pp.155–179.

company began to gain in sales. The year 1958 was a record one for the new corporation. Shipments of American Motors automobiles increased to 217,332 compared to 95,198 during 1954. Revenue rose to $470,349,000, and profits rose to $26 million. In the following years, revenue and profits grew even more. The company remained a healthy supplier of 6 to 7 percent of the nation's automobiles.

By 1960, the rapidly rising sales of the Rambler prompted responses from the "Big Three." Ford, General Motors, and Chrysler all introduced new compact cars in 1960. Ford's offering, the Falcon, was especially popular, selling over 400,000 cars during its first year. Even Studebaker experienced a resurgence with its 1959 Lark. Competition became very intense. Yet, American Motors actually picked up market share in both 1959 (up 2.06 percent) and 1960 (up 0.07 percent) and suffered only a very small decline (down 0.5 percent) in 1961.

What Romney did to keep American Motors competitive was to make sure that every part of the company ran smoothly and at low cost. The combination of design of products for manufacturability, manufacturing efficiency, general frugality, and intense market focus allowed American Motors to emerge with a position of low-cost leadership and reasonable product differentiation. Profits therefore increased. From 1958 to 1963, American Motors was profitable every year, with market shares from 5.1 to 7.25 percent.

It is important that American Motors was keenly interested in the health of its dealer organization during this period. Sales Manager Roy Abernathy trimmed weaker dealers and worked diligently to make those that remained healthier. The dealers continued to make money even during the years when AMC was itself yet emerging. When sales increased dramatically in 1958, the remaining dealers were strong and well positioned for further expansion (Edwards 1965, 68).

Late in 1962, George Romney left American Motors to become governor of Michigan; later he was a candidate for president and ultimately secretary of housing and urban development. In the meantime, American Motors continued to have many good years. At a later stage, the company lost its position as a low-cost producer of specialized cost-effective cars for a particular market. The company drifted and became a less vibrant producer of a wide assortment of medium- and low-priced autos with limited differentiation. Product quality became more sporadic and innovation subsided. Rapport with its workers diminished. The company survived as a separate entity until 1987, but not as the effective competitor it had been from 1955 to 1963.

During the time of the company's 1956 to 1963 recovery, however, American Motors' strategy focused on the efficient production of high-quality products for a particular market niche—an ambitious program that was made possible by a rigorous program of designing products for manufacturability. Very few financial steps were taken during the American Motors turnaround. During the recovery, the company issued only a minor amount of new common stock. The additions to net worth were gained almost totally through profits (Table 6-4).

Table 6-4. American Motors, 1953–1963

Year	Units	Sales	Profits	United market share, %
1953	213,762	$ 478,697	$ 3,712	3.48
1954	113,571	400,344	(17,274)	2.06
1955	161,790	441,127	(6,956)	2.04
1956	104,190	408,404	(19,746)	1.80
1957	114,084	362,234	(11,833)	1.87
1958	217,332	470,349	26,085	5.12
1959	401,466	869,850	60,342	7.18
1960	485,785	1,057,716	48,234	7.25
1961	372,485	875,724	23,579	6.75
1962	454,664	1,056,395	34,241	6.56
1963	480,365	1,132,356	37,807	6.29

American Motors Survived Because...

- Production was focused on fewer models.
- Lower costs were achieved through design.
- Top management understood how to break even in physical terms.
- Quality was maintained at high levels.
- Continuity was maintained with key historical markets.
- Ideals were present and were clearly articulated.
- Management played an exemplary role.

PART 3

The Value of Product Differentiation

Successful companies offer differentiated products—products that customers perceive as having value and uniqueness. Product differentiation is not accomplished merely through clever promotion or adroit management of the sales effort, although these are indeed desirable attributes. The products really are better—they have more meaningful features and benefits, higher reliability, better performance, and higher overall quality. In some cases, differentiated products are newly developed products with more modern features or superior performance. In other cases, they are enhanced older products, incrementally improved to add value while ensuring continuity with major historical markets. In all cases, differentiated products arise from experience in the industry, experience with customers, and experience in the proficient management of the development function.

The Strategic Value of Differentiated Products

Companies successful in turnarounds recognize the direct connection between differentiated products and profitability, the strategic value of making a good product or providing a good service. Differentiated products reduce volatility in unit sales and lower marketing expense by nurturing repeat business. Perhaps most important, differentiated products nourish the feelings of pride and confidence which organizations in trouble so desperately need. The effect of differentiated products on a troubled firm is holistic, an atmospheric effect that makes people want to belong to a class act.

What is surprising is how much effort and energy go into the attempted resurrection of companies in trouble without any serious investigation of the products being offered to the customer. Often, market strategies, production facilities, corporate officers, names, and financial arrangements change when products do not change. The usual result is sadness and despair for the loyal people in the affected organization and continued slippage of the firm.

Successful firms display an overwhelming resolve to bring differentiated products to market and then bracket this resolve with well-thought-out strategies and tactics. Unsuccessful companies seem to perceive the product as inconsequential to success or failure, for their energies are diverted to nonproduct matters. Successful firms make incremental improvements to produce differentiated products. Unsuccessful firms often fail to improve existing products even when product shortcomings are widely perceived. Successful firms put great emphasis on product quality, particularly in-process quality. Unsuccessful firms often neglect quality issues. Unsuccessful companies concentrate less on improving products, often making significant and abrupt marketing changes in search of new markets for marginal products, while successful firms avoid abrupt changes in market position but make more improvements in products being offered to familiar markets.

The continuous effort to improve products provides an ongoing strategic advantage not always apparent to unsuccessful managers, who commonly view their products as differentiated, most often incorrectly. Successful firms collect more data and talk to more people to ensure that their products are good, and then continue to make improvements even when the products are highly regarded. Unsuccessful companies fail to systematically appraise their product offerings in comparison to the competition's and therefore take no particular steps to improve them. Differentiated products provide a·strategic advantage that can vanquish high market-share positions of larger competitors.

Efficiency and Effectiveness of Product-Differentiating Resources

The achievement of product differentiation depends upon the company's internal efficiencies and effectiveness in the management of product-differentiating resources. Though product planning is very technical and is often based on sound scientific research at successful companies, major developments do not always consume large amounts of time and money. Product-differentiation efforts are conducted efficiently, often with the full cooperation of major suppliers to augment and amplify the skills of the firm itself. This results in rapid improvement of product offerings—accomplished on time and at affordable cost.

In contrast, unsuccessful firms often lack the skills to *economically* create product differentiation, an enormous practical liability for the firm in distress. Frequently, firms spend large sums of money to create unneeded products, develop features out of touch with the market, or else simply take too long to develop features and benefits fielded much earlier by the competition. Successful turnarounds do not depend so much on the allocation of product-differentiating resources but instead upon the adroit management of those resources. Product differentiation is achieved because small numbers of competent managers and technical people get the right things done quickly. Unsuccessful firms often lack the ability to interject quality and productivity into the product-differentiating process. Or, they are too slow.

Differences also exist in the planning for product differentiation. Successful companies utilize longer-range, proactive programs to incrementally differentiate their products by adding features in advance of or in sync with customers' expectations, by improving reliability, and by rigorously attending to product quality. In an interactive manner, product differentiation complements low-cost production, allowing a firm to insulate sales during recessions. In addition, successful companies reinforce product development activities by retaining continuity with key markets. Unsuccessful firms are far more likely to seek entry to some new market as a remedy to faltering sales and spend less time improving products.

The objective of Part 3 is to discuss the elements of product differentiation as they apply to the turnaround process. Chapter 7 examines the processes involved in developing distinguishing product features. Chapter 8 describes the steps successful companies have taken to achieve lasting product quality. Chapter 9 reviews how firms sustain continuity with their major markets.

7
Developing Distinguishing Product Features

Distinguishing features enable firms to sell their products when times are bad and to sell them for more money when times are good. For a company in trouble, these are pivotal advantages. However, achieving distinguishing features is not easy. The process demands that managers have a thorough understanding of the market and of the probable moves of both current and anticipated competitors. Product-differentiated features must be developed thoroughly, so that new features are reliable, and quickly, so that they hit the market in a timely manner.

Unsuccessful firms also attempt to develop distinguishing product features but often fail because they develop the wrong thing and take too long to do it. Often, they spend too much money on the process and involve too many of the wrong people. Yet, unsuccessful firms' difficulties with product development are not resource-based. Even the most technical companies seldom spend over 5 percent of revenue on research and development combined (Ford Motor Company, for instance, spends about 3.7 percent). Companies such as Hudson, Studebaker-Packard, Control Data, Computervision, and International Harvester had vast resources at their disposal. The development of products suitable for the firm's historical marketplace was clearly feasible, and indeed, product development did occur. Poor product development stems primarily from four strategic difficulties:

1. *Development activities focused on the past* rather than emerging trends.

2. *Development activities focused on products for new, unfamiliar markets* rather than for familiar markets.

3. *Development activities focused on gadgetry* rather than on product features and benefits that more accurately reflect user requirements.

4. *Development activities that are inefficiently executed* and take too long to satisfy the market being served, often resulting in products which are insufficiently tested and refined.

Managing Development for Future Trends

Successful companies skillfully detect future market trends and then time product enhancements that lead or at least equal the pace set by the market being served. Unsuccessful companies lag behind in the market. The product development activities of the major independent auto firms following World War II illustrate this point. The independent producers emerged from World War II in excellent financial condition and with good position in their markets. The war provided most of them with defense contracts substantial enough to reduce or eliminate many of their prewar liquidity problems. Both Packard and Studebaker, for instance, had about $32 million in cash at the end of 1945. In relative terms, their market position also improved. To some degree, 4 years without automobile production leveled the playing field regarding the public's perception of which companies were superior. Also, product differentiation achieved during the thirties worked in favor of the independents after the war. Packard, a favorite staff car for generals, still carried some of its prewar prestige. Nash's innovative unibody construction, excellent heating system, and quiet economical operation appealed to many buyers. Studebaker quickly adopted postwar styling, as did Kaiser-Frazer. Hudson got off to a fast start in production after the war and had an ample supply of cars available at the right time. Indeed, many sophisticated buyers appreciated the quality and engineering features the independents had been forced to develop during the 1930s in order to survive at all.

The anticipation of a strong market for cars also interested new candidates for dealerships. Kaiser-Frazer, with no prewar model at all, enlisted 4600 dealers by 1948. These favorable conditions allowed the independents (Nash, Hudson, Studebaker, Packard, Willys, and Kaiser-Frazer) to prosper, and all these firms operated profitably during the years immediately following World War II. In 1948, the independents produced 19.2 percent of the cars sold in the United States. By 1949, however, several of the independents were clearly failing to keep pace with key emerging trends in the marketplace, particularly in engine technology and car design.

The internal combustion engine underwent radical changes in the years following World War II. Affluent Americans, with rapidly expanding families, sought larger cars with more pep and more fuel efficiency in proportion to the power delivered. The L-head side-valve straight-cylinder configuration, which dominated the domestic auto industry during the 1930s, could accommodate neither need. However, only Chevrolet, Buick, and Nash offered overhead valves, and only Ford, Mercury, Lincoln, and Cadillac offered V8s. Most engines offered by the industry in 1946 had been designed at least 15 years earlier.

During this era, General Motors' research, under the direction of Charles F. Kettering, designed a lighter, more powerful, and more economical engine which became the standard design configuration of the industry during the 1960s and early 1970s. Beginning with the 1949 Cadillac and Oldsmobile models, GM led the automobile market trend toward more powerful and more fuel-efficient engines. Five emerging trends in engine design were of particular significance:

1. *Overhead valves* became the standard in the industry. After 1953, almost all domestic car manufacturers offered overhead-valve engines except Hudson, Willys, and Kaiser-Frazer. GM and Nash adopted this technology much earlier.

2. The industry average *bore-to-stroke ratio* (the ratio of the diameter of the cylinder to distance traveled by the piston) changed from about 0.75 in the late 1940s to about 1.1 in the 1950s (Figure 7-1). These higher revving short-stroke engines usually ran quieter, were more compatible with automatic transmissions, and indirectly increased horsepower by permitting the engine to operate smoothly at higher revolutions. Kaiser-Frazer, Hudson, and Studebaker all lagged behind this trend.

3. *Compression ratios* (with the piston at its low point, the ratio of the volume of the cylinder to the volume of the combustion chamber) also increased from an average of about 6.5 in the 1940s to as high as 11.0 in the mid-1960s (Figure 7-2). Here again, General Motors led this trend which greatly increased engine efficiency. Kaiser-Frazer, Packard, Hudson, and Studebaker followed.

4. *Cubic-inch displacement* (a measure of engine size) increased modestly in proportion to the weight of the cars from an average of about

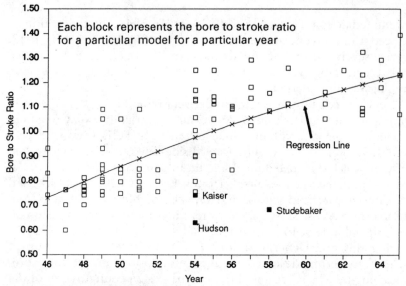

Figure 7-1. Bore to stroke ratios, 1946 to 1965. Engine geometry changed markedly in the highly competitive years from 1949 to 1965 as producers sought greater fuel efficiency and performance in engines compatible with automatic transmissions. The ratio of engine bore diameter to the length of the stroke increased by 50 percent during this period. Some producers, led by GM and later others, were well ahead of industry trends. Others, such as Kaiser, Studebaker, and Hudson, followed far behind industry trends in spite of new engine development programs.

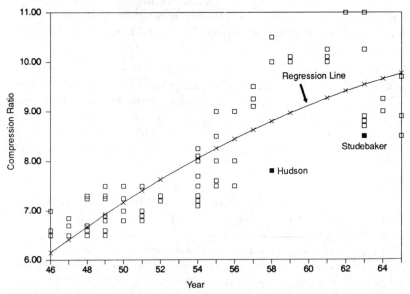

Figure 7-2. Engine compression ratios, 1946 to 1965. Compression ratios also increased, from an average of 6.5 in the late 1940s to 9.5 in the mid-1960s. Some compression ratios were even higher, but Kaiser, Packard, Hudson, and Studebaker lagged GM, Chrysler, Ford, and American Motors in this significant indicator of engine efficiency.

220 cubic inches in 1946 to about 300 inches 1956. During this time, Kaiser-Frazer retained only a modest displacement of 226 cubic inches in its rather expensively priced car. Hudson and Studebaker also offered medium-priced cars with small antiquated engines, although they did offer a few models more consistent with market trends.

5. *Horsepower per cubic inch* rose substantially because of the modern design characteristics of the engines delivered by the more progressive companies. In the 1940s, U.S. manufacturers averaged about 0.45 horsepower per cubic inch. In 10 years, several innovative manufacturers doubled the horsepower per cubic inch. Kaiser-Frazer, Hudson, and Studebaker still offered engines with under 0.6 horsepower per cubic inch.

The companies that lagged behind in automobile market trends did, in fact, develop new engines during this period. Hudson developed not one but *four* new engines, each with an L-head design, each with low bore-to-stroke ratios, and each with relatively low compression ratios. Though Hudson manufactured one durable 308-cubic-inch engine that established Hudson's fame in racing, it was not modern in design, it was not fuel-efficient, and it could not be used as a building block for more advanced products in the future. For its 1954 Jet, Hudson employed some of the same design features it used on engines built in the early 1930s. The company was the last manufacturer in the industry to offer a splash-oil system. During a time when Hudson showed good sales and profits and had the resources to develop modern products, the company adhered rigidly to design philosophies that lagged 20 and 30 years behind leading manufacturers.

Studebaker also developed an engine during the post–World War II period, but it was heavy, relatively small, and of relatively low compression. As late as 1963, it achieved horsepower per cubic inch of 0.69 as opposed to 0.9 with several Chrysler and GM engines. Packard also developed an overhead-valve V8, which hit the market a full 6 years after Cadillac. Packard unit sales were nearly 50 percent higher than Cadillac's before the GM overhead-valve V8 made its debut in 1949. Six years later, when Packard finally offered an overhead-valve V8, Packard sales had fallen to 40 percent of those of Cadillac.

Kaiser did not develop a modern engine, which it desperately needed, but spent vast sums to develop other products for unfamiliar markets. The development of the Henry J compact car, an unusual move for a high-cost producer, siphoned resources from products for Kaiser-Frazer's traditional marketplace, and as a result, the producer that led all independents in 1948 and individually held an 8 percent market share went out of business 8 years later. As with Packard, Hudson, Studebaker, and to some extent Chrysler Corporation of that era, Kaiser-Frazer dissipated its resources on projects which were strategically out of sync with changes in the market.

Nash (later AMC) was an exception to the preceding pattern. Nash engines featured overhead valves as early as 1918, and in 1946, some Nash engines had a bore-to-stroke ratio of 0.83 and a compression ratio of 7.3 – both relatively high for the industry at that time. Thus Nash entered the competitive period of the 1950s with engine characteristics more compatible with emerging trends than those of the other independents. More important, however, the firm did not stop there. In 1955, the firm offered a high-compression, overhead-valve V8 engine designed by Packard, followed by a V8 of their own design in 1956. In 1962, the firm announced two new six-cylinder engines, each with high bore-to-stroke ratios, higher compression ratios, and overhead valves. Since Nash (AMC) offered products to the economy-minded consumer, the need for powerful V8 engines was less critical than for the much higher-priced Kaiser-Frazer, Hudson, and Packard models. But Nash still designed V8s along with some of the most modern and best-developed sixes in the industry. Nash clearly led the rest of the independents in engine technology in the years following World War II. Whether this fact explains Nash's survival (as American Motors) is unclear, but the timely development of market-appropriate features and benefits certainly worked to the firm's advantage.

In addition to the trends specific to engine technology, drive train and styling trends also emerged during the postwar period:

1. *Automatic transmissions* became more common. In 1946, only Oldsmobile and Cadillac offered fully automatic transmissions. Buick and Pontiac followed in 1948, Chevrolet in 1950. Ford, Chrysler, and most of the independents offered automatics in 1951, but General Motors had exploited this development several years earlier.

2. *Pounds per horsepower* (a measure of total car weight to power available) declined from an average of about 33 in 1946 to 23 in 1954 and to 15 by 1962. As with engine technology, the independents lagged behind trends in the marketplace. In pounds per horsepower, the 1954 Kaiser, 1954 Hudson Jet, and the 1957 Studebaker Scotsman remained high, at 27. More powerful Hudson models had higher power-to-weight ratios but, by the mid-1950s, Hudson was severely out of step with industry trends.

3. The *width-to-height ratio* increased from 1.1 in 1946 to 1.4 in 1964 (Figure 7-3). Unsuccessful companies also lagged behind industry trends with respect to the external dimensions of the car they pro-

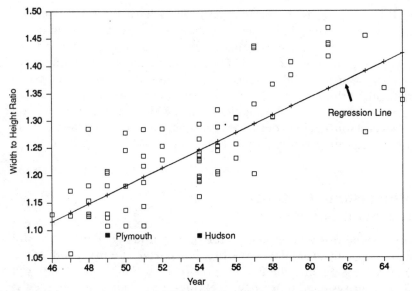

Figure 7-3. External width to height ratios, 1946 to 1965. The outside proportions of automobiles also changed with the styling changes initiated in 1948–1949. In marked departure from industry trends, Hudson and Chrysler Corporation significantly lagged industry trends even when new models were developed.

duced. At 1.28, the width-to-height ratio of Hudson automobiles was the industry's most advanced when "step-down" styling was announced in 1948. However, for reasons that are quite unclear, when the new Hudson Jet arrived in 1954, the width-to-height ratio was reduced to 1.08, thus producing a malproportioned car for the period.

Effective product development requires intense focus on the market being served. Duplicate or parallel product development programs are seldom affordable to the firm in trouble, but even successful firms must perceive and understand the trends taking place in the market and then patiently and thoroughly address these trends. Product development is, by nature, a future-focused activity.

Note that errors in the assessment of market trends can be made in either direction. No doubt, Hudson lagged behind the market in several of its key strategic decisions. But, Allis-Chalmers led the market in pursuing fuel cells and some other technological programs, as did Control Data in its pursuit of computer-based education. Quite commonly, companies overestimate market movement and thus prepare products for nonexistent trends. Perhaps the importance of comprehending market trends is one reason why people with experience in the industry being served do better as turnaround agents. They have more information. They have both formal and informal sources of information, and it is easier for them to cross-check that information. An experienced CEO remarked that he estimated only 60 percent of the information he received was accurate. With respect to the future, it is probably closer to 15 percent. If this level of accuracy is prevalent, the individual charting the course of product development will need to collect information from several sources in order to be reasonably certain of making correct decisions regarding future product offerings.

Distinguishing Features and Turnaround Success

Distinguishing features influenced the turnarounds of all the successful companies. Cadillac employed the first self-starter, the first production-volume V8 engine, and the first breaker-point ignition. Nash employed dual-ignition systems, more main bearings, and four-wheel brakes as standard equipment. During the 1957 to 1963 turnaround, American Motors used dual brakes, full-body rustproofing, and ceramic-coated mufflers. Deere tractors were highly reliable, maneuverable, and could run on cheap fuel. Packard products of the 1930s were quiet and had excellent styling. Chrysler's turnaround of the 1980s was in part due to the arrival of its innovative "minivan."

In contrast, the unsuccessful companies offered "me-too" products as late arrivals in the market and sometimes failed to detect important trends in the marketplace. Hudson modeled key elements of its 1948 styling after the 1942 Buick. Kaiser products offered innovative styling, but its drive train components were obsolete. Studebaker-Packard produced the last versions of the once-prestigious Packards by using the chassis of one of the least expensive cars in America. On one occasion after another, unsuccessful firms failed to deliver products that were perceived by customers as being *special*. In some cases, as with IHC's crawler tractors, Kaiser's engines, Hudson's antiquated splash-oil system, or Studebaker's antislip differential, substantial negative features were present in the products of the unsuccessful firms.

In their excellent book *Industrial Renaissance: Producing a Competitive Future for America*, Abernathy, Clark, and Kantrow (1983) tabulate some of the important innovations in the history of the U.S. automobile industry. The authors also weigh each innovation for its impact on production and then categorize it in accordance with the type of innovation (process, drive-train, body/chassis, or other). From this listing, the innovations that occurred during the recovery periods of both the successful and the unsuccessful firms were derived (Tables 7-1 and 7-2).

Process Developments as Well as Product Developments

The successful firms developed both process technologies and features and benefits that improved the differentiation of their products. Innovations like solid-metal wheels, full-body dip priming, and one-piece fiberglass headliners improved efficiencies while simultaneously adding distinguishing features. Other innovations such as oil filters, valve inserts, roller bearing universal joints, and ceramic-coated mufflers improved product durability and perceived quality. Some innovations, among them the electric starter, rubber spring shackles, and the side-hinged station wagon tailgate, were for convenience and customer comfort. Still other innovations such as the V8 engine, high-compression engines, and the vacuum spark advance improved performance. Companies adopted all the innovations listed in Table 7-1 during periods of recovery following severe financial difficulties.

In addition to the specific innovations listed in Table 7-1, the successful firms were also prompt in adopting innovations developed by others. Nash quickly adopted four-wheel brakes and overhead valves. Deere ceased production of its unsuccessful three-row tractor in favor of the more practical four-row configuration pioneered by International Harvester. American Motors became an early adopter of curved glass to improve internal spaciousness and styling. Overall, the successful companies were much more on the leading edge of both process and product innovations during their turnaround periods than were the unsuccessful firms. Further, many of these innovations had substantial impacts on the production process and were more difficult to implement. Yet, they were introduced by companies with limited resources and strained cash flows. In contrast, unsuccessful firms adopted fewer innovations and generally chose those which required fewer changes to the production process (Table 7-2). Several innovations, such as Hudson's electric hand transmission and Packard's nonslip differential, negatively impacted product differentiation because insufficient testing failed to detect reliability problems (Table 7-3).

Avoiding Development of the Unessential

A practical imperative for the company in trouble is to preserve development resources only for things that need to be done. As basic as this

Table 7-1. Innovation in the U.S. Automobile Industry, 1910–1981

Accomplished during the Period of Recovery—Successful Turnarounds

Weights	Categories
1 = Little or no impact on production	1 = Drive train innovation
2 = Minimal impact on production	2 = Process innovation
4 = Medium impact on production	3 = Body and chassis innovation
7 = Maximum impact on production	4 = Other innovation

Year	Producer	Innovation	Weight	Category
1910	Cadillac	Closed body	2	3
1912	Cadillac	Electric starter	4	1
1912	Cadillac	Generator battery	3	1
1914	Cadillac	Large-scale production V8 engine	7	1
1915	Cadillac	Adjustable steering wheel	3	1
1915	Cadillac	Tilt-beam headlights	2	4
1915	Cadillac	Thermostatic water-circulation contr.	2	1
1921	Buick	Solid-metal wheels	2	3
1922	Nash	Rubber engine mounts	5	1
1933	Nash	Directional turn signals	1	4
1925	Chrysler	High-compression L-head engine	4	1
1925	Chrysler	Replaceable-cartridge oil filter	2	1
1926	Chrysler	Engine isolated from frame	4	3
1927	Chrysler	Flexible-rubber engine mounts	2	1
1927	Chrysler	Rubber spring shackles	1	3
1930	Chrysler	Downdraft carburetor	4	1
1931	Chrysler	"Floating power"	2	1
1932	Chrysler	Cast iron brake drums	2	3
1932	Chrysler	Vacuum & centrifugal spark advance	2	1
1932	Chrysler	Valve-seat inserts	4	1
1933	Chrysler	Roller bearing universal joints	2	1
1934	Chrysler	One-piece curved-glass windshield	2	4
1934	Chrysler	Forward engine mounting (over fr. whls.)	3	3
1934	Chrysler	Airflow styling	4	3
1935	Chrysler	Synchronized front & rear springs	2	3
1935	Chrysler	Tubular frame seats	1	4
1938	Packard	Air conditioning	2	4
1942	Packard	Electrically controlled clutch	1	1
1948	Packard	Power-operated windows	1	4
1953	Nash-AMC	Concealed gas filter	1	4
1954	Nash-AMC	Air conditioner mounted under hood	1	4
1957	Amer. Motors	Full-body dip method of prime painting	3	2
1957	Amer. Motors	Fuel injection	3	1
1958	Amer. Motors	Variable-speed engine fan	1	1
1959	Amer. Motors	Individually adjustable seats	1	4
1960	Amer. Motors	Side-hinged rear station wagon door	1	4
1961	Amer. Motors	Ceramic-coated muffler & tail pipe	2	2
1961	Amer. Motors	One-piece fiberglass headliner	2	2
1961	Amer. Motors	Six-cylinder aluminum engine	4	1
1962	Amer. Motors	E-stick automatic-clutch transmission	3	1
1962	Amer. Motors	Factory front & rear seat belts	1	4
1962	Amer. Motors	Dual brakes	2	3
1963	Amer. Motors	Transistorized voltage regulator	2	1
1967	Amer. Motors	Collapsible steering column	2	4

Table 7-1. Innovation in the U.S. Automobile Industry, 1910–1981
Accomplished during the Period of Recovery—Successful Turnarounds (*Continued*)

Weights	Categories
1 = Little or no impact on production	1 = Drive train innovation
2 = Minimal impact on production	2 = Process innovation
4 = Medium impact on production	3 = Body and chassis innovation
7 = Maximum impact on production	4 = Other innovation

Year	Producer	Innovation	Weight	Category
1968	Amer. Motors	Headlight warning buzzer	1	4
1969	Amer. Motors	Fiberglass bias-belted tires	1	3
1969	Amer. Motors	Translucent battery case	1	4
1970	Amer. Motors	Granulating safety windshield	2	4
1970	AMC & others	High-back seats w/integral head rest	1	4
1978	Ford	Aluminum steering pump-housing	2	2
1978	Ford	Aluminum rack & pinion housing	2	2
1978	Ford	Electronic engine-control series	3	1
1978	Ford & others	Three-way catalytic converter	3	1
1979	Chrysler	Aluminum cylinder heads	3	1
1979	Ford	Aluminum brake master cylinder	2	3
1980	Ford	Automatic overdrive transmission	4	1
1980	Ford	Magnesium vacuum-advance housing on V-8 engines	2	2*
1980	Ford	Magnesium window-sail mirror plate	1	2
1980	Ford	Minifuse panel and plug-in fuse	2	4
1980	Lincoln	Magnesium steering column lock housing	1	2
1981	Ford	Magnesium louver for rear-quarter window	1	2*
1981	Ford	Magnesium rear-quarter window molding	1	2*
1981	Ford	Painted magnesium exterior mirror arm	1	2*

SOURCE: William J. Abernathy, Kim B. Clark, and Alan M. Kantrow, *Industrial Renaissance: Producing a Competitive Future for America*, Basic Books, New York, 1983.
*Dennis McCarthy of Ford Motor Company, who reviewed this chart prior to its inclusion in this book, suggests that the asterisked items did not reach full production volume. However, he also adds that one of the more significant accomplishments, the magnesium brake-pedal support, did reach production but was not included on the chart.

Table 7-2. Innovation in the U.S. Automobile Industry, 1932–1981
Accomplished during the Period of Recovery—Unsuccessful Turnarounds

Weights	Categories
1 = Little or no impact on production	1 = Drive train innovation
2 = Minimal impact on production	2 = Process innovation
4 = Medium impact on production	3 = Body and chassis innovation
7 = Maximum impact on production	4 = Other innovation

Year	Producer	Innovation	Weight	Category
	Willys-Overland	None listed		
1932	Hudson	Proferall camshaft	3	1
1933	Hudson	Vacuum-operated clutch	2	1
1935	Hudson	Rear trunk integral with body	1	3
1936	Hudson	"Electric hand" transmission select	2	1
1937	Hudson	Double automatic emergency brakes	1	3
1937	Hudson	Steel-torque steering arm	2	3
1939	Hudson	Safety hood latch	1	3
1940	Hudson	"Airfoam" seat cushion	1	4
1953	Packard	Four-way power seat	1	4
1955	Packard	Tubeless tires	1	3
1956	Packard & others	Push-button transmission selector	1	1
1956	Packard	Electric door latches	1	4
1956	Packard	Nonslip differential	3	1
1956	Packard	Torsion-bar suspension	4	3
1956	Studebaker	Ribbed brake drum	1	3
1957	Studebaker	Limited Slip differential	3	1
1958	Stud-Pack	Off-center rear spring mounting	1	3
1963	Studebaker	Front-wheel disc brakes	2	3
1947	Kaiser-Frazer	Gas tank beneath license	1	4
1950	Kaiser	Fold away rear-seat cargo area	1	4
1951	Kaiser	Narrow corner post & popout windshield	1	4
1951	Kaiser	Padded dash	1	4
1951	Kaiser	Molded plastic body	4	2
1974	AMC/Renault	Freestanding front & rear bumpers	1	3
1981	AMC/Renault	"Select drive"	2	1

SOURCE: William J. Abernathy, Kim B. Clark, and Alan M. Kantrow, *Industrial Renaissance: Producing a Competitive Future for America*, Basic Books, New York, 1983.

Table 7-3. Features and Benefits

		Strategically Successful			
Case	Feature developed	Feature significant	Alternative available	Feature timely	Feature reliable
Oldsmobile, 1949	High-compression OHV V8	Yes	No	Yes	Yes
Cadillac, 1948	High-compression OHV V8	Yes	No	Yes	Yes
Oldsmobile, 1941	Hydramatic drive	Yes	No	Yes	Yes
Chrysler, 1980	Minivan	Yes	No	Yes	Yes
AMC, 1957	Full-body rustproofing	Yes	No	Yes	Yes
Cadillac, 1912	Self-starter	Yes	No	Yes	Yes

		Strategically Unsuccessful			
Case	Feature developed	Feature significant	Alternative available	Feature timely	Feature reliable
Packard, 1950	Ultramatic transmission	Some	Yes	Yes	No
Packard, 1956	Torsion-bar suspension	Some	Yes	Yes	Yes
Hudson, 1936	Electric hand	No	Yes	Yes	No
Studebaker, 1957	Limited-slip differential	Some	No	Perhaps	No
Packard, 1955	V8 engine	Yes	No	No	Yes
IHC	Crawler tractor	Yes	No	Yes	No

caveat may seem, it is often overlooked. Control Data spent hundreds of millions of dollars developing products which were neither particularly useful nor of concern to the company's primary market. The result was that the one-time technical leader in the computer industry, with over 57,000 employees, suffered severe erosion in its customer base, market position, and employee loyalty. During the late 1940s and early 1950s, the Packard Motor Car Company invested heavily in two nonessential developments, a unique automatic transmission and torsion-bar suspension. The Ultramatic transmission turned out to be sluggish and underconstructed for the size of the car, resulting in reliability problems that were costly to both the company's cash position and the company's reputation. Torsion-bar suspension, although a meaningful feature, was not sufficiently meaningful to most potential customers and production totaled only 55,000 units the year Packard introduced it, as compared to 141,000 for arch rival Cadillac. While Packard's management focused development resources on features that could have been procured, or were not essential, it surrendered Packard's position in prestige automobiles to the more innovative Cadillac Division of GM.

Strategically successful features have in common the four attributes described on the next page.

1. The feature is significant. People perceive it as something that needs to be done.
2. Low-cost, suitable alternatives are not readily available. The decision to forgo development means not having the feature.
3. The feature is developed in a timely manner. The window of opportunity is not missed because decision or development times took too long.
4. The feature is reliable and well tested. The feature generates goodwill and not ill will.

Involving Top Management

Not only does it matter if the company has the resolve to innovate, it also matters whether competent technical people are left to do their job. Product differentiation is an essential survival attribute well deserving of the attention of top management. But often, ill-prepared members of top management become too involved in product differentiation to the exclusion of competent members of product development teams, as was the case with Hudson in its final years. A. E. Barit, the former stenographer who became president of the company when Roy Chapin died, had no flare for market analysis, product development, or design. Yet, he meddled in all three and failed to allow some of Hudson's competent product people to take the lead in their specialties. This resulted in missed opportunities, and resources were squandered on products aimed at markets the company had not served for many years.

Both Kaiser and Studebaker-Packard had similar experiences. During Studebaker-Packard's later years, its management showed little interest in genuine innovation but was fascinated with new gadgets — gadgets that customers did not always perceive as meaningful. Kaiser-Frazer's top management, although not experienced in the automobile industry, was heavily involved in the development of new products for new markets — unnecessary products for nonexistent markets. In successful cases, CEOs knew products but seldom meddled. Walter Chrysler, for instance, was quite technically knowledgeable, yet he allowed the chief members of his technical teams to chart the company's engineering direction. He was still involved but in a supportive way. Barit of Hudson, Nance of Studebaker-Packard, and some of the other unsuccessful CEOs of more recent times wanted not only involvement but authorship of product features and benefits. Unfortunately, they were often wrong.

Practical Lesson in Distinguishing Product Features

- Successful firms focus on emerging trends in the marketplace. They provide features and benefits ahead of or in sync with major market trends.

- Unsuccessful firms lag behind market trends or overanticipate market trends.

- Successful firms provide meaningful features and benefits, not gadgets.

- Successful firms avoid development of the unessential.

- Successful firms manage development tasks very well. Unsuccessful firms often take too long.

- Successful firms produce reliable new products. New products from unsuccessful firms are often poorly tested and unreliable.

- Successful chief executives are supportive of development staffs. Unsuccessful CEOs interfere with limited information and too much pride.

- Both successful and unsuccessful companies spend ample money on product development, but successful companies accomplish much more for the money.

Case Histories

From 1980 to 1982, the Ford Motor Company lost $3.3 billion as yearly car shipments dropped to less than half the levels of the late 1970s. Physical unit market share dropped during a time when the market itself became smaller. Five years later, Ford surpassed mighty GM in total dollar profits. Much of this turnaround was due to Ford's attention to distinguishing product features by virtue of its relentless goal to be "best in class." Kaiser-Frazer had the highest sales of any independent automobile producer in 1948, but 7 years later the firm had stopped domestic production. While Ford concentrated on meaningful features, Kaiser-Frazer concentrated on style and curiosities, which provided only short-term differentiation. The result was missed opportunities in historical markets and ultimate withdrawal from the business.

Case 6

Best in Class at Ford

As the Ford Motor Company entered the 1980s, the company experienced
competition more intense than at any time during its 80-year history. Over
time, Ford experienced occasional problematic relationships with
stakeholders but generally enjoyed resounding success in the marketplace.
By the 1970s, Ford no longer held the immense market share it had
enjoyed during the 1920s, but roughly one out of every four new cars sold
in the country was still a Ford. With the oil crisis of the mid-1970s, Ford
began to lose market position to imports. The imports' share of U.S. car
sales grew from 15.9 percent in 1974 to 26.7 percent in 1980, an increase
obtained almost totally at the expense of Ford and Chrysler. Ford's market
share declined from 25.1 percent in 1974 to 17.3 percent in 1980, while
Chrysler's share plummeted from 13.7 to 8.8 percent. Ford's before-tax
profit rate began declining in the mid-1950s and by the early 1980s had
turned substantially negative (Figure 7-4).

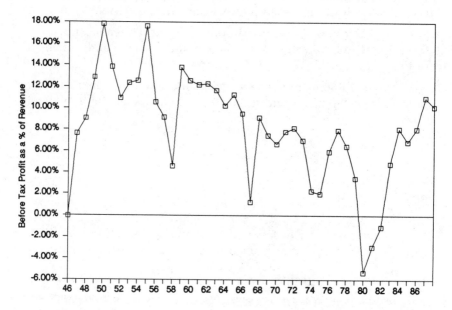

Figure 7-4. Ford Motor Company before tax profit rates, 1946 to 1988. Ford emerged from
lackluster financial performance and third position in U.S. sales before World War II to a strong
number two position by 1955. From that point, the profits of Ford and some other U.S. producers began to decline gradually, until they were negative in the early 1980s. As Ford passed
GM as the domestic leader in innovation, Ford profits rebounded until it became the dollar profit
leader in 1987 and 1988.

Ford lost nearly $2 billion in 1980, over $1 billion in 1981, and nearly $500 million in 1982. Car sales plummeted. In March 1980, Henry Ford II retired as Ford's chief executive, and Philip Caldwell was named as his successor. Caldwell exercised courage in marshaling support for product development from Ford's board of directors during a period when the firm was losing billions of dollars per year. Five years later, a product-development executive, Donald Petersen, was named president and later succeeded Caldwell as chairman.

Ford and Chrysler were both caught in a squeeze between fierce foreign competition and General Motors, whose earlier attention to downsizing gained it a temporary edge in strategic position. To meet the severe competitive demands confronting Ford, GM's management put in place strategically important proactive action plans. Ford actively sought, with both Chrysler and the United Auto Workers, a moratorium on imports. It established new product-development programs and initiated cost-reduction and productivity programs, often in cooperation with organized labor.

In March 1982, Ford reached a milestone agreement with the United Auto Workers wherein the workers agreed to a series of wage concessions saving Ford more than $300 million per year. The UAW conceded to the following (Harvard Business School 1983):

1. Gave up an annual 3 percent "improvement factor" in wages.

2. Gave up the equivalent of two weeks of paid time off per year.

3. Deferred cost-of-living adjustments for 18 months.

4. Allowed that newly hired and certain rehired employees would initially be paid 85 percent of the negotiated rate for the job classification.

In turn, Ford agreed to the following concessions (Harvard Business School 1983):

1. Give 6 months' notice of any plant closing.

2. Avoid closing any plant because of outsourcing for 2 years.

3. Review certain recently announced plant closings.

4. Guarantee workers with 15 years of service, 75 percent of their earnings and insurance benefits if they were laid off and remained unemployed.

5. Provide some senior employees with preferential placement.

6. Increase the company contribution to the laid-off workers' supplemental benefit fund.

7. Provide a share of North American before-tax profits exceeding 2.3 percent of sales to employees.

8. Experiment with "lifetime job security concepts" at two facilities.

However, during the early 1980s, Ford needed more than lower costs, it also needed cars that would sell. Ford quality was improved through programs involving Dr. W. Edwards Deming. Several new-product programs were initiated but chief among them was the Taurus/Sable program, which brought dramatic changes to car program management. Lewis C. Veraldi served as Ford's vice president of car program management during the development of the highly successful Taurus/Sable project, which became the model program-management system for the Lincoln, Thunderbird, and other Ford products at later times. Veraldi started with Ford as an apprentice tool-and-die maker in 1944 and then progressed through a variety of engineering and management positions while completing his engineering degree at night. Veraldi was well-equipped to handle the Taurus project because of his executive experiences in both manufacturing and engineering. The 7 years he spent in Europe heading the successful Fiesta project provided him with insights into foreign as well as U.S. product-development methods. A former tool-and-die maker himself, he was comfortable working with production people and other members of the Ford organization.

Ford's situation was extremely serious between 1980 and 1982, when the company lost $3.26 billion and witnessed a 50 percent decline in unit sales from 1978 levels. Yet the $3.3 billion project was approved, and much of the development effort took place when the company was experiencing its deepest losses. Veraldi remarked, "Ford had always followed General Motors' designs. We were never the pacesetter, but being in a loss position allowed us to do something innovative. It was almost a blessing. Being in the trenches helped us" (Mishne 1988).

Ford's Taurus team consisted of people throughout the Ford organization, and vendors and other stakeholders as well. Veraldi imported Jack Telnack from Ford of Europe to serve as the design executive. John Risk handled planning, and Al Gutherie served as chief engineer. It was an experienced crew, experienced not only in the engineering aspects of product development but also in dealing with the inner complexities of the Ford Motor Company. As experienced practitioners who had earned their spurs, they were trusted and therefore able to get things accomplished with a minimum of formality. Representatives from manufacturing engineering, product engineering, safety, production, legal, public relations, dealer relations, and many other constituencies combined efforts to design and produce a new car which would be simultaneously engineered—a car that would have lasting value to the customer, have superb features and benefits, be safe to drive, and inexpensive to produce.

As his first step in managing the Taurus project, Veraldi requested his staff to identify and document why various cars were perceived as good. The best automobiles in the world were identified and measured in each of 400 separate automotive features. The Taurus team examined each feature in detail and established a design objective to meet or exceed all competitors on each of these 400 attributes (a sample is displayed in Table 7-4). They tracked such factors as heater-switch feel, noise, foot comfort, glove compartment accessibility, handling characteristics, and hundreds of other design attributes to ensure that the Taurus would be the "best in class" in each of these characteristics.

The rigorous demands of the Taurus project required both the people skills and the managerial skills of Veraldi and others in the Ford organization.

Table 7-4. Ford Taurus/Mercury Sable Best-in-Class Expanded Images Sample Assessment of 400 Design Elements

Feature	Car line	Effort	DN05 objective	DN05 status	Remarks
Rear-seat comfort	Opel Senator		B-I-C*	B-I-C	DN05† is equal to Opel Senator for rear-seat comfort.
Wind noise	Audi 100		B-I-C	Less than B-I-C	Wind-noise improvement plan aimed at achieving B-I-C status to be in place by 8-87.
Perceived knee room	BMW		B-I-C	B-I-C	DN05 equivalent to BMW.
W/S wiper-system noise	Mazda 626 Honda Accord		B-I-C	B-I-C	DN05 is B-I-C.
Seat-belt buckling ease—front	Toyota Cressida		B-I-C	B-I-C	Toyota Cressida rated best due to passive system. BMW528E rated best among conventional continuous loop systems. DN05's adjust tongue-buckle assembly, antiroping D-ring and retractor design objectives will ensure excellent component accessibility and will allow single-handed latching of restraint system. This will make system equivalent to B-I-C competition.
Hood raising from pop-open	Toyota Cressida	9 #	8 #	7 #	DN05 objective is 8# using dual gas cylinders. Effort may vary on ambient temperature (as does Cressida). DN05 to be B-I-C overall.
Climate control operating efforts—rotary	Saab 900		B-I-C	B-I-C	DN05 efforts will be comparable to Saab.
Brake pedal—effort (at 15 feet per second, 2 from 60 miles per hour	Toyota Cressida	23 #	B-I-C	B-I-C	At the request of chassis engineering, a consumer survey was conducted at Dearborn test track by NAAO Marketing Research. The results indicate DN05 considered B-I-C.
Fuel-tank filling ease (spitback)	BMW/Mazda		B-I-C	B-I-C	Angle of fuel-filler pipe has been revised to make DN05 B-I-C. No spitback with ball check in fill pipe.
Clutch-pedal effort @ idle	Accord	9 # (rating)	B-I-C	B-I-C	Latest released level clutch shows pedal effort to be B-I-C.

*B-I-C = best in class.
†DN05 = Ford Taurus/Mercury Sable.

SOURCE: Ford Motor Company.

With 4000 new components and targeted quality levels substantially above what was customary for U.S. manufacturers, top performance was required of all team members. Veraldi remarked,

> The auto industry is constructed with "chimneys"—engineering, marketing, suppliers. The prevailing attitude has been, "Don't touch my field." Design would pass its ideas to manufacturing, then manufacturing would claim that the design didn't work. You have to get everything together working toward a common objective. If you don't have teamwork, then the work isn't devoted to the good of the product." (Mishne 1988. From "A Passion for Perfection," *Manufacturing Engineering*, November 1988.)

By involving the production people in the design process; by clearly understanding the legal, marketing, and financial requirements of the project up front; and by focusing on feature-by-feature superiority over competition, pride and confidence began to emerge within the ranks of the Taurus team. The team's slogan, "Do common things uncommonly well," reflected the thoroughness that began to typify the entire Ford organization. Veraldi explained, "Taurus is a vehicle used to show how people working together can accomplish more than people working apart. It's the obvious concepts that are always ignored" (Mishne 1988).

Ford's sales, profitability, and productivity improved with the Taurus and with the Continental, Thunderbird, and Lincoln TownCars, which also employed the Taurus team approach. By 1987, Ford's market share had risen substantially from its low in 1980. During the first year of production for the Taurus/Sable, production lines were producing 63 cars per hour versus 50 cars per hour with the same number of people on previous models (Mishne 1988).

Ford's reduction in incremental cost was substantial during the years of its recovery. Following reductions of $19 billion (1988 dollars) in annual expenses from 1979 to 1982, Ford was then postured to bring in additional revenue from a lower expense base. The efficiency and manufacturability resulting from the well-planned development activities of Ford, coupled with cooperative programs with organized labor, enabled the company to add incremental revenue at little additional cost. From 1982 to 1987, Ford added only $0.76 of incremental before-tax cost per dollar of incremental revenue—a very respectable rate of upside efficiency. Ford returned to profitability in 1983 with earnings of $1.9 billion. Profitability increased every year for the next 5 years until the $5.3 billion of 1988 exceeded that of much larger GM (see Figure 7-5).

The Ford turnaround resulted from much more than adroit management of new projects. Virtually all elements of the company improved within an atmosphere of labor and management cooperation. Relations greatly improved through a program of employee involvement launched jointly by Ford and the United Auto Workers, and by the late 1980s, Ford management and UAW representatives were sharing offices at some plants. One middle-ranking Ford manager summed up the atmosphere at the Ford Motor Company in the following way, "When I talk to Donald Peterson, I have the feeling he likes me."

At the heart of it all, however, was the overriding desire to produce better

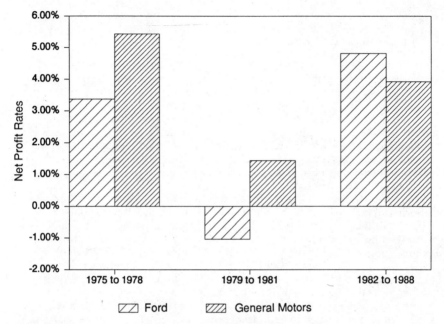

Figure 7-5. Ford and GM net profit rates. Ford's after-tax profit rate was approximately two-thirds that of GM from 1975 to 1978, and Ford operated unprofitably during the recession of the early 1980s. As both GM and Ford emerged from this very deep recession, Ford became the profit rate leader among U.S. producers.

products, to provide what the customer needed, to employ science and proper measurement, and to instill the desire to be "best in class" in all members of the Ford organization.

Ford Survived Because...

- Standards for product features and benefits were among the highest in the world.

- Top management knew a lot about cars and what it took to develop them.

- Development teams were composed of competent people from many areas of the company.

- Development proceeded on time and under budget.

- Product development people were left to do their jobs.

- Manufacturability was designed into the product.

Case 7

Cosmetic Surgery at Kaiser-Frazer

During the closing years of World War II, West Coast industrialist Henry J. Kaiser began to lay plans for a postwar automobile company. Kaiser had been a very successful defense and public works contractor. Among the accomplishments of the Kaiser industries and its associate companies were the building of Hoover Dam, Grand Coulee Dam, 1490 warships, the first steel mill on the West Coast, and numerous other spectacular construction and engineering feats — most of which were accomplished on schedule and under budget. Kaiser enterprises were extensive, including a substantial engineering and construction business, Kaiser Steel, Kaiser Aluminum & Chemicals, and other smaller enterprises.

In order to facilitate his goal of a postwar automotive company, Henry Kaiser ultimately teamed with another historic name in the automobile industry, Graham-Paige. In 1944, Joe Frazer, a respected and established sales executive who was involved in Chrysler's market penetration in the thirties, became president and chief executive of Graham-Paige, a firm that had suffered severely during the Great Depression. Frazer immediately began preparing for the resurgence of the automobile industry that many expected to emerge after World War II. Graham-Paige joined Kaiser Industries to form the Kaiser-Frazer Corporation in August 1945. Henry J. Kaiser was named chief executive and Joe Frazer, president. Kaiser-Frazer Corporation purchased the remaining Graham-Paige assets in February 1947.

The first Kaiser and Frazer automobiles were introduced in 1947. The two makes were nearly identical. The initial styling was modern for its time. Fenders were blended into the sides of the car. The car was wide and roomy inside with a large amount of room in the front passenger area due to an attractively designed concave dash. Visibility was excellent compared to other cars of this era.

Apart from the styling, the car's design was mainly prewar. The engine was designed by Continental Motors and was nearly identical to the Graham-Paige engines of the 1930s. It was not an especially durable engine, having only three main bearings and only moderate displacement for a full-size car. But the Kaiser-Frazer design was light in weight, and the cars had at least average performance for the late 1940s.

In order to provide a production facility for the automobile business, Kaiser-Frazer management arranged to lease (and later purchase) a huge surplus bomber plant at Willow Run, Michigan. At 4 million square feet under one roof, the Willow Run plant suddenly became the largest single automotive plant in the world. This huge plant, together with the Frazer's sales expertise and the construction and steel capabilities of the Kaiser industries generated enthusiasm for the industry's first new entrant in nearly 20 years. Kaiser-Frazer stock quickly tripled in value.

The early sales of Kaiser-Frazer automobiles were sensational. By 1948, Kaiser-Frazer was the sales leader among the six independent producers (see Table 7-5). Revenue for 1948 was $342 million and after-tax profits exceeded

Table 7-5. 1948 Sales in Units—
Independent Producers

Kaiser-Frazer	181,316
Hudson	142,454
Nash	118,621
Studebaker	102,123
Packard	98,898
Willys (cars)	32,635

$10 million. Clearly, this was an exceptional showing for a company many predicted would not get off the starting blocks.

Several important observations must be made regarding the success of Kaiser-Frazer during the postwar years, however. Most important, a seller's market prevailed because of the 4-year shutdown of domestic automobile production during World War II. Most companies were still production-bound, and materials were still scarce. The huge Willow Run plant plus its association with Kaiser Steel gave Kaiser-Frazer some advantages during this period. In addition, practically all the other producers were offering cars styled before World War II. Only Kaiser-Frazer offered new styling.

Kaiser-Frazer cars were relatively undifferentiated except for styling. Quality was below average, and the internal engineering of the actual production models was quite dated. Though Kaiser-Frazer engineers had experimented with a new V8 engine and front-wheel drive, these innovative concepts never reached production. When the other automobile producers announced new, more modern styling for 1948–1949, Kaiser-Frazer lost its key advantage. By 1949, Kaiser-Frazer was competing against lower-priced, attractively styled cars with modern overhead-valve V8 engines, good engineering, and automatic transmissions. Cadillac and Oldsmobile provided the most formidable competition.

Many members of the Kaiser organization were not experienced in the automobile industry, and production methods were oriented to the wartime requirement of finishing things quickly. The first Kaiser-Frazer automobiles went into production quickly, but the operation never became established as a low-cost producer. Kaisers were priced generally in the Buick and Chrysler range, while Frazer's prices compared with the Lincoln and the Packard. Even with these high prices, gross profit margins were low by industry standards (Table 7-6).

Joe Frazer expected that competitive automobile companies would be offering superior products during the 1949 model year, and he advocated reducing Kaiser-Frazer production schedules to an annualized rate of 70,000 cars, until Kaiser-Frazer announced its new car 18 months later. His production plan allowed for profitable operations at a much lower level of production. In sharp contrast, Henry Kaiser did not believe that sales would decline that substantially, and the company continued at full

Table 7-6. Gross Profit Rates of
Major Producers, 1947–1948

1947 Nash	21.8%
1947 GM	19.6%
1947 Kaiser-Frazer	11.1%
1947 Studebaker	8.9%
1947 Packard	7.0%
1948 GM	24.2%
1948 Nash	21.3%
1948 Packard	15.2%
1948 Kaiser-Frazer	12.5%
1948 Studebaker	11.1%

production for much of 1949. Frazer turned out to be correct. Kaiser-Frazer sold only 58,000 cars in 1949 and lost over $30 million.

In spite of Frazer's feel for the market, his influence began to erode at Kaiser-Frazer shortly after the 1949 experience. A philosophy of continued expansion was emerging at Kaiser-Frazer. A new full-sized car and a new compact car were being made ready. Henry J. Kaiser and his able son, Edgar, were convinced that they would ultimately prevail in the automobile business as they had in so many others. By 1950, Edgar Kaiser had replaced Joe Frazer as the company's president.

Basically skipping the 1950 model year, Kaiser-Frazer announced a new line of cars for 1951. The body of the Kaiser was completely new. The Frazer was to be new but retained the basic body shell of the 1949 models in order to use up an existing inventory of parts. Both were roomy cars with an innovative hatchback design available, but only the Kaiser sold well. The newly styled Kaiser sold 139,000 units. The modified Frazer sold 10,000.

The 1951 Kaiser was an attractively styled automobile. In many respects, the car resembled cars produced 15 or 20 years later. But, again, the car was differentiated only with respect to styling and a few innovative safety features. The car still had the same old prewar flat-head six-cylinder engine, and other engineering features were nearly identical to earlier models. Though the car did sell well immediately after its introduction, this high rate of sales was not sustained. Most manufacturers restyled again in 1952, and Kaiser's main edge again eroded.

During the 1950s, the firm also announced its new compact car — the "Henry J." This car was both small and sprightly but it was not inexpensive. Priced about the same as a Chevrolet with far less room, far fewer features, no trunk, and inexpensive plastic upholstery, it sold mainly to a curiosity market. About 120,000 were produced during the 4-year production run.

Though the new Kaiser and, to a lesser extent, the Henry J sold well at the time of their introduction, they were produced at very high cost. Kaiser automobiles had a limited number of body styles (no station wagon, no convertible, and no two-door hardtop), but the sculptured shape of the Kaiser body created some manufacturing problems and the company offered a huge assortment of exterior colors and styles of upholstery, some of them rather gaudy. Gross profit rates were under 5 percent for both 1951 and 1952. The inventory turns per year shrank to 4.8 for 1951. The company lost $12 million in 1951 and $5 million in 1952. Former vice president and secretary Hickman Price described matters in the following way:

> The money started to go out at a rate that was incredible. All sorts of research was done — but in general not basic research, not engineering research, of how to make a better product. It was what I would call a purifying operation, and at this Edgar [Kaiser] was good. But, the cost was unbelievable. The people working on a project like that you simply couldn't count. The plane fares alone, back and forth from California, plus plus plus plus plus, were out of this world. (Langworth 1975, 110)

During the same era, Willys-Overland had emerged from the war as an established producer of utility vehicles — primarily the Jeep. The Jeep sold modestly well and the firm was profitable from 1942 through 1953. The company began to experience substantial operating losses, however, when it began to produce a small conventional automobile, the Aero-Willys. Since Willys-Overland had been a supplier of engines to Kaiser, and Joe Frazer had, at one time, been president of Willys-Overland, considerable rapport already existed between the two firms. Kaiser-Frazer purchased the automobile-related assets of Willys-Overland in April of 1953, and with Joe Frazer out of the company and the Frazer automobile no longer in production, the company was renamed Kaiser Motors Inc.

Kaiser kept the Aero-Willys in production into 1955 — longer than the Henry J. The car itself was well designed and very economical. But, with list prices $200 above those of Ford and Chevrolet, it was also expensive. Again, Kaiser Motors was not equipped to build a low-priced car because the firm was a high-cost producer. Gross profits were negative for both 1953 and 1954, and net profits were substantially negative. After losses of $27 million in 1953 and $35 million in 1954, the decision was made to exit from passenger-car production to concentrate on the other Kaiser interests and on the manufacture of Jeeps. Five years later, in 1960, the remnants of the once-impressive Willys and Kaiser vehicle businesses were sold to American Motors in exchange for AMC stock.

In some respects, the Kaiser was an innovative car. The firm pioneered an interest in safety and produced one of the first practical hatchback automobiles. It was certainly well-styled. But, Kaiser management made the mistake of investing its differentiation resources in something that could change quickly — style. Management of the firm neglected to make investments in product development, process improvement, manufacturing engineering, and product quality. Kaiser's strategy was not internally consistent. The firm was never efficient enough to compete effectively in the low-priced field, even though huge investments were made to develop and purchase products for this market. A significant increase in internal efficiency was needed even for the medium-priced field, and this lack of internal efficiency absolutely precluded it from being a major factor in the low-priced field.

However, the main lesson in the missed opportunities of Kaiser-Frazer rests with the mishandling of product differentiation. True product differentiation, as with true beauty, must be more than skin deep. Kaiser automobiles were attractive for their time — some would say very attractive. But underneath the attractive exterior of the car were drive-train components nearly identical to those of a low-volume car of two decades earlier (Table 7-7). The absence of up-to-date engineering deprived the firm of the lasting differentiation necessary for the medium-priced field. From the start of the unsuccessful turnaround in 1949, the firm remained a high-cost producer of insufficiently differentiated products.

Table 7-7. Graham, Kaiser, and Oldsmobile Engines, 1936 and 1954

	Valve arrange- ment	Engine configu- ration	Engine bore	Engine stoke	Cubic- inch dis- place- ment	Com- pression ratio	Horsepower, r/min
1936 Graham	L head	In-line	3.25 in	4.375 in	217.8	6.70	85 @ 3300
1954 Kaiser	L head	In-line	3.32 in	4.375 in	226.2	7.30	118 @ 3650
1936 Oldsmobile	L head	In-line	3.31 in	4.125 in	213.3	6.00	90 @ 3400
1954 Oldsmobile	OHV	V8	3.88 in	3.438 in	324.3	8.25	170 @ 4000

Kaiser Failed Because...

- Product differentiation was limited to cosmetics and did not extend to meaningful technical features.

- Top management was competent but had little experience in the industry being served.

- Development and operational decisions were directed from levels which were too high in the company.

- Manufacturability was insufficiently considered.

- Expediting replaced operational efficiency.

8

Achieving Product Quality

The Cadillac Division of General Motors had a humble beginning as the failed experimental shop of Henry Ford. But rigorous attention to product quality allowed the Cadillac automobile to complete its evolution from a low-priced car with few sales to a prestigious marque with lasting presence in the world marketplace.

Fortunately for the firm in trouble, good quality lowers cost. The highest cost of bad quality occurs during the production process, when poorly made parts preclude efficient final assembly. Effective turnaround agents understand the cost of bad quality and make process changes that improve quality, at least to some degree, very quickly. Their approach is often rather simple, and often emotional. They display their feelings in ways that clearly convey their intentions to workers, vendors, and other managers. They express horror and indignation, not at the workers who produce the parts, but at the parts that are bad. They may use humor, expletives, or physical destruction of the part itself in order to illustrate the need for perfection, but they are not vindictive or personal. They determine causes of bad quality by thorough investigation. Then they effect corrections and reinforce them through ongoing systems of discipline. Turnaround managers who are successful attend to quality problems with vigor and dispatch.

In contrast, unsuccessful turnaround managers vacillate and are too polite. Production people tend to distrust overly polite managers when the company is on the brink of failure. The workers themselves want managerial action as an indication of corporate resolve. The workers do not want to lose their jobs because the products being produced do not meet customer expectations. They want the problems fixed, and they are most willing to participate in improvements. What workers detest most is the rationalization that no problems exist.

The human power to rationalize quality into one's own products is widespread, and many companies in trouble believe that they are unable to make suitable profits because other producers with lower-quality products underprice them. This rationalization is seldom verified, but its presence inhibits management from taking meaningful action to restore the firm's health. As an example, the top officers at a major manufacturer of potato harvesters felt that the firm's products were substantially better than any other products in the market, and if the agricultural economy would improve, prices could be raised and profitability restored. However, upon closer inspection, iron filings were found in the hydraulic tanks, the main frames of the units were welded up crooked, thus causing premature wear on working parts, the paint was peeling, nameplates were improperly mounted, and the company went 4 years without making a scheduled delivery on time. When some of the quality problems were corrected, the company did sell more because the basic design of the unit was adequate. But for many years, managers of the company had deluded themselves into believing that they had a quality product without ever checking. Ironically, it was the production workers who made the suggestions for improvement. The workers knew that the problems were there all along, but managers did not consider the employees' suggestions, insisting instead that the company already made the "Cadillac" of the industry.

Today's Cadillac automobiles are not alone in holding the lofty distinction the marque enjoyed in an earlier era, but the word *Cadillac* still connotes superb craftsmanship. It is more than a superlative, however; it has a technical meaning. Quality is a form of discipline relating to the institutionalization of product quality throughout the production process. Dr. Armand V. Feigenbaum defines quality as:

> The total composite product and service characteristics of marketing, engineering, manufacture, and maintenance through which the product and service in use will meet the expectation of the customer. (Feigenbaum 1983, 7)

Quality in the Product

There are several ways in which successful companies exploit quality as a distinguishing characteristic. First, they act cautiously but quickly in addressing quality problems. They do not delay or pretend that important problems do not exist. They resist the temptation to hide behind the weak excuse that additional information is required to verify the obvious fact that the product could be improved. Successful managers understand the technologies of their products well enough to know what can be done and what should be done. Then, they do it. They take action. Unsuccessful firms often let problems slide as they await further evidence that a problem exists, or they rationalize the problem as minimal.

Successful turnaround agents respond to quality problems quickly and with thoroughness, often incurring additional expense when the firm can least afford it. The result of prompt action on defects is not only a better product but reduced manufacturing cost. Ford's production efficiency improved with its quality initiatives as did those of Buick, Cadillac, and Nash, and American Motors in earlier times. By taking quick action to improve quality, the successful firms experienced the dividend of improved production efficiency.

The fact that unsuccessful companies take too long to address major quality issues results in a twofold penalty: negative product differentiation and high cost. Hudson machining tolerances and Kaiser door mountings were both examples of quality being neglected in ways that impacted process efficiencies. Product quality is often either neglected altogether or oriented to cosmetic features rather than in-depth quality. In a few cases, such as the Studebaker problems with rust, Kaiser problems with fit and finish, Firestone 500 Radial tires, or the lack of engine durability in Hudson's number-one seller—the Essex—blatant quality problems were either neglected or dealt with slowly by unsuccessful firms.

Sound product design provides the cornerstone for product quality, and successful firms treat quality as an iterative process involving engineering, manufacturing, and support organizations until the resulting product fully meets the expectation of the customer. The Ford Taurus, the Deere Model A tractor, the Chrysler K car, and the Rambler automobile are examples of this iterative approach to product development—these developments took time to fully implement but were constantly in a state of improvement.

Successful firms also understand, more completely, the economics of quality. Packard, for instance, understood that the proper heat treatment of steel could reduce both raw-material cost and processing cost while enhancing quality. Ford engineers understood that body fit and finish were closely tied to the design and size of stamping dies. Deere understood the mathematical reliability of fewer, well-made components. Nash engineers understood the advantages of heavier main bearings and dual ignition systems. In another industry, the IBM Corporation understood the qualitative advantages of lubrication-free nylon gears and more reliable ribbon cartridges in its typewriter products. Successful companies know more about their products and how they work so that they can be in a better position to improve quality while lowering cost. Unsuccessful companies are often headed by chief executives who do not know how their products work.

Successful firms also continue to improve the quality of products even when they are better than other products on the market. Charles Nash met with his chief managers and workers every week on the matter of product quality, meetings which began by reading any letters of complaint from customers. Whether the product was good was not the question. The question was, could the product be better? Ford used as its standard some of the highest-priced automobiles in the world and produced a sedan for the low-priced field, using the slogan "do common things uncommonly well." Programs of constant improvement have been present at Toyota, Honda, and Mazda but also at American producers such as Snap-On Tools Corporation, Maytag Corporation, Onan Corporation, and the 3M Company.

Quality in the Process

The mere determination to produce quality products is insufficient to restore a firm's competitive edge. Scientific investigation and discipline are the traits needed for a successful turnaround. Design characteristics, production processes, and user requirements must be scientifically examined in search of even minuscule contributors to low quality. Then, improvements must be implemented and carefully monitored to ensure that shipped products meet customer expectations. Though the firm may be teetering on the brink of liquidation, science and discipline must prevail to get things right prior to shipment of product.

Successful companies carry the concept quality through to completion in all aspects of the organization, not merely the final assembly of end products. Quality becomes systemic and proceeds from discipline. It applies to everything. Much emphasis is put on quality during the production process (as opposed to emphasis on end-product quality only). Henry Leland of Cadillac described this emphasis in the following way:

> It is the foreman's job to know that every piece of work turned out by his department is RIGHT, and it is his work to teach his men how to make it RIGHT. It doesn't cost as much to have the work done RIGHT the first time as it does to have it done poorly and then have a number of men to make it right afterward. (Automobile Quarterly Editors and Princeton Institute for Historic Research 1983, 26)

This emphasis on quality as an ongoing discipline is one factor which distinguished the successful from the unsuccessful turnarounds. End-product quality was meaningful because the successful firms sought to satisfy customers. But in-process quality impacts both end-product quality and unit cost. The successful turnaround agents understood that the highest cost of bad quality occurs during production, when defective components inhibit the product from moving to the next stage of assembly. They understood that it was not possible for the production process to move freely unless a discipline existed which required top quality at every stage in the production process. More recently, the Japanese have rediscovered the same concept.

The superior quality performance of the successful firms resulted from process consistency and constant improvement of both products and processes, but of these two, the discipline surrounding processes was primary. If the process, itself, is not predictable, mere rhetoric and company spirit will not provide customers with quality products.

Practical Lessons on Product Quality

- Both successful and unsuccessful companies believe their products to be of high quality, but credibility varies. Successful companies constantly check to ensure that products meet or exceed customer requirements. Unsuccessful companies presume that quality is high but do not check.

- Successful companies quickly take action on quality problems. Unsuccessful companies gather more evidence.

- Discipline in operations is prevalent among successful companies. Quality is maintained because precision is expected at every link in the value chain, and when quality is not forthcoming, changes are made. Unsuccessful companies lack discipline.

- Successful companies improve the product even when it is better than competing products. Unsuccessful companies become satisfied when quality is about the same as that of weaker competitors.

- In-process quality is the major emphasis at successful companies. At unsuccessful companies, more emphasis is on the end product.

- Top managers at successful companies are emotional about quality and other issues. Top managers at unsuccessful companies display less emotion and are hard for people to read.

- Top managers at successful companies instill pride in company and product by clearly articulating, through words and actions, what is important and by supplementing these articulations with outstanding technical knowledge. The combination of pride, technical competence, fairness, and experience helps organization members to believe that they are part of a class act.

Case Histories

In 1902, the financial backers of Henry Ford, exasperated by Ford's proclivity to tinker and the fact that only three cars had been produced in several years, sought the advice of a respected manufacturing manager to determine whether the firm should be salvaged or liquidated. The recommendation was that the firm should not be liquidated if quality and manufacturing could be improved. Many improvements were made in product design, quality, and manufacturability as the firm continued without Henry Ford under the name of Cadillac. Cadillac then rose from its early beginnings as a low-cost one-cylinder car to become one of the most prestigious and successful marques in the world. What enabled Cadillac to progress from its humble beginnings to the flagship position in the GM fleet was rigorous attention to product quality.

Twenty-five years later, the Hudson Motor Car Company was enjoying unprecedented success as one of the four largest producers of American cars. Hudson produced 276,000 cars in 1927, a market share of 8.96 percent. By 1929, sales had grown to over 300,000 units. The firm's popular Essex model had provided many innovative features to the moderately priced field, and Hudson stock appreciated greatly during the 1920s. Two years later, however, the Hudson Motor Car Company had entered a period of unprofitability which was to last, almost uninterrupted, until World War II. What caused Hudson to decline was not primarily the economy of the 1930s, for other producers fared better. What caused Hudson to decline was its failure to pursue top product quality, a shortcoming which resulted in a market share slippage of more than 50 percent.

Case 8

Getting It Right at Cadillac

Together with a group of prominent Detroit investors, Henry Ford formed the Detroit Automobile Company (later, the Henry Ford Company) in 1899. The financial backers were interested in producing a commercially viable passenger car, but Henry Ford found it difficult to complete the full design, develop, and produce a major product in the time allotted. After 3 years, only three prototype models had been produced. The company had largely exhausted its capital, and Ford's backers had lost interest in further support of his efforts. They no longer had faith that Ford could mold his product ideas into a workable business and decided to liquidate the company.

In order to reassure themselves that they had made the right decision, they sought the technical advice of Henry Leland of the machining firm of Leland and Faulconer. Leland and Faulconer was a major supplier to the then-infant automobile industry and manufactured the engines for Oldsmobile as well as component parts for other manufacturers. Leland had a strong background in precision machining, stemming from his long experience as a plant superintendent for the Brown & Sharpe Company, a prominent manufacturer of machine tools.

Leland was 56 at the time of the difficulties at the Henry Ford Company. Through the years he had developed the reputation of being absolutely fanatical about efficiency and precision in production. His son, Wilfred, worked with him. Wilfred was a highly competent technical person in his own right who had a flare for engineering and product design. Together, they trained, influenced, or encouraged by close association some of the most influential names in the early history of automobiles, including Horace Dodge, Fred Zeder (later head of Chrysler engineering), Alanson Brush (Pontiac/Oakland) and, at a later stage, Charles Kettering and Alfred Sloan. Together, the Lelands developed a highly respected position as perhaps the most qualified suppliers of precision parts to the then-infant automobile industry.

Henry Leland's disciplined and technological approach to machine design and production contrasted rather sharply with the informal trial-and-error methods employed by Ford (Nevins 1954). Leland's assessment was that the design of the Ford engine was neither advanced from an engineering standpoint nor cost-effective. A much better engine could be designed that would be far less costly to build — less costly by an amount which represented a significant percentage of the total cost of the automobile at the time. The financial backers bought Leland's product concept, and the firm of Leland and Faulconer was given a contract to manage the company, which was renamed the Cadillac Motor Company in honor of the founder of Detroit. Later, the two firms of Leland and Faulconer and Cadillac were combined. Thus, the Cadillac motor car rose from the ashes of Henry Ford's earlier unsuccessful efforts in the automotive industry.

The Lelands did indeed produce a highly reliable one-cylinder engine. This strong but small one-cylinder engine matched the needs of the marketplace, for the first Cadillacs were very small cars. In spite of the car's modest size, the Cadillac soon gained a widespread reputation for quality, reliability, and precision. In 1908, Leland had five Cadillacs shipped to a prestigious technical exhibition in Europe. The five cars were completely disassembled and the parts intermixed with some newly manufactured off-the-shelf parts. Then the cars were reassembled and driven 500 miles at full speed. All five Cadillacs ran perfectly — a magnificent accomplishment for 1908. The result was that the firm won the coveted DeWar Trophy for Manufacturing Excellence entitled Standard of the World — still the Cadillac slogan today.

Henry Leland understood at an early stage the important principle in manufacturing that the real cost of bad quality is in house in the form of inefficient production. He understood that parts that are not accurately machined do not fit together and cause delays in production as well as inconvenience to the customer later on. Leland insisted that parts be machined down to a tolerance of one-thousandth of an inch or even less for more critical parts. Leland would roam through the plant throwing parts away, breaking castings, and hiding poorly made parts so that they would not find their way into the production process. In this stirring and colorful manner, he exhibited the crucial leadership trait of being able to clearly articulate the importance of quality and accuracy.

Fred Zeder referred to Henry Leland as "a prince...the Grand Old Man of Detroit. He was indefatigable and so patient in his directing and guiding wherever needed" (Crabb 1969). Other individuals liked Henry Leland less well, but respect for his engineering abilities, his interest in quality, and knowledge of production was widespread.

Ultimately, many key innovations and inventions appeared in the Cadillac motor car first. The electric starter project was begun in 1910 after a close friend of the Lelands, Byron Carter of CarterCar, was fatally injured while cranking a car. At the time of Carter's death, Henry Leland made the following remark to close associates:

> I'm sorry I ever built an automobile. Those vicious cranks, I won't have Cadillacs hurting people that way. (Leland 1966, 131)

As with other successful turnarounds, production efficiency enabled the firm to add distinctive features and benefits. The industry's first electric starter, first generator and battery system, and the first coil ignition system were all projects sponsored by Cadillac when Charles Kettering was just beginning his Delco Laboratory. Cadillac introduced thermostatically controlled water circulation, tilt-beam headlights, and an adjustable steering wheel. Wilfred Leland developed the industry's first production V8 engine, which reached the market in 1915. Key advancements were made in lighting, engineering, and manufacturing processes.

Quality, workmanship, and production discipline built the Cadillac motor car into one of the most differentiated products in the industry. The advertising employed by Cadillac prior to World War I was highly technical. Prospective buyers were treated as competent, rational individuals who were interested in knowing why the Cadillac motor car was better. Cadillac advertisements often read more like an engineering manual than an advertisement for a motor car. Figure 8-1 displays some excerpts from a long and detailed advertisement covering the 1914 Cadillac Thirty.

As respect for the workmanship in the Cadillac motor car grew, sales increased dramatically, and Cadillac soon became the number three producer. Cadillac (along with Buick) became one of two chief contributors to the profit of the General Motors Company, which it had joined in 1909. It was Wilfred Leland's persuasive speech and the consistent profitability of Cadillac that

Motor

Cadillac pistons are gauged to similar accuracy. The result is that neither cylinders nor pistons can possibly vary in diameter even a hair's breadth. Consequently ANY piston will fit in ANY cylinder. They do not have to be "paired." If it ever becomes necessary to replace a piston, all the owner has to do is replace the piston. He is not necessarily obliged to replace the cylinder also, or possibly a pair of cylinders or the whole four as might be the case where they are cast in pairs or all together.

In finishing the cylinders and pistons, we do not stop at simply machining. Every one of them is ground to a polished surface resulting in practically perfect compression and consequently maximum power. The piston rings are finished with the same precision and are also made from our own special formula, different from that of which the cylinders and pistons are cast. This metal possesses exceptional spring qualities not easily affected by the heat of the motor. Therefore, they retain their efficiency long after the ordinary ring would be rendered practically worthless. The crank shaft is substantially supported by five large bearings, insuring that firmness and rigidity essential to a smooth running, vibrationless and durable motor.

Ignition

In the very essential matter of Ignition the Cadillac is equipped with two separate and complete systems, each with its individual set of spark plugs. Either system is efficient for operating the car, entirely independent of the other. For one system we use the Bosch high tension magneto. As an auxiliary ignition, we have adopted the new Delco Distributor System. We use this system not merely for starting but to afford Cadillac users a dependable reserve ignition that can be used for running any distance with satisfactory results.

Drive Shaft

The drive is direct by special heat treated high carbon steel shaft, fitted with two universal joins having hardened and ground bushings and pins. The joints are enclosed in spherical housings and run in oil baths. The forward joint, which is telescopic, is so constructed that it is self centering, resulting practically in the elimination of friction and bindings strains characteristic of ordinary construction. The drive shaft revolves on Timken bearings. The torsion member is V shaped tubular. When the car is carrying a normal load, the power is transmitted in practically a straight line from the motor to the rear axle, with the result that the maximum of generated power is delivered to the ground. The foregoing are some more reasons why the Cadillac shows more power than any other car having a motor of its size.

Figure 8-1. Excerpts from a Cadillac advertisement—1914. (*Source: David Q. Bowers, Early American Car Advertisements, Bonanza, New York, 1966.*)

Transmission

The Cadillac transmission is as superior to the usual transmission as the Cadillac motor is superior to other motors. It is more substantial, more positive, and by operators of long experience it has been pronounced the most easily operated of any they have ever used. It is our own design, manufactured in our own factory. It is the selective type of sliding gear. There are three speeds forward and reverse, direct on high. The gears, also the transmission shaft and clutch shaft, are made of chrome nickel steel. The construction is Cadillac quality throughout. The utmost skill is exercised in cutting and finishing the gears and other parts according to the Cadillac system of limit gauges which insures hair's-breadth accuracy. These parts are then treated by a special process which gives them extreme strength, toughness and wear resisting qualities.

The gear teeth are "backed off" or beveled by machinery especially designed for the purpose. This facilitates the shifting of the gears without the crashing and grinding characteristic of some construction. The main transmission shaft, the jack shaft and the clutch revolve on five annular ball bearings.

Figure 8-1. (Continued)

convinced the banking community to make a critical $15 million loan to General Motors in 1910. Cadillac production for those early years is shown in Table 8-1.

Cadillac's widespread reputation for quality and engineering moved it gradually into the flagship position in the GM product line. The automobile that initially began as a small, $750, one-cylinder car ultimately became the

Table 8-1. Cadillac Production

Year	Units
1902	3
1903	2,497
1904	2,457
1905	3,942
1906	3,559
1907	2,884
1908	2,377
1909	7,868
1910	10,039
1911	10,071
1912	12,708
1913	17,284
1914	7,818
1915	20,404

top-of-the-line make for the largest automobile company in the world. This rise had its foundation in sound manufacturing processes and superb product quality.

Henry Leland exhibited a strong-willed crusader mentality—not only with regard to the virtues of precision but also in both civic affairs and social issues. With others, he became engaged in a long and difficult struggle to clean up the city of Detroit. Leland and his compatriots campaigned for honest elections and even arranged, through their Civic Uplift League, to rate political candidates as "qualified," "preferred," or "recommended." He was active in the Westminster Presbyterian Church and was an active campaigner against alcoholic beverages. He vigorously promoted the establishment of a joint Thanksgiving Day sermon that featured clergy from the Protestant, Catholic, and Jewish faiths. He supported the YMCA activities for Chinese youth as well as Father McCarthy's Chinese Mission Society and was a patriotic American (Leland 1966).

Rigorous, conservative, and uncompromising as he was, Leland was also an early defender of trade unions. Although some authors question his sincerity in this regard (May 1975), the following quotes reflect his public statements on the matter:

> If tonight it was a question if every trade union in Detroit should be abolished, then I would stand with my rifle if necessary and say No! you don't do it. Because that is the only weapon they have against unscrupulous employers. Because there are many employers so unscrupulous that if it were not for the organization they would have been crushed, perhaps just as the agitators picture it. Therefore we must have organized labor, but we must also have organized employers.
> During my years as an employer I have always and constantly striven to increase wages. I have gone through several panics in which I have sweat blood to keep the men employed....I do not believe any man can say that during all the time I have treated my employees with anything but justice and consideration. Some of you know that the most humble employee who has a grievance is welcomed at the president's office. (Leland 1966, 168)

Even in advanced age, Leland remained technically up to date. He was president of the Society of Automotive Engineers from 1909 to 1914. He organized the National Foundry Association and the American Institute of Weights and Measures. He made many trips to Europe to examine the effectiveness of factories in Germany, France, and England. In 1920, Leland was awarded an honorary doctorate of engineering from the University of Michigan (Leland 1966, 169–170).

Although it is somewhat difficult to obtain complete financial information on the early history of Cadillac, we do know that it was quite profitable.

> The Cadillac purchase [by General Motors], in the light of its then current earnings and of its subsequent history, was exceedingly well advised. For the year ended August 31, 1909, the company reported earnings of $1,969,382—the equivalent of a forty-two percent return

on the amount of General Motors' investment; its net worth, after the payment of $675,000 in dividends, was $2,862,709. (Seltzer 1928, 135)

Cadillac continued to contribute heavily to the profits of General Motors for many years. In addition to being a consistent profit contributor, the operation also served as a font of technical expertise, particularly manufacturing expertise at critical points in GM's history.

In 1917, the Lelands left General Motors. Some historians say that it was to manufacture the Liberty aircraft engine, which was a World War I defense project temporarily spurned by Billy Durant. Some suggest that, as with Walter Chrysler and Charles Nash, there was a clash of philosophies between the Lelands and the individuals in charge at GM at the time. In any case, the Lelands left to form a new company to build 6500 Liberty engines in support of the U.S. defense effort in World War I. Later on, when Henry Leland was in his late seventies, the Lelands began production of another premium motor car, the Lincoln, which was later incorporated into Ford.

The Cadillac turnaround was based on production expertise, quality, and product innovation. Cadillac emerged from near-liquidation, prospered, and achieved lasting industrial prominence because it efficiently built better cars. The Cadillac organization became a source of production expertise that favorably influenced the state of the industry and the competitive position of American automobile manufacturers for a very long time. Cadillac's ability to focus on the lucrative high-priced segment of the market was a direct outgrowth of the division's reputation for quality.

Cadillac Survived Because...

- Standards for product quality were among the highest in the world.
- In-process quality was pursued as the key element in end-product quality.
- Products increased in their differentiation, and new markets were penetrated because of high quality standards.
- Operational efficiency was high.
- Ideals were present and were clearly articulated.
- Distinguishing features and benefits proceeded from a technical base.

Case 9

Leaving It Wrong at Hudson

The Hudson Motor Car Company was organized in 1909 by individuals who had been previously associated with several automobile companies, but primarily Oldsmobile. The principal financial backer and namesake for the firm was J. L. Hudson, the founder of the Detroit department store that makes up part of Dayton-Hudson Corporation today. The company established an early reputation for innovation by providing one of the industry's first counterbalanced crankshafts, reasonably priced closed cars, and engines noted for speed and endurance. The Hudson Super Six, an advanced engine for its time, became famous for its smoothness, endurance, and high speed. Hudson advertising featured the engineering orientation of the company and showed individual pictures of "the 48 engineers who designed the Hudson Motor Car." The advertising also described chief engineer Ned Coffin as "the foremost engineer in the industry" — a phrase which drew the objections of the Ford Motor Company.

The early history of Hudson was glamorous. The company lost $17,000 during its first year but then was consistently profitable for the next 22 years. By 1916, the company was producing over 25,000 cars per year and had accumulated revenues of over $20 million. Two years later, in 1918, the company launched a companion lower-priced car, the Essex. The Essex contained some of the advanced engineering features that characterized the early Hudson automobiles. The car was light but strong, was constructed from good materials, and was noted for its easy handling characteristics. The engine was a well-designed F-head four-cylinder of 143 cubic inches. At 50 horsepower, it was 2½ times more powerful than the similarly sized Ford engine. A moderate number of body styles was offered including one of the industry's first moderately priced closed automobiles.

During its early life, the Essex Four established several endurance and cross-country speed records. The combination of speed, durability, a closed configuration, and attractive price resulted in an instant market success. Sales during the first full year of production reached nearly 22,000 — an excellent record for a first-year car. By 1920, the combined Hudson and Essex production had risen to 46,000 cars — more than either Nash or Maxwell. Sales declined during the recession that followed World War I, but Hudson still operated profitably and was able to escape some of the difficulties that plagued both GM and Ford during the same period. By 1925, car production had reached 269,000 cars, and Hudson became the industry's third-largest producer. Owing to sales of 109,000 of the higher-priced Hudson, which the company described as "the largest-selling closed car in the world," profits stood at $21 million on sales of $209 million. Hudson stock was riding high, and it was comfortably one of the country's largest industrial companies.

The year of 1925, however, turned out to be the peak year for Hudson profits during its entire 45-year history. Production actually increased after 1925 to 276,000 in 1927, to 282,000 in 1928, and to 301,000 in 1929, but Hudson products gradually lost market share to various Chrysler models and the newly announced Ford Model A. Hudson's unit market share declined from 8.96 percent in 1927 to 6.28 percent in 1929. Profits for the years 1927, 1928, and 1929 were $14 million, $13 million, and $12 million.

On the surface, Hudson's situation appeared to be favorable. Sales were at record levels. Profits were at near-record levels. Hudson stock increased to $139 per share in 1925, and the principals in Hudson became wealthy. Some chose to travel and became less active in the business. Several became actively involved in the new field of aviation. Hudson CEO Roy D. Chapin was a prominent speaker, a director of several companies, a vice president of the Detroit Symphony, and active in a variety of civic affairs. Chapin had built one of the most lavish mansions in all of Michigan, a home later occupied by Henry Ford II. During Herbert Hoover's term as president, Chapin was appointed secretary of commerce. Beneath the surface, however, Hudson's product differentiation was slipping. As product differentiation slipped and the price premium for Hudson products declined, costs began to increase more rapidly than revenue. The new six-cylinder engine introduced for the Essex in 1925 was not a good one. The new engine was actually smaller than its four-cylinder predecessor, resulting in a small-displacement, high-revolution-per-minute engine in a full-sized car. In order to achieve sufficient power, final drive gear ratios were increased ultimately to 5.4 to 1. With engine revolutions roughly twice the level of those of modern automobiles, the car was very noisy at normal driving speeds and was prone to early wearout and low reliability. The antiquated thermosiphon cooling system and the splash-oil system with babbitted bearings were less sophisticated than the fully pressurized oil systems with precision bearings offered on many other models. With a very long stroke, high revolutions per minute, and only three main bearings, the engine quickly gained a reputation for ongoing trouble.

In 1930, Hudson management felt the need to offer a straight-eight engine to meet competitive pressures in a declining market. Yet, the company spurned the opportunity to design a completely new engine and, instead, used the components of the highly controversial Essex Six to produce a straight-eight engine that was actually smaller and less durable than the highly successful Super Six of the 1920s. The Super Six, holder of many speed and endurance records, displaced 288 cubic inches. At 214 cubic inches, the new Great Eight was 75 percent the size of the Super Six. The engine's durability was further compromised by its splash-oil system and easily worn valve lifters. Ultimately, the Great Eight was enlarged to 252 cubic inches to become the Commodore Eight and remained in production through 1952, but it was never a good engine from the standpoint of either quality or reliability.

Hudson had difficulty achieving low-cost operations as well. Between 1925 and 1929, revenue increased by only $174,000. Costs, however, increased by $9,957,000. On sales of 60 percent fewer automobiles, the Nash Motor Car Company was making 55 percent more profit. Chrysler's 1929 production was only about 25 percent higher than Hudson's, but profits were 108 percent higher. Hudson's gross profit rate in 1929 was meager compared to that of its competitors (Table 8-2).

Hudson entered the Great Depression in a weak strategic position. At a time when the market itself was shrinking, the company was losing market share because of quality and feature shortcomings. Hudson's physical unit market share declined from 9 percent in 1927 to 2.5 percent in 1933. Production

Table 8-2. 1929 Gross Profit Rate by Manufacturer

Packard	28.4%
General Motors	26.7%
Nash	23.0% (est.)
Chrysler	16.7%
Willys	13.9%
Hudson	7.9%

declined from 301,000 units in 1929 to 58,000 units in 1932. Revenue, in this highly competitive market, declined by 87 percent. The price of Hudson stock fell from more than $130 per share in the 1920s to less than $3 in 1932. With the Roosevelt inauguration in 1933, Secretary of Commerce Roy Chapin returned from Washington to again run the company.

Hudson had lost $5.5 million in 1933 and was operating at an 18 percent loss rate when Chapin returned. The company's serious problems were worsened by attrition among key managers. Chief engineer Ned Coffin had retired in 1930, Roscoe Jackson had died in 1929, and other key Hudson managers had left to pursue other interests. Chapin bravely shouldered the revitalizing of the firm that had been the industry's third-largest producer 6 years earlier.

In 1933, a new car, the Terraplane, was developed to replace the Essex — which by this time had achieved negative differentiation. Many components were actually the same as those on the Essex but the car's name and advertising promoted the image of higher speed. With the announcement of the higher-speed Terraplane in 1933, the company's market share began to increase. By 1934 it was back up to nearly 4 percent. By 1935, the company was again producing 100,000 cars, and by 1936, production reached 123,000 — still a far cry from the 301,000 units the firm produced in 1929.

Reflecting the austerity of 1933, the company revived the term *Super Six* and applied it to a somewhat larger Essex engine for placement in Hudson-designated cars. This marked the first time since 1929 that the Hudson marque had fielded a six, but it was not the quality of the older Super Six. Hudson's quality was still suspect. The company improved the Essex engine, but many of its weaknesses remained. In spite of being very expensive to produce, Hudson valve lifters were prone to early wear, which caused noise and loss of engine efficiency. The long-stroke design caused excessive piston travel. In addition, distributors were mounted directly in the path of water splashed by the front wheels, the result being many stranded and exasperated motorists.

In February 1936, Chapin died and was succeeded by Abraham Barit, who had previously been vice president and treasurer. Barit, who had joined Hudson in 1909 as a stenographic clerk, was also unsuccessful in making the company into a low-cost producer of quality products. From 1929 to 1941, the company enjoyed no year when gross profit rates exceeded 15 percent and for 9 of those years, gross profit rates were less than 10 percent. Hudson lost money in all but 3 years from 1931 to 1940. Combined losses for the period exceeded $18 million.

The arrival of World War II provided Hudson with some modest opportunities as a defense contractor. But, lacking the engineering talent of Packard or the production expertise of Ford or GM, the company was awarded only small defense contracts. Yet the firm did emerge after World War II to produce a well-designed modern sedan with a durable engine, superb roadability, and some excellent safety features. Hudson automobiles were consistently winning over half of the stock car races in the early 1950s — a tribute to the durability of Hudson automobiles of that period. The step-down Hudsons of 1948 to 1954 did sell well initially. Production rose to more than 140,000 units per year from 1948 to 1950. Hudson profits rose to more than $10 million for each of these years. Again, gross profits were low — usually around 13 percent. The company was still not a low-cost producer, and its product differentiation was not appreciated by all market segments. After 1950, Hudson began to experience increasing competition from models with more modern styling, more advanced engine design, and a wider choice of body styles. Chrysler, DeSoto, Oldsmobile, and Cadillac all had overhead-valve V8 engines, and virtually all the major competitors had them by 1955. Hudson's L-head six was a durable engine as well as a relatively new engine (1948 was its first year), but it was not as efficient as the engines that employed more modern engineering concepts. Hudson's management made only a few incremental improvements and no major replacements for the 1948 to 1954 models. Hudson's step-down sedans were good cars that were showing their age.

Under Barit's leadership the company neglected the incremental improvement of products in its main niche and squandered its few remaining reserves on developing a compact car (the Hudson Jet) to compete directly with other, more efficient suppliers in an unfamiliar market. The styling of the compact car was too high and unattractive. The technology of the newly designed Jet engine was traceable to the Hudson engines of the 1930s, and only 35,000 were ever produced.

Hudson was not efficient enough to persevere by offering products in the low-price class, nor was quality sufficient to attract more customers. The opportunity costs of the ill-fated Jet were damaging. The company failed to develop a modern fuel-efficient V8 engine, which was fully necessary for cars in Hudson's main market at the time. The company offered no station wagon. The belt line of the car was too high for that period (the car had been fashioned after the 1942 Buick), and visibility was restricted. Some individual features such as door latches and the antiquated L-head straight-eight engine fell far short of what the competition offered. Many of these problems could have been corrected with fewer resources than were consumed by the Jet.

By 1953, Hudson was again losing a substantial amount of money and merged with Nash to form American Motors Corporation. It was a merger in name only. The more efficient Nash-Kelvinator Corporation was clearly the acquiring parent. Within a matter of months, the less efficient Hudson plants were closed and the diminishing production of Hudson automobiles was shifted to the Nash plant at Kenosha. Three years later, in 1957, the Hudson name was laid to rest after a final production run of under 6000 units, one-fiftieth of the marque's all-time high.

In its prime, Hudson was one of the world's largest auto producers, with a domestic market share of over 9 percent. For short periods, it was the third-largest firm in terms of production volume and was clearly a major player. Company officers and owners became wealthy as the company prospered during its early years. Total employment reached 17,000 people. An additional 2200 businesses were involved in selling and servicing Hudson cars. At its zenith, Hudson was probably involved in nearly one-half of 1 percent of the gross national product of the United States. Now the company is gone. But, we can learn from the experience. Hudson's decline began in 1925, a full 29 years before operations ceased. While management became involved in other projects and other activities, the company failed to keep its quality high, its products differentiated, and its production efficient (Figure 8-2).

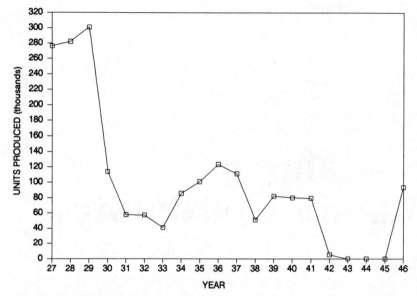

Figure 8-2. Hudson Motor Car Company—units produced. Hudson had been the third-largest producer of U.S. automobiles during the 1920s, but the firm's lack of attention to quality and operational issues caused its market share to drop markedly during the 1930s. During the first decade of Hudson's attempted turnaround, the firm lost money in all but 3 years.

Hudson Failed Because...

- Product differentiation was not based on quality and did not extend to meaningful technical features.

- Top management spent too much time on interests unrelated to the welfare of the firm.

- Known quality problems and product shortcomings remained in the product for years after they were discovered.

- Development and operational decisions were direct from levels which were too high in the company.

- Manufacturability was insufficiently considered.

- Efficiency seriously lagged that of competitors.

9
Sustaining Market Continuity

Most companies in trouble are short of customers. With this situation, it is not a bad idea to seek new customers, but it is a bad idea if old customers are lost in the process. Market continuity, the maintenance of continuity with historical markets, is a pragmatic necessity for companies in trouble. It could be briefly described as the propensity to focus on providing products for one very familiar market segment before expanding into any new markets or other new activities.

The development of markets is long and arduous, requiring the extra efforts of competent marketing personnel working with product development, manufacturing, and customer support. Once a market has been penetrated, it must not be neglected. Market share is never a static condition but instead requires constant attention to customers and the timely development of new products to suit their needs. Successful firms gracefully accept the idea that retaining markets is hard work, and they react with responsiveness and vigor to serve the present customer base. Even when new markets are cultivated, they are not cultivated at the expense of historical markets. Historical markets are nurtured and preserved as if they were the firm's only market even if new programs are contemplated, for the troubled firm can rarely afford a decline in its customary business as it pursues any new strategy.

Avoiding Strategic Drift

For reasons that are difficult to fathom, unsuccessful firms frequently exhibit a bizarre tendency to enter unfamiliar markets while neglecting familiar ones. The strategy of shifting distribution channels, selling systems, or markets is both complicated and inherently risky. Few firms can accomplish strategic shifts in the market served, especially during troubled times when cash from old markets is needed and the resources to develop new markets are limited. Beyond the resource considerations, there is the timing issue. It takes a long time to change markets, and few companies in trouble can afford the time it takes to thoroughly develop new markets and still work historical markets to their full potential.

A major insurance company provides a good example of market discontinuity. Fraught with cyclical economic problems in its home geography, the firm elected to move into new, faster-growing suburbs where the insured were more prosperous and actuarial factors were more favorable. The firm was so confident of the sound basis of its new strategy that it began to terminate some of its established agents with the thought of shifting the resources to the new market. Unfortunately, what the firm did not realize was that other, higher-caliber competitors also appreciated the advantages of serving this suburban market and that these able competitive firms had provided decades of reliable service. Understandably, the new entrant suffered major losses in both the new market and the old, which had sustained the company for more than 70 years. The planning logic employed in this tragic episode would be tantamount to the Detroit Lions transferring to the NFC Western Division because the San Francisco Forty-Niners do well there.

Instead of concentrating on gradual, incremental improvements, unsuccessful companies often make significant and abrupt changes in market position. They frequently jump from one market segment to another without fully understanding the requirements of either. In five of seven unsuccessful cases, management elected to bring out a low-priced car in the hopes of stimulating sales. Studebaker produced the Scotsman and then the Lark. Kaiser produced the Henry J. economy car. Hudson produced the Terraplane and then the Jet. Willys-Overland produced the Whippet. AMC/Renault produced the Alliance and the Encore. Often, these products were abridged versions of other company products that were not sufficiently differentiated for their own markets. The image that resulted was usually one of a "cheap" small car. Meanwhile, the new market initiatives consumed huge resources and impoverished programs directed toward familiar markets. The resulting losses in historical markets brought swift closure to firms that had previously been among the largest in their industries (Table 9-1).

During the time when Kaiser and Studebaker were actively seeking new markets, American Motors was concentrating its marketing efforts instead of diffusing them. AMC's target market was the same one that

Table 9-1. Important Strategic Shifts of Turnaround Candidates

Case	Historical market	New target market	Pace of change	Key strategy	Successful or unsuccessful
Cadillac	Low-priced, one-cylinder car	Low-priced one-cylinder car	Gradual	High-quality features and benefits	Yes
Buick	Medium-priced cars	Medium-priced higher-quality cars	Gradual	Fewer models in same market	Yes
Packard	High-priced cars	Upper-medium higher-quality cars	Medium	High quality and efficiency	Yes
American Motors	Conservative market and mid-range	Conservative market only	Medium	High quality, practical features	Yes
Kaiser-Frazer	Upper-medium price bracket	Low-priced economy car	Abrupt	Low quality, few features	No
Hudson	Upper-medium price bracket	Low-priced economy car	Abrupt	High quality, outdated features	No
Willys-Overland	Medium price bracket	Low-priced economy car	Medium	Heavy sales promotion	No
AMC/Renault	Conservative market	Low-priced economy car	Medium	Lower quality, ordinary features	No
Allis-Chalmers	Industrial and farm equipment	Filters and other products	Slow	Investment changes	No

its predecessor, Nash Motors, had served for years – the conservative market, the practical market, the functional market. This was a market the major firms in the industry had neglected. With their huge V8 engines, bulky exteriors, heavy bumpers, and gaudy embellishments, the traditional Fords, Chevrolets, and Plymouths had become much larger and less economical in response to perceived changes in the market. What American Motors understood, however, was that a significant fraction of the market had not changed and that a large pent-up demand existed because of neglect by the major producers. American Motors did not shift markets during the 1950s. With the arrival of the Rambler, the people at American Motors simply did what they always did, and they accentuated it with effective advertising that emphasized the firm's consistent practicality in contrast to the wasteful excesses of competitors.

American Motors managers also understood the emotional biases present among potential buyers and then nurtured those biases by supplying products that not only provided good service but also were advertised in a way that bestowed dignity upon the clear-thinking, patriotic American Motors customer. Foreign producers were beginning to penetrate the American market with products that delivered superior economy and, in the case of the Volkswagen, delivered quality and reliability as well. Yet, less than 15 years had passed since the end of World War II, and American Motors management correctly discerned that some Americans did not want to buy German or Japanese cars. Neither French nor English cars were very good, and the major American producers had leapfrogged this market segment to produce what George Romney described as the "dinosaur in the driveway." So, in an effort to strengthen its market continuity, American Motors announced a new model of an older car with a spirited new name, the Rambler American. It was a brilliant strategy directly targeted to the rational buyer who wanted to be practical but who did not want to buy a foreign car. The strategy was highly successful, and more than 90,000 Rambler Americans were sold during the model's second year in 1959.

The original Rambler American was not a new car. In reality, it was a car that had been in production from 1952 through 1955, when it was superseded by what became the Rambler Classic. George Romney's logic was straightforward. It was still a good car, and the company should build it again in 1958. So, the company pulled the old dies out of storage and produced, as a new model, a car they had taken out of production 3 years earlier. The strategy of the Rambler American not only minimized new tooling expense, but also cemented AMC's continuity with its historical market.

Unfortunately, 20 years later AMC's managers forgot these lessons. After 1970, the firm became increasingly inconsistent in dealing with its traditional market. Under the management of members of the family who at one time managed Hudson, the Rambler American and the Rambler Classic were dropped in favor of a new marque called the *Hornet*. The Hornet was named after an earlier higher-priced Hudson model unfamiliar in the traditional Rambler marketplace. The new Hornet had attractive styling, but it was less roomy than its predecessors and was particularly limited in its headroom. The station wagon model was far less utilitarian, and there was no convertible, long an American Motors strong point and the model that originated the Rambler. The colors were gaudy, and the models themselves looked cheap. To partly compensate for the Hornet's lagging sales, the firm announced the Rebel, which it later renamed the Matador, which then grew in length and bulk with no change in interior dimensions. The basic Matador was then supplemented with the Matador Coupe, which had entirely different tooling and looked altogether different from other members of the Matador family. It sold poorly, and the entire Matador line was dropped in 1977.

Meanwhile, AMC had developed a new marque with the name Pacer, a term borrowed from the defunct Edsel. The Pacer had some interesting design features, but the car came in 500 lb overweight, which reduced its value as an economy car during the oil crisis. The model departed from AMC traditions in other ways—by having limited and awkward seating, very heavy doors, and a tendency to rust. After sales declined to 10,000 units in 1979, AMC discontinued production the following year.

From 1968 to 1987, AMC developed very few new products and none that excelled. The Matador Coupe was a flop. The Pacer was an improperly managed project. In 1979, the company renamed its 9-year-old Hornet the *Concord,* the name of an unsuccessful Plymouth model produced in the early 1950s. Then, when the company did manage to locate the resources sufficient for a major new product program, continuity with the firm's traditional market was again destroyed by naming the car *Renault* in deference to its foreign partner. All this occurred as the American consumer, prodded by exceedingly high oil prices, was redeveloping an interest in the product philosophies that American Motors so successfully exploited during the 1950s.

Servicing the Declining Market

Historical markets must be treated with the utmost care and attention even if they are declining markets, because declining markets often provide robust opportunities as less conscientious firms neglect them. Crown Cork serves as an excellent example of a conscientious firm achieving success in a declining market. As Continental Can pursued other ventures and American Can became a brokerage house, Crown Cork was able to gain ground on less-interested competitors in the can market, which the competitors saw as pedestrian and unattractive. With fervent attention to product quality and customer service, Snap-on Tools continued to post record sales and profits in a market others saw as fiercely competitive and dominated by low-cost offshore suppliers. While Control Data diversified into new and uncharted waters, chief competitor Cray Research concentrated on providing state-of-the-art products to the market Control Data had historically served for many years. Cray stockholders prospered while Control Data stock declined to under $10 per share, down from $130 in 1968 and $78 in 1973.

One of the best examples of successful activity in a declining market is

Deere's performance during the early 1980s. Deere also experienced problems resulting from the devastated farm economy of that period. Deere did poorly, but everyone else did worse. When the smoke cleared, weaker and less focused producers such as Allis-Chalmers, White, and International Harvester had exited the business while Deere emerged with a 60 percent market share in what developed into a healthier industry later on.

In 1982, Hambrick, MacMillan, and Day published a useful analysis of industrial product businesses that provided interesting insights into the value of offering a dedicated service to declining markets. Using PIMS (Profit Impact of Market Strategy) data, the authors divided 1028 business units into the four boxes of the Boston Consulting Group (BCG) matrix and then examined the operational performance within each group: star (strong position in growth market), cash cow (strong position in mature or declining market), wildcat (weak position in growth market), and dog (weak position in mature or declining market). Some interesting conclusions were reached:

> The results do not support BCG's advice that Dogs should be promptly harvested or liquidated. This should come as a relief to many managers, because more and more of their industries are maturing and because all but the market leaders qualify as Dogs. What is needed is creative positive research and thinking about how Dogs can be managed for maximum long-term performance. (Hambrick et al. 1982, 528)

One of the more interesting aspects of their study was on the frequency distribution of the business units studied. It seems sobering that 71.3 percent of American industries would be reduced to the categories of *cash cows* and *dogs*. Using the BCG criteria, only 11.1 percent were stars. Whether we believe in the BCG analytical approach is not the central question here. The question is, do the theories of management that we have in place adequately address the needs of those companies striving to dramatically upgrade their performance in static or declining markets? We must address what can be done for the dogs, the cash cows, and even the wildcats to enable them to compete effectively against world-class competition, because they make up 89 percent of our companies.

Unquestionably, some businesses do not provide necessary services to the modern economy. However, as we review the list of companies having problems, many of them do provide necessary services—particularly by offering useful products and services to large, gradually declining markets. In many cases, these markets are declining not because we cannot compete in these worldwide markets but because we have neglected them. As Hambrick, MacMillan, and Day point out, many troubled companies have significant potential, and creative thinking is needed to discover how these troubled companies can be managed for maximum long-term performance. The mistake would be to assume that these important companies are not worth managing correctly.

The successful firms studied here survived in part because they displayed a less confusing and more consistent image to their current and potential customers. The unsuccessful firms often made changes that many people did not understand. Even in something as basic as what the products were called, the successful and unsuccessful companies displayed different approaches. The successful firms made a total of four major product-name changes while unsuccessful companies made 22 basic name changes. Successful turnaround agents, such as Iacocca, resisted the temptation to tamper with names even when image problems existed. Five of the eight successful firms made no name changes at all. When changes were made, they were made for nearly unavoidable reasons such as when the Henry Ford Company changed its name to Cadillac because Henry Ford was starting another company.

Unsuccessful firms often jumped from one market niche to another or into altogether new markets. Unsuccessful firms displayed a greater tendency to stray from familiar markets to acquisitions, divestitures, or other markets. The outcomes of these differing approaches provide evidence that active performance in familiar markets is a necessary condition for turnaround success.

The unsuccessful companies were not very good students of their own history. In fact, during his unfortunate reign at Studebaker-Packard, CEO James Nance had the corporate archives removed from the premises, an unfortunate cleavage with Packard's glorious past and Studebaker's lineage as the nation's oldest automobile manufacturer. Unsuccessful turnaround agents exhibited little appreciation for the many good things that were done to build some of the largest firms in the United States.

Unsuccessful turnaround agents also lacked an appreciation for the small consistencies that fostered consumer familiarity with historical markets. As International Harvester tractors moved from being red to gray and red, as Minneapolis-Moline moved from yellow to gray, and as Allis Chalmers from orange to white, Deere tractors remained green. Buick engines have sported overhead valves since 1902. The Packard name was one of the most revered in the industry, but within 5 years of the marque's demise, new models were called Clippers. These symbolic changes, though small, altered public perceptions of the products and confused customers. Successful companies knew more about their own history. When Japanese business manager Akiro Sueno returned to his bombed-out family business following World War II, his first act was to compose a company history. Knowledge of the company's history provides a meaningful anchor for sustaining continuity with key markets, particularly for companies short of customers.

Practical Lessons on Market Continuity

- Successful companies nurture, protect, and develop products for historical markets before moving into new markets. Unsuccessful companies often leave historical markets unprotected.

- Successful companies actively preserve product identifiers, such as names, product colors, advertising, or product attributes, that retain continuity with historical markets. Unsuccessful companies frequently change product identifiers.

- Successful companies assume that markets are captured on the basis of merit arising from better products and service. Unsuccessful companies overestimate the importance of the strategic selection of markets.

- Successful companies are able to more accurately gauge the rate of change in markets and provide products that are in phase with changes. Unsuccessful companies are frequently out of phase.

- In order to preserve investment and field a wide variety of products to cover different circumstances, successful companies are less inclined to totally discard products. Instead, they adroitly stash products and features that they believe will be useful at other times or extend product lines in other ways. Unsuccessful companies time product announcements poorly.

Case Histories

The severe recession of the early 1980s dealt harshly with both Chrysler and AMC/Renault. Both suffered harsh declines in unit sales and both lost money. AMC/Renault should have been better off because the combination of recession and higher oil prices was moving at least some buyers closer to the firm's historical market. As the customers approached, AMC/Renault began to shift position and outmaneuver the approaching customers by confusing them with new names, new styles, and unfamiliar products. Chrysler Corporation's situation was much more serious and more needed to be changed. Yet, Chrysler management doggedly clung to the protection of historical markets.

Case 10

Saving the Best of Chrysler Corporation

The revival of Chrysler Corporation in the 1980s is a story of triumph and tragedy. It was indeed a grand triumph for the firm to regain the profitability and prominence it had experienced at an earlier time in its history. It was tragic to see the economic difficulties of the early 1990s send the company into a new crisis.

Mistakes were made during the Chrysler turnaround, but most of them were made after 1986. During the earlier period of recovery, what was accomplished was remarkable. Several other authors (e.g., Abodaher 1985; Reich and Donahue 1985) have covered the Chrysler Corporation in great detail, so the full story will not be recounted here. But some interesting aspects of the Chrysler turnaround of the 1980s should be underscored so that it might be compared with other cases. In some important respects, the main themes were similar—efficiency, quality, innovation, leadership. But it was one of the most complicated and ambitious turnarounds in history. Chrysler Corporation had to greatly improve product quality, develop and bring to market entirely new models of cars, achieve more efficient production, nurture the loyalty of key vendors, mend fences with its anxious and depleted work force, and restore the confidence of its dealer network, all at lower cost.

The company's financial situation before the late 1970s was extremely severe and required dramatic steps in financial restructuring, which tended to dominate the news. However, the publicity surrounding the financial restructuring partly obscured the operational and cultural steps that were taken in order for the firm to survive. Certainly the loan guarantees and the financial restructurings were of some help in the revival of Chrysler Corporation. But Chrysler needed to restore the effectiveness of its dealer network, dramatically reduce overhead costs, trim losing operations, make investments to raise cash, and design cars that would sell before it could effect a full operational turnaround. In addition, Chrysler plants had to attain new levels of productivity and efficiency, all while workers and managers labored with reduced compensation.

The ability of Chrysler's leaders to establish credibility was key in implementing these crucial operational steps. Chrysler managers had to demonstrate their commitment to the principle of fairness. When overhead was trimmed substantially and executive pay was reduced, a workable arrangement with the union became possible—as did a deal with the banks and the government. However, as a part of these agreements, Chrysler had to establish that it could deliver completed designs of salable automobiles on time and in the face of massive personnel cuts. Ultimately, the success of the turnaround rested on a high degree of cooperation with organized labor and Chrysler's development of a whole new line of differentiated products, which were adroitly marketed to Chrysler's historical markets.

An extremely important element of the Chrysler turnaround strategy was the substantial reduction of cost. During the turnaround, Chrysler reduced costs from more than $16 billion to less than $10 billion. Adjusted for inflation, this represented a reduction of nearly 60 percent. Salaried and production staff were reduced in approximately the same proportion—each by about 50 percent. Worldwide, Chrysler employed more than 250,000 people in 1977 (Moody's 1984). By 1983, Chrysler's employment was down to 97,000. The Chrysler breakeven point was cut from 2.5 million cars to 1.2 million cars.

To achieve this increase in productivity along with a simultaneous reduction in cost, Iacocca sought and received the cooperation of the United Auto Workers, then headed by Douglas Fraser. Fraser helped immeasurably in working out delicate arrangements with the union membership, in exerting political pressure to obtain approval of the bank guarantees, and in serving as a highly competent, savvy, and experienced company director. In 1985, Douglas Fraser was awarded an honorary doctorate of laws by the University of Notre Dame for his many accomplishments including his role in the Chrysler turnaround. Lee Iacocca gives similar credit to Fraser and goes on to emphasize the need for government, management, and labor to work together in the revitalization of our basic industries (Iacocca 1984).

Few people recognize the sacrifices made by the Chrysler workers during the turnaround of 1979 to 1982. Not only had employment been decimated by the layoffs instituted under Ricardo and Iacocca, but wage concessions amounting to hundreds of millions of dollars were agreed upon on two occasions and in some cases required as covenants to the loan guarantees. In 1982, the average hourly wage for Chrysler workers was approximately 80 percent of what it was for Ford and GM counterparts.

Yet, even against considerable odds, and with a substantially reduced staff, the *new* Chrysler Corporation achieved its goals: revitalizing its dealer network and bringing out a new family of cars on time. Chrysler's decision to concentrate production on one basic platform, thereby reducing the number of parts needed to produce a variety of automobiles, was key to achieving these goals (see Table 9-2).

The character of Chrysler's leaders clearly played a role in the second Chrysler turnaround. Lee Iacocca's willingness to work for less pay, his ability to clearly articulate ideas, his willingness to accept the historical expertise of Chrysler Corporation as a building block for the infusion of new values, and his general love for the automobile all helped him enlist employees, dealers, creditors, and customers as partners in the turnaround process.

Table 9-2. Chrysler Manufacturing Statistics, 1980 and 1986

	1980	1986
Daily vehicle production (units per day)	4000/day	8000/day
Steel inventories at stamping plants (no. of days' supply)	32.6 days	6.0 days
Assembly plant inventory turn ratio (sales to inventory)	16.8	47.5
Total inventory turn ratio (sale to inventory)	6.6	8.0
Number of faults/front-drive vehicle		down 42%
Warranty work		down 25%

SOURCE: *Mechanical Engineering*, pp. 55–59, July 1987.

Both revenue and profits returned, and the company learned to make a profit on a much lower level of production. In 1978, Chrysler Corporation produced more than 1.1 million cars and lost $205 million. In 1984, the company produced more than 1.1 million cars and made a profit of $2.3 billion. Market share increased in 1984 and again in 1985. As can be seen from Table 9-3, there has been distinct improvement. This improvement was preceded by some financial restructuring, but the true strength of the turnaround lay in sound practices of manufacturing engineering, timely product development, wholesome working relationships with employees and vendors, and attention to the business the company was in at the time.

Unfortunately, as Iacocca himself has admitted, mistakes were made and his personal reputation for vigor and resourcefulness began to recede in the late 1980s. Preoccupation with other ventures, the Statue of Liberty, two books, and other personal involvements took some time away from Chrysler Corporation. Misguided strategic moves, including an expensive foray into the defense business, an aborted joint venture with Maserati, and the costly movement of Omni and Horizon production to an AMC plant on the verge of closure, siphoned resources away from the pressing problem of revitalizing Chrysler's mainstay products. The AMC acquisition worked out well regarding the Jeep but not well at all regarding the Renault-sponsored vehicles. The creation of an overlapping holding company confused channels and increased cost. Chrysler's breakeven point, which had declined to 1.1 million vehicles in 1985, had risen to 1.9 million vehicles by 1989.

The turnaround of Chrysler Corporation is still in process, and more time must pass before we can say that it was fully successful over the long term. However, substantial progress was made from 1980 to 1987. The Chrysler turnaround of the 1980s must, however, rank as one of the most ambitious in the history of the country. It had things in common with the

Table 9-3. Chrysler Corporation Unit Sales, Revenues, and Profits

Year	Domestic units	Total sales ($000)	Domestic prof-its ($000)	Unit market share, %*
1976	1,333,401	15,537,800	422,600	13.34
1977	1,236,359	16,708,300	163,200	11.19
1978	1,126,164	13,618,300	(204,600)	10.09
1979	928,618	12,001,900	(1,097,300)	8.79
1980	638,974	9,225,300	(1,709,700)	7.12
1981	749,648	9,971,000	(475,600)	8.78
1982	600,502	10,040,000	170,000	7.53
1983	903,533	13,240,400	700,900	9.84
1984	1,163,221	19,573,000	2,380,000	11.19
1985	1,219,931	21,255,400	1,635,000	11.05
1986	1,308,991	22,886,300	1,403,600	11.43
1987	1,091,904	26,279,100	1,289,700	10.62
1988	1,000,000	31,884,200	1,050,200	10.92

*Automobiles only, not minivans and light trucks.

Cadillac, Nash, Deere, and American Motors turnarounds in that a key element of the strategy was to develop a wide variety of products from the same set of common parts, while emphasizing product quality. And, as we have seen in other cases, fair play toward employees, creditors, suppliers, and customers was a central element in the progress made. But, in particular, the Chrysler turnaround avoided one mistake that is commonly made — the desertion of historical markets as new markets are cultivated. The capitalization on the already established Omni and Horizon, the nurturing and improvement of the K Car, the strengthening of relations with existing dealers, the retention of familiar Chrysler names such as New Yorker, Imperial, and Town and Country all helped to retain continuity with customers. In the specific sense of market continuity, the Chrysler turnaround of the early 1980s was laced with wisdom. It is to be hoped that the Chrysler Corporation will continue in the spirit of innovation and cooperation that made progress possible (Figure 9-1).

Turnarounds are never permanent. The tough economic times of the 1990s should not obscure the fact that the Chrysler turnaround of 10 years earlier was one of the most accomplished in the history of the industry.

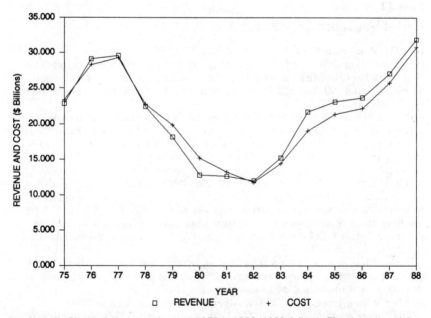

Figure 9-1. Chrysler revenue and costs—1975 to 1988 (1988 dollars). Chrysler survived the recession of the early 1980s because the company sustained continuity with its historical markets and then learned to produce quality products for these markets at reasonable cost. With massive sacrifices on the part of Chrysler professionals and workers, the company ascended from disaster to become a healthy contributor to American industry, until diversification programs and the weaker economy of the late 1980s affected the firm's core business.

Chrysler Survived Because...

- Labor and management worked cooperatively to restore the health of the company.

- Both labor and management played exemplary roles.

- Continuity was maintained with major historical markets.

- Costs were reduced to current levels of revenue. Revenue was not expanded to cover costs.

- A wide variety of products was produced from the same components parts.

- Operational efficiency dramatically improved.

- Inventory efficiency dramatically improved.

Case 11

Market Vacillation at AMC/Renault

In 1973, American Motors sold more than 500,000 vehicles, had roughly a 5 percent market share, and operated at a nearly 5 percent after-tax margin. Ten years later, the firm produced 383,000 vehicles and lost $146 million dollars. From 1980 through 1986, the firm lost $794 million; it was acquired by Chrysler in 1987.

It seems ironic that such hard times would fall on American Motors because, for much of the twentieth century, AMC and its predecessor, Nash Motors, enjoyed one of the strongest records of consistent profitability. From 1916 to 1931, Nash profit rates were among the best in the industry. During the depression, the firm conserved cash and emerged from World War II in excellent financial shape and again with excellent profits. The GM and Ford sales war of the 1950s put pressure on the independent producers. The merger with Hudson was in part a response to this pressure. The problems resulting from this competitive pressure were adroitly handled by George Romney, AMC's CEO from 1955 to 1963. The firm once again became both healthy and prominent.

Romney left American Motors in 1963 to become governor of Michigan. His successor was the company's sales manager, Roy Abernathy. Abernathy was in turn succeeded by the son of a founder of the Hudson Motor Car Company. Roy D. Chapin, Jr. became CEO of American Motors in the late 1960s.

The future looked bright for AMC during the early 1970s. The oil crisis was pushing buyers into AMC's traditional marketplace. The company sold a respected line of intermediate cars including a well-received economical but nearly full-size station wagon. There was some confusion in the marketplace because the highly successful Rambler had been replaced by a new car called the *Hornet* (the name of Hudson's leading model during the early 1950s). The rear of the Hornet was then truncated to produce the Gremlin subcompact, which shared most of its components with the Hornet. Even the AMC muscle cars, the Javelin and the AMX, were popular in the marketplace. The long-established AMC six-cylinder engines were well constructed, with seven main bearings and strong components, and were considered to be among the industry's most durable sixes. The company's V8s, which shared many components with the sixes, also performed well. Sales of the AMC models were robust, and the newly acquired Jeep operations broadened the company's product line even further.

In 1975, the firm announced an innovative new car called the *Pacer*. The Pacer was billed as the industry's first wide small car. The handling of the car was superb because of the wide tracking, rack and pinion steering, and disk brakes. An innovative electric overdrive gave the car very good performance and good economy. Visibility was excellent. The front seats were very comfortable, and the rear seats were on a par with today's models. To ease passenger entry to the rear, AMC engineers creatively made the right door 4 inches wider than the left door.

The Pacer was an initial sales success. About 150,000 were shipped during the first year of production, which was an impressive figure for an independent. Though industry sales declined, AMC's physical unit market share remained at 7.4 percent. But, the firm had difficulty producing the Pacer, and the positioning of the car in the marketplace was suboptimal. Though the Pacer shared many mechanical components with other AMC cars, it also had many differences. The engines and automatic transmissions were the same, but the front end, steering, suspension, and many body-hardware mechanisms were all different. When the early sales of the Pacer outstripped production, AMC was forced to make some awkward and time-consuming production changes.

Pacer's final design did not meet specifications; it came in almost 500 lb above the targeted weight. Manufacturing costs rose, and AMC's gross profit rate declined from 15.16 percent in 1973 to 8.7 percent in 1975. AMC lost $35 million in 1975 and $34 million in 1976, the peak sales year for the Pacer.

In addition to production problems with the Pacer, the car was probably not positioned properly in the marketplace. The original Pacer had weight, gearing, and performance characteristics similar to those of some popular models of sport sedans. It was a very good road car. But, the initial Pacers were marketed as a low-priced *small car*, and that is the image that took hold. These first cars had spartan interiors encased in inexpensive-looking plastic. The rear windows did not open, thus limiting ventilation, and the bottom one-third of the body, with its pronounced inward curvature, tended to rust.

AMC did offer some options that corrected many of these deficiencies, such as vent windows front and rear, attractive fender flaps, and, later on, an up-scale "Limited" edition with extra sound deadening, many convenience features, and all-leather premium upholstery. But, before these later programs took hold, the Pacer had been promoted as a cheap car. This problem was compounded by the fact that workmanship on some of these cars had declined to levels lower than usual for AMC products. The Pacer could have emerged as a well-designed lower- to medium-priced high-quality innovation car. What actually emerged was a cheap car of unusual design and poor construction which was manufactured at high cost and lacked the convenience features of traditional AMC products.

American Motors' management went through many transitions during the 20 years that followed Romney's departure. Roy Abernathy followed Romney as CEO. Under Abernathy, the Rambler's size increased while its quality decreased. Roy D. Chapin, Jr., the son of the former Hudson chief executive and AMC's first treasurer, was the next chairman. Chapin pushed new cars and new, unfamiliar names but at the expense of continuity in the marketplace. Following Chapin was Gerald Meyers, the former executive vice president and Roy Chapin's son-in-law. Meyers was the executive most closely associated with the Pacer's development and production. As American Motors became pressed for cash because of declining production efficiency and subdued product innovation, AMC sought a financial and technical partner. In 1979, AMC made an arrangement with Regie Nationale des Usines Renault for financing, joint marketing, and the joint development of a new car. The arrangement with Renault brought in another company leader, Jose. J. Dedeurwaerder, who represented the Renault interests. AMC cars became more like their European cousins. Joseph E. Cappy, formerly of Ford, served as AMC's chief executive officer in the mid-1980s. Many other officers changed as well. Along with these managerial changes came many changes in AMC's relationship to the marketplace.

For reasons that are difficult to understand, AMC seems to have had great difficulty offering a consistent set of products, names, and images to its marketplace. For more than 20 years, AMC did not have a consistent name for its make of automobiles. Under Romney, the focus was clear—the company made Ramblers. Ramblers sold well and gained a well-recognized identity. But under Chapin, a Hudson man, Rambler was replaced by the Hornet (a heavier Hudson model produced in the early 1950s). The Hornet was replaced by the Concord, which in turn was replaced by the Renault Alliance and the Renault Encore. The names of its intermediate-sized cars also created confusion. First, the make of the car was the Rambler and the model was the Ambassador. Then the make was called the Rebel and then the Matador, and then production was cut. During this same time, the competition was presenting a more consistent image of its products.

American Motors management under Romney in the 1950s and early 1960s displayed a far more cultivated feel for the marketplace being served. These people realized that a considerable number of American consumers liked the attributes of a compact economy car, but they did not want to buy a foreign car. The Rambler American was designed for this audience. When AMC dropped the Concord and renamed its successor the Renault Alliance, many AMC loyalists were alienated.

In addition to the problem of names, the firm over time withdrew some of its most successful models from the marketplace without offering successor models. The well-designed intermediate station wagons of the late 1960s grew longer during the 1970s and then were dropped in the late 1970s. Suddenly, a company whose models sold well to the station wagon marketplace had no real station wagon (on a car chassis) except the very small and not very utilitarian Hornet wagon—which was more like a less practical hatchback. The Javelin and AMX sports cars were curtailed without replacement. The whole intermediate series was canceled. Finally, the rather popular Concord series was dropped at about the same time that Ford introduced two new models that were nearly identical in appearance and dimensions—the Ford Tempo and the Mercury Topaz.

During the past few years, AMC did build some cars that had the potential for differentiation. But, the confusing and inconsistent manner in which they approached the marketplace made it difficult to develop continuity with potential buyers. In addition, the firm's historical emphasis on quality and value declined.

While these actions were unfolding, AMC's market share shrank substantially. The sale of conventional automobiles (not Jeeps) declined from 485,000 in 1970 to 150,000 in 1985. Market share had gone from over 7 percent without Jeep to 4 percent with Jeep. From 1974 to 1985, total unit sales had declined from 545,000 to 392,000, and market share had slipped from 7.5 percent to 4.6 percent. The worst was yet to come.

Sales drifted still lower in 1986 and 1987 and in early 1987, AMC's passenger cars fell to under 1 percent of total industry sales. In 1987, what was left of what at one time had been one of the most profitable and successful firms in the industry was absorbed by Chrysler Corporation.

What happened, of course, is along the way American Motors lost its historical legacy of internal efficiency. Gross profit rates were well above 20 percent for much of Nash-AMC history. By the early 1980s, gross profit rates had declined to 7.6 percent. Inventory turns per year, once a hallmark of Nash production expertise that often approached 20 to 1, declined to 5 to 1 in the early eighties. The central theme of earlier Nash strategy had been to operate efficiently and then use some of the savings to improve product quality and differentiation. This successful strategy was lost during the 1970s and 1980s, when the firm became a high-cost producer of insufficiently differentiated products which were offered without regard to market continuity.

AMC/Renault management became involved in many issues unrelated to the initial core business of producing high-quality reasonably priced fuel-efficient automobiles. The company acquired Jeep, AM General, Wheel Horse Products (garden tractors), and other companies. The company sold Kelvinator and, later on, AM General. It formed a long-term joint venture with Renault and with the People's Republic of China. But it couldn't generate enough internal cash to develop a smaller-displacement fuel-efficient engine, an essential requirement to the markets being served. By the early 1980s, AMC six-cylinder Renault engines had approximately twice the displacement of those of other manufacturers in their price class. The penalty paid in fuel consumption eroded a long-standing AMC competitive edge. Though durable, the engine's basic design was over 50 years old.

As with many other unsuccessful turnaround cases, the AMC/Renault case is a sad one. AMC began the 1960s with a clearly articulated mission which was being executed in an efficient manner by creditable managers with extensive industrial experience in the markets being served. What transpired over time was a lack of attention to detail, a dearth of incremental improvements, and vacillation as to how to address the markets being served. By the mid-1980s, AMC/Renault employment had declined to less than two-thirds of its peak employment of 33,000 and was still dropping. Sales of passenger cars in early 1987 fell to less than 1 percent of the market. The company could have done much better (Figure 9-2).

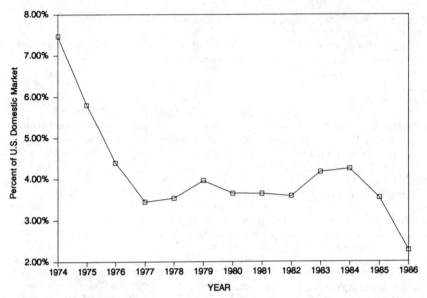

Figure 9-2. AMC/Renault market share—1974 to 1986. In 1974, AMC/Renault produced 1 of every 13 U.S. cars. After an almost systematic neglect of historical markets, AMC/Renault's market share dropped to under 2 percent by 1987, when the firm that had been, at one time, one of the most efficient producers in the industry ceased operations as a separate company.

AMC/Renault Failed Because...

- Continuity with major historical markets was not preserved.

- Operational efficiency declined.

- Manufacturability was lacking in key high-volume products.

- Quality declined.

- The company failed to develop new products with technically meaningful features and benefits.

- Managerial stability was lacking.

- Old values were not used as the foundation of new beliefs.

- Historical markets were starved by unproductive diversification.

PART 4

Leadership and the Turnaround Organization

Money, low-cost operation, product quality, and distinguishing features are all helpful to the company in trouble—but they may not be forthcoming if the firm lacks leadership. Yet *leadership* is a term open to interpretation. Some people take leadership to mean an impressive, outgoing personality, yet many of our greatest leaders are quiet and contemplative and not very imposing as public speakers. Some people equate leadership with notoriety or general business experience, although the evidence suggests that notoriety wears out quickly and that general business experience does not always indicate whether the person knows what to do in certain industries. Others liken leadership to goal direction, objective setting, and the creation of formal plans and strategies. Yet, evidence also suggests that the best plans are flexible and adaptive, often blended with the culture of the firm, and conveyed informally via unwritten messages and managerial actions.

Leadership is undeniably of crucial importance, and successful turnaround managers exhibit distinctive leadership characteristics which are seldom present in managers of unsuccessful turnarounds. Effective turnaround agents focus the attention of the firm on operational issues, such as enhancing the product, reducing cost, and improving product quality and customer service. Ineffective turnaround agents lead the firm to acquisitions, financial restructurings, or other activities less central to the firm's major business. Successful turnaround leaders are often people with extensive experience in the industry being served, while unsuccessful turnarounds are often headed by people from other industries. The functional background of successful turnaround leaders is often technical—either manufacturing or engineering—perhaps because these disciplines provide a basic grounding in products and customer requirements. Unsuccessful turnaround managers frequently have functional backgrounds in finance or marketing. Successful managers conscientiously seek sufficient knowledge in areas crucial to important decisions, rather than relying solely on readily available information. Successful turnaround leaders utilize the company's historical skills as a basis for new strategic initiatives and are alert to industry trends. Unsuccessful turnarounds often involve inconsistent strategies, poor forecasting, and a lack of awareness of technological and industry trends. Successful turnarounds often involve a high degree of managerial stability in which the top leadership remains constant for many years, often more than 10 years and occasionally more than 20. Finally, although it is difficult to obtain hard evidence, there are sample suggestions that successful turnaround agents often foster an atmosphere of traditional morality involving characteristics such as sobriety, thrift, hard work, and honesty and exhibit greater fairness in dealing with employees, creditors, stockholders, and customers.

Both successful and unsuccessful turnarounds do some things well and some things less well. Most turnarounds experience a mixed set of difficulties, skills, strategies, and luck. Successful turnarounds involve more consistency and a greater propensity to focus on managerial basics such as operational efficiency, product improvement, and the work ethic of the organization. As they work through a much longer list of top managers, unsuccessful turnarounds occasionally manifest these same traits, but usually not for long periods.

Part 4 discusses the qualities of successful leadership and the turnaround organization. Chapter 10 describes the practical aspects of outfitting the management team. Chapter 11 entreats the turnaround manager to focus on present operations. The pivotal role of fair play in turnaround management is covered in Chapter 12.

10
Outfitting the Management Team

Though the leadership qualities of the CEO profoundly affect successful turnarounds, one person alone seldom reverses the adverse fortunes of a corporation. Turnaround success requires teamwork, and the team's makeup is decisive. Thus, most companies that succeed have deep teams, with many individuals sharing both responsibility and the spotlight. In the wars for corporate survival, the victorious CEOs are often trustworthy, mild-mannered people with good negotiating skills who can share center stage and motivate others to reach for greater accomplishments. They seldom act alone.

Because the company in trouble cannot afford additional failures, all elements of the company must be competent. Seldom are enough resources available to permit success if even some departments are operating poorly. The turnaround process is a team event, and each functional area must do its job well. Sales must sell, manufacturing must produce quality products efficiently, and the financial team must keep the company operating within its resource base. Each element of the team must be effective and have special characteristics.

The Management Team

The Chief Executive

The characteristics needed by the chief executive reflect both the nature of the company's difficulties and the special organizational dynamics surrounding turnaround situations. Because of the typical requirement to improve quality while costs are being reduced, the individual should

have industry and technical experience, as well as managerial experience. Because of the frequent need to obtain further cooperation from
creditors, employees, dealers, and investors, he or she needs to radiate
fairness and honesty. The individual needs to explore the environment
and determine what information he or she needs in order to address
the weighty questions being faced and must be able to separate what the
firm does well from what it does less well. The individual should also
have stamina and perseverance. Companies in trouble do not react well
to frequent managerial changes.

Beyond these tangible qualifications, turnaround CEOs should have
another, more subtle and somewhat contradictory attribute: The chief
turnaround agent must attract enough attention to be noticeable and
distinguishable, yet not so much attention that all the credit redounds to
this one person. This is a delicate balance for what is often a high-
profile job. If the CEO is an overly polite, amorphous functionary, with
few technical ideas and little experience with the company's business, it
is doubtful that people within the company will see the CEO as credible.
On the other hand, if the CEO monopolizes all the credit when progress
is made, the hard-working people who contribute to that progress may
feel that their extraordinary efforts are not being recognized. The CEO
must be a visible champion of ideas and an advocate for change but in a
nurturing way that makes it possible for others to share in accomplishments.

Experience in the industry being served eases the difficulty a CEO
has in turning a company around. Regardless of the intellect a turnaround manager may possess, there are some elements of knowledge
that simply cannot be derived from logic. In seven of the nine successful
cases discussed in this book, the turnaround agents had extensive experience in the industry. The other two had extensive experience in
closely related industries. In the seven unsuccessful cases, the turnaround agents were often unfamiliar with the industries in which they
were operating. Successful firms displayed a greater inclination to promote from within, while unsuccessful firms exhibited a proclivity to
bring in outsiders.

Technical experience is also helpful to the CEO because of the pressing need to lower costs while simultaneously providing better products.
Six of the nine successful turnarounds were headed by manufacturing
people. One was headed by a product development engineer. The other
two were headed by individuals with extensive product experience in
the industry. None of the successful turnaround agents were financial
people, and only Iacocca had a functional background primarily in
sales. Iacocca's sales experience, however, was preceded by a bachelor's
degree in engineering from Lehigh and a master's degree in engineer-

ing from Princeton—all accomplished in 4 years. Also, his first assignments at Ford were in engineering. Financial people and salespeople were more numerous among the unsuccessful cases (Table 10-1).

Successful turnarounds also involve a much greater degree of managerial stability—an average of 16 years on the job for successful turnaround agents versus 4.3 years for the unsuccessful. While top management remained constant for many years at the successful firms, unsuccessful companies occasionally fielded a new chief executive every year or two or three. Greater consensus among top executives and the board of directors is also present at successful companies. Bickering between and among managers and directors was the case with Studebaker, Kaiser-Frazer, and several other unsuccessful firms.

Differing viewpoints often emerge during a troubled business situation, and in order to reverse the adverse trends of a company in trouble, some changes must be made. What needs to change and what does not is, of course, one of the CEO's most delicate decisions. Successful

Table10-1. Backgrounds of Chief Turnaround Agents

	Name of chief turnaround agent	Main functional areas	Industry or related experience
	Successful Cases		
Cadillac	Leland	Manufacturing	Yes
Buick	Nash/Chrysler	Manufacturing/ Manufacturing	Yes/Yes
Jeffery (Nash)	Nash	Manufacturing	Yes
Maxwell-Chalmers	Chrysler	Manufacturing	Yes
Packard	Macauley	Law and manufacturing	Yes
Deere	Wiman	Engineering	Yes
AMC	Romney	Manufacturing	Yes
Chrysler	Iacocca	Engineering and sales	Yes
Ford	Petersen	Engineering and product development	Yes
	Unsuccessful Cases		
Willys-Overland	Chrysler/Willys/others	Mainly sales	Yes
Hudson	Chapin/Mcean'y/ Chapin/Barit	Finance and sales	Yes
Studebaker-Packard	Nance/Francis/ Churchill/Egbert/others	Finance, sales, and manufacturing	Some
International Harvester	McCardell/Menk/ Lennox	Finance and then manufacturing	Little
Allis-Chalmers	Scott/Bueche	Sales and engineering	Little
Kaiser-Frazer	H. Kaiser/E. Kaiser	Construction and sales	Little
AMC/Renault	Chapin/Meyers/ Deudeweader/Cappy	Sales, manufacturing, and other	Yes

managers spurn sweeping changes in favor of incremental changes in strategies, policies, and managerial appointments. Old values are used as a foundation for new beliefs, and appreciation is shown for the positive contributions of people who were part of the organization at the time problems developed.

The ability of chief turnaround agents to gain the trust of employees, creditors, and customers was a positive force in several turnaround successes. For the successful and unsuccessful firms alike, the trustworthiness of the top management team became a factor in rallying the troops to put forth the extra efforts needed for a turnaround. CEOs like Petersen, Wiman, Romney, Chrysler, Iacocca, and Nash were somehow able to elicit enough trust to mobilize the companies, whereas organizations remained suspicious of unsuccessful CEOs (Table 10-2).

The Financial Team

Top financial people need not have exhaustive knowledge of the more exotic branches of corporate finance, but they do need to know the

Table 10-2. Top Management Characteristics of Turnaround Organizations during the Period of Recovery

	Top management industry experience	Top management technical experience	Managerial stability	Knowledge exploration	Incremental change
Successful Cases					
Cadillac	Yes	Yes	Yes	Yes	Yes
Buick	Related	Yes	Yes	N/A	Yes
Jeffery (Nash)	Yes	Yes	Yes	Yes	Yes
Maxwell-Chalmers	Yes	Yes	Yes	Yes	Yes
Packard	Yes	Yes	Yes	Yes	Yes
Deere	Yes	Yes	Yes	Yes	Yes
AMC	Yes	Yes	Yes	Yes	Yes
Chrysler	Yes	Yes	Yes	Yes	Yes
Ford	Yes	Yes	Yes	Yes	Yes
Unsuccessful Cases					
Willys-Overland	Yes	No	Some	No	No
Hudson	Yes	No	Some	No	No
Studebaker-Packard	No	No	No	No	No
International Harvester	No	No	No	No	No
Allis-Chalmers	No	Some	Some	No	No
Kaiser-Frazer	No	No	Some	No	No
AMC/Renault	Yes	No	No	No	No

business. They should also possess good negotiating skills and be regarded as dependable by the present and potential creditors. But most important, they must know the business. During Chrysler's successful period in the 1930s, B. E. Hutchinson, who was in charge of financial operations, knew the business very well. An experienced production supervisor, he could interpret terms like direct labor, material cost, overhead, and productivity in realistic terms. The great inventor Charles F. Kettering once noted that organizations lose their effectiveness when they begin substituting symbols for things. Kettering suggested that it is all right to use a symbol for a thing if you fully understand what the thing is. The inability to comprehend the organizational and technical factors behind symbols appears to be a fundamental problem with many financial and accounting people at unsuccessful firms. They simply do not understand the crucial dynamic relationships underlying the financial reports, and often they are disinclined to find out.

George Gleeson, a financial consultant for troubled companies, shares Kettering's caution against short-cutting a thorough understanding of the business. He deplores the inappropriateness of discussing strategy, mission, business segments, and long-range plans when nobody is selling the product or collecting the money. Gleeson once described the unspecific globalism rampant in some corporations today as "like trying to paint the Sistine Chapel with a four-inch brush."

Just as American students need a more thorough understanding of science and mathematics in order to compete in today's global economy, financial staff members of troubled companies must thoroughly understand the business in physical and scientific, as well as symbolic, terms. This need affects where financial people spend their time. You will not find Gleeson pouring over the latest standards of the American Institute of Certified Public Accountants, nor will you find him researching the latest techniques of financial manipulation. You will find him out talking to the production people about reducing scrap and inventory or working with dissatisfied customers to resolve whatever problem is keeping them from paying their bills. These actions bring long-term success.

Robert Townsend once described the position of controller as the conscience of the organization, and he implored the controller not to treat the CEO as the chief customer. The operating people are the customers. The financial team must have the respect and participation of the operating units.

The Product Team

The product team must not only be able to develop new products, it must be able to develop substantially better products which can be produced at much lower cost, and it must accomplish this in shorter periods of time. These are the requirements of today's marketplace—even for companies in the strongest market position. Some companies take the task too lightly and develop products which are only different, not better and not lower in cost. Often, they compound these errors by taking too long.

As Ford's fruitful experience with the Taurus/Sable project demonstrated, today's product teams are composed of people of various ranks and responsibilities across the corporation. Effective product development involves manufacturing and engineering along with purchasing, legal, marketing, service, and other support activities. The product team must work with all these constituencies in a collaborative manner and still take charge of the project. Ford's term for it was *program management*. In other circles, the term *simultaneous engineering* has been used to describe the process of developing the product in an iterative manner involving many disciplines.

Unsuccessful firms often have dogmatic product teams, occasionally headed by the CEO. Many times their vision is clear but, unfortunately, incorrect. Unsuccessful product teams frequently think that they are brilliant, and thus they employ fewer of the interrogating techniques and cross-checks that typify successful projects like the Taurus. The Taurus project was successful because Ford paid painstaking attention to the requirements of many constituencies and then realistically appraised the design of Ford products versus that of competitors. Unsuccessful product teams often profess to know all the answers, thereby denying themselves valuable insights from associates and customers.

Product teams may commit another error—taking too long. Most probably, it would have been in the best interest of GM to field an earlier response to the Ford Taurus, but the immensity of GM's bureaucracy worked against the timely completion of this important development program. By the time the product hit the sales floor, the U.S. car market was in decline. So it was also with Packard's V8, Hudson's replacement for the step-down sedan, Control Data's replacement for its Cyber series, and many other projects.

These dual problems of conceit and procrastination hinder the corporation's ability to survive in troubled times. A good product team avoids both. Team members, including top management, must be knowledgeable about the industry and should possess up-to-date scientific and technical knowledge, as well as managerial skill. They must be open to new ideas and be willing to study how other competitors or industries solve their problems.

The Sales Team

Lyle Altman, CEO of Network Systems, describes it simply. A good salesperson is one who sells. For the struggling firm without much time, this may mean knowing the customers in personal, as well as conceptual, terms. This distinction is important.

The revenue-expansion strategy is both risky and time-limited as the sole remedy for a troubled firm. Yet, attaining sufficient revenue is clearly preeminent, and good salespeople are indispensable to a firm's survival. Unfortunately, limited understanding of both the sales process for the industry and the specific customer base of the company leads many companies in trouble to seriously mishandle their sales organizations at the most unfortunate times. They sometimes make too many changes, at the wrong time, and for the wrong reasons—with disastrous results.

Sales are most often slow at troubled companies because of low product quality, lack of differentiating features, high prices, a bad economy, distress on the part of key customers, or even ineffective sales administration. Often, the sophomoric answer is to bring in "stronger" sales or marketing executives. In some circumstances, this may be warranted. In other cases, it may create problems for these reasons:

1. The new sales or marketing executives may not be competent. They may be in the job market because they were ineffective in their last job. Some sales and marketing people are far more effective at selling themselves than they are at selling the company's goods. Personnel changes in marketing or sales will not necessarily improve anything, though sometimes they may.

2. The old salespeople may be well respected within the organization. Good salespeople tend to be well liked inside, as well as outside, the organization. The chief executive or the board of directors may believe that stronger marketing people are needed, but the replacement of good salespeople may hurt morale, particularly if the salespeople are hard-working.

3. New sales and marketing people may not know any customers. Selling often results from the salesperson's intimate knowledge of what a specific customer needs. It takes a great deal of time to accumulate this knowledge, and the pressing demands of the turnaround situation may not permit enough time to bring new people through their learning curves. New sales and marketing people may not sell enough, soon enough.

4. New salespeople almost always spend more. Their very presence, which is seldom inexpensive, often represents a signal to the organization that additional expenditures on marketing are now in vogue. If the new programs work, the company may (or may not) improve (see Chapter 4). However, the programs may not work better, and the company may spend more money on the sales function, sell less, and operate less profitably.

If the company is doing quite poorly, it may be necessary to make some changes in the marketing and sales organizations. However, most successful turnaround agents find it unwise to change too many things at once, lest the organization lose its orientation. Most companies have some good people in sales and marketing. Effective turnaround agents work to keep them.

Special Teams

Companies in trouble often have special problems which need attention. These problems are often significant enough so that they should not be treated as the routine responsibilities of the functional departments of the company. The Packard turnaround of the 1930s, which involved offering a medium-priced car, required a resource to finance cars and an ability to move larger volumes of used cars. Previously, most Packard customers had paid cash, and the low-volume sales of "senior" Packards meant that used-car sales were not an important determinant of dealer profitability. Packard management recognized these two needs as integral to its medium-priced car strategy and recruited people who could address them. Similarly, the special teams at Ford during the 1980s were instrumental in developing new concepts of stamping-die design, which permitted a reduction in the number of body side stampings from nine to two. This improved both the quality of the fit and the profitability of the Taurus/Sable products. During the 1980s, Chrysler Corporation used special teams to work out the complicated financial rearrangements. During the 1920s, Walter Chrysler utilized special teams to make full use of the well-equipped Dodge Brothers manufacturing facilities.

During the hectic periods of a turnaround, many things must be done, and some of them are unusual. Unsuccessful firms often miss the opportunity to concentrate special attention on important main events, which, in some cases, may require carefully chosen additional skills. Special teams are important because they divide responsibility along practical lines. Turnarounds are hectic enough without line managers becoming distracted with new special tasks. Carefully selected, modest, easy-to-work-with special teams can take care of some unusual special requirements while the rest of the organization remains focused on the main business.

Personal Characteristics

Skills and competencies of the management team provide the foundation for organizational improvement, but skills and competencies alone are not enough. The traumatic circumstances of a turnaround require the presence of certain character traits.

Pride versus Ego

With respect to turnarounds, there are two types of pride. One is helpful and one is not. It is helpful for the members of the organization to have pride in their company and for the management team to reflect this pride. It is not helpful for the management team to be overly preoccupied with its own importance. Charles Nash epitomized what was important in running a business: "Oriental rugs, factory administration buildings with imposing granite columns and uniformed office attendants have no place in the successful conduct of the automobile manufacturing business," he would say. "I belong to the common people and I'm proud I do. I honestly treasure the good-will and the respect and the confidence of the men working with me and for me more than all of the money I have ever made. If I didn't have that—if I gave them cause to lose it…well I guess I wouldn't sleep nights"(Kimes 1977).

Chester Barnard suggested that each executive possesses a "zone of indifference" with respect to the organization. Unless the decision is especially controversial, the organization will tend to go along. Barnard also suggested that the zone of indifference varies greatly from one executive to another because some are more trustworthy and more confidence exists with respect to their leadership. In spite of what some executives think, members of organizations do not think about them very much. Most members of organizations are busy people, busy with their responsibilities, their customers, their families, and their own personal needs. Members of organizations simply do not have the time to worry a great deal about executives unless their behavior falls outside a normal band of typical behavior. Nor is there great emotion regarding who should have executive jobs.

The fact that their existence is not material comes as a shock to some executives, who are amazed when their directives are not followed or their messages are not clearly understood or people do not know who they are. Nobody thinks about Chester A. Arthur very much any more. Yet his civil service reforms have outlasted his personal notoriety as president of the United States. The capable executive recognizes that the only lasting notoriety results from selfless dedication to the ideals of the organization and its people and its customers. The only lasting personal reward comes from the intrinsic quality in performing the managerial task. All members of the organization feel that they are important and they are quick to pick up the sincerity, idealism, and humility of top management.

Justice

Unavoidably, the turnaround agent becomes the purveyor of either justice or injustice, in hiring, firing, promotions, and retention. If justice prevails, an organization's morale improves and the probability of a successful outcome is enhanced. If injustice prevails, organization members become disenchanted and success is far less probable.

Most companies in trouble employ highly dedicated, competent people as well as individuals of lesser talent and fidelity. Almost always, in a turnaround situation, more people are employed than the company can afford. Choices must therefore be made regarding who goes and who stays. At this juncture the opportunity exists to either promote or retard justice.

Actions taken by management during this critical stage of headcount retrenchment send profound messages to members of the organization. If management uses the occasion to correct long-term problems of poor attendance, theft, laziness, incompetence, and other weaknesses, it conveys the message that the organization is serious about correcting its problems, and morale improves. If headcount reductions are arbitrary or unjust or penalize the individuals most respected for their forbearance and expertise by the informal organization, they can hurt morale very deeply. Most people in organizations want to be part of a class outfit, and successful turnaround agents grasp this subtlety and work to provide an atmosphere of justice even as costs are reduced. Unsuccessful turnaround agents tend to be arbitrary, rather than just, and further damage morale with poorly thought-out promotions or enlistments.

Perseverance

Turnaround efforts are long and arduous and require stamina on the part of both managers and workers. Some people are not up to it. They don't work hard enough or long enough.

Hard work, in a turnaround setting, means something different than simply putting in long hours. Often, the people who are most respected for being conscientious are not the people who spend night and day at work. Such people are often viewed as narrow and incapable of balancing personal goals involving family and other considerations with professional goals. Instead, the people with perseverance budget their time very carefully. They seldom golf during the workday. They don't usually play racquetball at lunch. They stick to business. They don't spend too much time in meetings, but they do put in an honest day's work, often visiting customers or suppliers. Then they go home to do something else, and return early the next day to pursue objectives with renewed vigor. That is perseverance in a turnaround setting.

Chester Barnard once mentioned that it is virtually impossible to get members of an organization to support a decision which conflicts with their own personal moral beliefs. This is especially true regarding the building of perseverance in an organization in trouble. Most people have no difficulty with putting in extra hours, without additional compensation, when the company is in desperate need. However, the prudent manager will recognize that turnarounds go on for very long periods (usually about 4 years). Hence, to maintain perseverance, they avoid wasting people's time, so that energies can be preserved for the most critical main events. Unsuccessful firms often waste people's time and diminish perseverance by holding poorly planned meetings for long periods without taking action on the problems discussed, by attempting to gain consensus on trivial issues, or by foot dragging on those key decisions that do need to be made. Too often, these actions only make people late for supper, thereby compounding the company's problems by reducing support from the families of organization members—a cardinal mistake. The quality and timeliness of managerial actions affect both organizational commitment and perseverance.

Mostly, however, perseverance applies to the managers themselves. The turnaround process is long, and key managers simply must stick with it. The track record of turnarounds involving many changes in management is quite poor.

Temperance

It is not fashionable in business schools to discuss sobriety as an attribute of management. As a practical matter, however, personal temperance does play a role in turnaround success. The evidence gathered among the cases examined here coincides with the author's personal experience that many business problems could be averted by a more widespread adoption of personal temperance. It does not seem circumstantial that the key turnaround agents at Cadillac,

Packard, Nash, Deere, and American Motors during the 1950s all enjoyed generally temperate reputations, and several were active campaigners against alcohol. Organization members, creditors, and other associates are quite likely to distrust people who drink excessively or behave immodestly in other ways. Alan K. "Bud" Ruvelson, one of the nation's more experienced venture capitalists, describes the four horsemen of the apocalypse of company problems as "the four B's: booze, boy/girl problems, bucks, and ballots (people running for office, either internally or externally)." Whether the personal behavior of executives should be a material consideration in turnaround success is not the issue. Concerns regarding personal behavior cannot be evaluated within a narrow legalistic framework. Motivation operates within a framework of perceptions. Organization members will decide for themselves what they regard as relevant qualities in executives, and what a legalistic framework suggests they ought to consider is not of much interest to them. The fact is that intemperate executives are not popular with organizations in trouble, and we should resist the temptation to exclude from our business analyses nonbusiness variables that do indeed affect the business. The process of turnaround is difficult enough without incurring additional problems which the organization does not need.

Successful companies often sustain a culture of traditional morality involving characteristics such as sobriety, thrift, hard work, and honesty. IBM's policy of sobriety during its formative years drew some remarks and wisecracks, but IBM became one of the most formidable corporations in history. Cadillac and Deere, in particular, hired at least partly on the basis of character traits, as did General Motors at various times. Most successful turnaround agents had reputations of being fundamentally honest and trustworthy and of having fairly wholesome personal lives.

Yet, unsuccessful firms often violate this simple precept of temperance during times of corporate stress. Intemperance often occurs in out-of-town travel and company meetings—even meetings called to discuss ways out of the crisis. It is amazing how managers will justify meetings at expensive resorts some distance from headquarters to discuss the adversities of troubled companies. The liquor, the golf, the entertainment, and the expensive surroundings are probably not of material accounting cost to major corporations, but the cost in terms of organizational cohesiveness is often exceedingly high. Members of organizations often evaluate the mannerisms of executives in very simple terms. If the company is in trouble, executives should not compound the trouble by staying in too-expensive places or by indulging themselves at corporate expense. Many people see indulgence as evidence that the seriousness needed during troubled times is lacking.

Practical Lessons on Outfitting the Management Team

- Successful turnaround leaders clearly articulate ideals, purposes, and procedures using unambiguous language. Unsuccessful turnaround leaders are often polite, but vague.

- Successful turnaround leaders have widespread reputations for honesty and trustworthiness. Unsuccessful turnaround leaders are often shrewd, but untrusted.

- Turnaround leaders who are successful over the very long term share center stage and the credit for success with other members of the organization.

- Successful turnaround teams include salespeople who know customers, visit customers, and like customers — and who also sell.

- Successful turnaround teams include financial and accounting people who understand and appreciate the technical and managerial aspects of the business.

- Special teams are used for one-time projects, in part so that the rest of the organization can remain focused on the main business.

- Successful turnaround teams rarely include people who drink too much, spend too much, or are indulgent in other ways.

- Successful turnaround leaders are purveyors of justice, especially during downturns when expenses must be cut. They sustain morale by protecting the conscientious, dedicated worker to the maximum degree possible. People who do not work hard or who are not conscientious are usually dismissed.

Case Histories

The cases we will examine in this chapter provide an interesting contrast in the makeup of management teams. Allis-Chalmers was certainly an innovative company at one time and indeed had vast technical resources. However, the makeup of the management team was vastly different from that of the successful Maxwell-Chalmers turnaround of the 1920s. In one case, the team was very experienced, rather basic in its

approach and beliefs, scientific in its development of products, and focused on what needed to be done at the time. Idealism certainly existed,
but it was constrained to the here and now. In the other case, management took bold steps without possessing a thorough knowledge of what
would happen. Experience played less of a role, and more was left to
the intuition of fewer people—intuition that was often wrong.

Case 12

Professionals in Place at Maxwell-Chalmers

During the early 1920s, the Maxwell-Chalmers Company sank deeply into
crisis. Unit sales declined to less than one-fourth the level of 1916, as dealers
and customers together became disenchanted with the slipping quality and
sporadic performance of Maxwell-Chalmers products. The management team,
though experienced in the automobile industry, did not appear to know what
to do to restore profits and consumer confidence. After heavy losses in 1920
and 1921, financial backers elected to bring in Walter Chrysler, who was then
engineering a temporary resurgence of Willys-Overland. Over time, Chrysler
brought in a deep and experienced management team composed of people
who did know what to do. The firm survived and prospered, and within 12
years U.S. production had exceeded that of the mighty Ford Motor Company.
The firm survives today as Chrysler Corporation.

Jonathan Maxwell started out in the bicycle business with another auto
pioneer, Elmer Apperson, and later was involved with the Haynes,
Oldsmobile, and Northern automobile operations. In 1903, he teamed with
Benjamin Briscoe to form the Maxwell-Briscoe Motor Car Company, which
soon became an established producer of automobiles. However, Benjamin
Briscoe's ambitions were immense, and in 1910, the Maxwell-Briscoe Motor
Car Company was combined with 129 others to form the ill-fated United
States Motor Car Corporation. The new firm offered 28 models of
automobiles produced under seven trade names (Seltzer 1928). A shortage of
capital and lack of organizational cohesiveness forced the company into
bankruptcy in 1912, and Benjamin Briscoe left the firm. Walter Flanders,
formerly of Ford and Everitt-Metzger-Flanders (EMF), was called upon to
reorganize the company as the Maxwell Motor Car Company (Rae 1965, 44).

Walter Flanders had some understanding of production but was reputed to
be flamboyant, intemperate, and in possession of few engineering skills. His
namesake firm, EMF, enjoyed the dubious nicknames of "Every Morning
Fixit" and "Every Mechanical Fault." Reliability and quality problems also
surfaced at Maxwell during the Flanders era (Rae 1965, 84). Maxwell's
technical capabilities were further compromised by forced sell-off of some of
its most valued assets, and one of the major Maxwell plants was sold to Billy
Durant's new company, Chevrolet, as part of the financial restructuring of
1914 (Crabb 1969, 326). Perhaps in an effort to augment its reduced
production capabilities, which were caused by the sale of a major plant, the
Maxwell Motor Car Company engaged in a quasiofficial relationship with the

Chalmers Motor Company in 1917. This "leasing" of the Chalmers facilities provided a modest resolution to Maxwell's need for production capacity. However, the arrangement produced a legion of organizational "turf" issues along with the problem of updating an additional model. These problems proved stressful to the company's already thin resource base. However, in spite of its problems, the Maxwell-Chalmers Company enjoyed several years of strong unit sales and emerged as one of the more significant producers of automobiles (Table 10-3). By 1917, output rose to 90,000 units, and profits exceeded $5 million. Maxwell-Chalmers' market share climbed to 6 percent.

After 1917, Maxwell-Chalmers' unit sales, market share, and profits all declined. The recession following World War I accentuated the decline, and by 1921, the company was experiencing heavy losses. The financial backers of Maxwell sought a more lasting solution to the company's problems. Some of Maxwell-Chalmers' backers had worked with Walter Chrysler and approached him with a proposal to take over the management of the Maxwell-Chalmers company in addition to his responsibilities at Willys-Overland. A short time later, Chrysler devoted his full attention to the Maxwell-Chalmers turnaround. In contrast to his assessment of Willys-Overland, Chrysler saw more potential in the Maxwell-Chalmers enterprise and elected to take a much lower fee along with a percentage of the company's stock.

Chrysler approached the Maxwell-Chalmers turnaround in the same manner he had employed at Buick and Willys-Overland. He walked around the company assessing people, looking for ways to improve products and to increase production efficiency. He improved relations with the company's creditors and tried to develop a more competent cadre of trusted associates.

Table 10-3. Maxwell-Chalmers/Chrysler Corporation Output, Sales, and Profit, 1904–1921

Year	Units produced Maxwell	Units produced Chalmers	Profits ($000)	Unit market share, %
1904	10			
1905	823			
1906	2,000			
1907	3,785			
1908	4,455			
1909	9,490			
1910	10,000	6,350		9.03
1911	16,000	6,250		11.16
1912	(company bankrupt)			
1913	17,000	6,000		5.33
1914	21,000	6,200	2,500	5.00
1915	44,000	9,800		6.00
1916	69,000	21,000	5,426	5.90
1917	75,000	(low)	5,507	4.58
1918	34,000	(low)	2,292	4.13
1919	50,000	(low)	1,500	3.32
1920	34,168	10,000	(heavy losses)	2.32
1921	16,000	(low)	(heavy losses)	1.38

When asked by Bertie Forbes, "What is the secret of your ability to make going concerns out of these bankrupt companies?" Chrysler replied,

> The first thing I do when I start to look into the affairs of a failing company is to study the personnel of the organization and the individuality of the men. I am concerned first of all with executives, because if their principles are not right it is useless to look at the results of men. When I have measured up in my own mind the capacity of the executives, I get out into the operation of the plant and watch the men. I look around to see how many of them are standing still and how many of them are moving around the plant. Highly paid men should be busy with accomplishment, not useless motion. If there is a lot of [useless] movement I know the plant is badly operated.
>
> I do not believe in idle machines or idle men. Outside of the idle investment involved, it is bad policy. If a man is working next to an idle machine it not only has a bad effect on him mentally, but he takes less care of his own machine because he thinks he has a ready substitute. I believe in keeping people out of temptation, for many cannot resist it.
>
> I have the floor space measured and estimate the amount of its productive capacity and then check up to see whether it is overcrowded or is running under its capacity, also whether the plant is overmanned. If it is overmanned and we are producing, I reduce the force arbitrarily.
>
> I proceed to get the organization into shape by cutting out every unnecessary expense and wasteful practice the moment I discover it.
>
> Men should look forward, and progress stops when they refuse to listen to other people's opinions, although they should make their own decisions. I never want to get to the place where I so dominate the job that no one under me dares to make suggestions.
>
> I gauge men through my intuition and experience.... Then, too, these cuts in the organization give me a big opportunity to learn something about my manpower. I find out how much fight the men have in them and learn a lot about their individual force. By cutting to the quick I get rapid contacts and am able to measure up my men's resourcefulness under emergency conditions without delay. (Forbes 1972, 37–39)

Walter Chrysler had the respect of his organization. He roamed through the plant asking workers how he could help them. He stayed late with the development engineers and took an interest in their work, but he did not take charge of their efforts. When talking to the press, he heaped praise upon his management team and his development engineers. Chrysler was an executive comfortable with sharing center stage.

The Maxwell-Chalmers turnaround involved many people. Almost immediately after taking over, Chrysler employed the services of Fred Zeder, Owen Skelton, and Carl Breer, who designed Willys-Overland's new car during Chrysler's association with that company. After Chrysler left, John North Willys sold the design and the factory to Durant Motors to raise cash, and as a result, Zeder, Skelton, and Breer were back on their own. In 1922, they moved to Michigan to work exclusively for Walter Chrysler.

Zeder, Skelton, and Breer soon began work on a new automobile which was

highly differentiated from other automobiles of that day, a car which later
evolved into the first Chrysler automobile. Building the first Chrysler car was
very much a team effort. Zeder and Breer worked primarily on engines;
Skelton handled axles, transmissions, and brakes; Breer designed many
essential miscellaneous parts; George Mason (later president of Nash-
Kelvinator) took care of production. Many other individuals were involved on
other projects (Rae 1965; Langworth and Nordbye 1985). Yet, informality
prevailed and many activities overlapped as the company's mode of operation
closely paralleled that of a skunk works.

In the first Chrysler car, modern materials were used to ensure strength
and reduce weight; the result was a quick, economical, and durable car. The
car was designed with particular concern for manufacturing cost. As with
some other successful turnarounds, considerable emphasis was placed on the
commonality of parts and design for manufacturability. The innovation
displayed by the Chrysler engineering staff, headed by Fred Zeder, allowed
the company to produce a broad spectrum of products from a basic catalog of
primary components. Although the car featured modern attributes such as a
high-compression engines and hydraulic brakes, its designers spurned exotic
processes and trendy design elements and instead opted for dependability,
manufacturability, quality, and the ability to make maximum use of the
machinery in the Chalmers factory (Langworth and Nordbye 1985, 28).

Most of the people involved with the turnaround of Maxwell-Chalmers and
the emergence of Chrysler were technically trained and experienced, but
other disciplines were well represented. Chrysler, Mason, and K. T. Keller
(Chrysler's successor as president) were production people. Zeder, Skelton,
Breer, and Clark were engineers. Herbert Henderson was an industrial
designer. Joe Fields, the sales manager, was a former agricultural equipment
salesperson who had spent time with National Cash Register. B. E. "Hutch"
Hutchinson, in charge of finances, was trained as an accountant at MIT and
then Ernst & Ernst. However, he was also an accountant who came out of
school to take a job shoveling coal into a blast furnace. Later, he rose to the
position of superintendent of the open-hearth furnace section of that
company (Chrysler 1937, 178). The market planning activities of the early
Chrysler Corporation attracted the attention of the highly academic
Econometric Society. In all, the management team was seasoned,
well-educated, and eclectic.

In contrast to the rather dashing profiles of contemporary Hudson and
Willys-Overland executives, an informal atmosphere of traditional down-home
values permeated the management team in the early days of Chrysler
Corporation. Walter Chrysler and George Mason liked to fish and hunt and
generally spurned social activities. Chrysler put great importance on the
security of his family and continued association with old friends such as A. B.
Sloan, William Durant, and Charles Nash. He took extra pains to let the
employees of the company know that he was not special. He had a good
rapport with workers in the organization and chatted with them often about
many subjects. Fred Zeder was a religious person who often attended church
daily. B. E. Hutchinson was reputed to be a kind and professional person who
was fond of saying: "Gentlemen, let's have less heat and more light in this
discussion." K. T. Keller was a conservative who believed that dependability,
passenger comfort, and quality were more important to an automobile than
style. While the managers of other companies grew wealthy and sought

diversions, the people at Chrysler worked hard at developing an exciting industrial company.

The fortunes of the company began to improve. Output jumped from fewer than 45,000 cars in 1922 to 182,000 in 1927. Profits grew from the severe losses of the 1919–1921 era to more than $19 million in 1927. The market share of the company grew to nearly 6 percent, and the company occupied sixth place in sales (Table 10-4). But, the Chrysler turnaround was still gathering momentum. On July 30, 1928, the company was asked to purchase Dodge Brothers, Inc., thus increasing Chrysler's market share, further enabling it to become the unchallenged number-three producer.

The Dodge brothers had figured crucially in the emergence of the American motor car industry in several ways. Both John and Horace Dodge were excellent machinists, and Horace Dodge worked under the wise stewardship of Henry Leland at Leland & Faulconer. With this expertise in hand, the two brothers opened the Dodge Brothers Machine Shop in 1901 to provide component parts to the fledgling auto industry. One of their earliest customers was the Ford Motor Company, and John and Horace Dodge became two of only a handful of stockholders in that company. For many years, they played a significant role in the emergence of Ford. As late as

Table 10-4. Chrysler/Maxwell-Chalmers Output, Sales, and Profit, 1921–1941

Year	Units produced	Total revenue ($000)	Profits ($000)	Unit market share, %
1921	16,000	(low)	(heavy losses)	1.38
1922	44,811	46,123	832	1.89
1923	49,546	58,138	2,678	1.50
1924	79,144	81,364	4,115	2.46
1925	132,343	137,321	17,126	3.42
1926	162,242	163,891	17,400	4.11
1927	182,195	172,344	19,500	5.90
1928	313,769	315,305	34,167	7.82
1929	375,094	375,033	24,207	7.82
1930	230,904	207,789	922	7.93
1931	244,916	183,805	3,421	12.02
1932	204,416	136,547	(10,131)	17.23
1933	397,373	238,676	16,555	24.42
1934	512,554	362,255	12,496	22.57
1935	738,319	516,830	44,948	21.79
1936	926,165	667,138	73,443	24.33
1937	997,315	769,808	60,000	24.51
1938	478,126	413,250	19,000	22.50
1939	657,538	549,806	42,000	22.10
1940	934,959	744,561	58,000	24.60
1941	878,356	888,366	65,000	23.37

NOTE: Shipments and financial figures for Dodge Brothers, Inc., are not included for the time preceding the acquisition of that company by Chrysler Corporation in 1928.

1914, the Dodge Brothers Machine Shop built all the components for Ford cars, except the body, tires, and wheels.

In 1914, however, Henry Ford decided to reduce his dependence on outsiders. The giant Ford complex at Highland Park came into full production, and with that Ford began to systematically cut off his old, and sometimes faithful, suppliers. The Dodge brothers were affected not only because of the falloff in Ford business but also because the dividends in the Ford Motor Company were cut to zero. Some authors suggest that Henry Ford wanted to plow the full proceeds of Ford profits directly into the company. Others imply that he wanted to diminish the possibility of Dodge Brothers becoming a viable builder of automobiles. In any case, the combination of the two moves resulted in the Dodge Brothers building its own car, and later a successful suit was brought against Henry Ford for nonpayment of dividends (Seltzer 1928).

The first Dodge car sold 45,000 units. By 1920, production grew to 141,000, and Dodge emerged as one of the nation's larger producers, with profits of $24 million in 1919 and $18.4 million in 1920 (Heasley 1977, 20–21). Dodge cars garnered an early reputation for dependability and good value.

Although the Dodge brothers were excellent machinists and were generally fair in dealing with their business associates, their personal lives were less orderly (Nevins 1954). Both John and Horace Dodge died in 1920 at an early age, some say of diphtheria, a malady perhaps worsened by what some authors have suggested was a less than temperate lifestyle. Their widows sold the company to an investor syndicate headed by Dillon Read.

Dodge sales were strong during its early history but fluctuated wildly during the Dillon Read period. In 1921, sales dropped to 81,000, then recovered to 265,000 in 1926, and then dropped to 67,000 in 1928. In 1928, the investors' syndicate approached Walter Chrysler to see whether he had an interest in purchasing Dodge Brothers, Inc., an inquiry that resulted in the Chrysler Corporation buying Dodge Brothers in a transaction financed by Dillon Read.

Chrysler purchased Dodge Brothers primarily because of its production facilities. The Dodge plant was well-equipped, complete with a fine foundry and forge. It provided Chrysler Corporation with a building block to expand and strengthen its position in the industry and to broaden the company's product line. In 1928, Chrysler produced both the DeSoto and the Plymouth (named, in part, after a popular brand of binder twine well known to the farm people at Chrysler). With the arrival of a fuller product line and better production facilities, the Chrysler Corporation began to grow. By 1929, unit sales had risen to 375,000 units and profits exceeded $24 million.

A steady stream of quality automobiles and product innovations contributed to a substantial cushioning of sales during the Great Depression. The company introduced overdrive to increase gas mileage while reducing noise and engine wear, the downdraft carburetor, floating power, vacuum-spark advance, more reliable universal joints and brake drums, and many other innovative features which were user-oriented. The company pioneered many significant engineering and product features. Hydraulic brakes improved safety, tubular axles added strength and reduced weight, and floating power reduced noise and vibration. The advanced aerodynamics of the 1934 models improved gas mileage and performance. Standardized parts improved production efficiency and lowered cost. These fruits of Chrysler's engineering staff allowed the company to increase market penetration greatly during a period of severe economic difficulty. In 1928, Chrysler production lagged that of Willys-Overland and unit sales for 1929 were only about 20 percent higher than those of Hudson. Hudson's sales dipped to under 18,000 in 1931, and Willys-Overland's sales dropped to 6552 in 1934. Chrysler sales remained relatively strong, dropping only to 204,000 in 1932, the only year of the Great Depression when Chrysler Corporation operated at a loss.

Meanwhile, by 1940, Ford's market share slipped to well under 20 percent (16 percent in 1940 and 18.3 percent in 1941). Chrysler Corporation had surpassed the Ford Motor Company and moved into a strong number-two position in the U.S. market (Figure 10-1).

The Maxwell-Chalmers turnaround was headed by a broadly based managerial team composed of conscientious individuals who understood the practicalities of production, product innovation, and organizational teamwork oriented to quality and function rather than style. In their own way, and in a manner consistent with their values, the people at Chrysler produced products they thought society needed. They were interested in economy, durability, and passenger comfort rather than fashion.

Not all Chrysler innovations were well received by the marketplace. But enough were to move the company to a strongly profitable number-two

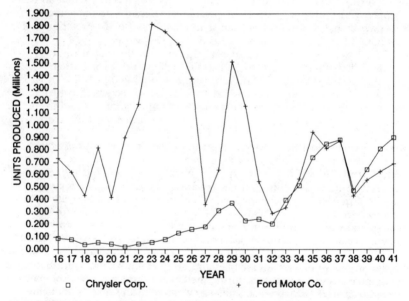

Figure 10-1. U.S. auto production of Chrysler and Ford. The domestic sales of Ford Motor Company peaked at 1.8 million units in 1923, a year when predecessors of Chrysler Corporation produced under 50,000 units. By 1929, Chrysler production had risen to 375,000 units, while Ford production of the new Model A had rebounded to over 1.5 million. Ford sales suffered badly during the depression, however, while Chrysler sales continued to grow. By 1936, Chrysler had moved ahead of Ford to become the nation's second-largest producer, a condition which prevailed for the next 14 years.

position. The company developed solid competitive advantages: production efficiency, product innovation, superb engineering, and its basic down-home approach to supplying products for the market. With this formula, Chrysler Corporation was perhaps the best-run automobile company during the 1930s and certainly showed the most stability during a disastrous depression. From a position of near bankruptcy in 1921 (which would have been its second bankruptcy), the company emerged as the country's second-largest producer only 12 years later.

At a later stage, when the original Chrysler management had died or retired, the company moved away from its position of supplying well-built, reliable cars to conservative people with an appreciation for engineering. Less flashy than the postwar GM and, perhaps, less gifted at marketing than the refinanced and newly managed Ford, Chrysler Corporation faltered in the early 1950s. A few years later, Chrysler corporation began to compete directly in the high-performance, high-style arena. Performance improved, styling became more exotic, fuel economy plummeted, and quality declined. Consequently, traditional Chrysler customers looked for other alternatives whereas customers in the new market remained loyal to other producers. But, from 1924 to 1941, the deep and technically competent management team at Chrysler Corporation enabled the company to emerge from disaster to become the best-run automobile company of the period.

Maxwell-Chalmers Survived Because...

- Managers were experienced in the industry being served.

- Talent, competence, and goodwill were distributed broadly throughout the organization.

- Top managers were technically competent.

- Products became differentiated in advance of industry trends.

- Product features and benefits were rooted in technical advances rather than cosmetics.

- Each major part of the company did its job well. Engineering developed good products, manufacturing efficiently produced quality products, sales sold, and finance understood how to make money in physical terms.

Case 13

Witless Dissipation at Allis-Chalmers

The Allis-Chalmers corporation began operations in the Milwaukee area of Wisconsin in 1847 as the Reliance Works—a machinery and foundry company and a producer of specialized machinery. A successful local businessman, William P. Allis, purchased the firm in 1861 and later renamed it the William P. Allis Company. The firm expanded and became well known for its ability to produce large machinery—particularly in support of the nearby lumber and flour industries.

The William P. Allis Company soon developed a distinctive business philosophy which emphasized excellence in engineering and efficiency of production. The buildings were flimsy, but the production equipment was first-rate, allowing the company to produce large-scale equipment such as pump engines, saw mills, flour mills, and other specialized machinery. One of the firm's primary technical accomplishments was the refinement of a huge band saw that, for most lumber-making operations, was both faster and far more efficient than the alternative technologies of the time. By the 1870s, the company had become a major manufacturer of stationary steam engines and gigantic blowing engines for use in the manufacture of steel. On the basis of these technologies, the firm then manufactured electrical generating equipment. In 1901, the William P. Allis Company acquired three other companies including the Frazer & Chalmers Works in Chicago. The name of the company was then changed to the Allis-Chalmers Company.

The Allis-Chalmers Company had considerable manufacturing prowess involving more than 3 million square feet of manufacturing space and some first-rate equipment. By 1906, the West Allis plant alone consisted of 1,416,000 square feet of floor space on 113 acres of land, and the firm had additional major plants in Chicago and Scranton, Pennsylvania.

Although a decade of technical accomplishment followed the formation of Allis-Chalmers, the company experienced difficulty in managing its business and entered receivership in 1912. A local successful business leader and a member of the German community of Milwaukee, General Otto Falk, acted as the company's receiver. Falk soon reorganized the company to improve efficiency and upgrade the training of company personnel. The company prospered as a quality manufacturer of specialized generators and other machinery. In order to utilize all of the company's huge manufacturing capacity, Otto Falk chartered the development of an Allis-Chalmers tractor, and by 1935, tractors and farm equipment accounted for more than half the company's sales. The innovative and practical designs of Allis-Chalmers agricultural products were especially appealing to medium- and small-scale farmers, and by the mid-1930s, Allis-Chalmers was quite comfortably established as one of the industry's most significant producers. By 1966, total Allis-Chalmers sales rose to $857 million, and the company became number 130 of the *Fortune* 500.

By the 1960s, however, the strains of being such a widely diversified manufacturer began to show. Although the company continued to be an innovator by building nuclear power plants, an experimental tractor powered by fuel cells, a popular low-cost hay baler, which featured more-weather-resistant round bales, and a line of tractors with power-shift wheels and other innovative products, profit rates were not high. From 1963 to 1966, net after-tax profit rates averaged 2.6 percent. In 1967, sales dropped by 4.3 percent but after-tax earnings declined by 81 percent.

During the mid-1960s, Allis-Chalmers became embroiled in a costly series of untimely hostile takeover attempts. The first company to express an interest in acquiring Allis-Chalmers was Ling-Temco-Vought, Inc., a company later renamed LTV—an active acquirer of many businesses during the 1960s, most of which it later sold. LTV filed for bankruptcy in 1986. But in 1967, the LTV offer was a traumatic event to Allis-Chalmers. Initially, talks were held with a rival merger candidate, General Dynamics. Later, Allis-Chalmers management decided to actively resist any takeover. With some help from the Wisconsin state government, and by filing a complaint against LTV, the CEO of LTV, James Ling, withdrew the offer to acquire Allis-Chalmers in August of 1967.

The LTV episode alerted the investment community to the possible undervalued financial condition of Allis-Chalmers, and other companies began to buy Allis-Chalmers stock. CEO Robert Stevenson then began to hold exploratory talks with other possible merger partners as a defense against further hostile takeovers. None of these discussions reached fruition, and in June of 1968, the Allis-Chalmers board of directors elected David G. Scott as president. A former executive of Colt Industries and General Electric, Scott was experienced in acquisition matters.

The takeover battles continued, with other companies involved. Ultimately, Allis-Chalmers prevailed, but the company began to experience operational problems—perhaps resulting from management's preoccupation with other issues. Peterson and Weber (1978) describe the situation as follows:

> Allis-Chalmers had many obsolete, inefficient plants; it was burdened with high labor costs for some products relative to its competitors, and its share of market and sales volume was insufficient in some areas to operate its plants efficiently or to invest in modern facilities. Salaried overhead was high, and the company feasted or starved in its capital goods markets. New technological developments which created sales opportunities required heavy investment and research expenditures. Finally, the company's reentry into steam turbines was devastated by new environmental and economic forces. (Peterson and Weber 1978, 397)

In 1968, revenues declined again from $821 million to $767 million. Gross profit declined as well to 6.4 percent. But, selling and general and administrative expenses rose from $100 million in 1967 to $131 million in 1968—in part due to additional reserves set aside by the new CEO. The company reported an after-tax loss of $55 million for the year, but the actual 1968 loss of $122 million was much greater than the reported loss because $60 million worth of future tax benefits resulting from the 1968 loss were booked into current profits (Bhattacharyya 1969). This unusual accounting treatment drew critical comment from the business press (*Fortune* 1969).

David Scott then took some initial steps to put the company in a more competitive position. He reduced total headcount by 8000 people, including a reduction of more than 1000 people in the headquarters staff. He also spent substantially on plant rearrangement. Some plants were decommissioned, at very high one-time costs, while new facilities were opened at the rate of about one per year. About $40 million per year was reportedly expended for capital improvements (Peterson and Weber 1978, 397).

Along the way, however, Allis-Chalmers became involved in a highly complicated series of acquisitions, divestitures, joint ventures, and special transactions with other companies, often foreign companies, which added

further ambiguity to the company's mission. These transactions are listed in
Table 10-5.

The lackluster performance of Allis-Chalmers continued in spite of the
aggressive diversification program. The company was only marginally
profitable in the years from 1969 to 1974, when profit rates ranged from 0.6
percent to 2.2 percent. During the same time period, Deere profits ranged
from 4.0 percent to 8.4 percent.

For a brief period from 1976 to 1979, earnings rose to record levels ($81
million in 1979) and profit rates approached average levels. The peak year
was 1977, with an after-tax profit rate of 4.36 percent. However, these were
also peak years for the other agricultural-equipment producers such as Deere
and International Harvester, which also enjoyed record earnings. By 1980,
however, the robust sales of the late 1970s had waned and Allis-Chalmers
experienced a 43 percent decline in earnings. By 1981, the company was
again operating at a loss of $28 million. By 1982, the loss grew to $207
million. The year 1983 was marginally less poor, with a loss of $142 million.
Things worsened again in 1984, with a loss of $261 million. An additional
$169 million loss occurred in 1985, and the company's net worth became
negative. In response to the severe losses of the 1980s, the company had to
sell off many of its better operations in order to raise cash or to realize capital
gains. Along the way, many workers were displaced, several facilities were
closed, and part of the savings was made at the expense of the company's
retirement fund. The company's auditors soberly inserted the following
excerpt in their qualified opinion of the 1985 operations of Allis-Chalmers:

Table 10-5. Allis-Chalmers Ownership Transactions,
1969–1981

Year	Transaction
1969	Write-down of assets of $124 million
1969	Sale of preferred stock to Fiat
1969	Acquired Standard Steel
1969	Acquired Lantz International
1972	Acquired Pennsylvania Electric Coil
1972	Acquired ACO Paulista S.A.
1974	Acquired Svedala-Arba
1974	Acquired Stephenson-Adamson
1974	Joint venture with J. M. Voith G.m.b.H
1975	Acquired Material Movement
1976	Acquired an electric motor repair shop
1977	Reduced equity in Fiat-Allis in exchange for Allis-Chalmers stock held by Fiat
1977	Acquired Clough Manufacturing
1977	Acquired Sala International of Sweden
1977	Acquired EMMISA of France
1978	Acquired American Air Filter
1979	Acquired Barron Industries
1980	Acquired Hartman Metal
1981	Purchased Houston Dynamic Service

As described in the Termination of Pension Plans note on pages 20 and 21, during 1985, the company terminated several pension plans having aggregate unfunded benefits of $170 million. As a result of these terminations, the Pension Benefit Guarantee Corporation may assert a claim for up to 30 percent of the company's net worth...(*Moodys* 1986)

From 1968 to 1985, Allis-Chalmers made 20 major acquisitions, joint-venture arrangements, or divestitures. In the process, the number of company employees declined from 33,500 in 1963 to 12,000 in 1985, and has declined further since. A total of 29 manufacturing plants were sold or closed in the downsizing of Allis-Chalmers (Allis-Chalmers Corporation Annual Report 1985).

Allis-Chalmers' workers were concerned about the viability of the company long before the problems became public and were frustrated with their inability to engage in meaningful dialogue regarding resolution of the problems. Representatives of the United Auto Workers eagerly sought a meeting with David Scott. Finally, after several months, word arrived that Scott would be at the next meeting. He was, but in the form of a videotape. Understandably, worker representatives were somewhat underwhelmed with the prospect of dialoguing with a videotape.

In contrast to the close association with workers enjoyed by Charles Nash and Walter Chrysler, David Scott fostered an air of remoteness in dealing with the organization of Allis-Chalmers, as typified by the special entrance enabling him to reach his office without passing by either workers or company operations. At year end 1985, David C. Scott retired as the CEO of Allis-Chalmers Corporation, and his successor, Wendel Bueche, set about to salvage what was left of a company that at one time was a respected and innovative producer of technically advanced special machinery and practical farm equipment. The dramatic changes Allis-Chalmers experienced from 1967 to 1985 are summarized in Table 10-6.

Allis-Chalmers was almost systematically managed downward. Although the company was not a substantial profit maker in the early 1960s, it was at least profitable and it did enjoy the reputation of a technically respected producer of special-purpose machinery and farm equipment. Allis-Chalmers has since completely exited these two industries; it filed for bankruptcy in 1987. Most of its plants have been sold or closed, and the site of the once-mighty West

Table 10-6. Allis-Chalmers Corporation, 1967 and 1985

	1967	1985
Revenue (in current $000)	821,765	886,064
Revenue in 1988$ ($000)	2,577,760	953,167
Profits ($000)	5,002	(169,383)
Profits in 1988$ ($000)	15,690	(182,211)
Stockholder Equity ($000)	360,000	(22,625)
Equity in 1988$ ($000)	1,129,235	(24,338)

Allis plant now houses a K-Mart. Stockholders' equity has become substantially negative. The number of employees is minuscule compared to what it was at peak levels. Retired employees now find that their pension fund is in dispute, and it is clear that either the workers or the U.S. taxpayers will lose the money. The largest employer in the state of Wisconsin is gone.

The demise of Allis-Chalmers did not have to happen. Along the way the management of the company focused on acquisitions, restructuring, joint ventures, divestitures, accounting manipulations, and a variety of other activities not central to producing differentiated products at the lowest cost. Management's preoccupation with unrelated issues weakened the company's rapport with its employees. Had Allis-Chalmers focused its energies on reducing cost, product differentiation, and fair play with employees, creditors, suppliers, and customers, the company might still be a major producer in its major markets (Figure 10-2).

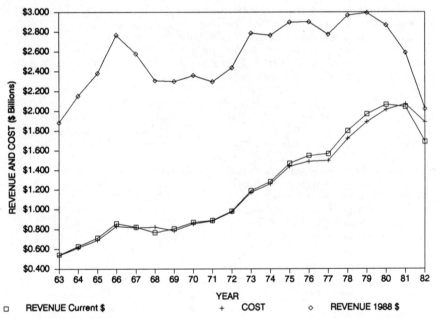

Figure 10-2. Allis-Chalmers' real revenue and cost. As is the case with many companies during periods of inflation, Allis-Chalmers continued to post record sales and earnings when revenue was static or declining in real terms. In reality, aggressive strategic measures instituted by Allis-Chalmers management were not working. By 1985, real revenue had declined to 40 percent of the levels of the 1960s and stockholders' equity had become negative. The company later filed for bankruptcy.

Allis-Chalmers Failed Because...

- Top managers lacked experience in the industry being served.

- Management did not focus on day-to-day operational matters.

- Management diversified into new and unfamiliar ventures while neglecting familiar markets.

- Product differentiation was not sustained.

- Too much money was spent on items unrelated to what the customer was buying.

- Top management appeared to be uninterested in either the company's main products or the people who designed, sold, and produced them.

11
Focusing on Present Operations

An experienced professional football coach once remarked that it was embarrassing to lose to the Green Bay Packers under Vince Lombardi because they had only six plays. In ways similar to Lombardi's Packers, successful turnaround agents focus attention on the basics—blocking and tackling. They center the company's attention on the business it is in at the time, and they scorn diversions. They focus on operational issues such as improving the product, reducing production cost, and improving product quality and customer service. They do this daily, not weekly or monthly or during planning periods. Habits, gestures, memorandums, and meetings focus on immediate events. Planning tends to be, as Robert Hayes (1985) says it should be, an incremental extension of today's small steps rather than a grand plan long into the future.

Unsuccessful turnaround agents often lack sufficient understanding of their business to manage operations in a detailed way. They may pressure their sales organizations for higher sales without understanding that variable costs may be higher than prices. They tend to have meager knowledge of both products and production processes and therefore miss the potential that superior performance in these areas can have for enhancing performance. They are inclined to spend more time in meetings discussing overall corporate strategy and less time with customers or key employees in the operating units in search of incremental improvements. They have a great propensity to make deals to get into new businesses or get out of old businesses without any deep understanding of what is required to have any of these businesses operate profitably. The planning logic appears to be, if we can't manage what we've got, we had better manage something else.

Why companies in dire straits choose to dissipate scarce resources in oblique activities remains a mystery. There is plenty to do just to keep the business functioning, and most companies in trouble have imperfections that need to be remedied in order to restore health. The activities that really count are making better products, selling, gaining cooperation with vendors, training staff, and collecting money. Successful managers spend time in performing these tasks, and they are careful to continue performing them.

In one instance, a *Fortune* 500 company was grappling with profit problems in an operation that was later dismantled after losing tens of millions of dollars. At that time, the division was losing roughly a million dollars a month. Morale was low, and the decision was made to sponsor a company necktie to improve morale. That might have been a suitable project if it had taken 5 minutes. But, practical obstacles surfaced. For instance, the necktie manufacturer was located in Hong Kong, and the matter became an international transaction. Also, necktie styles were changing and an internal debate broke out as to how wide the necktie should be. The project dragged on and on, month after month, and while losses mounted, the necktie matter was featured at divisional staff meetings. It was ridiculous, and company management suffered an enormous loss of respect for these and other diversionary actions.

Companies in trouble must focus on what needs to be done. Management cannot afford to spend time on vague global concepts or unrelated trivial issues. This need to focus begins with company ideals but affects strategic planning, decision making, and organizational change.

Focus on Needs in Turnarounds

Clearly Defined Ideals and Executive Responsibility

The superiority of flourishing companies begins with ideals and is reinforced by executive responsibility. The ideals of successful firms are easily understood basic concepts that emphasize service to the community. An example might be Du Pont's slogan: "Better things for better living through chemistry." Note that it is specific, not open-ended, and it implies community well-being as an objective. Unsuccessful companies' ideals are often less specific and usually espouse objectives rather than service. Compare the Du Pont statement with the "strategic evolution" of

Allis-Chalmers, which had as its objective to "redeploy our assets and investments for efficient utilization and worldwide optimization" (Allis-Chalmers 1985).

Harrington Emerson (1960) listed "clearly defined ideals" as the first of his 12 principles of efficiency. In turnaround work, it is especially important for members of the organization to understand the mission of the company and its reason for existence. Philip Selznick (1957) noted that the ideals of the company become "institutionalized" as a step in the development of leadership. As a practical matter, when the difficulties of an organization are intense, members of the organization need an important, noble purpose in which to believe.

In the case of American Motors in the 1950s, the noble purpose was the building of a high-quality practical compact car that did not consume so many natural resources. In the case of Chrysler, it was the survival of the American industrial system against the onslaught of imports. In the case of Deere, it was building durable products with low-cost operation for use by the wellspring of American wealth—agriculture.

People involved in turning a company around need something to get excited about. They need ideals. These ideals must be clearly understood by organization members. Reinforcement of these ideals can come from any level in the organization.

Lew Veraldi of Ford provides a meaningful example of clarity in the promotion of ideals. An arm-waving, foot-stomping, gregarious Italian with a big heart and a huge sense of responsibility, he would emit sparks if development projects were not proceeding with sufficient dispatch to ward off foreign competition. If they were, however, he was all heart and quite willing to note how individual accomplishments fulfilled the Taurus/Sable mission. As one seasoned Ford manager noted: "I don't think anyone was ever confused about what Veraldi wanted."

Good leaders can cultivate ideals, but the leaders must be believable as individuals and appear to be operating within their own framework of idealism. With the special tensions of a turnaround situation, the individual managers have to be perceived as fair, honest, and appreciative of the need to integrate the goals of the organization with those of the individual (Follett 1941). If the leaders receive excessive personal compensation or indulge in superfluous ostentation, the organization is likely to think that the leaders do not believe in "the cause."

This link between ideals and the personal credibility of the leader was recognized by Chester Barnard in his concept of the "zone of indifference," which theorized that members of the organization will grant to executives some considerable range of operating freedom. March and Simon (1963) referred to this same concept as the "zone of acceptance."

Barnard added another thought that is often overlooked in human relations within organizations. What matters is how all people and all stakeholders are treated — not necessarily how the specific individual is treated. It doesn't matter who the victim is. People will use how others are treated as an index of how they will be treated. Barnard was very interested in the effect that opportunism could have on an executive's ability to mobilize the organization. He addressed this in two chapters, "The Theory of Opportunism" and "The Nature of Executive Responsibility," in *The Functions of the Executive*. The following quote is indicative:

> Executive responsibility, then, is that capacity of leaders by which, reflecting attitudes, ideals, hopes, derived largely from without themselves, they are compelled to bind the wills of men to the accomplishment of purposes beyond their immediate ends, beyond their times. Even when these purposes are lowly and the time is short, the transitory efforts of men become a part of that organization of living forces that transcends man unaided by man; but when these purposes are high and the wills of many men and many generations are bound together, they live boundlessly. (Barnard 1953, 283–284)

Ideals and executive responsibility frame the discipline system so essential to a focus on present operations.

Strategic Planning

David Scott of Allis-Chalmers and Charles Nash of the Jeffery turnaround approached strategic planning in opposite ways. Scott examined the profitability trends in different business segments and then attempted to veer the company toward arenas of perceived opportunity. Nash looked at the business he was in and tried to find ways his firm could do better. For Scott, strategic management meant working out a new joint venture, selling off an old business, or buying a new one. Nash's idea of strategic management is reflected in the subject matter of his meetings. He began the meetings, which often involved whoever wanted to attend from the plant work force, by reading aloud any letters of complaint from customers and then asking for suggestions to keep the problems from happening again. The second item of discussion was how the company could improve its efficiency and be more cost-effective. The third item was how the company could utilize some of the savings from the efficiencies just discussed to make a better-quality product. Nash continued this focused practice for the years during which the firm progressed from being a minor player in the industry to a leader in innovation, inventory management, and profitability (Brown 1981). With similar focus, George Romney engineered the American Motors turnaround of the 1950s and Henry Leland guided the reconstruction of Cadillac. Few successful turnaround agents spend much time on general strategic planning.

With respect to the markets they entered, successful firms also more accurately gauged their ability to fully implement their strategic plans. Unsuccessful firms often had strategic plans that were internally inconsistent—such as expansion plans that outran finances or a low-priced car being marketed by a high-cost producer, as happened with Willys-Overland, Kaiser, and Hudson. Successful firms developed internally consistent plans which more realistically considered the firm's resources. Often, they modified strategies to consider the firm's resources in physical as well as financial terms. An example occurred with the design of the first Chrysler car when managers determined that the Chalmers factory was not equipped to efficiently manufacture an overhead-valve engine, so an L-head engine was produced instead.

The literature on strategic planning is long and reflective. One of the best definitions of strategy was provided by Igor Ansoff (1965): *Strategy* is the act of matching the firm to its environment. This paraphrase is a fitting description of the strategic planning process in turnarounds.

In a *Harvard Business Review* article entitled "Strategic Planning—Forward in Reverse," Robert Hayes (1985) noted that an incremental approach leads to an improved strategic system because the strategy is tested sequentially as it is being developed. Hayes suggests that the traditional ends-ways-means logic of planning should be reversed. Instead of concentrating on end objectives first and then determining what methods, resources, and procedures are required to obtain the objectives, companies should critically examine their current methods and resources first and then see what research and development activities would best complement the present resources. Since a feedback loop is involved, the ability does exist to modify the present situation in order to meet a more attractive set of objectives. The successful turnaround consists of incremental steps to improve the effectiveness of the organization one day at a time.

Styles of Decision Making in the Turnaround Process

A seasoned expert remarked that "anyone can manage if they have the facts," and, indeed, facts are seldom plentiful in turnaround situations. Yet, the need for decision making does not change. The turnaround manager is often forced by circumstance to make decisions with something less than full information. Mintzberg (1978) described three different modes of decision making: planning (analytical), adaptive (political), and entrepreneurial (intuitive). He suggested that these three modes are often intermixed at different levels in the organization and at different stages in the organization's development. Kilmann and Mitroff (1976) proposed that information gathering and decision making employ qualitative as well as quantitative analyses along two scales: thinking versus feeling and sensation versus intuition. Their theory held that it is through the interaction of these qualitative and quantitative forces that the decision-making process takes place. Bibeault (1982, 372) also found that intuition was a common style of decision making in troubled situations in his 1978 survey of 81 turnaround company chief executives. In response to the question, "Were the major turnaround moves accomplished according to a formal plan or mostly by intuitive management action?" the responses were "intuitive action first = 19.3%; intuitive action followed by formal plan = 50.6%, and formal plan followed by implementation = 30.1%."

One obvious question, however, is, how informed is the intuition? Intuition in the hands of competent individuals with extensive experience in a related industry is one thing. Intuition in the hands of rank amateurs is quite another. March and Simon (1963) developed the theory of "bounded rationality" and thereby delineated a lack of exposure which can surface in turnaround environments. Practitioners can make intuitive decisions outside the boundaries of their rationality (their domain). They may depend too much upon intuition and present knowledge and not enough upon experience and required knowledge. This is the fundamental dilemma for turnaround agents needing to make difficult decisions. Time pressures may create an inclination to use intuition outside the manager's domain, the province over which one's experience is functional. Intuition amortized over a very small domain usually leads to unfavorable results during a time of crisis. For these reasons, the effective turnaround manager will wish to complement intuition with knowledge exploration.

Knowledge Exploration

Knowledge exploration is a concept difficult to measure, but meaningful to the study of turnarounds, and can briefly be described as a systematic appraisal that has to be made regarding what information is necessary (as opposed to what is available) in order to make a proper decision. The key elements of this necessary information are actively sought. In his description of "the program planning model," Andrew Van de Ven (1980) explained that this necessary step of "knowledge exploration" is key to effective decision making.

Decision making in unsuccessful firms is frequently too intuitive and insufficiently grounded in fact. Successful firms are more studious about obtaining the information necessary for good decisions. The successful companies arranged to gather, or to know, that information which was critical to the making of key strategic decisions. Unsuccessful firms frequently had significant gaps in their information flows and tended to make decisions mostly on what information was available rather than on the basis of what information was needed. Forecasting and market information was particularly lacking at International Harvester, Studebaker-Packard, Willys-Overland, and Kaiser. The unfortunate decisions made on the basis of inaccurate but available information were very costly to the firms involved and contributed to their demise.

The depth and relevance of the background of key turnaround agents are other factors in the usefulness of the intuition as it is applied to the decision-making process. The intuition needs to be specifically experienced rather than general or amateurish. In addition, professional analysis, usually involving data external to the firm, should be performed as part of the intuitive process.

Organizational Change

Incremental Changes

Gradual and consistent incremental improvement was the operative style in place during the successful turnarounds. Improvements were made one day at a time by improving one thing at a time. The Monday afternoon meetings of Charles Nash are a case in point. Great changes in corporate strategy were not discussed at these meetings. What was discussed were any letters of complaint from either dealers or customers and ideas presented by employees as to how the product could be made less expensively and how quality could be improved. Gradual, incremental improvements turned Deere's unsatisfactory Model GP tractor into the highly successful models A and B, which had production runs of more than 20 years. Gradual incremental changes were made at American Motors under Romney, at Cadillac under the Lelands, and at the Japanese companies today.

The practice of incremental change extended far beyond product changes. Incremental changes aided the process of organizational learning as old values were used as a foundation for new beliefs (Quinn

1980). Change resistance (Tichy 1983) was more fully understood by the successful turnaround agents. More of an appreciation was shown for the positive contributions of people who may have been a part of the organization at the time problems developed.

In contrast, the unsuccessful firms made many abrupt, drastic changes in plant location, markets served, products, and members of managerial teams. Examples of nonincremental change are the substantial infusion of Continental Can and Xerox management into International Harvester, or Kaiser's invasion of the unfamiliar low-priced car market, or the failure of AMC/Renault to provide follow-up on products for historical markets. Other examples might be the changing of the Packard assembly plant or the aggressive acquisition of unfamiliar businesses by Allis-Chalmers.

Incremental change is the long-established process of testing small operational improvements as a part of the process of continual organizational improvement. In their classic book *Organizations,* March and Simon (1963) describe in detail the cognitive limits to the rational model of decision making and also put forth some cogent arguments for why an incremental approach is necessary and practical:*

> An individual can attend to only a limited number of things at a time....Rational behavior involves substituting for the complex reality a model of reality that is sufficiently simple to be handled by problem solving processes....
>
> A large complex task is broken down into a sequence of smaller tasks, the conjunction of which adds up to the accomplishment of the larger. The factorization of a large task can be more elaborate for an organization than for an individual, but the underlying reason is the same: the definition of the situation at any one moment must be sufficiently simple to be encompassed by the human mind. (March and Simon 1963, 151–152)

At the root of the need for incremental change is the fact that insecurity and uncertainty permeate the troubled organization. Confidence is usually low. If too many things change too quickly, two problems develop. First, people in the organization lose their orientation, and they may respond with behavior that is neither predictable nor constructive. Second, they may simply get confused about what to do. Bibeault puts it another way in his book *Corporate Turnaround:*

> In all probability, you will not have all of the facts, or, in the organization's seasoned eyes, the seasoned judgment to take on all matters of policy and industry practice in the first month or two. Making

*Reprinted with permission from James G. March and Herbert A. Simon, *Organizations,* Wiley, New York, 1963.

premature decisions increases the likelihood of making erroneous decisions. At best, you will be viewed as a meddler. At worst, you'll rupture the normal chains of command and confuse the organization. (Bibeault 1982, 178)

By keenly focusing on day-to-day operational matters and by constantly making small incremental changes for the better, the wise manager builds team confidence and gradually builds competitive strength. Old values provide a useful and effective base for the building of new values.

Bringing about Change

Obviously, turnarounds involve some changes in the manner in which the firm conducts its business, and some of these may need to be quite major changes. Yet, as experienced managers know, concluding that changes are necessary is quite a different matter than getting things to actually change. We can benefit from the contributions that others have made in examining successful changes under turbulent conditions.

Tushman and Romanelli (1985) have proposed a "punctuated equilibrium" model of organizational evolution wherein organizations progress through convergent periods of minimal change punctuated by reorientations involving more change. These reorientations set the directions for the next convergent period. Convergent periods may be quite long. Reorientations tend to be relatively short periods of discontinuity during which power, structure, and systems are realigned to adapt more readily to the newly perceived environment.

Pettigrew (1985) found a similar need for change interspersed by stabilization when he examined the practical aspects of implementing change in large, and often older, organizations. He observed that the implementation of change was a longer-term process interlaced with political behavior and organizational behavior. Pettigrew divides an effective change process into five steps:

1. Problem sensing
2. The development of concern
3. The acknowledgment and understanding of the problem
4. Planning and action
5. Stabilizing the change(s)

In his book about Imperial Chemical Industries, *An Awakening Giant*, Pettigrew describes the ineffectiveness of moving from step 1 (problem sensing) to step 4 (planning and action), without deliberately taking the time to cultivate step 2 (the development of concern) and step 3 (the acknowledgment and understanding of the problem).

Pettigrew's analysis, however, is far more thought-provoking and subtle than a mere caution against proceeding too quickly. Rather, it is a scholarly treatise concerning the workings of organizational change within organizations that need to change very much. Several points warrant additional comment. First, it is not necessarily true that the need to change will be acknowledged even by those individuals who will be most adversely affected if changes are not made. Second, analysis is a necessary part of formulating the turnaround strategy. This analysis needs to be thought-provoking and should involve new information. A systematic appraisal has to be made regarding what few facts have to be either known for certain (rarely) or interpolated (often) in order to make a proper decision as described by the "knowledge exploration" step advanced by Van de Ven.

Noel Tichy (1983) describes three sets of dynamic forces that influence the ease with which changes can be introduced. These forces are:*

1. Technical resistant forces
   a. Resistance due to habit
   b. Resistance due to fear of the unknown
   c. Resistance due to absence of skills
   d. Resistance due to organizational predictability
   e. Resistance due to sunk costs
2. Political resistant forces
   a. Resistance due to need for power
   b. Resistance due to overdependence on others
   c. Resistance due to competition for power
   d. Resistance due to threats to powerful coalitions
   e. Resistance due to sunk costs
   f. Resistance due to resource limitations
3. Cultural resistant forces
   a. Resistance due to selective perception (cultural filters)
   b. Resistance due to values and beliefs
   c. Resistance due to security by regression to past
   d. Resistance due to conformity by norms
   e. Resistance due to climate for change

The accomplishment of essential change is one of the most pressing tasks of the turnaround agent. To deal with the many aspects of resis-

*Reprinted with permission from Noel M. Tichy, *Managing Strategic Change: Technical, Political and Cultural Dynamics*, Wiley, New York, 1983.

tance, the turnaround agent must be an effective teacher using old values as a foundation in order to reduce cultural resistance to change. New ways of achieving objectives must be taught with technical credibility as well as managerial credibility in order to further reduce change resistance. Negotiating skills are indispensable in order to weave a workable pattern through the forces of political resistance.

Power

Power can influence the change process, and some turnaround agents have a great deal more power than others. French and Raven (1959) described the five bases of power:

1. Reward power, whereby the influencer has the ability to reward another person.
2. Coercive power, whereby the influencer has the ability to punish others.
3. Legitimate power, which corresponds to a concept of authority or legally granted power.
4. Expert power, based on the perceived special knowledge of the influencer.
5. Referent power, which is accrued to the influencer because others desire to imitate the influencer.

The amount of power the turnaround agent has depends in part upon the personal history and characteristics of the individual and the circumstances surrounding how he or she arrived on the scene. If the individual is considered to be competent in certain products or processes or is especially skilled in dealing with difficult situations, the expert power may be great. If the individual has full authority from financial backers or owners, reward (or coercive) power may be great. When Walter Chrysler arrived at Maxwell, for instance, he possessed a broad base of power involving expert power, coercive power, referent power, and legitimate power. Though Harold Churchill at Studebaker was probably a good manager, he was unfortunately endowed with a much narrower power base, which contributed to his much shorter stay as chairman. Some measure of power is often necessary to bring the change process through to fruition.

Acquisitions

Acquisitions are very time-consuming and distracting events. The literature on acquisitions generally suggests that the yields accrue to the seller. Whether a firm should, or should not, acquire other firms is not the issue here. The issue is whether acquisitions are helpful to the turnaround process. The successful companies made very few acquisitions of any consequence, and several acquisitions, such as Chrysler's foray into aerospace, probably hindered success much more than they helped. Several unsuccessful firms made acquisitions, and generally they did not work out either. In the cases studied here, the inclination of successful turnaround managers to concentrate on managing the present business versus looking to new areas is reflected in their general disinterest in diversification. Acquisitions played almost no role at all in the turnarounds of any of the successful companies. The merger of Nash and Hudson to form American Motors occurred during year −2 of the first American Motors turnaround, and the assumption of Hudson liabilities may have hurt Nash. The acquisition of Dodge by Chrysler Corporation came 7 years after the Maxwell-Chalmers period of crisis, and after the firm had enjoyed several years of profits in excess of 10 percent and a quadrupling of market share. The Dodge firm was offered to Chrysler Corporation because a banking syndicate had problems managing the company in a consistent manner, not because Chrysler was actively seeking acquisitions.

Nor did divestitures play much of a role with the successful companies. There were some consolidation efforts by Storrow, Nash, and Chrysler when they were with GM, but they focused mostly on operating efficiently or they simply stopped producing certain products. There was little interest in either buying or selling portions of the business.

In contrast, the unsuccessful turnaround agents were almost frenetic about changing the company's mission. From 1968 to 1985, Allis-Chalmers made 20 major acquisitions, joint-venture arrangements, or divestitures. In the process, the number of company employees declined from 33,500 in 1963 to 12,000 in 1987, when the firm entered bankruptcy.

Practical Lessons in Focusing on Present Operations

- Strategic planning at successful companies is rudimentary and near-term. The focus is on operational issues such as improving the product, reducing production cost, and improving product quality and customer service.

- Successful turnaround leaders center the company's attention on the business it is in at the time, and they scorn diversions. Acquisitions, divestitures, diversifications schemes, and new ventures attract very little attention.

- Planning at successful companies tends to be an incremental extension of today's small steps rather than a grand plan long into the future. Unsuccessful turnaround leaders are more inclined to forecast the future, but their forecasts are often wrong.

- Ideals play more of a role at successful companies. People at companies in trouble need something to get excited about. Unsuccessful companies are unexciting.

- Old values and old beliefs form the basis for new beliefs at successful companies. Unsuccessful companies often discard the past, thereby denying senior organization members a sense of pride.

- Change is introduced both continuously and sporadically at successful companies. Incremental improvements are made constantly. Radical changes are made less frequently and are interspersed by period of stabilization.

Case Histories

The two cases selected for this chapter involve the same company but 20 years apart. The Packard Motor Car Company turnaround of the 1930s was a masterfully executed example of strategic planning, thorough implementation, and incremental improvement. Twenty years later, under different leadership, the same company flitted from one manufacturing plant to another, from one corporate structure to another, from one chief executive to another, and from one strategy to another until finally two of the most prominent names in the history of the auto industry went out of business. It did not have to happen. The Studebaker-Packard turnaround of the 1950s lacked the attention to detail, the consistency, and the focus on operations that characterized earlier efforts.

Case 14
Cars for the Methodists at Packard

During the prosperous period of the late 1920s, the Packard Motor Car Company sold more than half of U.S. high-priced motor cars. Profits were enormous—sometimes more than 20 percent of sales. The company had achieved what was perhaps the most extensive product differentiation in the industry, owing to a solid reputation for high product quality, advanced engineering, distinctive styling, and refined manufacturing processes including the very sophisticated heat treatment of metals. The strong technical capabilities of the company enabled it to obtain business as a defense contractor in addition to its profitable automobile business. Packard engineers designed the most important aircraft engine of World War I, the Liberty, of which nearly 20,000 were produced. Packard also produced marine engines and a highly reputable line of trucks.

Packard's strong tradition of engineering excellence and product quality dated back to before the turn of the century, when James Ward Packard chose to build his own car after experiencing unsatisfactory performance from his Winton. The early Packards had interesting features including an automatic spark advance and a modern-style sliding-gear transmission. The cars were also reliable; in 1903, a Packard Model F was driven from San Francisco to New York. In 1904, a new four-cylinder Packard Model K set a new 1-mile speed record of 77.6 miles per hour. Packards of this era were fine, quality cars for the day, and their reputation soon spread. Instead of relying on artistic promotional literature, the firm confidently adopted the slogan "Ask the man who owns one."

The two Packard brothers, James Ward Packard and William Dowd Packard, had another business which survives today as Packard Electric, so their primary interest did not remain in automobiles. They soon enlisted a partner, Detroit business leader Henry B. Joy. By 1902, the firm had moved from Warren, Ohio, to Detroit and into a modern factory designed by Alfred Kahn, later the designer of many of the Ford assembly plants. The assets of product quality and good engineering were then combined with some of the industry's most efficient manufacturing facilities. Packard sales and production grew, and by 1906, production exceeded 1000 four-cylinder units. By 1911, Packard was producing six-cylinder cars in the $4000 to $7000 price range, and in 1915, the firm startled the industry with the announcement of an advanced V-12 engine called the *Twin-Six*. The Packard Twin-Six sold well and helped to establish the company as the technical leader in the high-priced field. By 1923, Packard registrations reached 13,382. By 1927, registrations rose to 31,355 very expensive automobiles.

During the 1920s, Packard consolidated and strengthened its position in the high-priced market where the Packard automobile was widely recognized as one of the most prestigious marques in the world. The accompanying comparison of 1929 registrations illustrates the relative significance of Packard versus other manufacturers in the high-priced field.

1929 Registrations	
Packard	44,634
Cadillac	14,936
Pierce Arrow	8,386
Peerless	8,318
Lincoln	6,115

During the 1920s, the company made huge profits. Although Packard's physical unit market share was modest, the automobiles sold for very high prices—often 10 times the price of a Ford and 4 times the price of a Buick. The firm was in excellent financial condition; after-tax profit rates often approached 20 percent of revenue.

But the depression dealt harshly with Packard in two ways: the absolute size of the luxury market was severely reduced, and many people who could afford a luxury car were reluctant to flaunt their prosperity. Packard continued to be a strong force in the high priced market, but between 1929 and 1932, this market declined by close to 90 percent. Packard sales tailed off with the market, and by 1934, Packard sold only 6552 units. This represented a more than 85 percent decline from 1929 levels.

During the mid-1930s, Packard and Packard dealers lost money for several years running. Though the Packard motor cars of this era were among the most distinctive automobiles ever produced, the number of Packard dealers had declined from 900 in 1930 to 500 in 1933 (*Fortune* 1937, 43). The financial figures for those years are shown in Table 11-1.

Packard's chief executive since 1916 had been Alvin Macauley. Macauley was educated as an engineer and patent attorney and joined National Cash Register in this capacity early in his career. He was formal but personable and practical, and his potent interest in mechanics led him to spend most of his time in the factory and the experimental shop improving the inventions that came before him. In time, his interests in product development gained him an important engineering position at the Burroughs Adding Machine

Table 11-1. Packard Registrations, Revenue, Profits, and Unit Market Share, 1926–1941

	Registrations	Revenue ($000)	Profits ($000)	Unit market share, %
1926	29,588	77,364	13,207	0.74
1927	31,355	71,659	9,831	1.02
1928	42,961	94,677	19,198	1.07
1929	44,634	107,542	21,695	0.93
1930	28,318	57,690	9,034	0.97
1931	16,256	29,987	(2,909)	0.79
1932	11,058	15,517	(6,824)	0.93
1933	9,081	19,230	107	0.55
1934	6,552	17,315	(7,291)	0.29
1935	37,653	49,967	3,316	1.11
1936	68,772	73,053	7,053	1.81
1937	95,455	109,572	3,052	2.35
1938	49,163	50,655	(1,618)	2.30
1939	62,005	75,560	546	2.08
1940	73,794	82,242	774	1.94
1941	69,653	115,319	2,061	1.78

Company. Later, he was made responsible for that company's production. In 1910, he left Burroughs to become General Manager of Packard, then a producer of 2000 cars per year. With him, he brought an enterprising young tool and die maker, Jesse Vincent, who emerged as one of the most reputable engine designers of all time (Forbes 1972, 178–192).

Under the leadership of Macauley and Vincent, Packard improved its product development program and the efficiency and quality of its production. The company formalized and organized duties. It provided "Packard principles" and "Packard standards" to guide the organization on matters relating to operating procedures and product quality. The company was also somewhat paternalistic. Packard treated its employees well but encouraged particular character traits such as a good work ethic and individual sobriety. President Macauley was strongly against drink.

Macauley accepted the declining nature of the luxury car market with grace and resolved to adapt to the changing times. In 1933, he gathered his managers together and with great professionalism and decorum he proclaimed:

> Gentlemen, our company has an Episcopalian reputation. And, it is time we do business with the Methodists. (*Fortune* 1937, 44)

The managers of Packard then began to implement one of the most structurally difficult turnarounds in the history of the automobile business. It involved the simultaneous penetration of new and old markets, a radical change in the production system, a blending of new cultural values with old, a revitalizing of the dealer network, and a whole new family of products.

In the 1920s, Packard management recognized the likelihood that the then-burgeoning high-priced market might not endure forever. Packard developed a Light Eight, which made its debut in 1932, as a lower-priced car than those Packard had offered previously. Although it was a well-engineered, quality automobile, Packard's manufacturing facilities and methods were not appropriate to a new-product offering in the upper-medium-priced field. Packard needed a radically new approach to manufacturing products for this new market.

To accomplish this transition, Alvin Macauley imported one of General Motors' most reputable production people, George Christopher, who had formerly headed production at Pontiac. With Macauley's permission, Christopher gutted the old body plant, bought some additional equipment, and laid out one of the most efficient plants in the industry at the time. Packard's fastest production workers were transferred to the new plant, while the most meticulous remained at the senior plant.

The product which emerged from the new plant and succeeded the Light Eight was called the *Packard 120*. It was still a quality automobile but in the high-medium-price category. The styling of the car was distinctly Packard, and some of the engineering features were later utilized by higher-priced models. Yet, the Model 120 sold for approximately one-third the price of the Super Eight and one-fourth the price of the Packard Twelve. Later it was joined by two more models in the midrange price class: the Packard 115 and the Packard 110.

In support of the medium-priced car strategy, Packard painstakingly rebuilt its dealer network to meet the higher-volume marketing requirements of the new car. To do this, Macauley selected a hard-driving, brash New Yorker whose personal image was somewhat out of character with the patrician reputation of Packard. But Max Gillman could sell cars and, in spite of his brusque manner, was actually well groomed in the Packard tradition, having been associated with the firm since 1919. He was known locally for his attention to business and his cold realism as reflected in the most famous Gillman quote: "Ya, I've read Babbitt. So what?" (*Fortune* 1937, 43).

Packard had always had good relations with its dealers and fostered several industry innovations including:

1. A uniform accounting system
2. An allied real estate business that enabled the dealers to enjoy good business locations
3. Frequent newsletters and personal contacts with the members of Packard management including Macauley
4. Special discounts to liquidate year-end inventories
5. A special program on spare parts which allowed certain parts to be available only from Packard dealers

Gillman used the foundation of these good relationships and the new Packard products to build the number of dealers from 500 in 1933 to 1980 (1700 in the United States and 280 overseas) by 1937. Packard needed to develop another skill in order to implement its turnaround: the selling of other models of used cars. During the 1920s, 80 percent of Packard trade-ins were other Packards. During the mid-1930s, as the company gained market share, 65 percent of trade-ins were other makes (*Fortune* 1937, 47). To accomplish this conversion, Macauley recruited another GM manager, Bill Packer, an individual especially knowledgeable in the practical problem of handling step-up sales. The company also expanded its installment sales program. Previously, most Packard customers had paid cash.

With detailed attention to product development, production efficiency, marketing, and short-term sales performance, the Packard 120 was a success. Packard production for the Twelfth Series (mid-1934 to mid-1935) grew to almost 32,000, of which approximately 25,000 were 120s (Table 11-1).

However, Macauley was not so naive as to neglect old markets as he pursued the new. The senior Packards continued to be produced with great care. After all, they had earned the company an after-tax profit rate of more than 20 percent in 1929. The majestic Super Eights and Packard Twelves of the 1930s were among the most prestigious automobiles in the world at the time. Packard management reasoned that a viable medium-priced car would help rebuild the Packard dealer network, which would also sell the highly profitable senior models. A key element of Macauley's strategy was that Packard remain the market leader of the lucrative luxury automobile market.

The strategy of parallel marketing of both junior and senior Packards worked especially well during the middepression years. Senior Packards of this era were marvelous machines, and almost all are full classics today. Packard even pioneered the development of air conditioning—first offered in 1938. The Packard Twelves continued to outsell the Cadillac V12s and V16s of the period by a substantial margin. The Super Eights also continued to be automobiles of high distinction.

But, the depression continued. The severe economic contraction of 1938 sharply lowered auto sales and again reduced the size of the luxury market. For a relatively small producer like Packard, it became increasingly difficult to fund the production of several distinct models of automobiles. Intense competition emerged within the company for the funding that was available. George Christopher, who later became president of Packard, did not grasp the marketing subtleties Macauley did, and support for the senior Packards gradually began to decline. With this came a corresponding decline in profitability and a limitation of the company's potential to attract people to the Packard showrooms. However, Packard remained a significant producer and a reputable defense contractor.

After World War II, the market for automobiles turned around and became a seller's market. Packard built some fine cars after World War II, but they did not carry the distinction of earlier Packards. The prestigious senior Packards would probably have sold well during this postwar period and no doubt would have added profits. But Packard's leadership had changed, and Packard's main competitors were now Buick, DeSoto, Hudson, and Chrysler. Packard was no longer a low-cost producer in comparison with this new competition, and without the senior Packards providing an umbrella of prestige, the products were not sufficiently differentiated. The company fell far short of its full potential. Management changed again. A former GM president, Charles E. Wilson, then secretary of defense, pulled the defense contracts. An inappropriate acquisition of Studebaker, the unnecessary and expensive development of the Ultramatic automatic transmission, an ill-timed move to a different manufacturing plant, and a tardy development of the V8 were all managerial mistakes that the firm made in later years. Finally, the last of the once-glorious Packards were produced with Studebaker bodies in 1958.

Still, the Packard turnaround of the 1930s is perhaps one of the most ambitious. In order for the turnaround to be effective, Packard had to develop new products to match the market, it had to restructure its distribution system, establish an entirely new production system, set up financing programs, and create trade-in remarketing systems. Considering its encompassing nature, the Packard turnaround of the 1930s was indeed a major accomplishment.

It also had some familiar aspects. The leading characters were technically competent. Products were highly differentiated. Costs were systematically lowered and controlled. Old values and old products were retained and appreciated as new products and values were cultivated. Product quality was paramount and proceeded from traditional morality and discipline. Mostly, however, it was a turnaround of intense focus on present operations (Figure 11-1).

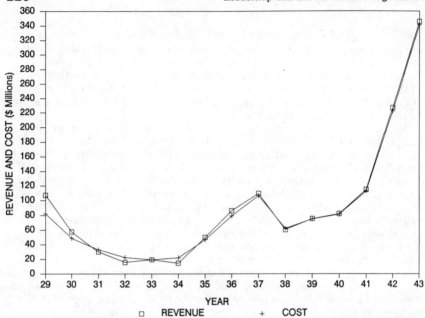

Figure 11-1. Packard Motor Car Co. revenue and cost. The Packard Motor Car Co. suffered acutely from the decline in the luxury automobile market brought about by the depression of the 1930s. Packard regrouped, however, by focusing intently on day-to-day operations and by capitalizing on the firm's well-accepted reputation for quality products. By the late 1930s, the company had emerged from disaster to regain profitability and to become one of the country's respected defense contractors.

Packard Survived Because...

- Management focused on operational matters.

- Management focused on the business the firm was in and resisted the temptation to diversify.

- Highly differentiated products were developed at very low cost.

- Talent and competence were distributed broadly throughout the organization.

- Management fostered and articulated noble ideals.

- Efficiency and quality were rigidly maintained.

- Costs were lowered through design.

- Historical markets were nurtured and protected as new markets were cultivated.

Case 15

Last Hurrah in South Bend

Henry and Clem Studebaker began operating their wagon-making shop in South Bend, Indiana, in 1852. The firm prospered first as a producer of horse-drawn vehicles and later as a respected manufacturer of motor cars, and market share rose to 3.6 percent in 1927. Some difficulties surfaced in the 1930s, when President Albert Erskine sought to support the price of Studebaker stock by paying dividends in excess of earnings. As the depression increased in severity and length, this practice depleted the company's cash reserves. The firm entered receivership in 1935 but emerged in time to participate in the upward trend of the later thirties. The arrival of World War II brought extensive business to Studebaker for the manufacture of trucks and other defense products. The firm ended 1944 with nearly $32 million in cash.

As was the case with the other automobile manufacturers, Studebaker's first postwar models were virtually identical to the 1942 models which had been discontinued shortly after the war began. But Studebaker was the first established manufacturer with true postwar styling. The 1947 Studebakers were low, attractive, and very modern in appearance. Studebakers of these years were also known for their excellent visibility and high gasoline mileage. This combination of attributes was well received by the public, and sales rose from 103,000 in 1947 to nearly 200,000 in 1949. The company prospered from car sales but was also a significant manufacturer of trucks. In 1948, revenue grew to $384 million, with profits of $19 million. Shipments and revenue grew again in 1949, and profits grew still further, to $27.6 million. Studebaker had established itself as an innovative supplier of well-designed, stylish products. Referring to the progress the firm was making toward becoming accepted as a price-class participant with Ford, Plymouth, and Chevrolet, the firm adopted the slogan "Four to see instead of three."

Shipments and revenue grew again in 1950, when Studebaker produced 268,000 units. Profits were high but lower than in 1949. Studebaker had begun to exhibit one of the telltale signs of the slipping firm, costs increasing faster than revenue.

In 1951, in celebration of the firm's upcoming one-hundredth anniversary, Studebaker announced a new overhead-valve V8 engine and its own automatic transmission—an achievement of sufficient technical credibility to elicit an offer from the Ford Motor Company to purchase Studebaker transmissions for use in Ford products. The new engine and transmission, coupled with the attractive styling of Studebaker products, initially provided a creditable offering to the marketplace. Over 200,000 units were shipped in 1951, and it appeared that Studebaker would be a factor in the automobile market well into the future.

Meanwhile, the Packard Motor Car Company was having some good years as well. Packard was also a highly respected defense contractor during World War II, and though the profits on these contracts were small, the firm finished the war in excellent financial condition with $32 million in cash at the end of 1945. Postwar Packards sold well, with production reaching a high of 105,000 units in 1949 as opposed to 81,000 for rival Cadillac. The company did miss an opportunity by failing to offer a "senior Packard" in the true sense of the term. In the seller's market that existed after the war, automobiles of the type offered by Packard before the war would have sold well and probably at higher margins. But still, the Packards of the 1940s were good cars that outsold both Cadillac and Lincoln.

The efficiency and innovation of these two older firms varied over time. Packard had attained a respected level of efficiency in its turnaround during the 1930s, and the firm's excellent history of significant engineering accomplishments added credibility to the firm's reputation as an innovator. Among the many Packard achievements were automatically adjusted torsion-bar suspension, the first straight-eight engine, the first 12-cylinder engine, the first car with air conditioning (1938), a front-end suspension system that was to be rigorously copied later by Rolls Royce, one of the first four-speed gearboxes, the first car with spiral (quieter) gears, and the first hypoid rear axle. Packard designed and built aircraft, marine, and jet engines. The company's quality control laboratory and its advanced understanding of the heat treatment of steel were nationally recognized.

But after World War II, many key Packard personalities were advanced in age. Macauley and Vincent, perhaps the two most influential members of the management team, had joined the company during the World War I era and were nearing retirement, as was Max Gillman, the sales manager who organized the sales activities during the resurgence of the 1930s. The gross profit rates listed in Table 11-2 describe the differences between Packard following World War I and the Packard of the 1930s.

Studebaker's efficiency and innovation ebbed and flowed as well. Following its emergence from receivership during the depression, the company entered into an incentive wage system with the CIO (United Auto Workers). The company did pay wages above the industry average, but it never succeeded in obtaining the commensurate productivity improvements (Craypo 1984). The period immediately following World War II probably represented a high point in Studebaker's production efficiency, but gross profits were still well below those achieved by other firms (see Table 11-3).

Table 11-2. Packard Gross Profit Rates

Year	1937	1939	1947	1948	1949
Gross profit	24.0%	19.6%	7.0%	15.2%	11.9%

Table 11-3. Studebaker Profitability and Inventory Efficiency

Year	Company	Gross profit, %	Inventory turns per year	Net profit on sales, %
1947	Nash	21.8	7.1	7.2
1947	GM	19.6	5.5	5.5
1947	Studebaker	8.9	8.5	3.4
1947	Packard	7.0	6.6	2.8
1949	GM	26.4	7.9	11.5
1949	Nash	21.6	8.7	7.2
1949	Studebaker	12.2	12.5	5.8
1949	Packard	11.9	8.0	3.6

After the seller's market subsided, Ford and Chevrolet began a feverish struggle for the first-place sales position, increasing pressure on Chrysler and the independents. Nash chairman George Mason began to hold exploratory talks with other independent producers in the hope of strengthening the market positions of Nash and a prospective partner. Because of the firm's historic engineering expertise and reputation in the marketplace, Mason's number-one choice for a merger partner was Packard.

Unfortunately for Mason, the Packard Motor Car Company had recently gone outside to find a new chief executive officer and chose James J. Nance, an executive formerly with the Hotpoint Appliance Division of General Electric. Nance, a flamboyant outgoing individual, had a definite eye toward expansion. When Mason approached Nance concerning a possible merger, Nance resisted, perhaps because Mason would not guarantee his position as chief executive officer. Though the merger would probably have been much better than the Nash-Hudson and Studebaker-Packard combinations that ultimately came about, Mason's offer was rejected.

In 1954, Hudson and Nash merged (Nash actually acquired Hudson) to form American Motors Corporation. Packard and Studebaker then merged (Packard actually acquired Studebaker) to form the Studebaker-Packard Corporation with James Nance as CEO. Both mergers were friendly. Even though the American Motors consolidation was only two-thirds the size of Studebaker-Packard, it had a much clearer sense of direction.

The combined size of Studebaker and Packard before the merger was very substantial. Peak employment was more than 38,000. Revenue was nearly $1 billion in 1953 (a $4 billion corporation in 1988 dollars).

The Studebaker-Packard merger had dubious synergy. The two companies served quite different markets, and their products utilized different components. Both companies had considerable unused manufacturing capacity. The Studebaker facilities in South Bend were huge in size and very old, with an inflexible, out-of-step layout. Packard added two new facilities shortly before the Studebaker merger. The combined plant sizes of the two firms reached 14 million square feet—an enormous capacity both then and now. The combination of many plants at several locations reduced Studebaker-Packard's efficiency. Also, the new firm, and the Studebaker firm before it, was unable to work productively with the employees and their bargaining units to improve the efficiency of the company's operations. Combined gross profits declined as seen in Table 11-4.

The early years of the Studebaker-Packard Corporation were fraught with confusion, misunderstandings, unstable leadership, and a failure to address some of the firm's major operational needs. The acquisition of the vast and inefficient Studebaker facilities plus two other plants during a period of declining demand aggravated the company's cash-flow problems. Studebaker-Packard hired outside consultants to find a solution, but they approached operational problems only in portfolio terms. They provided a list of strategic selections asking whether it would be better to be in this plant or that, in this business or that. They failed to address the questions of how

Table 11-4. Studebaker-Packard Gross Profit Rates

1950	1951	1952	1953	1954	1955	1956
10.9%	8.5%	8.8%	6.2%	6.6%	2.0%	0.5%

any of the businesses or plants ran. Meanwhile, the company's products attained an unfortunate reputation for skimpy design, poor quality, and a marked propensity to rust prematurely.

In an effort to attract volume while market share was shrinking, the firm marketed its newly developed V8 engine to American Motors in return for a tacit agreement to utilize some of Hudson's unused metal-stamping facilities. When Nance failed to follow through with the counterpurchase, American Motors chief executive George Romney canceled the arrangement and AMC developed a more efficient engine on its own.

The Studebaker-Packard Corporation lost more than $120 million from 1954 through 1958. The magnitude of these losses necessitated a curtailment of many company programs—among them the Packard program. In 1957, the final model of the once-prestigious Packard automobile appeared on a Studebaker chassis. In 1958, the make was entirely dropped.

During the years shortly before and immediately following the merger, the managers and directors of the Studebaker-Packard operations failed to proactively address significant problems of manufacturing efficiency, product differentiation, and day-to-day sales. Studebaker body designs went essentially unchanged after 1953, as did Packard bodies after 1951. Incremental improvements were not made on critical engineering projects. Both companies produced their own automatic transmissions when alternatives were available, and both had problems with them. The long-awaited Packard V8 was too heavy, as was the earlier Studebaker V8. In addition, difficulty in dealing with Nance caused a prominent customer, American Motors, to build its own engine. Quality problems were neglected at both Studebaker and Packard operations.

Instead of concentrating on the problems facing the company and working out action plans to address them, the board of directors offered a confusing and often contradictory set of directions for the company to follow. The company had five presidents in the 11 years from 1954 to 1963, the year when the U.S. automobile operations of Studebaker were permanently shut down. Much internal bickering occurred among members of the board of directors. An acquisition strategy emerged, and several significant acquisitions were made at an enormous cost of precious cash. One of these acquisitions, Franklin Manufacturing, cost the company more than $41 million at a time when cash was scarce. Others such as Trans-International Airlines and Domowatt (an Italian maker of appliances) were complete failures. Some helpful acquisitions did go through, but at an enormous cost to the main business and the company as a whole.

An unexpected problem emerged when each new acquisition brought with it some new personalities in the corporate management of Studebaker-Packard and to the board of directors. Many of these people thought they could run the company better than the present management. So, the bickering increased. For a while, the Curtis-Wright company looked like a savior, but in the end, that firm lost interest as well. Studebaker stopped all automobile production in the United States in 1963 and stopped its Canadian production in 1966—114 years after Henry and Clem started it all.

There was a brief respite when Harold Churchill ran the company in the late 1950s. Churchill, a manufacturing executive, concentrated on improving internal efficiency rather than expansion. He was interested in the present business rather than diversification, and the temporarily successful

Studebaker Lark was developed during his tenure. The firm was profitable and made $30 million in 1959 and remained profitable until 1962. But the bad managerial decisions of his predecessors and the board of directors had created a situation that was difficult to address. A dispute arose among board members as to whether the profits from the Lark should be used to improve the present business, which Churchill favored, or whether they should be used for acquisitions. Churchill did not have the political base to continue. In November 1960, he was replaced by a board member who favored an aggressive acquisitions policy.

Many lessons can be learned from the unsuccessful Studebaker-Packard turnaround: Focus on efficiency, customers, and products; enlist the participation of organization members; and strive to become a low-cost producer (particularly if you are in the low-priced field) of products that customers can respect. In a turnaround situation, most other activities are secondary. But the management of Studebaker-Packard elected to concentrate on other things. As a result, a firm that had proud historical antecedents, dating back 60 years in one case and more than 100 years in another, ceased to exist. Over time, 30,000 people lost their jobs, the town of South Bend has still not fully recovered, and foreign producers have moved in to fill the niches that at one time belonged to these two proud firms (Figure 11-2).

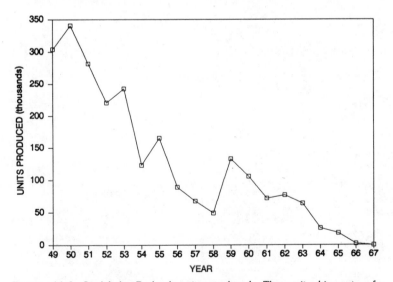

Figure 11-2. Studebaker-Packard units produced. The unit shipments of Studebaker and Packard automobiles exceeded 340,000 units in 1950, more than the units of the Oldsmobile division of GM. But, as the company dissipated its resources on ill-fated acquisitions, and managers and directors squabbled among themselves, two long-respected marques lost potential and existing customers. While quality was neglected and internal efficiencies were left to chance, customers left for other makes. In 1966, the company ceased vehicle production, after having been in business for 114 years.

Studebaker-Packard Failed Because...

- Management failed to concentrate on the business the firm was in.

- Resources were diverted into new ventures while historical markets were neglected.

- Managerial stability was lacking.

- Ideals were lacking.

- Little regard was shown for the company's past achievements and for the company's latent strengths.

- Top management lacked experience in the industry being served.

- Top management failed to play an exemplary role.

- Labor and management did not work together.

12
Fair Play

In our modern world of strategic analysis and portfolio management, the more traditional values of fairness and decency do not receive much attention in the management literature. Yet, in situation after situation, evidence suggests that adherence to concepts of basic fairness is as important to a successful turnaround as strategic direction, marketing experience, or other managerial attributes. Though fair play is a very difficult concept to measure, the proxy indicators available on the sample companies in this study suggest that successful turnaround agents are generally perceived as dealing fairly with employees, creditors, suppliers, and customers. The perception of fairness (or lack of it) influences the willingness of organization members to expend the extra effort necessary to mobilize a turnaround. Successful turnaround agents exhibit honesty and trustworthiness, downplay their own importance, and allow others to share in accomplishments. The firm in trouble needs managers who have an appropriate and balanced perspective of their personal value and their personal responsibilities.

Quite often, we see highly successful business executives who do not necessarily look the part. They don't dress well. They drive very ordinary cars. They stumble over words. They do not exude brilliance. Their public statements seem simple and unrefined. But, within their own organizations, they possess one essential attribute key to the entire motivational process: people perceive them as trustworthy. This perception is not easily achieved. An image of trustworthiness takes time to develop and requires many tests. But, over time, the organization comes to appreciate the reliability of its leaders. These leaders may or may not be flamboyant, but organization members know that they possess knowledge of the business, sound judgment, and a willingness to teach and that they will evaluate employees fairly and give equitable rewards. Organization members see them as people of fundamental goodwill. These qualities are often difficult to determine by those with only casual exposure to the company, such as members of the board of directors or stock analysts. They may be overlooked by aloof, out-of-touch members of higher management and may not be observable at all by members of the corporate staff. Yet, integrity and trust are firmly entrenched in our most scientific understanding of motivation.

Fairness as Discussed in the Earlier Literature on Management

Managerial thought is rich in the evaluation of fairness as a variable in organizational performance. Mooney and Riley emphasized the importance of fair play in their book *The Principles of Organization* (1939):

> The leader must be sensitive to the rights of the led and he must take measures to ensure that they are maintained for every individual throughout the organization. In other words, he must hug closely to the policy of "fair play." To this end, the leaders must begin by playing fair with each other.*

Members of the scientific management school viewed fair play as an essential factor in managerial effectiveness, organizational efficiency, and incentive compensation systems. Taylor spoke about the need for a "great mental revolution," fundamental to the concepts of efficiency, which could be realized only through the legitimate coincidence of interest between workers and management. Harrington Emerson (1913) listed "fairness" as one of his 12 principles of efficiency. Lillian Gilbreth devoted much of her 1919 classic, *The Psychology of Management,* to the need for moral training within organizations:*

> Moral development according to scientific management results from the provisions for cultivating:
>
> 1. Personal responsibility
> 2. Responsibility for others
> 3. Appreciation of standing
> 4. Self-control
> 5. "Squareness"

> This squareness is exemplified first of all by the attitude of the management. It provides, in every way, that the men are given a "square deal," in that the tasks assigned are of the proper size, and the re-

*Courtesy Macmillan, New York.

ward that is given is of the proper dimensions, and is assured. (L. Gilbreth 1919)

Years later, Oliver Sheldon (1960) wrote of the necessary integration that must take place between the goals of the organization and those of the society as a whole. In her many lectures of the same period, Mary Parker Follett stressed the need for goal integration between workers and management (Follett 1941). These theories produced a central premise that underscored the linkages between the integrity of members of the organization and the success of the organization itself. When events take place which alter the ways in which success is earned and distributed, motivation of the individuals in the organization is affected. If the events are opportunistic or unsavory, they represent an affront to the individual's most powerful needs, and demotivation takes place. We may wish to reflect upon the following excerpt from Chester Barnard's chapter "Executive Responsibility" in *Organization and Management:*

> Now we shall confine our thoughts to the second aspect of leadership—the more general; the more constant; the subjective; that which reflects the attitudes and ideals of society and its general institutions. It is this aspect of individual superiority in determination, persistence, endurance, courage; that determines the quality of action; which often is most inferred from what is not done, from abstention; which commands respect, reverence. It is the aspect of leadership we commonly imply in the word "responsibility," the quality which gives dependability and determination to human conduct, and foresight and ideality to purpose. (Barnard 1948)

If fairness is not present in organizations, it does not matter who is adversely affected. People tend to see the way others are treated as an index of how they will be treated. Much of the motivational process is built around trust, more specifically, the perceptions of trust. Trust in managers as purveyors of fairness is crucial to long-term achievement.

Equity Theory

Managing a turnaround is often like dealing with children. Equity is paramount. In dealing with our own children, few of us would be surprised if we experienced outcries of indignation as a result of giving one M&M to one child and 40 M&Ms to another. Yet, on occasion after occasion, we distribute the rewards, perquisites, and remuneration of declining organizations in ways that violate our most primitive understanding of the equity principle. Some executives (not all) earn more, travel more luxuriously, spend more, receive more personal service, and require more maintenance than other valuable people within the organization. Often these additional costs are remitted without commensurate competence or responsibility being received in return. Turnaround specialist George Gleeson has noted: "We are paying for crepes suzette but we are getting chicken salad." In contrast, the welfare of others is often disregarded as people are laid off, endure pay reductions, or are reassigned under distressing circumstances.

People expect executives to be reasonably paid, of course, and no one is going to argue for total parity among organization members, even of a company in trouble. However, we may have moved beyond the point of reasonableness in compensating our executives, particularly those involved in troubled situations. First Bank Systems, for instance, wrote off several hundred million dollars because of imprudent bond-trading strategies as both the president and then the chief executive received executive compensation well in excess of a million dollars per year. For several years, executives of Midwest Federal were proudly listed among the highest-paid executives in the upper Midwest while that institution was accumulating a negative net worth of more than $900 million. Control Data once suffered the indignity of having one of its officers earn more than the corporation. Similar extreme situations have occurred at Allegheny International, E. F. Hutton, and other companies. Less flamboyant breaches of equity exist elsewhere and are widespread.

Some retrenchment is no doubt essential to the survival of some firms, and such emergencies are recognized by organization members, but equity is necessary as an operating principle. Miner (1980) describes Adams' fundamental concepts of equity theory in the following way:*

> Although the term equity is used to describe the theory, it is at least as appropriate to describe it as inequity theory. The major motivating force considered is a striving for equity, but some degree of inequity must be perceived before this force can be mobilized.
>
> The theory starts with an exchange whereby the individual gives something and gets something in return. What the individual gives may be viewed as inputs, or investments in the relationship....
>
> On the other side of the exchange are various things the individual may receive, the outcomes of the exchange relationship....
>
> The third type of theoretical variable, in addition to the inputs provided and the outcomes received is the reference person or group used in evaluating the equity of one's own relationship....

Excerpts from *Theories of Organizational Behavior* by John B. Miner, copyright © 1980 by The Dyrden Press, a division of Holt, Rinehart and Winston, Inc., reprinted by permission of the publisher.

Inequity is said to exist when the ratio of an individual's outcomes to inputs departs to a significant degree from the ratio perceived for the reference source....

Equity, balance, or reciprocity exists when outcome/input ratios for the individual and the reference source are equal, and the motivating force can arise when there is a departure either way from this steady state....

Inequity, when perceived, results in dissatisfaction either in the form of anger (underreward) or guilt (overreward). A tension is created in proportion to the amount of inequity. This tension in turn serves as a motivating force to reduce the inequity and move it to zero. (Miner 1980, 107–110)

Similarly, Chester Barnard (1938) decried individual opportunism as a demotivating force in organizations. Opportunism is clearly perceived by the informal organization, and it diminishes the willingness of organization members to actively participate in the attainment of the organization's objectives.

With her "law of the situation," Mary Parker Follett (1941) asserted that people interpret a wide variety of meanings from the same event. She cautioned practicing managers to make sure that the "situations" around important decisions are thoroughly understood by organization members. The simple act of making the right decision is not sufficient to enlist the cooperation of the organization. On important matters, the organization needs to understand the rationale, the situation, and the reasoning processes that go into the making of a decision. By providing organization members with full knowledge of the background conditions, both the perception and the realities of fairness can be cultivated in the organization.

The Manager in an Exemplary Role

Walter Chrysler said it best. "If the spirit is not right, it is useless to look at results." The key strategy for turnaround sometimes boils down to retaining the most honest people who want to work hard, who know something about the business they are in, and who want the company to succeed. This strategy implies the need for these traits on the part of top management. In this study, most if not all of the successful turnarounds were headed by people who exhibited character traits involving old-fashioned honesty, morality, and hard work.

Observing the variance in executive behavior during periods of cost reduction is of interest. The cost reduction programs of successful turn-arounds begin with top management's voluntarily shouldering a disproportionate share of the cost-reductions. The management teams of unsuccessful turnarounds in the cases studied here did not typically include themselves in cost reductions. Occasionally, they continued to consume or waste corporate resources when it was crucial for the organizations to reduce costs. Even when their firms faltered badly, some executives displayed inflated views of their own value and less conscientious views of their responsibilities. In some cases, the firm's board of directors reinforced these misperceptions by approving lucrative compensation packages or severance packages at inopportune times. A few weeks into the very critical strike at International Harvester, in which the company was asking for concessions from the union, the board of directors voted to forgive $2.7 million in loans to the two top officers of the company. The strike became the longest in the history of the industry, and the company lost as did the other stakeholders. We should wonder about the role of managerial arrogance in the demise of the firm. As one employee in the truck engineering department noted:

> Morale is low. We see Lee Iacocca working for a dollar a year and the general feeling is that our top guys are lapping up the gravy. (Marsh 1985, 248)

Ironically, executive compensation may have attenuated the momentum of Chrysler Corporation in later years. Huge compensation packages to Iacocca, though appropriate by some standards, may have reduced the corporate resolve to operate profitably. One Chrysler board member, Douglas Fraser, did express concern as to how Iacocca's compensation would affect cooperation from other constituencies, such as organized labor. In expressing this concern about whether the compensation was good for the company, Fraser was correct in fulfilling his responsibilities as a corporate director.

In the successful turnaround cases, including Chrysler Corporation in the early 1980s, management often played exemplary roles in cost reductions. Packard, Nash, and Deere all trimmed executive compensation during the 1930s, as did American Motors during the 1950s and other well-managed firms subsequently. Even during profitable periods, executives from highly successful companies such as 3M and IBM rarely receive salaries among the nation's highest. Even within the small state of Minnesota, 3M's chief executive has rarely ranked among the state's 10 highest-paid executives, although the company makes more profit than all of the next 10 largest companies in the state combined. George Romney's golden parachute from American Motors nets him $42 per month, while less capable executives of failed enterprises exit with tens of millions of dollars.

The manner in which company executives handle costs sets the appropriate tone for the turnaround process. If management is frugal, members of the organization are more likely to conserve resources. Similarly, if management spends carelessly, others will too. Successful turnaround agents such as those at Deere, Buick, Maxwell, and Jeffery knew how to practice fair play and avoided many of the awkward and unnecessary disorders that impacted the unsuccessful firms.

Fair Play Extended Outside the Firm

Fairness is as essential in the external affairs of the company as it is inside the organization. In some cases, the presence or absence of fair play in external matters can have even a more immediate effect on the outcome of the turnaround attempt than some internal affairs. Those who have actively participated in actual turnaround attempts understand that there are a great many matters beyond the turnaround agent's control, such as creditor committees, environmental matters, regulatory matters, and the private behavior of key lenders, suppliers, and customers.

Responsible turnaround agents will work productively with each of these groups but will not try to control them. The cooperation of one or more external stakeholders is almost always a necessary condition to a firm's turnaround success. Most of the time, these external stakeholders are being asked for something they would prefer not to give. The request may be for extended terms from a major supplier or perhaps a partial write-down of amounts owed or the option to pay much later without interest. Other requests might be the shipment of goods well beyond normal credit limits or the conversion of debt into speculative stock. Rarely are any of these ideas popular with the creditors involved, and usually these people have the freedom to cooperate or not as they see fit.

Some observers representing the rational perspective might argue that external stakeholders will opt to pursue their own best interests. My experience suggests that the rational perspective is a gross oversimplification. Much depends upon whether fairness is, or is not, perceived. Often external stakeholders have granted concessions in the past but have never received what was promised them in return. Or, they may be sick of the entire situation and simply wish to be done with it. Their attitude toward further cooperation may depend on whether they have set aside sufficient reserves for an unfavorable outcome, the number of other, similar events they are facing at the time, constraints imposed on them by their own external stakeholders such as regulators, and whether they believe that they are being dealt with fairly by the organization that owes them money.

The wise turnaround agent will recognize that there is honor among creditors. Most creditors make mistakes at some time during their career, and some of these mistakes are the result of incomplete knowledge of the situation at the time the credit was extended. But, creditors are busy people, and few of them have the time available to judge every situation with the expertise they could apply if they had to. To supplement their own thin resources, creditors often rely on informal networks to gain information and make decisions. Thus, rationality may be only part of the picture. If creditors perceive a company's unfairness as serious enough, they may decide to put the company permanently out of business so that the people involved will not bother them any more. Creditors may fail to cooperate — even if it results in a personal loss. What matters in critical dealings with external stakeholders is this vague, highly subjective, and highly individualized perception of fairness.

Fairness is a concept so universal and so precious that it impacts executives and workers alike. Walter Chrysler ultimately left General Motors in part because he felt that a competent supplier was being unfairly treated by the GM chief at the time, Billy Durant. Similarly, key executives left companies like Bendix, First Bank Systems, Control Data, and other companies because of their belief that fair play was not in evidence. When fair play is perceived as being absent during a time when others are asked for sacrifice, the esprit de corps of fellow executives, middle managers, and factory workers alike is severely reduced.

Practical Lessons in Fair Play

- Successful companies operate with consistent and exemplary standards of fairness in their dealings with employees, creditors, suppliers, and customers. Unsuccessful companies often have reputations of unfairness.

- If fairness is not present, it does not matter who is the victim. People view the treatment of others as an index of how they will be treated.

- Unsuccessful companies attempt to use suppliers as sources of cash (by lengthening out payables) and as sources for new processes and concepts (often developed at supplier expense in anticipation of future business). Successful companies value suppliers as extensions of their own organizations and rarely become involved in opportunistic transactions with them.

- The wise turnaround agent will recognize that there is honor among creditors. Noble creditors may refuse to cooperate with the ignoble troubled company even if it means greater personal loss.

- Successful turnaround leaders set an example for the organization during times of misfortune by accepting less pay as the first step in cost reductions and by handling the affairs of their office in a frugal manner.

- Successful turnaround leaders value the economic and social stability of the company associates and attempt, as best they can, to minimize disruption.

Case History

During the Great Depression, Deere had suffered a revenue decline of more than 90 percent from its peak of 1929. The economy was in terrible condition, and on top of that, Deere products were not meeting the needs of the marketplace. From 1931 to 1933, company losses were nearly 40 percent of company revenues. Deere was only one-eighth the size of International Harvester, which dominated the industry at the time, and Deere stock had tumbled from $690 per share to $3.50. As things looked their bleakest, Deere officers, owners, and managers personally sacrificed in a manner that illustrates the role of fair play during the turnaround process.

Case 16
Midwestern Ethic at Deere

By 1932, Deere & Co. was 95 years old. The company was known for its close attention to customer needs and its steady supply of quality farm equipment. The traditions and values of the original John Deere had been passed on through family members who, individually, had run the various operating units of the company since its inception in 1837. "You can't sell plows to a hatter," William Butterworth would say. He and the other members of the Deere family were always in touch with what the farmer needed. In order to ensure that these important perceptions were not lost, many members of the Deere management team engaged in farming themselves.

The ever-present attention to the customer served Deere well through the years. The company had become a significant number-two producer in its industry. It was, however, still well behind the huge International Harvester, which was several times the size of Deere. Deere was highly profitable during some periods but experienced difficult times shortly after World War I. Receivable problems, problems with the local economies in large overseas markets, and the general economic conditions at home combined to cause Deere an 80 percent revenue decline in the years following the war. During 1920 and 1921, more than 150 Deere dealers went bankrupt, and the company was in a precarious financial position. The later years of the 1920s were not as robust for the agricultural sector as they were for other segments of the economy, but Deere did recover, and by the late 1920s profits were once again healthy as revenues reached $80 million.

By 1932, however, the situation had dramatically changed again, resulting in the company's worst crisis ever. Not only did the bottom drop out of the farm economy, but the usually attentive and customer-oriented management of Deere failed to match one of its key products to the marketplace. For most of the company's history, each Deere plant enjoyed considerable autonomy in developing, marketing, and producing products for particular markets (Broehl 1984). Each Deere plant served its own particular market, and the staff at each specialized plant maintained a high degree of contact with their respective customers. Key decisions were made at the plant level. This informal structure served the company well, and Deere was normally highly responsive to its markets. The one exception was with the general purpose (GP) tractor, one of the few Deere products developed by the central research and development department. Unfortunately, this centralized department failed to develop a product adequately matched to its market, a product which served Deere poorly.

Prior to 1924, most tractors were powerful, built low to the ground, and cumbersome. They had little crop clearance and were hard to maneuver. They were not bad for plowing, but they were not designed for cultivating, planting, and other fieldwork. During this era, the Fordson tractor, with its low cost and basic operation, accounted for more than 70 percent of total tractor sales and 76 percent in 1923 (Broehl 1984, 478). During the early 1920s, International Harvester designed a tractor which was far more maneuverable and far better adapted to a much wider variety of general farm work. The tractor had greater crop clearance, was of moderate size, showed better economy, and was of the four-row tricycle type for better maneuverability. It was called the *Farmall*. The International Harvester Farmall sold very well and soon displaced the Fordson as the leading tractor in a much larger and more rapidly expanding market. By 1928, International Harvester had garnered 68 percent of the tractor market (*Fortune* 1933).

In the meantime, Deere attempted to field a general-purpose tractor of its own, and the GP project was eagerly taken on by the central research and development department. The result was a product inappropriate to the marketplace. The GP tractor was a three-row model, not a four-row, and not as maneuverable or productive in terms of either fuel or time. It failed to develop the horsepower it was rated, and other important details were overlooked. During a time when tractor sales were increasing and the economy was sound, Deere was left with a suboptimal product (Broehl 1984). Fortunately, other Deere products sold well during the 1920s, and Deere had enough other people who understood what the market needed so that the company was still prosperous. But, some valuable time had been lost, and by the time the depression arrived, the company had been weakened by not offering a better general-purpose tractor to the marketplace.

To make matters worse, the quality of the competition had improved. A series of mergers and other consolidations had enabled Oliver, Minneapolis-Moline, and Massey-Harris to become larger and stronger competitors. The innovative and well-equipped Allis-Chalmers Corporation announced its own general-purpose tractor called the *All-Crop*. Under experienced management, the well-known J. I. Case Company emerged as an efficient producer of new products. The number of tractor manufacturers shrank from 186 in 1921 to 38 in 1930, but the tractors produced were better units made by larger and more competitive long-line manufacturers. By 1932, Deere's market share among the seven major long-line manufacturers (International Harvester, Allis-Chalmers, Case, Massey-Harris, Oliver, Minneapolis-Moline, and Deere) had dropped to 9.1 percent, from more than 17 percent in 1929. Deere fell to one-eighth the size of International Harvester in revenue (Table 12-1).

By 1932, Deere was in severe difficulty. Revenues had dropped from $81 million in 1929 to less than $10 million in 1932, an 85 percent decline. In 1932, the company lost $6,714,000, and between 1931 and 1934, it lost a total of $11 million. But, Deere & Co. still had production efficiency, a close relationship with its dealers and customers, and a strong balance sheet. Perhaps more important, the company had systematically cultivated the moral character of its managers and employees.

Kindly old William Butterworth, the son-in-law of Charles Deere (John Deere's son), was president of the company until 1928, when he retired to spend more time with the U.S. Chamber of Commerce. His regime was marked by thrift, honesty, and hard work, but he was also generous in his treatment of employees. He believed that people of character were needed to carry on the traditions and standards of Deere. Under his leadership, Deere employees gained financially and in the quality of working life. In 1928, he

Table 12-1. Percent of Long-Line Market

Company	1929	1930	1931	1932	1933
International Harvester	60.8	57.9	62.5	69.4	71.3
Deere	17.3	17.8	13.9	9.1	9.1
Case	6.4	7.2	7.0	5.3	5.2
Oliver	6.4	6.9	8.1	5.1	4.7
Allis-Chalmers	2.5	3.6	3.3	7.4	5.8
Minneapolis-Moline	3.4	3.4	2.2	2.5	2.1
Massey-Harris	3.3	3.3	2.9	1.2	1.8

SOURCES: Federal Trade Commission, 1938; *Moody's Industrials Manual*, 1932.

was succeeded by John Deere's great-grandson, graduate engineer and former shop worker Charles Wiman.

For many years, Deere employed people on the basis of moral character and good personal habits including sound work habits, sobriety, and thrift. In addition, the management of Deere had urged employees to save money against a reversal in the farm economy. Many employees followed this advice, and sizable amounts of their savings were deposited in the People's Savings Bank of Moline, Illinois. But during the depression, the Peoples Savings Bank experienced the same problems banks generally have during depressions. Loans were hard to collect and deposits were scarce. In the midst of the depression, in 1932, the People's Savings Bank was hit by a disgraceful embezzlement of $1.25 million. The bank seemed destined to fail—and with the failure, much of the savings of the Deere employees would vanish.

Key managers and owners of Deere felt that it would be a travesty if the Deere employees lost the savings that the company had encouraged them to accumulate. So, they gathered together the members of the Deere family and the company and bank directors (some individuals served on both boards). Collectively it was decided that an assessment should be levied on each of these people individually. Then the money was put into the bank to preserve the bank and the savings of the community.

Of course, during the Great Depression, Deere & Co. was suffering on its own. In response to its huge losses (67 percent of revenue in 1932), management had initiated many severe cost-reduction measures. Dividends on preferred stock had been cut from $7 to 20 cents. Common dividends had been eliminated. Deere stock had fallen from a high of $690 in 1930 to $3.50 (Broehl 1984; *Fortune* 1936). Executive compensation was cut by 25 percent, managers' salaries were cut by 10 percent, and employees' hourly wages were cut by 4 percent. Then, elaborate schemes were worked out to give each family some work. Yet it was in this atmosphere that the management and owners of the company elected to use their personal resources to salvage the savings of the community in general and company employees in particular. The strains of the depression continued to work on the bank and region, but the intervention by Deere & Co. management and owners brought at least some temporary relief to the community and attracted the interest of the national press.

The clannish nature of the Deere organization, coupled with the fact that many Deere managers were farmers, enhanced a close relationship with dealers and customers. Five branch managers were directors in the company, and one of them, C. C. Webber of Deere & Webber of Minneapolis and also a Deere grandson, was the company's second-largest stockholder. The company was so interested in personal contacts with its customers that it insisted that 1.5 million copies of the company magazine, *The Furrow*, be hand-addressed by members of the Deere organization (*Fortune* 1936).

Deere's primary distinction, however, was the efficiency of its factories. Deere factories reflected a clear-cut strategy that emphasized quality, peak efficiency, and employment of people of good character, with each factory making its own decisions in the manner that best served a particular set of customers. In the very early days, the company adopted the practice of producing equipment with a small number of rugged and common component parts. Deere tractors had two cylinders for some very explicit engineering reasons, which sales manager Frank Silloway articulated in 1918:

1st: A two cylinder tractor can be built cheaper than a four and price is an important factor, because the tractor business is a business that must win its economy.

2nd: The tractor, unlike the automobile, must pull hard all the time. The bearings must be adjusted for wear. There are half as many bearings on a two cylinder tractor and half as many valves to grind.

3rd: There are less parts to get out of order and cause delay.

4th: The bearings are more accessible on a two cylinder horizontal engine than on a four cylinder vertical engine.

5th: Two cylinder engines will burn kerosene better than four.

6th: Four cylinders are not necessary on tractors. The fact that a tractor is geared 50 to 1 instead of 4 to 1 eliminates all jerky motion. The engine of a tractor can be made heavy and have a heavy fly wheel and can be mounted on a rigid strong frame. Therefore, a two cylinder tractor is satisfactory in a tractor and when it is, why go to the four cylinder type. (Broehl 1984, 405)

Deere continued with this same engineering concept for its tractors through 1960. This clearly articulated philosophy continued to provide production advantages to Deere for those many years. The Deere tractor had approximately 1400 fewer parts than its comparably powered counterparts from Allis-Chalmers, Case, or International Harvester.

Deere factories were efficient as well. Even during the tough years of the depression, Deere's gross profit rates continued at levels near the top of all producers (Table 12-2). Likewise, the Deere sales organization was efficient. In 1929, selling expense was roughly comparable to that of the industry leader, International Harvester, but Deere enjoyed a 12-point advantage in production cost (Broehl 1984, 805).

Charles Wiman, a Yale engineering graduate, was very careful to preserve

Table 12-2. Percent of Gross Profit Rates of Long-Line Companies

Company	1927	1928	1929	1930	1931
Deere & Co.	41.65	41.67	43.19	40.33	34.53
J. I. Case	45.95	46.45	40.61	39.54	31.78
Oliver			34.75	31.03	28.49
International Harvester	27.39	30.62	30.96	28.85	24.52
Massey-Harris	25.58	22.67	23.40	18.39	23.74
Allis-Chalmers	21.28	28.13	16.51	19.87	21.62
Minneapolis-Moline			28.62	29.01	13.77

SOURCES: Federal Trade Commission, 1938; *Moody's Industrial Manual,* 1932.

the company's new-product development effort during the harsh times of the 1930s. He continued to preach caution and thrift on a daily basis and insisted that the managers and executives of the company operate in spartan surroundings. But he actively promoted new-product development and was personally involved in reviewing the progress. Wiman would often drive up and down the testing fields to closely examine the performance of experimental tractors and implements. By 1932, Deere was offering a new, more powerful, and better-engineered general-purpose tractor called the *Model A*, of which 293,000 were sold during its 20-year production run. The following year Deere introduced the Model B and sold 309,000 over a 19-year period (Broehl 1984, 520–521). The Models A and B, with their high quality, reliability, and low cost of operation, resulting from the ability to burn "anything you can pour into the tank" (Broehl 1984), provided a winning combination for Deere. Profits and revenue began to grow.

In parallel with Deere's progress in product development and manufacturing efficiency, the firm adopted a strategy of very technical and factual advertising. The advertising stressed the technical virtues of Deere products in terms of simplicity, reliability, operator convenience, and cost of operation.

By 1937, sales had climbed back to more than $100 million, and after-tax profits rose to $14.9 million—still below 1929 levels but far better than the severe losses of 1932 and 1933. By 1941, the company was earning before-tax profits of $25 million on sales of $125 million, but taxes had increased to keep after-tax earnings at the $15 million level.

The engineering accomplishments associated with the Models A and B, together with many other technical achievements, established Deere as a dependable and practical supplier of quality and innovative products to the agricultural industry.

The Deere turnaround was in reality a long process of readjustment following the problems experienced after World War I. The turnaround was successful, and the company went on to improve profits and gain market share. By 1971, the company had overtaken International Harvester in profits. By 1982, it was larger in terms of revenue. Today, the company survives as a respected worldwide producer of agricultural machinery, with a roughly 60 percent market share in North America. Its former, much larger competitor International Harvester, which at one time was eight times its size, has departed the business.

The themes of the Deere turnaround come as no surprise: familiarity with markets, innovative products, low-cost operation, spartan surroundings, a focus on operations, and the selection of employees on the basis of work ethics and character traits. But perhaps the most significant characteristic of the Deere turnaround was the presence of fair play during a time of deprivation. It is one thing for managers and owners to give from their surplus; it is entirely another matter to make sacrifices for the benefit of others when there is less to give. Strong character traits among leaders, the cultivation of traditional values among both managers and workers, and a sense of managerial responsibility are the attributes that helped to make the Deere turnaround successful.

Deere Survived Because...

- Top management exhibited fair play.
- Operational efficiency was very high.
- Product quality problems were quickly corrected, and quality became excellent.
- Top management had extensive experience in the industry being served.
- Top management had technical experience.
- Product features and benefits were distinctive.
- Continuity was preserved with historical markets.

PART 5

The Turnaround Experience

Looking Ahead

The world economy is being ravaged by collective rapacity and institutional neglect. For 40 years, we have shifted resources from industrial companies that historically have provided jobs for much of the population to other programs, some meritorious. But, as the industrial economy shrinks and as resources are dissipated on activities unrelated to tangible production, the American standard of living is slipping from our grasp, sustained with difficulty only by huge borrowings from other countries. The approach of emphasizing the service economy and the activities of government is doomed to failure because it is neither practical nor without risk. In order to survive as a nation, and to avoid the social and economic problems of twentieth-century Germany or eighteenth-century France, we will have to produce.

Yet, much of our productive capacity is in disarray. As problems with the world economy deepen, as layoffs multiply, as financial markets become increasingly volatile, and as more and more people and companies file for bankruptcy, it is clear that we need new, more specific approaches to economic revitalization. General, economywide approaches involving fiscal, monetary, tax, and regulatory policies have potential, but they are hard to organize. The problem with macro-level policies is that they are all coordinated through ungainly governments which often drift aimlessly in response to cumulative political considerations and fail to do what needs to be done. In a manner consistent with the case studies reviewed here, revitalization demands character, technical competence, and fair play, along with small incremental steps oriented to increasing the competitive edge of individual firms participating in key strategic industries. Millions of individually helpful actions to improve the performance of individual companies have more likelihood of happening than any conceivable colossal act of government, however desirable it may be.

Developed economies can regain their strength and vitality only if we learn to fix some of the large industrial enterprises that played such a major role in the initial building of national economies. It is simply too costly, both in money terms and in people terms, to allow the productive sectors of our societies to continually drift toward oblivion. We are not prepared for the social upheaval and political consequences that will result. Remedial skills—the skills to repair, to resurrect, and to enlist the cooperation of diverse interests—are in demand.

The chapters in Part 5 briefly summarize some of the strategic aspects of turnaround management and then look ahead to the future of turnarounds as key ingredients to restorative action in our modern society. The discussion of the strategic profiles of successful companies in Chapter 13 should be helpful to managers, investors, workers, and other stakeholders. Chapter 14 examines the intricate connections between corporate revitalization and industrial renewal at the national level. Chapter 15 offers some recommendations for the future.

13

The Strategic
Profiles of
Turnaround Cases

Companies successful in turnarounds achieve both the attributes of low-cost production and product differentiation through the enlightened leadership of top management. These attributes are crucial to turnaround success; however, the sequence of movements toward these objectives is also of interest as successful companies appear first to become efficient, low-cost producers and then to progress toward product differentiation. Though there are exceptions, this sequence of low-cost production followed by product differentiation is the most common path toward an improved strategic position.

Foreign producers have often employed the same sequence in entering markets in the United States. Sony television sets and Toyota automobiles first appeared as low-cost products. Later, after many investments in product characteristics made possible by internal efficiencies, the offerings of these same manufacturers were broadly perceived as high-quality differentiated products. The same could be said of Japanese bearings and machine tools and other foreign products as well. We see this same sequence employed by American producers such as Nucor, Loctite, Maytag, 3M, and Autodesk.

Successful
Turnaround Profiles

The successful turnarounds in our sample also followed the strategic sequence of low-cost production followed by product differentiation (Hall 1983), although the combinations of low cost and differentiation certainly

251

varied. During the turnaround process, most successful companies initially moved upward and then diagonally to the right (Figure 13-1). Note that this is really a two-step process. Charles Nash had the clearest perception: become highly efficient at manufacturing and then use some of the savings to differentiate the product by adding quality and differentiating features. Cadillac moved from an inefficient producer of modest undifferentiated cars to a highly efficient producer of one of the most prestigious marques in the world. Cadillac moved from box 9 to box 1 in what was probably the most dramatic shift (Figure 13-2).

Buick automobiles sold well and possessed some differentiation. What was needed was to organize production so that it could be accomplished at a lower cost. By consolidating product lines and improving efficiency, Buick moved upward along the low-cost-of-production axis from box 5 to box 2. To some degree, Deere's situation was perpendicular to that of Buick's. Deere was always a low-cost producer. With the advent of the Models A and B tractors and other product improvements, Deere moved laterally along the product differentiation axis from box 3 to box 1.

The early Thomas B. Jeffery Company ranked medium in terms of

C O S T O F O P E R A T I O N	L O W	Marginal Survival Position (3)	Good Survival Position (2)	Best Survival Position (1)
	M E D I U M	Poor Survival Position (6)	Possible Survival Position (5)	Good Survival Position (4)
	H I G H	Worst Survival Position (9)	Poor Survival Position (8)	Marginal Survival Position (7)
		Low	Medium	High

PRODUCT DIFFERENTIATION

Figure 13-1. Strategic positioning for survival. Survival is most likely when a company is a low-cost provider of differentiated products or services and least likely when undifferentiated products are expensively produced (Hall, 1983). A firm's survival position is enhanced if either product differentiation or low-cost operation is present, but both attributes seem to be necessary to ensure turnaround success.

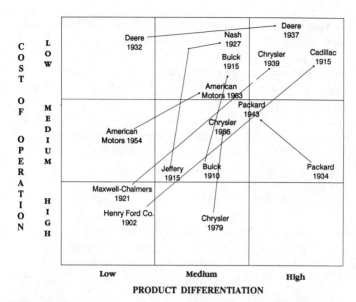

Figure 13-2. Strategic profiles—successful cases. Successful turnarounds often first achieve low-cost operation and then enhance product differentiation in a two-step process. Charles Nash had the clearest perception: become highly efficient at manufacturing and then use some of the savings to differentiate the product by adding quality and features.

both differentiation and production cost. With the arrival of Charles Nash, the company became one of the lowest-cost producers in the industry while simultaneously improving product differentiation. The new Nash Motors moved to the very top position in box 2. During the low point of its period of crisis, when bankruptcy was imminent, Maxwell-Chalmers was a high-cost producer of negatively differentiated products. Efficiency was low, and Maxwell products had earned a poor reputation in the marketplace. With the arrival of Chrysler, Zeder, Skelton, Breer, Mason, and Hutchinson, the company began to make substantial progress on both production cost and product differentiation. The first Chrysler car marked a 20-year progression toward high-differentiation low-cost production, which resulted in the firm's becoming the nation's second-largest producer.

American Motors had achieved low-cost operation earlier in its history, but this favorable attribute was retarded by the acquisition of Hudson. As the intense competition of the 1950s spurred the rapid development of more powerful engines, additional convenience and performance features, and styling innovations on the part of competitors, American Motors moved to a less favorable differentiation position.

During the American Motors turnaround from 1958 to 1963, the company greatly reduced its costs and concentrated its product-differentiation efforts on a particular market segment. The resulting specialization economies, the firm's quality emphasis, and the selling of the compact car concept (as opposed to "cheap car") all helped the move to a more favorable position in box 2.

During the late 1970s, Chrysler Corporation was a high-cost producer with a breakeven point of 2.5 million medium-quality cars per year. Six years later, Chrysler emerged as one of the industry's most innovative producers, with a breakeven point of 1.3 million cars. Chrysler moved from near insolvency to a strongly competitive position before losing much of this advantage with the diversification program of the late 1980s. Beset by intense international competition during the same period, Ford Motor Company was also forced to radically alter both its cost structure and its processes of innovation. Using product design as the main vehicle to improve quality and reduce cost, Ford moved from box 5 to box 1 to achieve the best strategic position of any U.S. producer.

Packard was the only one of our successful cases to move to a lower level of product differentiation. Packard products enjoyed one of the most prestigious positions in the industry at the start of its turnaround. Packard moved into box 5 with its new medium-priced 120 and 115 models. In doing so, the company moved into a much larger market. What is important is that all the companies that executed a lasting turnaround emerged with a favorable strategic profile involving some combination of low-cost production and product differentiation (Figure 13-2).

Unsuccessful Turnaround Profiles

The unsuccessful firms were unable to manifest a favorable strategic profile involving low-cost production and product differentiation. Willys-Overland showed better performance temporarily because of actions initiated during the short stewardship of Walter Chrysler, but the company's lack of long-term efficiency in manufacturing precluded it from surviving during a major downturn. The Willys-Overland turnaround began with a company that was a high-cost producer of undifferentiated products. With the arrival of Walter Chrysler, the company temporarily moved to a more favorable position. After his departure, the company continued to sell vast quantities of cars, but production costs rose and the company's numerous products were not sufficiently differentiated to sustain sales under less favorable conditions. Ultimately, Willys-Overland moved back to box 9 and entered receivership. After a promising start, the Willys-Overland turnaround strategy put too much emphasis on marketing and sales and not enough on production efficiency and product differentiation (Figure 13-3).

The same was true of Studebaker-Packard Corporation during the 1950s. Studebaker (together with Packard) entered the decade selling more than 340,000 cars per year. Combined market share was nearly 6 percent in 1949. One decade later, Studebaker-Packard was essentially out of business. Product differentiation and operating costs were such that profitability could be sustained only during a boom period, and even then with only third-rate results.

Within 3 years of its formation, Kaiser-Frazer became the leading independent producer of automobiles in the United States, a position the firm attained by offering attractive styling during a seller's market. The rest of the car had basically prewar engineering, and styling proved to have a limited life as a differentiating feature. When other producers restyled, Kaiser-Frazer's main competitive edge was lost. Operating costs were too high. In the final analysis, the company could not sustain

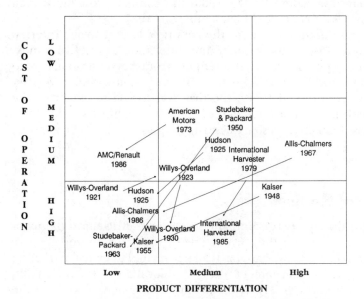

Figure 13-3. Strategic profiles—unsuccessful cases. Unsuccessful firms are seldom able to exhibit a favorable strategic profile involving low-cost operation and product differentiation. Costs remain high while product quality, features, and benefits remain poor. Under these conditions, failure is an almost universal outcome.

its competitive position because of high costs of operation and limited long-term product differentiation.

Hudson products had differentiating features which were both favorable and unfavorable. The full-size Hudsons made from 1948 to 1954 were good automobiles produced at high cost. However, from 1929 to 1947, the company experienced a long period of low efficiency and medium-to-low product differentiation. This important period sapped resources as the company lost money for 7 years out of 10, from 1931 to 1940. In only 1 year, 1936, did profits exceed 4 percent of revenue. By the mid-1930s, the antiquated splash-oil systems and three main-bearing six-cylinder engines were obsolete. The company gradually moved to a position of a high-cost producer with mixed differentiation.

Allis-Chalmers entered the 1960s as an innovative and efficient producer of electrical and agricultural machinery with high gross profits. But, after being involved in a hostile takeover attempt during the late 1960s, the company spent the next 15 years diverting its resources into a wide range of activities which were not related to the company's major businesses. Product cost and product differentiation were neglected, and by the end of the 1970s, Allis-Chalmers ceased to be competitive in its major markets. From 1981 to 1986, the company lost more than $800 million. The firm entered bankruptcy in 1987.

After several decades as one of the country's largest firms, International Harvester lost both efficiency and innovation as the firm's inexperienced management diverted attention from key operational matters, such as product development, efficiency, sales, and inventory management. By the mid-1980s, the firm was forced to exit from the market it had dominated for much of its 150-year history. The once-mighty International Harvester was struggling to remain in business by producing large trucks.

Summary of Findings

The ability of the successful companies to remain efficient in the manufacture of products was the cornerstone of their turnaround success. Their ability to compete was not particularly related to exotic marketing programs, portfolio management, the cost of local taxes, financial skills, or sales expertise. It was largely a function of managerial skills in the fields of production and product differentiation, along with industry and technical experience and a basic sense of fairness in dealing with employees, customers, and others. No substantial differentials in production wage rates existed between the companies that emerged and those that did not. The fact is that people like Charles Nash, Walter Chrysler, the Lelands, and the people at Deere knew how to run industrial companies. The people at Willys, Hudson, Allis-Chalmers, Studebaker, and several of the rest, including International Harvester, did not know how to run such companies — even when the companies were among the largest producers in their industries.

But efficiency and innovation may not be sufficient conditions for turnaround. Trustworthiness and fairness were factors as well. Most of the successful turnaround people were from rather humble origins. They were not interested in high salaries or fancy offices or heavy involvement in high society. They were people who worked hard, knew their jobs, fostered an atmosphere of trust, and generally enjoyed wholesome personal reputations. They tended to be people who appreciated the contribution of others, even those who may have been a part of the company when the problems began. Successful turnaround agents allowed recognition of others. It takes more than one person to turn a company around. The successful chief turnaround agents were people who could share center stage.

The chief findings of this research into the nature and causes of successful turnarounds are summarized in the following sections.

Relating to the Nature and Severity of Economic Difficulties

1. *Large dominant firms as well as smaller producers failed.* Large size did not seem to be a factor in turnaround success.

2. During the early years of the turnaround experience, the *successful turnarounds experienced more pronounced business declines and deeper loss rates* during the low points of their principal periods of crisis. This may reinforce the Schendel and Patton (1976) hypothesis that a severe decline in profits and/or revenue will motivate positive management action. Slow stagnation will not.

3. *Improved performance on the part of the successful companies was not immediately apparent.* During the period of decline and the period of crisis, the unsuccessful companies generally looked better financially. From year 2 forward, the successful companies began to emerge as much more consistent and much more profitable.

Relating to Being a Low-Cost Producer

4. The *successful companies were noticeably more efficient in operations* than the unsuccessful firms. Gross profit rates and inventory turn

ratios were significantly higher. This difference in operational efficiency accounted for more than 70 percent of the differences in profitability between successful and unsuccessful firms.

5. The successful companies stayed with their cost-reduction programs longer and made deeper cuts. They *brought the costs down to the then current levels of revenue.* Unsuccessful firms attempted to increase the level of revenue to cover existing costs, either by selling into new markets or by making acquisitions.

6. Cost-reduction programs during the successful turnarounds were pragmatic, disciplined, and even-handed. *Management often played an exemplary role in the cost reduction* programs of successful firms by accepting less pay.

7. *Successful companies handled money conservatively* on an ongoing basis. Cost consciousness was more likely to be a cultural characteristic of successful firms than unsuccessful firms. When the successful firms spent money, it was primarily to improve current operations rather than for expansion into new areas or for corporate image.

8. The *successful companies spent less on* selling, general and administrative expense, and other *non-cost-of-sales expense.*

Relating to the Differentiation of Products

9. Successful companies took painstakingly detailed steps to continually provide differentiated products. Unsuccessful firms often failed to incrementally improve existing products even when product shortcomings were widely perceived.

10. Unsuccessful companies often made significant and abrupt changes in the positioning of their products in the market. Successful firms avoided abrupt changes in market position.

11. *Successful firms put greater emphasis on product quality.* Unsuccessful firms often neglected quality issues.

Relating to Leadership and the Turnaround Organization

12. Successful firms more accurately gauged their ability to implement fully their strategic plans. *Unsuccessful firms often had strategic*

plans that were either *internally inconsistent* or inconsistent with the company's resource base.

13. *The successful firms concentrated on internal operational issues* such as product quality, organizational productivity, product differentiation, and day-to-day sales. Unsuccessful firms often focused on external expansion, acquisitions, or financial restructuring.

14. Successful turnarounds experienced *greater managerial stability* and greater consensus between the officers and directors. Unsuccessful turnarounds experienced more managerial turnover and less cohesion.

15. The chief turnaround agents at the *successful firms had extensive industrial experience* in the particular industry or in a closely related industry. The chief turnaround agents at the unsuccessful firms had less experience in the industry being served.

16. *Experience in manufacturing and/or engineering* was prevalent among the chief turnaround agents in all of the successful cases. Sales or finance experience was more prevalent among the unsuccessful cases.

17. Some subjective narrative information suggests that successful companies embraced *traditional concepts of morality and fairness*. Unsuccessful turnarounds often exhibited problems in relationships with employees, customers, or others.

18. *Both successful and unsuccessful turnarounds involved doing some things well and some things less well.* No one turnaround went perfectly in all respects. No one firm failed in all respects. But sharp contrasts did exist in managerial emphasis, in the procedures used, and in the strengths and styles of the management.

Generality of the Findings

One obvious question regarding this study is, How general are the findings? Only the automotive and agricultural equipment industries were studied here. These two industries have many similar characteristics in that they require similar production equipment and skills, they have had similar financial profiles over time, companies in both industries sell through dealers, and both tend to be located in and to draw employees from similar geographic areas. The question is, Can conclusions regarding the turnaround performance of companies in these two industries be applied to distressed companies in other industries?

It must be remembered that one of the findings of this study was that experience in the industry being served was found to be a powerful determinant of turnaround success. Therefore, it would not be entirely consistent with the findings to suggest that the recommendations are universal to all industries. The author has a deep appreciation for the subtleties necessary to manage successfully in any industry. However, many of those findings are consistent with the research work of others and should have application to other situations, including service industries and transportation and distribution companies.

Several previous studies of turnarounds (Schendel et al. 1976; Hofer 1980; Taylor 1982/1983) have indicated that cost-reduction and internal efficiency strategies appear often among the successful turnaround cases. Other studies (Schendel and Patton 1976; Schendel, et al. 1976; Hofer 1980; O'Niell 1981, 1986; Taylor 1982/1983) found that product differentiation and market-focus strategies appear often among successful turnaround cases. Porter (1980) has advanced the theory that successful companies concentrate on the three generic strategies of low-cost operation, product differentiation, and market focus.

As part of the initial investigation for this study, other industries were reviewed as potential candidates for analysis. The scope of this study did not permit the examination of industries beyond the two selected. However, a cursory review did reveal sharp differences in cost positions and product differentiation in the steel (Nucor and Carpenter Technology vs. LTV), paper and forest-products (Kimberly-Clark vs. International Paper), and appliance industries (Maytag vs. Allegheny International). In addition, some of the same variations in leadership qualities that characterized the turnaround cases selected here also seem to exist in other industries.

At the time of this writing, there are signs of trouble brewing in several industries that have been rather immune to periods of economic upheaval in the recent past. The finance industry is experiencing massive losses and layoffs in its frantic efforts to provide differentiated products at a cost affordable to customers. Insurance companies and health providers are also experiencing stresses not previously experienced. High-technology companies have become subject to the same competitive pressures our industrial companies experienced during the early 1980s, sometimes to an even greater degree. Though I do not claim that the lessons of this study will apply to all circumstances, it is hoped that the material presented here will be useful to practitioners in other industries.

Alternative Explanations

The possibility also exists that there may be other explanations for why the successful companies emerged from the turnaround experience in far better condition than those who were unsuccessful. Among these possible explanations are luck, environmental forces, and other theories of management.

Luck has long played an influential role in the history of business. The case could be made that the emergence of General Motors was at least assisted by the extraordinarily poor relationships that existed between Henry Ford and many of his key associates (one of whom later nurtured the development of Chevrolet and later became president of GM) and Ford's general disregard of trends in the market. Had the Ford Motor Company been a more comfortable long-term place of employment for key managerial and technical people, and had the company been more responsive to customers, the position of GM might be different today. The role of luck should be respected.

However, the cases studied here were examined over very long periods of time. The successes and failures tended to be based on an accrual of positive and negative experiences over many years in many situations. If luck was a factor in the systematic decline of International Harvester, from industry dominance to industry exit, or in the emergence of American Motors during the highly competitive recession years of the late 1950s, there had to be a lot of it.

Luck did play a role in some situations. But in every one of the unsuccessful cases there was some other company in the same industry at the same time that was handling similar situations better. If luck does play a role, it is quite likely to be bidirectional. It seems doubtful that luck operates consistently in the same direction and thereby victimizes only unsuccessful firms. The successful firms had some good and some bad luck, as did the unsuccessful firms.

Environmental factors have been at least partly corrected for in the design of this study. The periods examined run 86 years, from 1902 to 1988. Both successful and unsuccessful cases were found in depression years, recession years, and prosperous years. Government policies, changes in consumer tastes, and other environmental forces affected the companies studied here. But both successful and unsuccessful firms were involved. In some cases, environmental forces provided help to unsuccessful firms, but the firms did not always take advantage of it. For instance, the Arab oil embargo pushed consumers toward the historical market niche of AMC/Renault during the 1970s, when management of the firm was pushing the firm toward unfamiliar upscale large-car markets.

Other theories of management may provide acceptable alternative explanations. The punctuated equilibrium model of Tushman and Romanelli (1985) may provide an interesting perspective as to why the successful companies swung into action the way they did. Schendel and Patton's (1976) first hypothesis, that a radical downturn is more likely than gradual drift to promote action, is also of interest.

Many theories of management are complementary to this analysis, and none of them should be discredited. However, what is interesting about successful turnarounds are the technical steps taken to achieve low-cost operation and product differentiation. Turnaround success was not achieved solely by employing appropriate managerial concepts but by very specific and often very technical managerial actions. With the importance of technology thus obvious, theories of management must allow sufficiently for technology.

The branch of management theory that relates to the escalation of commitment may have some relevance to the examination of turnaround success. It does appear that the commitment of organization members varied widely. All the companies studied had manufacturing plants, but some were far more productive than others. All had product-development departments, but some of these departments were not effective, while others were able to introduce a wide variety of new products during times of staff reductions and expense curtailments. The allocation of resources was not the principal decision variable. The yield on the allocated resources ranged greatly. Perhaps the research surrounding commitment can provide further insights.

Need for Improved Analysis of the Declining Firm

As more of our companies reach advanced age in mature or declining markets, we will need to enrich our understanding of the declining firm. We will no doubt find, as many of the European firms have found, that the declining firm is too important to the nation's employment and the supply of needed goods to be left to drift without a methodology for correction. We will need to develop ways to remedy the fortunes of these crucial elements of our society, and further research into the special questions surrounding the declining firm will be required. Fortunately, remedial management is a branch of our broader theory of management, so we will be able to rely heavily upon what has been accomplished in the past. However, there are some circumstances unique to the declining firm, and time and resource limitations provide further constraints. It is hoped that the evidence provided here will be a useful supplement to the rest of management theory, which is fully applicable to the turnaround situation.

A Final Caveat

One caveat remains: *Turnarounds are never permanent.* Constant vigilance is required to remain competitive. Several companies managed highly successful turnarounds, experienced high rates of profitability, and enjoyed renewed market presence for several years only to experience a new predicament 15, 20, or 30 years later. The same is true of companies that have not faced crisis. Managers can never rest assured that their companies are out of the woods (Figure 13-4).

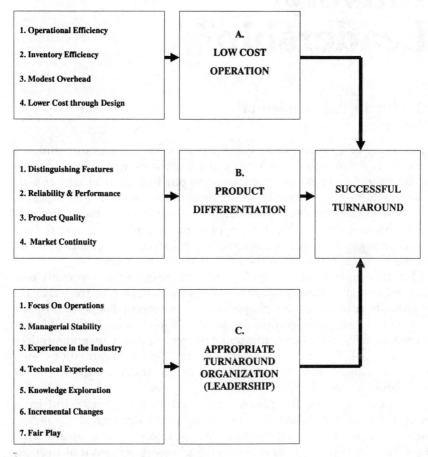

Figure 13-4. Framework of a successful turnaround process.

14
Real or Illusory Leadership?

Quality in the Managerial Process

This study of 16 turnaround cases provides both reassurance and sadness. It is reassuring to see companies come back from disaster to become strong and healthy contributors to our industrial society. It is reassuring, also, to see *how* the companies turned around. The processes involved would seem to be available to most companies facing financial crisis, because the key characteristics of turnaround success were business strategy, managerial competence, technical skills, and personal character traits rather than the availability of resources.

But this study of turnarounds is also sobering, because so many people and so many other companies and communities were affected by the failure of the unsuccessful companies. During their peak periods of employment, these major companies directly employed more than 270,000 people (Table 14-1). Many additional people, probably several hundred thousand people, were associated with the dealer organizations, supplier companies, and other businesses in the communities where the companies operated.

In some instances, the people employed by the unsuccessful firms were ultimately absorbed by other companies, although the numbers were probably small. The competitive positions of the unsuccessful firms had already seriously deteriorated when other firms took over the remnants of these once-major companies. With the demise of the un-

Table 14-1. Employment Changes of Unsuccessful Turnaround Cases

	Peak employment (estimate)	1989 employment (estimate)	Percent of peak employment
Willys-Overland	21,000	0	0
Hudson	21,000	0	0
Studebaker-Packard	38,000	0	0
International Harvester	105,000	17,000	16
Allis-Chalmers	33,500	1,000	3
Kaiser-Frazer	20,000	0	0
AMC/Renault	33,000	8,000	24
Total	271,500	26,000	9.6
Number of cases	7	3	

successful firms came the inevitable decline in the number of people gainfully employed in the continuation of these businesses – even under different names. Hudson's major plants were closed completely. The Willow Run plant of Kaiser-Frazer was sold to General Motors for an entirely different purpose. Many International Harvester plants now stand idle. The West Allis, Wisconsin, plant of Allis-Chalmers, which at one time employed more than 20,000 people, is now a modest shopping center.

Some people may suggest that no special problem exists in this regard. Old businesses are constantly failing as new businesses are born. Through this ongoing process of failure and rebirth, the economy strengthens itself and adapts to changing conditions and changing markets. This perspective has validity for analyzing some problems, but at this time in our present economy, we need answers to some fundamental questions. Is rebirth really happening, or are some of our basic and essential industries in the process of failing permanently, with no suitable replacement in sight? What will our economy and our society be like when they are gone? We should remember that the once-glamorous, high-tech industries are now under feverish attack and that the service industries have proved to be poor substitutes for profitable and vibrant basic industries in terms of providing employment.

Also, we must be concerned about quality in the managerial process. How can we be satisfied with failure? If we give the turnarounds before us our most serious study and our most conscientious efforts and we still fail, perhaps that is one possible outcome. But, as professionals, we must be concerned with the quality of our managerial process.

Our recent economic history supports an argument for greater precision in the turnaround process. South Bend has never really recovered from the demise of Studebaker. Several cities have been seriously damaged by the problems of International Harvester. Our trade balance gets more serious every year. Unemployment has ranged between 9 and 12 million people in recent years. Governments face ongoing deficits of enormous magnitude with the present level of receipts from our malfunctioning economy.

Does Management Understand Its Job?

This study of turnaround cases surfaces important questions regarding the quality of our managerial execution during times of stress: How well does management understand its job? Do the managers of companies undergoing difficult times know what needs to be done?

In the successful cases, this knowledge *did* exist—at least most of the time. Management trimmed cost, improved efficiency, nurtured the improvement of products, and concentrated on crucial events which were pertinent to the firm's business at the time. Management encouraged the successful firms to focus on familiar market segments and spurn diversions. Management provided leadership based on technical expertise, on relevant experience in the industry being served, and on personal integrity. During times of cash shortage, managers set examples by taking less pay.

Regarding the unsuccessful cases, there is evidence that *management often did not know what needed to be done and did not know how to do what was needed.* Management diverted scarce resources into poorly thought-out plans for expansion while critical day-to-day problems of high cost and low quality were neglected. Management allowed the unsuccessful firms to drift ineffectively from one market segment to another without sufficient proactive attention to historically important markets. Management approved the adoption of inconsistent strategies which were beyond the resource base of the firm. Management changed more frequently, played less of an exemplary role, and exhibited less appreciation of old values as foundations for new beliefs.

This is a serious indictment, of course, but the problems are serious too. All the unsuccessful companies were, at one time, substantial components of the industrial complex of the United States. None ranked lower than the fourth-largest firm in their industries at some point in their history, and most reached higher levels. Now, they are virtually gone. Many factors played a role in the demise of these once-substantial firms, but one question that should arise is whether management knew what to do.

This question of whether management knew what to do should not be viewed as too simple or too basic. Consider the evidence in the cases studied here. International Harvester built up huge inventories, against the advice of experienced company personnel, to support out-of-date production methods and in response to an utterly false reading of the market demand for the company's products. Management did not know enough about the business to structure an appropriate forecasting system or to organize a critique of its own perceptions. The lack of good forecasting, coupled with limited knowledge of the business, led to an enormous buildup in inventories that severely pinched cash and played a major role in the demise of the company's historical mainline business. Studebaker and Hudson both remained high-cost producers for decades prior to the actual demise of the firms. Allis-Chalmers, Kaiser-Frazer, and AMC/Renault (in recent years) were all high-cost producers at critical times during their attempted turnarounds. In none of the unsuccessful cases did management display sufficient expertise in organizing the firm's production or in managing the firm's major business.

The inability of management to manage efficiently affected product differentiation as well. In several cases (IHC, Kaiser-Frazer, Studebaker, and Hudson) the high cost of operations limited funding so severely that programs of product differentiation were either eliminated or severely curtailed. These same companies then worsened their situations by dissipating shrinking resources on poorly planned new ventures — with disastrous results. The successful companies were also short of funds, but these companies had the advantage of resource savings from production efficiencies and, in addition, they found ways to develop better products within the framework of limited resources. Top management in the unsuccessful companies lacked these skills.

There is also evidence that management of the unsuccessful companies was not sufficiently in touch with markets to effectively deliver well-thought-out product strategies. In the case of International Harvester, much of the company's top management was unacquainted with the businesses the company was in, and the lack of appreciation for the views of the more experienced Harvester executives contributed to a growing mismatch between the company's actions and the needs of the marketplace. Similar events took place at Studebaker, Kaiser-Frazer, and AMC/Renault in recent years. In other cases, such as Hudson and Willys-Overland, top management had industry experience (although not in product development or manufacturing), but then compounded problems by dabbling in outside affairs. The executives of these firms were not trained in the habits of efficiency. They did not know how a plant should operate. With respect to understanding the theories and practicalities of low-cost production and product differentiation and being able to mobilize effective competitive offerings, management was operating outside of its domain.

In the cases where management was operating outside of its domain, the results were internally inconsistent strategies — strategies which did not hang together logically. Some strategies presumed that the fortunes of the companies would rebound with increased sales when variable costs were close to or above 100 percent of revenue. Some strategies involved high-cost producers offering products in the low-priced field. Some strategies involved offering brand-new products to new markets when the products being offered were rushed into production, were poorly tested, and were of shoddy quality. There were strategies involving actions which almost systematically alienated the firm from its historical customer base.

The successful firms operated differently. They knew the markets. They had experience in serving the markets. They knew how to build the products at an acceptable cost, and they knew how to differentiate the products from competitive offerings. Successful companies had *real leadership*.

What seems to have emerged in the unsuccessful companies was not leadership but the *illusion of leadership*. The companies were paying for leadership. James Nance of Studebaker-Packard made more money than the entire officer corps *combined* at Nash Motors when that company faced troubled times in the 1930s. The compensation of the executives of International Harvester was high enough to exacerbate relations with company employees during a time of crisis. Roy Chapin of Hudson had one of the largest houses in Michigan, but the company was crumbling from within. Managers of the unsuccessful companies had adequate incentives available to them. They just didn't know what to do.

This illusion of leadership was not an easy situation to detect initially because many of the unsuccessful managers were impressive-looking and impressive-sounding people. Roy Chapin of Hudson was impressive enough to become secretary of commerce. John North Willys of Willys-Overland became an ambassador. Several of the unsuccessful turnaround agents had reputations for being impressive, outgoing public speakers, but there is no long-term evidence that outwardly impressive people necessarily have sufficient depth, sufficient experience, and sufficient character or generate sufficient trust to effectively manage a turnaround. What in fact happened is that these once-noble companies were ruined as viable competitors in their principal markets.

The long-term notoriety of one unsuccessful turnaround agent can be described by an incident extracted from Barbara Marsh's book *Corporate Tragedy*, which described the demise of International Harvester:

> Inside the milk house, where several [farmers] have stopped for fresh pie, one man asks if anybody remembers the name of the ex-

ecutive who didn't know anything about tractors who ran the company into the ground. (Marsh 1985, 299)

The question being raised here is fundamental to the system of recruiting managers in the United States. As Hayes and Abernathy (1980) pointed out, a decline has taken place in the number of top managers who have technical and marketing backgrounds, whereas the number with legal and finance backgrounds has increased. However, the question is only partly related to the experience of the individuals. The problem isn't as simple as having too many people in finance, for the expertise of the finance departments varied widely too. Some finance people, such as B. F. Hutchinson with the early Chrysler Corporation, Red Poling with Ford, or Gerald Greenwald with Chrysler in later years, were thorough, trustworthy people who understood very well the technical details of the business. In order to turn companies around, managers with meaningful technical knowledge are needed in all aspects of the business. It is important for people in the finance or accounting departments to have an intimate understanding of what drives the costs they are measuring. Hutchinson understood what influences real cost in part because he, at one time, had been a production supervisor himself.

The successful turnaround agents understood how to design products for both low cost and product differentiation. During its 1956 to 1964 turnaround, American Motors built five basic engines, three sixes and two V8s, from one very similar set of pistons and valves. Cars of different sizes had the same door frames—which greatly reduced tooling expense. Right and left taillights, front and rear bumpers, and many other parts were often identical. These actions led to a tooling cost per unit that was substantially lower than that of any other manufacturer in the business, and the firm survived.

In contrast, when Chrysler Corporation was getting into trouble in the 1960s and 1970s, as many as eight different engines were offered with certain car models. Product development took too long, which often resulted in the firm's being out of step with the market. When the Chrysler turnaround became successful, it was to a very large degree because of the innovative handling of product design and manufacturing engineering. Chrysler's design teams learned how to make a broad spectrum of product offerings from a smaller assortment of component parts. The Chrysler turnaround was not a financial restructuring. It was a major engineering and production accomplishment, which resulted in vastly improved product differentiation at a much lower cost of production, a turnaround made possible by the accommodating cooperation of organized labor.

The unsuccessful turnaround agents did not understand these things. They were busy with other matters. They were pressuring their sales organizations to sell more without understanding that variable costs were near to or above the prices received for the products. They were making deals to get into new businesses or out of old businesses without any deep understanding about what was required for any of these businesses to operate profitably. The planning logic seemed to be, If we can't manage what we've got, we had better manage something else.

The successful turnaround agents appeared to differ in character traits as well as in industry awareness and technical knowledge. The perception of fairness (or lack of it) influenced the willingness of members of the organization to put forth the extra effort necessary to mobilize a turnaround. The proxy indicators available in these cases suggest that the successful turnaround agents exhibited honesty and trustworthiness, were not preoccupied with their own importance, and allowed others to share in the accomplishments. Further, when things were not going well, these executives first reduced their own compensation and then prevailed upon the organization to reduce costs.

Many people, not just one or two, played key roles in the successful turnarounds. The successful turnarounds had deep managerial teams. Similarly, the blame for corporate failure cannot be laid at the door of one or two people. Many people were involved in both the successful and the unsuccessful cases. The seeds of failure or success are sowed over long periods of time. That is why we need longitudinal studies to examine business situations.

We do need to keep in perspective the fact that no one company did everything perfectly and no one company did everything wrong. Mistakes were made in successful cases, and there were high points in the attempts that failed. But, certain patterns did emerge. Successful turnaround agents exhibited industry knowledge, production knowledge, engineering knowledge, rapport with customers and dealers, incremental improvements, an appreciation for the company's history, honesty, humility, and a sense of fair play. These are some of the factors that distinguished the successful firms. Of these, the most prominent were low-cost operation, product differentiation, and leadership. It could be that a more thorough study at another time will find that character traits and value systems have great untapped potential to mobilize the organizational learning necessary for a successful turnaround.

Turnaround Management as a Skill

The economic and financial problems we have before us collectively suggest that we must greatly improve our industrial performance if the citizens of the United States are to continue to enjoy the social stability that has blessed our country in the past. We do have the capability to get some of our problems resolved, but this capability exists only in potential form. We must transfer it to the kinetic form, and that means developing the skills not only to analyze problems but to remedy them.

Our business schools, our business publications, our informal networks within business itself, and our government have deluded us into thinking that mere analysis of the problem is the principal skill. It is not the principal skill, though it is helpful. To cope effectively with today's problems, we need skills that may be entirely different from those which served our nation during better times. We must develop skills that will equip us to remedy troubled situations when they occur, and at cost levels that are affordable to stockholders, employees, creditors, and communities. We must know more about how to accomplish more with less. We must be more efficient in our practice of management, more cost-effective, and more professional. In order for us to continue as a meaningful participant in the world economy, we must modify our behavior, particularly our managerial behavior.

The evidence provided in this study should be reassuring because many individuals have demonstrated the remedial skills sufficient for the task before us. But we need more people with remedial skills, and we need them in positions of influence. One of the more sobering aspects of this study is that many of the individuals who have most actively demonstrated the remedial skills we so desperately need are either sick, old, or dead. Lewis Veraldi passed away in the fall of 1990. Donald Petersen has retired from Ford. George Romney is in his eighties. Iacocca is nearing retirement. Hans Matthias has retired for a second time. It is to be hoped that new people are being trained to take their places. Surely a country with the vast population of the United States can field suitable replacements. But perhaps the early conditioning of these people—the deprivation of the 1930s, the hardships of the World War II, the long climb from immigrant status to positions of influence—was in fact preparing them with the remedial and survival skills that the country now so desperately needs.

Those of us in education may wish to believe that education is the appropriate vehicle for preparing leaders for the future. After reflecting upon the evidence gathered here, I am less sure. Indeed, there may be reasons to question whether education, as we presently practice it here in the United States, is a help or a hindrance to the development of remedial skills. Even the recipients of our most technically advanced degrees seldom receive first-hand experience with production as a part of their training anymore. Their knowledge of theory is well-developed, but we may wonder whether we are falling into the trap identified by Charles Kettering, one of our greatest inventors: We may be "confusing symbols for things." Veraldi started out as an apprentice tool-and-die maker in 1944 and then got his engineering degree in night school. By the time he ascended to the position of vice president of Ford, he intimately knew many of the tasks that needed to be done at Ford, and he knew the people who could do them well. Walter Chrysler, Henry Leland, B. F. Hutchinson, George Mason, Charles Nash, William Knudsen, and Charles Kettering had similar beginnings. None of these great industrialists were exposed to the style of education that exists in our modern world today.

Now our conditioning is different. We graduate from college and move directly into management without the benefit of first-hand execution of some of the tasks we are managing. Instead of learning about real management in courses like operations management, we learn the ground rules for selecting unit, batch, or mass production systems, probably a once-in-a-lifetime decision for most companies. In courses on strategy we learn a *style* of portfolio management, the implication being that management is basically a selection process and not an accomplishment process. We learn how to detect and analyze problems, but we learn less about how to remedy them. Even in engineering programs, we are learning less about how goods are actually designed and produced. In our marketing programs we seldom cover how to get an order, and in our finance courses, we seldom cover how to collect money. Perhaps the remedial skills will unfold from our present educational system. In many ways it is a good system, and one that is certainly capable of making corrections.

As the United States continues to struggle with its economic and industrial difficulties, higher levels of managerial professionalism will be needed, not only to analyze but to remedy the problems being faced. Remedial management will become an increasingly precious skill. Whether it is a skill that emanates from an elaborate formal education system or one that is nurtured and developed by thorough first-hand exposure, interspersed with periods of deprivation, remains to be seen.

15

Recommendations for the Future

During the late 1980s, the economy of the United States was robust and growing. Inflation was at an acceptable range, and unemployment had declined from the appalling levels of the early 1980s. On the surface, there was prosperity. However, few would suggest that the economic system was in equilibrium. Unprecedented consumer debt, government deficits several times what we formerly regarded as astronomical, the quick transition of the United States from the world's largest creditor to its largest debtor, volatile capital markets, monumental trade deficits, and a plethora of unfriendly and underanalyzed corporate takeovers all provided testimony that the U.S. economy, though prosperous, lacked equilibrium.

As we progress into the 1990s, we must develop the skills to turn companies around and restore America's competitive edge one company at a time. That is not easy, but it is the only practical option open to us. Industrial companies and productive individuals are the source of America's wealth. If we want to sustain the prosperity and social stability of the United States, we must improve the performance of individual companies.

The recommendations that follow pertain to business, education, government, and finance. All these activities must function with greater reliability, more creativity, and an understanding of the informal linkages between the key elements of our economy. Successful resolution of the problems before us will involve a systematic interleaving of technical, sociological, and managerial concepts. These recommendations are divided into four groups:

Recommendations for Businesses Involved in Turnarounds

Find Managers Who Understand the Business

Don't assume that being smart is a qualifying asset in the long term. Successful management during a turnaround is partly a matter of domain. Key people should understand the business and the company's individual business in particular. The most successful turnaround agents were those who had experience in the industry being served.

Be Respectful of the People Who Were Involved in the Company

People who were involved in the company when the problems developed may have done some things very well. The turnarounds that succeed often involve an appreciation of past accomplishments. The firms that have difficulty often run roughshod over old values and bring in too much new management. Some of the best turnaround agents are from within the company.

Cultivate Both Formal and Informal Forecasting Techniques

Either may be wrong. In a situation as chaotic as a turnaround, the cross-checking of forecast information is critical. Ineffective cross-checks on forecasting systems often result in major strategic mistakes in inventory levels, staffing levels, plant locations, or other factors essential to survival. Successful turnaround agents are respectful, but they gather information from more than one source.

Ensure That the Entire Organization Is Part of the Turnaround Process

The process of turnaround is one of organizational learning. The entire organization must develop together and in parallel. It is not simply the task of selecting the appropriate leader. Even though the leader is important, so are the other members of the organization. The entire organization must progress in order to become an effective competitor in the modern industrial world.

Examine the Environment on the Basis of Essential Information

Examine the environment on the basis of information that is essential in formulating the appropriate approach to organizational turnaround. *Don't rely on information that is available, because it may not be enough.* One of the most serious mistakes in a turnaround is to try to solve problems on the basis of what information is available rather than what information is necessary. There will still be a need to make decisions expeditiously during a turnaround. The above comments apply to the information that is sought rather than the need to obtain it quickly. One reason why turnaround agents with experience in the industry do better is because they often have quick access to outside information.

Hire and Retain People Partly on the Basis of Character Traits

Walter Chrysler said it best: "If the spirit is not right, it is useless to look at results." The successful turnarounds are most often headed by people who exhibit strong preferences for character traits involving old-fashioned honesty, morality, and hard work. The key attribute of a successful turnaround sometimes boils down to retaining the most honest people who want to work hard, who know something about the business they are in, and who want the company to succeed.

Get Efficient First—Sell Later

Efficiency is crucial to turnaround success. Rarely will higher levels of revenue greatly increase company prosperity if the company is inefficient. Without efficiency, incremental costs eventually consume incremental revenue. In order to succeed, the first priority of the troubled firm should be to improve efficiency, conserve precious resources, and use those resources to differentiate products. After these steps are taken, additional revenue will help restore corporate profits.

Use Efficiency Savings to Differentiate the Products and Improve Quality

Product differentiation must be enhanced every day through innovative programs of constant improvement funded and made possible by high levels of internal efficiency. Product feature and benefit improvements must be timed with market trends and must be meaningful, not gadgetry or limited to cosmetics. Product quality must proceed from discipline and must include attention to in-process quality.

Systematically Withdraw Resources to Improve Performance

Too many people and too much inventory—maybe even too much money—can get in the way of turnaround success. Most successful turnarounds do not have and do not seek excess resources that might get in the way of efficient performance. If steps can be taken to promote broadly based organizational learning, improved performance with fewer resources is distinctly possible. Beyond this, the very condition of resource scarcity can promote organizational learning and lead to greater innovation.

Concentrate on the Basic Business

Don't get diverted. The track record of turning around a company by entering a new field is very poor—particularly when the company shows no capacity to manage its old field. If we cannot keep our basic business healthy, what shred of evidence is there to suggest that we can manage anything else?

Make Small, Incremental Improvements, Constantly

Successful companies only rarely attempt bold new initiatives into unchartered waters. They effectively work on myriads of small problems every day, month after month, for years and decades. Turnarounds commonly take several years to reach fruition. Success involved constant programs of incremental improvement interspersed with occasional well-executed new product programs—programs that arose from science and involved many constituencies.

Recommendations for Boards of Directors

One cannot review the histories of these once-great companies without wondering what role members of the boards of directors played in the successes or failures of the firms they helped direct. In some cases, the role of certain directors was very positive. In other cases, one wonders why the directors did not press for earlier action as these important industrial companies showed signs of declining. As an experienced director who has served on the boards of 10 companies, I realize the practical difficulties of wishing to support the company while exercising fiduciary responsibility. However, the information gathered in this study, coupled with the experiences of others including the author, suggests that our present systems of corporate directorship could be improved. The following recommendations might be helpful.

Cultivate the Acceptability of Voting Conscience and Judgment

Let management and directors feel more comfortable in proposing ideas that are controversial. Presently, the system is similar to the English parliamentary system. The CEO must win every vote of confidence, and there is much informal pressure to support management on every vote, even on trivial issues. There seems to be some muted reasoning that suggests that if a director ever votes differently from management, the director is not supportive of the company and perhaps should not serve. In reality, the directors most needed are those who do have a mind of their own and who have the courage to express their convictions, particularly at times of crisis. This need not be a hostile situation, any more than was the case with the often opposing votes cast by George Aiken and Mike Mansfield during their years as responsible leaders of their respective parties in the U.S. Senate. The fact was that they were close personal friends who usually had breakfast together, even though they often voted differently on major issues. Yet, in business, this informal convention of consistent support of management often leads to the curtailment of healthy expression on the major issues facing the firm. The system is no better for the CEO than for the directors. What we need is greater candor about where we stand and some fresh ideas about how to improve our situation, not overly courteous, informally stifled discussion. With the loss in international market share that we are presently experiencing, we cannot be satisfied with the ways we conduct the corporate affairs of America.

Upgrade and Round Out the Board of Directors

Invite people on to the board who are insightful, studious, and fair and who understand at least something about the business the firm is in. Also, avoid reciprocity appointments or appointments in which other conflicts of interest exist. For instance, some venture capitalists suggest that a top manager of one of their portfolio companies be appointed to sit on the board of another investment. Too many interrelationships among directors can impede the systematic review of the situation that must take place for a firm in trouble to develop a lasting solution.

Be Alert to Strategic Conflicts of Interest

Remain skeptical of new strategic initiatives that seem to compete in resources or time with the management of the basic business. Existing businesses must be treated with priority, at least until new programs have been successfully launched, are capable of carrying the organization, and are functioning reliably. Too often, the desire to expand markets or enter new markets compromises success in present markets and causes the firm to decline. Directors must preserve the firm's historical business.

Retest the Forecasts

If the firm relies heavily on forecasts to establish its strategic direction, insist that it employ both formal and informal forecasting systems. Then, insist that both the forecasts and the assumptions are cross-checked. The best firms do not rely so heavily on forecasts, opting instead for strategies adaptable to many conditions. When forecasts are used, they flow from knowledge exploration, from a systematic analysis of critical questions that need to be answered, rather than from conveniently available internal information.

Hold Board Meetings and Annual Meetings at Reasonable Places

Numerex, a quality producer of precision coordinate measuring machines, holds its annual meetings on the factory checkout floor, amid the company's workers and products. The best annual meetings are held in places that can be easily attended by employees, creditors, suppliers, and customers. The most inappropriate places for meetings are at expensive hotels and resorts.

Remedy Obvious Ethical Problems When They Occur

Fire people who are dishonest or unethical and do not give them any severance pay. There is nothing that can reduce the collective resolve of the company more quickly than the retention of known crooks, or alternatively, their departure under lucrative circumstances. Do not worry about the lawsuits. They will be even bigger if the company fails.

Get Realistic on Executive Compensation

Most really good executives don't care about it anyway. If the company does regain profitability (for several years running), it is reasonable for managers and others to share in the rewards. But when the company is still in difficulty, and many are being asked to sacrifice, management should lead the way.

Help Formulate Public Policy

People in government in the United States need to have a closer association with and a better appreciation of the industrial segment of our society, as is the case in Europe and Asia. Many of the pressing problems facing industry in the United States result from inappropriate industrial policies or the lack of scientific knowledge on the part of policymakers. Some government officials will help if representatives from industry can articulate the way in which industry is linked to the social fabric of our society. But corporations and companies are remarkably passive. The CEO will most often be too busy running the business to be active in the political arena, but directors can help clarify the inner workings of an industrial economy to a political structure that has been less interested than has been the case in other industrialized countries.

Recommendations for Business Schools

Schools of business have much to offer, but unfortunately, U.S. trade and federal deficits have not declined as the number of business school graduates has increased. It is time for business schools to undergo an organized critique of their own performance. The following suggestions are constructively offered to incrementally improve some aspects of business school education.

Study the Way Companies Operate over Longer Periods of Time

Of the cases involved in this study, the successful companies experienced steeper revenue decreases and deeper loss rates and emerged more slowly. In several of the unsuccessful cases, such as Willys-Overland, Allis-Chalmers, or International Harvester, the companies' true problems did not become apparent until several years into the turnaround attempt. During the principal periods of crisis, the best companies quite often looked worse, and the worst companies quite often looked better. It was only after several years that the superior effort of the successful firms enabled them to look better statistically. Company performance and managerial practices must be evaluated over long periods of time. Our principles of management should be derived from longitudinal analysis.

Integrate Technical Knowledge into Business Curriculums

We must *integrate technical knowledge of products, materials, production methods, and customer service procedures into the curriculum of business schools.* The subjects we now cover are too simplistic to prepare people for global competition. We have to understand, in much greater detail, what is required to have true performance over a lasting period of time. We must understand the processes of product differentiation, low-cost production, and customer satisfaction in *technical as well as managerial terms.* Through long-term managerial competence we must preserve our basic industries, which are the lifeblood of our economy.

Study Specific Industries in Greater Detail

In order to compete internationally, we must study our competitors in much greater detail. The Harvard case method lends itself to in-depth understanding of some situations, and many schools use the method. We must understand more about the technologies, production methods, and marketing systems, and how they operate to establish a stronger competitive position in important major industries. We must develop a more thorough understanding of why some firms (both national and international) in a particular industry do well, whereas others do poorly. Our present business school curriculum should be far more detailed and substantially more industry-specific to provide modern managers with the skills necessary to prevail in today's highly competitive global economy.

Study Companies in Decline as well as Those That Are Growing

Our society is faced with difficult structural problems relating to issues with the environment, emerging technologies, the society, and worldwide political stability. Any of these can impact the growth rates of individual firms and industries. Our primary case examples should not be only of companies that are temporarily successful and growing. We must know more about the processes of decline and possible remedies. Some excellent work has been performed, for instance, John Argenti's book *Corporate Collapse*. But we need more.

Integrate Character Development and Managerial Education

The case for value-free managerial education can be made only if there is evidence that all values are equally effective in dealing with particular situations. There is at least some evidence that certain values are a factor in turnaround success. These values are not that controversial. They involve basic honesty, some minimal levels of temperance, traditional morality, and a genuine appreciation for others. Maybe these qualities are not the domain of the management schools, but some of us are more optimistic about what might be accomplished if character traits became topics of discussion. Perhaps we could turn out managers who would be more in tune with their organizations.

As more businesses find themselves in turnaround situations, business schools must cultivate the skills their students will need to solve turnaround problems. Business schools have a great deal to offer, but they should examine whether their own products are sufficiently differentiated. Intense global competition and other industry stresses require greater precision in the managerial process. Executives need to study more, and business schools need to provide them with current, well-researched information about turnarounds.

Recommendations Regarding Public Policy

Those involved with public policy may also benefit from an appreciation of the remedies used by the successful turnaround companies. Many local communities within the United States have been adversely affected by the eroding competitive edge of their major industries. In some cases, public policy, though very well intentioned, has greatly retarded the readaptation of local industry. The following suggestions for those involved in formulating public policy are designed to foster the economic revitalization of industrial communities.

Focus on Tangible Production

Tangible production is the ultimate source of our entire society's standard of living. Without strong world-class productivity on the part of agriculture, mining, construction, and manufacturing, the rest of our society can only lose ground economically, socially, and politically. The services, government, and trade segments of our society, though important, cannot produce wealth in real terms. Support services and educational institutions will perish in the absence of an underlying base of competitively viable production. Programs that focus on race tracks, lotteries, shopping centers, and office buildings are not really economic development programs but instead often become long-term economic liabilities as they wither from the lack of real function. Only carefully nurtured tangible production can ultimately provide the capital accumulation needed to improve the competitive position of the United States and provide its population with a meaningful standard of living. Yet, at the present time we devote much of our economic development resources to peripheral activities which are, in some cases, totally unrelated to lasting economic development. Resources should be explicitly directed away from these false providers of short-term employment and toward improving the region's capability as a low-cost supplier of needed products.

There are plenty of good products that need to be produced. Modern societies need better and more economical pollution-control systems, more efficient energy generation and transmission systems, more cost-effective transportation systems, more versatile production systems, newer materials that have as their main ingredient fewer strategic resources, more environmentally sound packaging systems, better health-care products, and a wide variety of other needed products. There is plenty for us to do, but we must focus on doing it.

Formulate Policy on the Basis of
Input/Output Economics

Modern industrial economies can best be understood and measured by employing the principles of modern input/output economics. The underlying concepts of input/output economics are straightforward. The goods and services each industry requires to produce its own products must either be produced within the same economy or be imported and financed. Thus it becomes important to pay attention to the supplier elements of our economy and to nurture and encourage those industries that have the maximum favorable impact on the performance of the overall economy.

As we examine our national economy, we must ensure that the industries we encourage with our limited public resources are in fact crucial to overall performance. Improvement in the U.S. balance of payments depends on our ability to improve the competitive positions of the individual firms participating in key strategic industries. These key strategic industries employ large numbers of people in activities related to the tangible production of goods (and services) most integral to the development of a strong industrial infrastructure. We cannot expect to regain prosperity by diversifying into new areas where we have little experience. Instead, we must cultivate the skills necessary to restore the competitive edge of key strategic industries and their supplier networks.

The strategy of concentrating on the efficiency of the supplier network does not work against the important economic principle of comparative advantage. Comparative advantages are built over long periods of time and involve the expertise of supplier organizations as well as end-product companies. Yet, an input/output road map to industrial prominence is scarcely evident in our industrial policy-making. Recent public initiatives place little emphasis on developing the underlying capabilities for efficient tangible production. At the national level, changes in the U.S. 1986 tax law shifted taxes from indirect service industries to industrial companies and to capital formation, exactly the opposite of what we should do if we are concerned with economic stability. At the local level, industrial revenue bonds and tax increment financing seem, more frequently, to subsidize office buildings, convention sites, and shopping centers rather than to build a solid industrial base which will provide meaningful high-value employment long into the future. Many states now use the proceeds of gambling (which is probably quite harmful to both our human capital and our economy in total) to fund projects that are either totally unrelated to an industrial economy or remarkably indirect. Although the objective of creating employment is worthwhile, it is doubtful that many of these programs will provide the underlying industrial strength we need to regain our competitive position. In many cases, the programs themselves are costly and counterproductive and divert attention from what should be done. To achieve economic stability, we must develop our industrial infrastructure one company at a time.

Improve the Competitive Edge of Present Industries

Our primary task is to improve the competitive edge of present industries rather than to attract new industries to take their place. The individual firm is the key unit of analysis in the study of the competitive position of developed economies. One can hardly find an American TV set or an American videocassette recorder, yet imported electric tools are quite rare. We know of the penetration of the Japanese auto, yet we make almost all our major appliances here. We import large amounts of textiles but not much carpet. When we examine the production processes employed in the manufacture of these various products, we see similarities among both imported and domestically produced goods. The same sort of stampings, die castings, plastic-injection moldings, wires, switches, transmissions, actuators, and finishings used in the manufacture of major appliances, where we have almost no imports, are used in automobiles, where competition from imports is extensive. We make small electric tools with some of the same materials and some of the same processes as consumer electronics; yet we make most of our electric tools and import most of our small appliances. Clearly, the United States has the engineering and scientific capability to produce products at favorable costs in markets where we are presently not doing well, but we must focus our efforts.

Yet, because of our narrow perspective, we have not always focused on improving the effectiveness of our present industries. In response to the strains on our present economy, industrial communities have adopted vigorous programs to attract new industries to replace industrial jobs lost through plant closings or staff reductions. These programs are unlikely to be successful because little significant industrial movement occurs during a single year and the approach does not build on the strengths of the local community. It also takes too long. For practical reasons, present industries, not other industries, must be competitive for a developed economy to flourish.

Improve Everybody's Quality and Productivity

Tangible production can be advanced by improving the work quality and productivity of those involved in tangible production and of those who provide goods and services. Improving the productivity of education, law enforcement, accounting, finance, and social services is as important as improving the effectiveness of manufacturers. In dollar terms, it is more important because, at·this time, only about 10 to 15 percent of the GNP of the United States is for the labor associated with tangible production.

Programs oriented to improving the nation's competitive position have largely ignored the productivity of the nation's infrastructure. Yet, it is in the indirect segments of our economy that improvements are most urgently needed. We cannot allow the indirect segments of our economy to continue to siphon money from our industrial sector and expect that sector to remain competitive in world markets. We must objectively appraise our position and then make innovative improvements in these indirect segments of our economy. The quality and productivity improvements instituted at Deere, Chrysler, Ford, and 3M provide worthwhile examples for governments, financial institutions, insurance companies, educational institutions, and suppliers of needed services. Economic development programs should be restructured to expect and achieve significant improvements in quality and productivity on the part of all of us.

Push for Similar Benefits, Reasonable Compensation Levels, and More Work

The work-time requirements, fringe benefits, and compensation for various occupations and participants within our society should bear some logical relationship to one another. We cannot have vast differences in place more because of tradition or randomness than because of merit, and still have maximum cost-effectiveness. Although many firms behave responsibly, there is room for considerable improvement. Higher executive salaries often occur at marginally performing S&Ls, risk-oriented financial services firms, pyramiding retailers, industrial firms where market share is slipping, or as golden parachutes in takeovers where the company has already been lost. We all need to review what we take from the system. Executive compensation may be a good place to begin because it is highly visible and because moderate executive pay could have a highly beneficial effect on our economy by setting an appropriate example. However, we are all part of the compensation problem because our country consumes more than it produces. Our best interest is served when *all* of us do more work and exercise moderation in the use of resources and in personal compensation. In many cases, we need realistic compensation and more work.

Seek Individual Solutions
Not Class Solutions

No individual category of workers (production workers, lawyers, schoolteachers, etc.) is to blame for the current difficulties of the United States. Our problems exist because of quality and productivity shortfalls on the part of people within every profession. The appropriate remedy is to address the quality of individual participation within each profession (occupation) rather than trying to shift wealth from one group to another.

Fortunately, most fields, including education, the services, and industry, have many highly dedicated professionals. But, we need a great deal more dedication generally. The task before us is to significantly improve quality while costs are simultaneously reduced. Creative solutions and new systems will be needed to accomplish such aggressive goals. However, the challenges also mean that more must be expected from individuals. We are now forced by economic circumstance to pay a great deal more attention to the character traits, quality of performance, and productivity of individuals as key ingredients to global economic stability.

The pursuit of individual solutions is difficult but not impossible. Although individual rights are basic to our identity as a nation, these individual rights should not include the right to jeopardize an entire firm because of marginal performance, to endanger the future resources of a firm by extracting absurd compensation, or to endanger public safety, the ecology, or the workplace of fellow citizens by operating under the influence of drugs or alcohol. Problems in individual performance are too costly to ignore. We have to more systematically evaluate individuals on the basis of contribution, not credentials, and we as individuals must work more reliably.

Resist the Temptation to Solve
Problems by Spending More

With respect to the nation's industrial infrastructure as well as companies, we must learn to improve both quality and productivity simultaneously. In many instances, our infrastructural organizations are enormous consumers of resources, even their own resources. We must learn to do more with less. Additional communications, resources, and control mechanisms pose severe burdens which our already stressed economy cannot afford. Our econonomy needs not more but less money spent on infrastructure in order to adapt to a changing world.

Operating with fewer resources provides an important holistic advantage. Small units with focused responsibilities operate more effectively because the participants can see problems in their entirety. Organizational learning permits the company, or the community, to achieve more with fewer resources. If we can promote broadly based organizational learning, improved performance with fewer resources is distinctly possible.

Lack of resources is not our primary problem in industrial development. The United States remains one of the wealthiest nations on earth, but we cannot afford many of the things we do. Our primary problems include lack of organization, low efficiency, limited real competence, a propensity to duplicate at public expense resources already available through private institutions, and disparate work-time requirements among occupations. We simply cannot afford these things. We must find ways to accomplish a great deal more with fewer resources.

Obtain an Adherence to Sound
Turnaround Principles in Exchange
for Economic Assistance

Many ineffective competitors ultimately turn to the government for economic assistance in their efforts to remain viable. Because these companies often employ a significant number of people from a local labor force, there is often considerable public sympathy for some form of assistance. Unfortunately, state or local governments grant assistance without requiring that the company adhere to sound turnaround principles. Often, the money is used to replicate the patterns of the past. Governments should insist that specific and tangible steps toward low-cost production, product differentiation, and appropriate turnaround leadership be undertaken as part of the terms of any assistance.

Set the Example by Applying Turnaround Principles to Governmental Performance

Few institutions on earth currently operate with a more unfavorable relationship between revenue and cost than some governmental units. Governments have an advantage in their extraordinary powers to unilaterally extract revenues and to borrow money even under the most undeserving conditions. Governments are in an excellent position to provide examples to our basic industries by turning around their own performance. Many governmental units are blatantly irresponsible in their exercise of the public trust. Absurd, self-interested, inappropriate actions are jeopardizing the economic security, social stability, and peace of the entire world.

Conclusion

Tangible production is the ultimate source of the standard of living for the entire society. Without strong world-class productivity on the part of agriculture, mining, construction, and manufacturing, the rest of our society can only lose ground economically, socially, and politically. The services, government, and trade segments of our society, though important, cannot produce wealth in real terms. Only carefully nurtured tangible production can ultimately provide for the capital accumulation needed to improve the competitive position of the United States and provide its population with a meaningful standard of living.

Because tangible production is so integral to the economic well-being and social stability of our citizens, we need to develop better methodologies for the revitalization of industrial companies experiencing decline and stagnation. We must develop the skills to turn around these crucially important contributors to our economy and culture.

Remedial skills will be needed also for those companies providing services to our industrial economy. The providers of needed services will find it necessary to become more cost-effective to obtain business from an industrial economy that is becoming more discriminating as it faces its own competitive pressures. Increasing efficiency on the part of service providers is central to the resurgence of our industrial sector.

Sound turnaround principles are at least as applicable to service providers as they are to manufacturers.

At the same time, we should develop some basic principles to guide our industrial development programs and our turnarounds. We must employ more refined economic models and a more qualitative form of economics. We must work within a framework of ethics, morality, and self-sacrifice at every level in business and government—and personally. We must promote industrial development programs aimed at improving the competitive edge of our present industries—programs that are more specific, more oriented to the production of needed tangible goods and services, and more practical. We must learn to accomplish far more at far less cost by employing a far greater efficiency. We must develop industrial procedures that are more compatible with our environment.

We must formulate our public, private, and personal policies with the perspective that, in order to provide a stable economy in the future, we must alter our behavior. Our situation is serious. We must systematically appraise our present situation and take those actions that will provide economic stability for those who follow us. We cannot continue to drift. However, as we yearn for more coordinated activities at the national level, we must also live for the here and now. Severely troubled companies have faced dire circumstances and still survived. The resurgence of these companies should be heartening to the rest of us.

Appendix

Table A-1. The Turnaround Sample

Successful Cases	
Case 1	Buick, 1906–1925
Case 3	Jeffery (Nash Motors), 1911–1930
Case 5	American Motors, 1951–1970
Case 6	Ford Motor Company, 1975–1988
Case 8	Cadillac, 1897–1916
Case 10	Chrysler Corporation, 1975–1988
Case 12	Maxwell-Chalmers, 1916–1935
Case 14	Packard, 1929–1948
Case 16	Deere & Co., 1927–1946

Unsuccessful Cases	
Case 2	International Harvester, 1966–1985
Case 4	Willys-Overland, 1916–1935
Case 7	Kaiser-Frazer, 1944–1956
Case 9	Hudson Motor Car Company, 1927–1946
Case 11	AMC/Renault, 1971–1987
Case 13	Allis-Chalmers, 1963–1986
Case 15	Studebaker-Packard, 1949–1966

Building the Comparative Database

Once the cases were selected, the database was restructured into a format that would facilitate comparisons among individual firms and between the successful and unsuccessful groups of firms. This task was complicated because of several factors. The different turnarounds occurred at quite different times in the history of these industries. The dollars measured in the financial statements therefore possessed different relative values. Also, since most turnarounds occur over a period of many years, the presence of inflation made it difficult to compare data—even for different years of the same turnaround attempt. This was a particular problem during the 1970s, when the inflation rate was very high. Further, firm sizes varied widely, thus creating a problem of weighing the comparisons. A few firms consolidated with other companies during the periods of interest. This posed a problem of consistency from one accounting period to another. Finally, data were not always available for a constant number of years because of several factors:

1. Some firms ceased operations before others.

2. Some turnarounds were rather recent, and fewer years had passed since the turnaround was attempted.

3. Some turnarounds were attempted many years ago, when financial reporting conventions were less developed.

4. In a few turnaround cases, financial data on the firm's performance were not public during the period of interest.

Several steps were taken to reduce the problems mentioned above. The first was to examine the data in terms of the "virtual year" of the turnaround. Financial figures were then converted into constant dollars (1988 dollars) using the implicit GNP deflator as provided by the U.S. Bureau of Economic Statistics. The next step was to normalize the data for each case so that comparison between cases could be made. The normalization procedure was accomplished by adjusting the revenue for each case to an average of $1 billion per year. It was not practical to obtain information for all cases for all time periods for the reasons given. Still, for the years most proximate to the low point, most financial data were available for all but the very earliest cases.

Obviously, it would have been better if we had been able to obtain sample data for all time periods for all companies. However, if we consider the two earliest cases (Buick and Cadillac) separately, the database did turn out to be reasonably complete for the years most proximate to the period of crisis. After-tax earnings information was available for all remaining firms for years + 1 through + 8. After these years, the sample began to decline as the unsuccessful firms thinned out, or, as in the case of Chrysler and Ford, the turnaround attempts were recent.

The earnings information for the earliest years was not available for the Jeffery Company because it was a private company before the turnaround was attempted. However, both narrative information and unit shipment figures were available. Cost-of-sales data were not available for the years 1917 through 1926 and were estimated for these years based on other financial, production, and narrative information. A similar problem occurred for the Maxwell-Chalmers cost-of-sales data for the year 1922, which were also estimated. Because of some important developments in the case, data for Allis-Chalmers were collected for 23 years.

The Cadillac and Buick cases have not been included in the financial comparisons because financial information was not available for these very early firms which were later incorporated into General Motors. However, a great deal of narrative and physical units data were available for both these cases, as was some financial information on the early history of GM.

The database and the narrative information were analyzed together in order to reach conclusions about what happened during the turnaround attempts. In total, approximately 2000 individual quantitative data elements were collected on these 16 companies. Additional information on the performance of the industries and the national economy during the periods studied was also collected. This quantitative information, together with the narrative information, provided a picture of what happened during these important turnaround attempts.

Of the nine successful turnarounds studied, the survival time ranges from 9 years (Chrysler Corporation—a relatively recent turnaround) to 85 years (Cadillac). Of the seven unsuccessful cases studied, two (Allis-Chalmers and Willys-Overland) have filed for bankruptcy. Four others (Hudson, Kaiser, Studebaker-Packard, and International Harvester) have departed what was once their major industry and have turned these operations over to others or closed them. Of the unsuccessful turnarounds, only American Motors, at one time an excellent company, remained in business in its major industry in 1987. However, from 1982 to 1986, AMC/Renault lost $683 million, and the firm was absorbed by Chrysler Corporation that year.

Examining the Variables in Turnaround Success

The proposition advanced in this study is that a successful business turnaround is primarily a function of three principal factors:

1. A business strategy that focuses primarily on improving the firm's effectiveness as a *low-cost producer.*

2. A business strategy that focuses at a later stage on improving the firm's effectiveness as a producer of increasingly *differentiated products.*

3. *Leadership* involving turnaround agents who possess managerial competencies, technical skills, industrial experience and value orientations; enjoy generally favorable personal reputations; and employ a sense of fair play in dealing with employees, creditors, suppliers, and customers.

Some comments are in order regarding the procedures employed to examine the relevance of the three independent variables listed above.

Variable A: Low-Cost Operation

The first independent variable, low cost of production, was examined as a necessary ingredient to the successful turnaround process. Among quantitative measures examined to indicate the presence of the low cost of production characteristic were the following:

Gross profit rate (percent)

After-tax profit rate (percent)

Inventory turn ratio

Inventory dollars per unit produced (for automobile producers)

Incremental increase in cost as revenue increases (percent)

Incremental decrease in cost as revenue decreases (percent)

Before-tax non-cost-of-sales expense as a percent of revenue (percent)

After-tax non-cost-of-sales expense as a percent of revenue (percent)

Narrative information was then utilized to supplement the quantitative information.

Variable B: Product Differentiation

The second independent variable examined, product differentiation, was more difficult to assess. However, considerable quantitative information was available regarding specific product features, and narrative information was available on other aspects of product differentiation.

To measure the presence of product differentiation, feature-by-feature comparisons of competitive product offerings during the same time periods were employed. Product specifications and narrative information from manuscripts and histories were used to provide additional proxy indications of product quality, major product features, and other differentiating characteristics. Each case was then studied to assess the firm's product differentiation as exhibited in distinguishing features, superior performance, product reliability, product quality, and customer service. Following the collection of the historical and proxy material, the degree of product differentiation was assessed. Of necessity, this assessment was partially subjective.

Variable C: The Turnaround Organization—Leadership

The third variable examined was the turnaround organization and, in particular, its leadership. With respect to the turnaround agents and other members of the turnaround organization, the following characteristics were examined:

1. Functional background (finance, sales, engineering, production, service, etc.) of key turnaround agents (usually top managers within the firm)
2. Experience of top managers in the industry served
3. How the key turnaround agents spent their time
4. Operational emphasis and specific steps taken to improve the firm's position
5. Processes and styles of implementing change
6. Reputation for fairness (or unfairness) in dealing with employees, creditors, suppliers, and customers

In order to obtain information on these important characteristics, historical evidence from manuscripts, documents, testimonials, and other histories were used to provide proxy indicators of their presence. Information about the character traits of key executives and about the operational steps taken during the turnaround process was obtained through reviewing the historical works covering these two industries and by collecting industry material. A visit to the archives of General Motors Institute was most helpful, as were several interviews with people closely associated with this major industry.

The database helped to clarify the narrative material. The availability of information on such factors as gross profit rates, registrations, inventory turn ratios, and incremental cost ratios helped to quantify some managerial actions described in the narrative material.

Table A-2. Summary of Changes through Three Turnaround Periods
Successful Turnarounds

	Preturnaround situation	Period of crisis	Period of recovery
Normalized Revenue in 1988 dollars (000)*			
Sample size in number of cases (N)	5	6	7
Mean (M)	849,500	499,175	1,094,134
Range (R)			767,853–1,466,661
Physical Unit Market Share			
Sample size in number of cases (N)	8	8	8
Mean (M)	10.87%	7.72%	7.15%
Range (R)			2.16–9.70%
After-Tax Profit Rate			
Sample size in number of cases (N)	5	7	7
Mean (M)	4.85%	−5.38%	6.50%
Range (R)			1.57–16.33%

*Normalized revenue is a unitless measure used to adjust the financial figures for the individual firms to a similar size to facilitate comparisons. The term *dollars* is used because all financial figures were converted to 1988 dollars, as a part of this normalization procedure to provide for greater comparability from one time period to another.

Table A-3. Summary of Changes through Three Turnaround Periods
Unsuccessful Turnarounds

	Preturnaround situation	Period of crisis	Period of recovery
Normalized Revenue in 1988 dollars (000)*			
Sample size in number of cases (N)	6	6	7
Mean (M)	1,202,519	1,029,306	953,629
Range (R)			590,148–1,176,377
Physical Unit Market Share			
Sample size in number of cases (N)	5	5	5
Mean (M)	5.68%	3.90%	2.54%
Range (R)			0.78–4.30%
After-Tax Profit Rate			
Sample size in number of cases (N)	6	6	7
Mean (M)	3.51%	−1.97%	−1.03%
Range (R)			−4.2– 2.56%

*Normalized revenue is a unitless measure used to adjust the financial figures for the individual firms to a similar size to facilitate comparisons. The term *dollars* is used because all financial figures were converted to 1988 dollars, as a part of this normalization procedure to provide for greater comparability from one time period to another.

Table A-4. Revenue in 1988 Dollars (000)

	Year −3 revenue	Year 0 revenue	Percent change
	Successful Cases		
Packard	255,735	141,788	−44.6
Deere	524,929	73,403	−86.0
American Motors	2,831,395	1,613,062	−43.0
Chrysler	29,586,933	12,822,971	−56.7
Ford	67,009,582	51,548,055	−23.1
	Unsuccessful Cases		
Hudson	1,416,263	245,541	−82.7
Studebaker-Packard	2,960,349	2,498,741	−15.6
International Harvester	7,631,616	7,568,679	−0.8
Allis-Chalmers	2,382,644	2,305,472	−3.2
Kaiser-Frazer-Willys*	406,487	1,166,233	186.9
AMC/Renault	4,078,281	4,339,100	6.4

*Kaiser's revenue declined from $2,419,606 in 1948 to $1,166,223 in 1949 (1988 $).

Table A-5. Change in Number of Units Produced

	Year −3 units produced	Year 0 units produced	Percent change
	Successful Cases		
Cadillac	0	3	
Buick	8,820	13,389*	
Jeffery	4,435	4,608†	
Maxwell-Chalmers	39,000	21,000	−46.2
Packard	16,256	6,071	−54.2
American Motors	213,762	104,190	−51.3
Chrysler	1,236,359	638,974	−48.3
Ford	2,555,866	1,306,950	−48.9
	Unsuccessful Cases		
Hudson	300,962	57,550	−80.9
Willys-Overland	88,753	48,016	−45.9
Studebaker-Packard	281,589	123,507	−56.1
Kaiser-Frazer-Willys	80,317	141,309‡	+75.9
AMC/Renault	514,046	439,524	−14.5

*Although Buick sales in year 0 were actually greater than the sales for year −3, the company did experience a 57 percent decline from 30,525 units in 1910 to 13,389 units in 1911.

†Jeffery automobile sales had declined from 10,417 in 1914 to 4608 in 1916.

‡Kaiser's unit sales declined from 317,963 in 1948 to 141,309 in 1949.

Table A-6. Objective Information on Low-Cost Operation during the Period of Recovery

	Gross profit rate over 15%	Inventory turn ratio > 8	Non-cost-of-sales expense < 14% of revenue
Successful Cases			
Cadillac	Yes	N/A	Likely
Buick	Yes	Likely	Likely
Jeffery (Nash)	Yes	Yes	Yes
Maxwell-Chalmers	Yes	Yes	Yes
Packard	Yes	Yes	Yes
Deere	Yes	No	No
American Motors	Yes	Yes	Yes
Chrysler	Yes	Yes	Yes
Ford	Yes	Yes	Yes
Unsuccessful Cases			
Willys-Overland	No	No	No
Hudson	No	Yes	Yes
Studebaker-Packard	No	No	No
International Harvester	No	No	No
Allis-Chalmers	Yes	No	No
Kaiser-Frazer	No	Yes	Yes
AMC/Renault	No	Yes	No

Table A-7. Narrative Information on Low-Cost Operation during the Period of Recovery

	Cost reduction deep and lasting	Design for manufacturability	Commonality of parts
Successful Cases			
Cadillac	N/A	Yes	Yes
Buick	N/A	N/A	Yes
Jeffery (Nash)	Yes	Yes	Yes
Maxwell-Chalmers	Yes	Yes	Yes
Packard	Yes	Yes	Yes
Deere	Yes	Yes	Yes
American Motors	Yes	Yes	Yes
Chrysler	Yes	Yes	Yes
Ford	Yes	Yes	Yes
Unsuccessful Cases			
Willys-Overland	No	No	No
Hudson	Fair	No	Yes
Studebaker-Packard	No	No	No
International Harvester	No	No	No
Allis-Chalmers	Yes	N/A	No
Kaiser-Frazer	Fair	No	Some
AMC/Renault	No	No	Legacy of past

Table A-8. Classic Automobiles Manufactured by
Packard Motor Car Company, 1930–1939
(Officially Recognized by the Classic Car Club of America)

1930 Packard Standard Eight, models 726 and 733
1930 Packard Speedster, model 734
1930 Packard Custom Eight, models 740 and 745
1931 Packard Standard Eight, models 826 and 833
1931 Packard Custom Eight, model 840
1931 Packard Deluxe Eight, model 845
1932 Packard Light Eight, model 900
1932 Packard Standard Eight, models 901 and 902
1932 Packard Deluxe Eight, models 903 and 904
1932 Packard Custom Twelve, models 905 and 906
1933 Packard Eight, models 1001 and 1002
1933 Packard Super Eight, models 1003 and 1004
1933 Packard Twelve, model 1005
1933 Packard Custom Twelve, model 1006
1934 Packard Eight, models 1100, 1101, and 1102
1934 Packard Super Eight, models 1103, 1104, and 1105
1934 Packard Twelve, models 1106 and 1107
1934 Packard Custom Twelve, model 1108
1935 Packard Eight, models 1200, 1201, and 1202
1935 Packard Super Eight, models 1203, 1204, and 1205
1935 Packard Twelve, models 1206, 1207, and 1208
1936 Packard Eight, models 1400, 1401, and 1402
1936 Packard Super Eight, models 1403, 1404, and 1405
1936 Packard Twelve, models 1407 and 1408
1937 Packard Super Eight, models 1500, 1501, and 1502
1937 Packard Twelve, models 1506, 1507, and 1508
1938 Packard Six, model 1600
1938 Packard Eight, models 1601 and 1602
1938 Packard Super Eight, models 1603 and 1604
1938 Packard Twelve, models 1607 and 1608
1939 Packard Super Eight, model 1705
1939 Packard Twelve, models 1707 and 1708

Notes

Part 1

Page 8.   Several industries were examined as possible candidates for this study including chemicals, steel, consumer products, food products, aerospace, automobiles, and agricultural equipment. The decision was made to concentrate on the automobile industry and the agricultural equipment industry because extensive information existed about both the companies and the people involved during periods of crisis.

Page 20.   Peter Lorange and Robert Nelson suggest that organizational decline is commonly preceded by early warning signals including excess personnel, tolerance of incompetence, cumbersome administrative procedures, disproportionate staff power, replacement of substance with form, scarcity of clear goals and decision benchmarks, fear of embarrassment and conflict, loss of effective communication, and outdated organizational structure. Indeed, one or more of these maladies may plague the company in trouble. However, it is not always true that managerial incompetencies are rampant throughout the troubled organization. Economic and market conditions also stress corporate resources and cause revenues, cashflows, and profits to decline. These misfortunes affect capable as well as incapable firms, and it cannot be assumed that because a company is in trouble it has no sound management and no distinctive competencies. Organizations, like people, get sick but some recover—in part because they may not be sick all over.

Page 20.   Some authors have focused on the organizational characteristics of the troubled firm. In *How to Manage a Turnaround,* Stanley Goodman describes processes often present among companies in need of change.
  Operating the same way as in the past, independent of the operating environment
  Contentment with lackluster performance
  Little self-criticism
  Company accustomed to falling short of sales and profit plans
  Poor interdepartmental communications
  Dictatorial CEO with submissive managers
  No firm plans for corrective action (Goodman 1982)

Page 20. Danny Miller (1977) discusses four common failure syndromes:

1. The impulsive syndrome: running blind, involving overambitious, incautious, and oblivious strategies
2. The stagnant bureaucracy which disregards customers, competitors, and new technologies
3. The headless firm with a leadership vacuum and the absence of a clearly defined strategy
4. Swimming upstream: the aftermath of suffering from depleted resources, eroded market positions, and the neglect of plant and equipment

Miller's findings suggest that organizational failure resembles organic illness where the symptoms need to be distinguished from the disease and is often traceable to many separate factors, which may combine to generally weaken the firm.

Page 20. Donald Hambrick (1985) suggests that turnaround situations have four common features: limited resources, poor internal morale, skeptical stakeholders, and urgency. These common features combine to create awesome responsibility for the turnaround manager, including custodial responsibility for jobs, careers, and financial and physical resources.

Part 2

Page 40. This question of revenue expansion versus cost reduction in turnarounds has been examined by Dan Schendel and G. R. Patton (1976), Hugh O'Niell (1986), and others, and is reexamined here.

Page 45. Previous studies of turnarounds generally support the importance of efficiency moves rather than entrepreneurial moves as a recovery strategy. Hugh O'Niell (1986) examined the turnaround strategies of 13 companies involved in attempted turnarounds during the 1970s. Of these 13, nine were successful and four were not. Although O'Niell draws many conclusions about turnaround strategy, he found that most companies pursued several turnaround strategies simultaneously; cutback strategies were present in 12 of the 13 cases. Growth strategies were present in eight cases and three of these were unsuccessful.

Bernard Taylor (1982/1983) identified several possible strategies for turnaround and recovery:

1. Undertaking mergers and cooperative supply agreements
2. Selling assets and reducing overhead
3. Cutting back in central administration
4. Implementing a business strategy and tight budgetary control
5. Pruning the product line and introducing new cost-effective products
6. Achieving dramatic improvements in productivity
7. Developing a highly productive and well-paid work force
8. Setting up new structures for employee participation and communication
9. Establishing a strong public affairs operation

As with other studies of turnarounds, Taylor attributes greater success to internal efficiency than to revenue expansion.

Page 81. Several methods are commonly used to determine inventory turn ratio. The method used here is total sales (or revenue) divided by the inventory at the end of the fiscal year.

Part 3

Page 116. Studebaker-Packard's exit from the high-priced car market, where it once accounted for over half the sales, was related less to the availability of resources (Studebaker-Packard was a huge company in its time) than to incremental improvements made by major competitors. The firm had plenty of resources but opted to deploy them on acquisitions, the expansion of capacity, and for product features which were not sufficiently meaningful. During the company's unsuccessful turnaround attempt of the 1950s and 1960s, Studebaker-Packard neglected or mismanaged product-differentiating activities while competitors made constant product improvements. Cadillac and Lincoln each developed efficient, high-performing V8 engines while Packard offered only a 1000-pound L-head straight-eight designed a quarter of a century earlier. Cadillac bodies became rigid and strong whereas Packard bodies degenerated in both quality and dependability. In part because it outsold both Cadillac and Lincoln during the early life of these new competitive products, Packard opted to rest on its reputation. However, as competitors' products improved and Packard's remained unchanged, it lost its one-time dominance of the luxury market. Packard developed a new engine, but it came 6 years too late, was not distinctive, and was too heavy for the remaining parts of the running gear. Studebaker-Packard managers failed to realize that product differentiation is an ever-present ongoing obligation requiring maximum attention and there is never any rest.

Page 117. For example: Cadillac/Delco developed the breaker-point ignition system and the self-starter, Cadillac developed the V8 engine, Packard used air conditioning in its 1938 (during the firm's successful period), and Chrysler developed the high-compression engine. These innovations, among others, contributed to product enhancement and to turnaround success.

Page 117. International Harvester spent lavishly on research and development and produced very few sustainable products. During the 1980s, AMC/Renault spent large sums of money on products that did not retain customer interest. Willys-Overland produced, at very high cost, a revolutionary engine that was not significantly better than conventional engines. Hudson developed a new car for a new market with which they were unfamiliar while ignoring the critical needs of the firm's historical market.

Pages 125–126. Professors Cooper (1976) and Schnaars (1989) provide examples of trends that took many decades to develop, trends that some managers mistakenly saw as immediate.

Part 4

Page 205. Telephone interview with Ralph Amerling of the United Auto Workers, 1989.

Page 205. *Ibid.*

Part 5

Page 252. The author is especially indebted to the enlightened work of William K. Hall, "Survival Strategies in a Hostile Environment, in Alan M. Kantrow (ed.), *Survival Strategies for American Industry,* Wiley, New York, 1983.

Bibliography

Introduction

Ackoff, R. A., *Creating the Corporate Future*, Wiley, New York, 1981.

Ackoff, R. A., *Redesigning the Future*, Wiley, New York, 1974.

Adams, John S., "The Regional Service Economy—A Contemporary Mirage?," *The Journal of Applied Manufacturing Systems*, vol. 3, no. 1, p. 3, Spring 1990.

Bluestone, Barry, and Bennett Harrison, *The Deindustrialization of American Industry*, Basic Books, New York, 1982.

Botwin, J. W., et al., *No Limits to Learning: A Report to the Club of Rome*, Pergamon, Oxford, 1979.

Chandler, Alfred D., Jr., *Scale and Scope, The Dynamics of Industrial Capitalism*, Harvard Belknap Press, Cambridge, Mass., 1990.

Cohen, Stephen S., and John Zysman, *Manufacturing Matters: The Myth of the Post-Industrial Economy*, Basic Books, New York, 1987.

Gantt, Henry L., "The Parting of the Ways," in Harwood F. Merrill (ed.), *Classics in Management*, American Management Associations, New York, 1960, pp. 151–160.

Gantt, Henry L., "Training Workmen in Habits of Industry and Cooperation," in *Classics in Management*, Harwood F. Merrill, (ed.), American Management Association, New York, 1960.

Gantt, Henry L., *Industrial Leadership*, Yale University Press, New Haven, Conn., 1916.

Gilbreth, Frank B., "Science in Management for the One Best Way to Do Work," in *Classics in Management*, Harwood F. Merrill (ed.), American Management Associations, New York, 1960.

Glasnall, William, "The World's Top 50 Banks: It's Official—Japan Is Way Out in Front," *Business Week*, no. 3058, p. 77, June 27, 1988.

Hayes, Robert H., and William J. Abernathy, "Managing Our Way to Economic Decline," *Harvard Business Review*, vol. 58, no. 14, July–Aug., 1980.

Hayes, Robert H., and Steven C. Wheelwright, *Restoring Our Competitive Edge: Competing through Manufacturing*, Wiley, New York, 1984.

Hayes, Robert H., Steven C. Wheelwright, and Kim B. Clark, *Dynamic Manufacturing*, Free Press, New York, 1988.

Kilmann, R. H., and I. I. Mitroff, "Qualitative Versus Quantitative Analysis for Management Science: Different Forms of Psychological Types," *Interfaces*, vol. 6, no. 2, Feb. 1976.

Lawrence, Paul R., and Davis Dyer, *Renewing American Industry*, Free Press, New York, 1983.

Leontief, Wassily, "The Ins and Outs of Input/Output Analysis," *Mechanical Engineering*, vol. 109, no. 1, Jan. 1987, p. 29.

Morgenstern, Oskar, *Economic Activity Analysis*, Wiley, New York, 1954.

Morgenstern, Oskar, *International Financial Transactions and Business Cycles*, Princeton University Press, Princeton, NJ, 1959.

Thorow, Lester C., *The Zero Sum Society*, Penguin, New York, 1980.

U.S. Department of Commerce, *Statistical Abstract of the United States 1988*, U.S. Government Printing Office, Washington, D.C., 1989.

Chapter 1

Whetten David A., "Organizational Decline: A Neglected Topic in Organization Science," *Academy of Management Review*, vol. 5, no. 4, 1980, pp. 577–588.

Chapter 2

Argenti, John, *Corporate Collapse: Causes and Symptoms*, Wiley, New York, 1976.

Bibeault, Donald B., *Corporate Turnaround: How Managers Turn Losers into Winners*, McGraw-Hill, New York, 1982.

Cooper, Arnold C., and Dan Schendel, "Strategic Responses to Technological Threats," *Business Horizons*, Feb. 1976.

Federated American Engineering Societies, *Waste in Industry*, McGraw-Hill, New York, 1921.

Follett, Mary Parker, *Dynamic Administration*, Henry C. Metcalf and Lyndall Urwick (eds.), Harper, New York, 1941.

Goodman, Stanley, *How to Manage a Turnaround*, Free Press, New York, 1982.

Hall, William K., "Survival Strategies in a Hostile Environment," *Survival Strategies for American Industry*, Wiley, New York, 1983.

Hambrick, D. C., "Turnaround Strategies," *Handbook of Business Strategy*, W. H. Guth (ed.), Warren, Gorham and Lamont, Boston, 1985.

Hambrick, D. C., and Richard A. D'Aveni, "Large Corporate Failures as Downward Spirals," *Administrative Science Quarterly*, vol. 33, March 1988.

Hambrick, D. C., I. MacMillan, and D. Day, "Strategic Attributes and Performance in the BCG Matrix—a PIMS Based Analysis of Industrial Product Businesses," *Academy of Management Journal*, vol. 25, no. 3, 1982.

Hambrick, D. C., and C. Schecter, "Turnaround Strategies for Mature Industrial Product Businesses," *Journal of Business Strategy*, Fall 1980.

Hayes, Robert H., "Strategic Planning—Forward in Reverse," *Harvard Business Review*, vol. 63, no. 6, Nov.–Dec. 1985.

Hofer, Charles W., "Toward a Contingency Theory of Business Strategy." *Academy of Management Journal,* vol. 18, no. 4, 1975.

Hofer, Charles W., "Turnaround Strategies," *Journal of Business Strategy,* pp. 19–31, Summer 1980.

Hofer, Charles W., and M. J. Davoust, *Successful Strategic Management,* A. T. Kearney, Chicago, 1977, p. 138.

Hofer, Charles W., and Dan Schendel, *Strategy Formation: Analytical Concepts,* West, St. Paul, Minn., 1978.

Lorange, Peter, and Robert T. Nelson, "How to Recognize — and Avoid — Organizational Decline," *Sloan Management Review,* pp. 41–48, Spring 1987.

Miller, Danny, "Common Syndromes of Business Failure," *Business Horizons,* Nov. 1977, pp. 43–53.

Moody's Industrial Manual, 1915, 1920, 1922, 1924, 1926, 1928, 1929, 1930, 1933, 1935, 1937, 1938, 1939, 1942, 1946, 1948, 1952, 1953, 1954, 1955, 1958, 1961, 1964, 1968, 1972, 1975, 1977, 1978, 1979, 1980, 1981, 1982, 1983, 1984, 1985, 1986.

O'Niell, Hugh M., "Turnaround and Recovery: What Strategy Do You Need," *Long Range Planning,* vol. 19, no. 1, 1986.

O'Niell, Hugh M., *Turnaround Strategies in the Commercial Banking Industry,* UMI Research Press, Ann Arbor, Mich., 1981.

Pettigrew, Andrew W., *An Awakening Giant: Continuity and Change in Imperial Chemical Industries,* Basil Blackwell, New York, 1985.

Richardson, Peter R., *Cost Containment: The Ultimate Advantage,* Free Press, New York, 1988.

Schendel, D., and G. R. Patton, "Corporate Stagnation and Turnaround," *Journal of Economics and Business,* vol. 28, no. 3, pp. 236–241, Spring–Summer 1976.

Schendel, D., G. R. Patton, and J. Riggs, "Corporate Turnaround Strategies: A Study of Profit Decline and Recovery," *Journal of General Management,* pp. 3–11, Spring 1976.

Starbuck, William H., Arent Greve, and Bo L. T. Hedberg, "Responding to Crisis," *Journal of Business Administration,* vol. 9, pp. 111–137.

Taylor, Bernard, "Turnaround, Recovery and Growth: The Way through the Crises," *Journal of General Management,* pp. 5–13, Winter 1982/1983.

U.S. Federal Trade Commission, *Report to the Seventy-Fourth Congress on the Agricultural Implement and Machinery Industry,* U.S. Government Printing Office, Washington, D.C., 1938.

Zimmerman, Frederick M., "Managing a Successful Turnaround," *Long Range Planning,* vol. 22, no. 3, June 1989.

Zimmerman, Frederick M., "Turnaround — A Painful Learning Process," *Long Range Planning,* vol. 19, no. 4, Aug. 1986.

Chapter 3

Allis-Chalmers Corporation, *1985 Annual Report,* Allis-Chalmers Corporation, Milwaukee, Wis., 1986.

Allis-Chalmers Corporation, *1984 Annual Report,* Allis-Chalmers Corporation, Milwaukee, Wis., 1985.

Allis-Chalmers Corporation, *1986 Form 10-K,* Allis-Chalmers Corporation, Milwaukee, Wis., 1986.

Allis-Chalmers Corporation, *1985 Form 10-K,* Allis-Chalmers Corporation, Milwaukee, Wis., 1986.

Allis-Chalmers Corporation, *1984 Form 10-K,* Allis-Chalmers Corporation, Milwaukee, Wis., 1986.

Allis-Chalmers Corporation, *News Release #116-87,* Allis-Chalmers Corporation, Milwaukee, Wis., 1987.

Allis-Chalmers Corporation, *News Release #106-87,* Allis-Chalmers Corporation, Milwaukee, Wis., 1987.

Allis-Chalmers Corporation, *News Release #105-87,* Allis-Chalmers Corporation, 1987.

Broehl, Wayne G., Jr., *John Deere's Company,* Doubleday, New York, 1984.

Chandler, Alfred D., *Giant Enterprise: Ford, General Motors and the Automobile Industry,* Harcourt Brace, New York, 1964.

Edwards, Charles E., *Dynamics of the United States Automobile Industry,* University of South Carolina Press, Columbia, S.C., 1965.

Fortune "Packard," Jan. 1937. Reprinted in *Packard's International Motor Car Club,* vol. 18, no. 4, Winter 1981.

Harvard Business School, "Ford Motor Company (C)," #9-382-165, Harvard Business School, Boston, 1983.

Harvard Business School, "Ford Motor Company (D)," #9-382-166, Harvard Business School, Boston, 1983.

Heasley, Jerry, *The Production Figure Book for U.S. Cars,* Motorbooks International, Osceola, Wis., 1977.

Kennedy, E. D., *The Automobile Industry: The Coming of Age of Capitalism's Favorite Child,* Reynal & Hitchcock, New York, 1941.

Kimes, B. R., and Henry Austin Clark, Jr., *The Standard Catalog of American Cars 1805–1942,* Krause, Iola, Wis., 1985.

Kimes, B. R., and Richard M. Langworth, *Packard: A History of the Motor Car and the Company,* Princeton, Princeton, N.J., 1978.

Langworth, Richard M., *Kaiser-Frazer: The Last Onslaught on Detroit,* Princeton, Princeton, N.J., 1975.

Langworth, Richard M., *The Milestone Car Number Seventeen,* Dragonwyck, Hopewell, N.J., Autumn 1976.

Langworth, Richard M., and Jan P. Nordbye, *The Complete History of Chrysler Corporation 1924–1985,* Publications International, Skokie, Ill., 1985.

Moody's Industrial Manual, 1915, 1920, 1922, 1924, 1926, 1928, 1929, 1930, 1933, 1935, 1937, 1938, 1939, 1942, 1946, 1948, 1952, 1953, 1954, 1955, 1958, 1961, 1964, 1968, 1972, 1975, 1977, 1978, 1979, 1980, 1981, 1982, 1983, 1984, 1985, 1986.

Schendel, D., and G. R. Patton, "Corporate Stagnation and Turnaround." *Journal of Economics and Business,* vol. 28, no. 3, pp. 236–241, Spring–Summer 1976.

Seltzer, Lawrence, *The Financial History of the North American Automobile Industry*, Houghton Mifflin, Boston, 1928.

U.S. Federal Trade Commission, *Report to the Seventy-Fourth Congress on the Agricultural Implement and Machinery Industry*, U.S. Government Printing Office, Washington, D.C., 1938.

U.S. Federal Trade Commission, *Report to the Seventy-Fourth Congress on the Motor Vehicle Industry*, U.S. Government Printing Office, Washington, D.C., 1938.

Wards Automotive Yearbook, 1977, 1985.

Part 2

Schoeffler, S., R. Buzzell, and D. Heany, "Impact of Strategic Planning on Profit Performance," *Harvard Business Review*, vol. 52, no. 2, March–April 1974.

Chapter 4

Automobile Manufacturers Association, *Automobiles of America*, Wayne State University Press, Detroit, 1968.

Automobile Quarterly Editors and Princeton Institute for Historic Research: *General Motors: The First 75 Years of Transportation Products*, Automotive Quarterly, Princeton, N.J., 1983.

Chandler, Alfred D., *Giant Enterprise: Ford, General Motors and the Automobile Industry*, Harcourt Brace, New York, 1964.

Chandler, Alfred D., *Strategy and Structure*, MIT Press, Cambridge, Mass., 1962.

Chandler, Alfred D., *The Visible Hand: The Managerial Revolution in American Business*, Harvard University Press, Cambridge, Mass., 1977.

Chandler, Alfred D., and Stephen Salsbury, *Pierre S. DuPont and the Making of the Modern Corporation*, Harper, New York, 1971.

Chilton's Automotive Multi-Guide Spring 1931, Chilton Book Company, Radnor, Pa., 1970.

Christiansen, C. Roland, Kenneth R. Andrews, Joseph L. Bower, Richard G. Hamermesh, and Michael E. Porter, *Business Policy: Text and Cases*, Irwin, Homewood, Ill., 1982.

Chrysler, Walter P., *Life of an American Workman*, Dodd, Mead, New York, 1937.

Coleman, Richard N., and Keith W. Burnaham, "Milestones in the Application of Power to Agricultural Machines," *An Historical Perspective of Farm Machinery*, Society of Automotive Engineers, Milwaukee, Wis., 1980.

Crabb, Richard, *Birth of a Giant: The Men and Incidents that Gave America the Motorcar*, Chilton, New York, 1969.

Cray, Ed, *Chrome Colossus: General Motors and Its Times*, McGraw-Hill, New York, 1980.

Dunham, Terry B., and Lawrence R. Gustin, *The Buick: A Complete History*, Princeton, Princeton, N.J., 1985.

Dyke, A. L., *Dyke's Automotive and Gasoline Engine Encyclopedia*, A. L. Dyke, St. Louis, 1946.

Fink, James J., *The Car Culture*, MIT Press, Cambridge, Mass., 1975.

Forbes, Bertie Charles, *Automotive Giants of America*, Books for Libraries Press, New York, 1972.

Ford, Jeffrey D., "The Occurrence of Structural Hysteresis in Declining Organizations," *Academy of Management Review*, vol. 5, no. 4, pp. 589–598, 1980.

Fortune, "International Harvester – Supremacy," Aug. 1933.

Hambrick, D. C., and C. Schecter, "Turnaround Strategies for Mature Industrial Product Businesses," *Journal of Business Strategy*, Fall 1980.

Hamner, W. Clay, "Reinforcement Theory and Contingency Management in Organizational Settings," in *Motivation and Work Behavior*, Richard M. Steers and Lyman W. Porter (eds.), McGraw-Hill, New York, 1983.

Hamner, W. Clay, Jerry Ross, and Barry M. Staw, "Motivation in Organizations: The Need for a New Direction," in *Motivation and Work Behavior*, Richard M. Steers and Lyman W. Porter (eds.), McGraw-Hill, New York, 1983.

Harbison, Frederick H., and Robert Dubin, *Patterns of Union-Management Relations: United Auto Workers* (CIO, GENERAL MOTORS, STUDEBAKER), SRA, Chicago, 1947.

Hayes, Robert H., and Steven C. Wheelwright, *Restoring Our Competitive Edge: Competing through Manufacturing*, Wiley, New York, 1984.

Hayes, Robert H., Steven C. Wheelwright, and Kim B. Clark, *Dynamic Manufacturing*, Free Press, New York, 1988.

Heasley, Jerry, *The Production Figure Book for U.S. Cars*, Motorbooks International, Osceola, Wis., 1977.

Hofer, Charles W., "Toward a Contingency Theory of Business Strategy," *Academy of Management Journal*, vol. 18, no. 4, 1975.

Hofer, Charles W., "Turnaround Strategies," *Journal of Business Strategy*, pp. 19–31, Summer 1980.

Homans, James E., *Self Propelled Vehicles: A Practical Treatise on the Theory, Construction, Operation, Care and Management of All Forms of Automobiles*, Theo. Audel, New York, 1906.

Hunt, R. Douglas, *American Farm Tools from Hand Power to Steam Power*, Sunflower University Press, Manhattan, Kan., 1985.

Jardim, Anne, "The First Henry Ford," #9-373-308, Harvard Business School, Boston, 1973.

Jelinek, Mariann, and Michael C. Burstein, "The Production Administrative Structure: A Paradigm for Strategic Fit," *Academy of Management Review*, vol. 7, no. 2, pp. 242–252, Apr. 1982.

Jennings, Eugene E., *An Anatomy of Leadership*, Harper, New York, 1960.

Kennedy, E. D., *The Automobile Industry: The Coming of Age of Capitalism's Favorite Child*, Reynal & Hitchcock, New York, 1941.

Kimes, B. R., and Henry Austin Clark, Jr., *The Standard Catalog of American Cars 1805–1942*, Krause, Iola, Wis., 1985.

Kimes, B. R., and Richard M. Langworth, *Packard: A History of the Motor Car and the Company*, Princeton, Princeton, N.J., 1978.

Langworth, Richard M., and Jan P. Nordbye, *The Complete History of Chrysler Corporation 1924–1985*, Publications International, Skokie, Ill., 1985.

Leland, Mrs. Wilfred C., and Minnie Dubbs Millbrook, *Master of Precision — Henry M. Leland*, Wayne State University Press, Detroit, 1966.

Marsh, Barbara, *A Corporate Tragedy: The Agony of International Harvester Company*, Doubleday, Garden City, N.Y., 1985.

May, George S., *A Most Unique Machine: The Michigan Origins of the American Automobile Industry*, William B. Eerdmans, Grand Rapids, Mich., 1975.

Moody's Industrial Manual, 1915, 1920, 1922, 1924, 1926, 1928, 1929, 1930, 1933, 1935, 1937, 1938, 1939, 1942, 1946, 1948, 1952, 1953, 1954, 1955, 1958, 1961, 1964, 1968, 1972, 1975, 1977, 1978, 1979, 1980, 1981, 1982, 1983, 1984, 1985, 1986.

Morgenstern, Oskar, *Economic Activity Analysis*, Wiley, New York, 1954.

Morgenstern, Oskar, *International Financial Transactions and Business Cycles*, Princeton University Press, Princeton, N.J., 1959.

Naul, G. Marshall, and R. Perry Zavitz, *The Specification Book for U.S. Cars 1930–1969*, Motorbooks International, Osceola, Wis., 1980.

Naylor, James C., Robert D. Pritchard, Daniel R. Illgen, *A Theory of Behavior in Organizations*, Academic Press, New York, 1980.

Nevins, Allan, *Ford: The Times, the Man, the Company*, Scribner, New York, 1954.

O'Niell, Hugh M., "Turnaround and Recovery: What Strategy Do You Need." *Long Range Planning*, vol. 19, no. 1, 1986.

O'Niell, Hugh M., *Turnaround Strategies in the Commercial Banking Industry*, UMI Research Press, Ann Arbor, Mich., 1981.

Pound, Arthur, *The Turning Wheel: The Story of General Motors through Twenty-five Years*, Doubleday, Garden City, N.Y., 1934.

Rae, John B., *The American Automobile: A Brief History*, University of Chicago Press, Chicago, 1965.

Rae, John B., *The American Automobile Industry*, G. K. Hall, Boston, 1984.

Richardson, Peter R., *Cost Containment: The Ultimate Advantage*, Free Press, New York, 1988.

Roberts, Peter, *The History of the Automobile*, Exeter, New York, 1984.

Ross, Joel E., and Michael J. Kami, *Corporate Management in Crisis: Why the Mighty Fall*, Prentice-Hall, Englewood Cliffs, N.J., 1973.

Rothberg, Robert R., *Corporate Strategy and Product Innovation*, Free Press, New York, 1976.

Schendel, Dan, and Charles W. Hofer, *Strategic Management: A New View of Business Policy and Planning*, Little Brown, Boston, 1979.

Schendel, D., and G. R. Patton, "Corporate Stagnation and Turnaround," *Journal of Economics and Business*, vol. 28, no. 3, pp. 236–241, Spring–Summer 1976.

Schendel, D., G. R. Patton, and J. Riggs, "Corporate Turnaround Strategies: A Study of Profit Decline and Recovery," *Journal of General Management*, pp. 3–11, Spring 1976.

Schisgall, Oscar, *Eyes on Tomorrow: The Evolution of Procter & Gamble*, Doubleday, New York, 1981.

Schnaars, Steven P., *Megamistakes: Forecasting and the Myth of Rapid Technological Change*, Free Press, New York, 1989.

Sears, Stephen W., *The Automobile in America*, American Heritage, New York, 1977.

Seltzer, Lawrence, *The Financial History of the North American Automobile Industry*, Houghton Mifflin, Boston, 1928.

Slappey, Sterling G., *Pioneers of American Business*, Grosset & Dunlap, New York, 1970.

Sloan, Alfred B., Jr., *My Years with General Motors*, Doubleday, Garden City, N.Y., 1964.

Smith, Philip H., *Wheels within Wheels: A Short History of American Motor Car Manufacturing*, Funk & Wagnalls, New York, 1968.

Society of Automotive Engineers, *An Historical Perspective of Farm Machinery*, SAE, Warrendale, Pa., 1980.

Southwick, Lawrence, Jr., *Managerial Economics*, Business Publications, Plano, Tex., 1985.

Taylor, Bernard, "Turnaround, Recovery and Growth: The Way through the Crises," *Journal of General Management*, pp. 5–13, Winter 1982/1983.

U.S. Federal Trade Commission, *Report to the Seventy-Fourth Congress on the Agricultural Implement and Machinery Industry*, U.S. Government Printing Office, Washington, D.C., 1938.

U.S. Federal Trade Commission, *Report to the Seventy-Fourth Congress on the Motor Vehicle Industry*, U.S. Government Printing Office, Washington, D.C., 1938.

Wendel,C. H., *150 Years of International Harvester*, Crestline, Sarasota, Fla., 1981.

White, Lawrence, J., *The Automobile Industry Since 1945*, Harvard University Press, Cambridge, Mass., 1971.

Chapter 5

Abernathy, William J., Kim B. Clark, and Alan M. Kantrow, "The New Industrial Competition," *Survival Strategies for American Industry*, Wiley, New York, 1983.

Abernathy, William J., Kim B. Clark, and Alan M. Kantrow, *Industrial Renaissance: Producing a Competitive Future for America*, Basic Books, New York, 1983.

Automobile Manufacturers Association, *Automobiles of America*, Wayne State University Press, Detroit, 1968.

Barnard, Chester I., *The Functions of the Executive*, Harvard University Press, Cambridge, Mass., 1968.

Beatty, Michael, Patrick Furlong, and Loren Pennington, *Studebaker: Less than They Promised*, and books, South Bend, Ind., 1984.

Bowers, Q. David, *Early American Car Advertisements*, Bonanza, New York, 1966.

Brent, Sandor B., "Prigogine's Model of Self Organization in Nonequilibrium Systems," *Human Development*, no. 21, 1978.

Brown, Arch, "Almost a Classic: 1932 Nash," *Special Interest Autos*, no. 66, Dec. 1981.

Brown, Arch, "An Interview with Governor George Romney," *Special Interest Autos*, no. 66, Dec. 1981.

Chrysler Walter P., *Life of an American Workman*, Dodd, Mead, New York, 1937.

Crabb, Richard, *Birth of a Giant: The Men and Incidents That Gave America the Motorcar*, Chilton, New York, 1969.

Dawes, Nathaniel T., *The Packard 1942–1962*, A. S. Barnes, New York, 1975.

Dykes, A. L., *Dyke's Automotive and Gasoline Engine Encyclopedia*, A. L. Dyke, St. Louis, 1946.

Fink, James J., *The Car Culture*, MIT Press, Cambridge, Mass., 1975.

Forbes, Bertie Charles, *Automotive Giants of America*, Books for Libraries Press, New York, 1972.

Goodman, Stanley, *How to Manage a Turnaround*, Free Press, New York, 1982.

Hall, William K., "Survival Strategies in a Hostile Environment," *Survival Strategies for American Industry*, Wiley, New York, 1983.

Hambrick, D. C., I. MacMillan, and D. Day, "Strategic Attributes and Performance in the BCG Matrix—A PIMS Based Analysis of Industrial Product Businesses," *Academy of Management Journal*, vol. 25, no. 3, 1982.

Homans, James E., *Self Propelled Vehicles: A Practical Treatise on the Theory, Construction, Operation, Care and Management of All Forms of Automobiles*, Theo. Audel, New York, 1906.

Jennings, Eugene E., *An Anatomy of Leadership*, Harper, New York, 1960.

Kennedy, E. D., *The Automobile Industry: The Coming of Age of Capitalism's Favorite Child*, Reynal & Hitchcock, New York, 1941.

Kimes, B. R., and Henry Austin Clark, Jr., *The Standard Catalog of American Cars 1805–1942*, Krause, Iola, Wis., 1985.

Lawrence, Paul R., and Davis Dyer, *Renewing American Industry*, Free Press, New York, 1983.

Lee, Albert, *Call Me Roger*, Contemporary, Chicago, 1988.

Mahoney, John Thomas, *The Story of George Romney: Builder, Salesman, Crusader*, Harper, New York, 1960.

Marsh, Barbara, *A Corporate Tragedy: The Agony of International Harvester Company*, Doubleday, Garden City, N.Y., 1985.

May, George S., *A Most Unique Machine: The Michigan Origins of the American Automobile Industry*, William B. Eerdmans, Grand Rapids, Mich., 1975.

Meredith, Alex, "Willys Small Success: 1927 Whippet," *Special Interest Autos*, no. 66, Dec. 1981.

Moody's Industrial Manual, 1915, 1920, 1922, 1924, 1926, 1928, 1929, 1930, 1933, 1935, 1937, 1938, 1939, 1942, 1946, 1948, 1952, 1953, 1954, 1955, 1958, 1961, 1964, 1968, 1972, 1975, 1977, 1978, 1979, 1980, 1981, 1982, 1983, 1984, 1985, 1986.

O'Niell, Hugh M., "Turnaround and Recovery: What Strategy Do You Need," *Long Range Planning,* vol. 19, no. 1, 1986.

O'Niell, Hugh M., *Turnaround Strategies in the Commercial Banking Industry,* UMI Research Press, Ann Arbor, Mich., 1981.

Peterson, Walter F., and C. Edward Weber, *An Industrial Heritage: Allis-Chalmers Corporation,* Milwaukee County Historical Society, Milwaukee, Wis., 1978.

Rae, John B., *The American Automobile: A Brief History,* University of Chicago Press, Chicago, 1965.

Rae, John B., *The American Automobile Industry,* G. K. Hall, Boston, 1984.

Schonberger, Richard, *Japanese Manufacturing Techniques,* Free Press, New York, 1982.

Sears, Stephen W., *The Automobile in America,* American Heritage, New York, 1977.

Seltzer, Lawrence, *The Financial History of the North American Automobile Industry,* Houghton Mifflin, Boston, 1928.

Sloan, Alfred B., Jr., *My Years with General Motors,* Doubleday, New York, 1964.

Smith, Philip H., *Wheels within Wheels: A Short History of American Motor Car Manufacturing,* Funk & Wagnalls, New York, 1968.

U.S. Federal Trade Commission, *Report to the Seventy-Fourth Congress on the Motor Vehicle Industry,* U.S. Government Printing Office, Washington, D.C., 1938.

Zimmerman, Frederick M., "Turnaround—A Painful Learning Process," *Long Range Planning,* vol. 19, no. 4, Aug. 1986.

Chapter 6

Abernathy, William J., Kim B. Clark, and Alan M. Kantrow, *Industrial Renaissance: Producing a Competitive Future for America,* Basic Books, New York, 1983.

Abernathy, William J., Kim B. Clark, and Alan M. Kantrow, "The New Industrial Competition," *Survival Strategies for American Industry,* Wiley, New York, 1983.

Abodaher, David, *Iacocca: America's Most Dynamic Businessman,* Kensington, New York, 1985.

Automobile Manufacturers Association, *Automobiles of America,* Wayne State University Press, Detroit, 1968.

Broehl, Wayne G., Jr, *John Deere's Company,* Doubleday, New York, 1984.

Brown, Arch, "1948–1954 Hudson: Step Up to a Step Down," *Collectible Automobile,* vol. 3, no. 1, pp. 50–70, June 1986.

Brown, Arch, "An Interview with Governor George Romney," *Special Interest Autos,* no. 66, Dec. 1981.

Chrysler, Walter P., *Life of an American Workman,* Dodd, Mead, New York, 1937.

Conde, John A., *The Cars That Hudson Built*, Arnold Porter, Keego Harbor, Mich., 1980.

Edwards, Charles E., *Dynamics of the United States Automobile Industry*, University of South Carolina Press, Columbia, S.C., 1965.

Fink, James J., *The Car Culture*, MIT Press, Cambridge, Mass., 1975.

Forbes, Bertie Charles, *Automotive Giants of America*, Books for Libraries Press, New York, 1972.

Fortune, "Packard," January 1937. Reprinted in *Packard's International Motor Car Club*, vol. 18, no. 4, Winter 1981.

Harbison, Frederick H., and Robert Dubin, *Patterns of Union-Management Relations: United Auto Workers* (CIO, GENERAL MOTORS, STUDEBAKER), SRA, Chicago, 1947.

Heasley, Jerry, *The Production Figure Book for U.S. Cars*, Motorbooks International, Osceola, Wis., 1977.

Hofer, Charles W., "Turnaround Strategies." *Journal of Business Strategy*, pp. 19–31, Summer 1980.

Kimes, B. R., and Henry Austin Clark, Jr., *The Standard Catalog of American Cars 1805–1942*, Krause, Iola, Wis., 1985.

Langworth, Richard M., *The Milestone Car Number Seventeen*. Dragonwyck, Hopewell, N.J., Autumn 1976.

Leland, Mrs. Wilfred C., and Minnie Dubbs Millbrook, *Master of Precision — Henry M. Leland*, Wayne State University Press, Detroit, 1966.

Mahoney, John Thomas, *The Story of George Romney: Builder, Salesman, Crusader*, Harper, New York, 1960.

May, George S., *A Most Unique Machine: The Michigan Origins of the American Automobile Industry*, William B. Eerdmans, Grand Rapids, Mich., 1975.

Mayborn, Mitch, and Ted W. Mayborn, *Hudson: An Historical Account of the Hudson, Essex, and Terraplane Automobiles*, Highland Enterprises, Dallas, 1975.

Moody's Industrial Manual, 1915, 1920, 1922, 1924, 1926, 1928, 1929, 1930, 1933, 1935, 1937, 1938, 1939, 1942, 1946, 1948, 1952, 1953, 1954, 1955, 1958, 1961, 1964, 1968, 1972, 1975, 1977, 1978, 1979, 1980, 1981, 1982, 1983, 1984, 1985, 1986.

Naul, G. Marshall, and R. Perry Zavitz, *The Specification Book for U.S. Cars 1930–1969*, Motorbooks International, Osceola, Wis., 1980.

Roberts, Peter, *The History of the Automobile*, Exeter, New York, 1984.

Schonberger, Richard, *Japanese Manufacturing Techniques*, Free Press, New York, 1982.

Sears, Stephen W., *The Automobile in America*, American Heritage, New York, 1977.

Wards Automotive Yearbook, 1977, 1985.

White, Lawrence, J., *The Automobile Industry Since 1945*, Harvard University Press, Cambridge, Mass., 1971.

Zimmerman, Frederick M., "Managing a Successful Turnaround," *Long Range Planning*, vol. 22, no. 3, June 1989.

Chapter 7

Abernathy, William J., Kim B. Clark, and Alan M. Kantrow, *Industrial Renaissance: Producing a Competitive Future for America*, Basic Books, New York, 1983.

Edwards, Charles E., *Dynamics of the United States Automobile Industry*, University of South Carolina Press, Columbia, S.C., 1965.

Fuller, Mark B., "Ford Motor Company (B)," #9-382-162, Harvard Business School, Boston, 1982.

Fuller, Mark B., "Ford Motor Company (A)," #9-382-161, Harvard Business School, Boston, 1982.

Harvard Business School, "Ford Motor Company (D)," #9-382-166, Harvard Business School, Boston, 1983.

Harvard Business School, "Ford Motor Company (C)," #9-382-165, Harvard Business School, Boston, 1983.

Heasley, Jerry, *The Production Figure Book for U.S. Cars*, Motorbooks International, Osceola, Wis., 1977.

Kimes, B. R., "Blueprints and Balance Sheets—The Company that Charlie Built," *Automotive Quarterly*, vol. XV, no. 2, Second quarter 1977.

Kimes, B. R., and Henry Austin Clark, Jr., *The Standard Catalog of American Cars 1805–1942*, Krause, Iola, Wis., 1985.

Langworth, Richard M., *Kaiser-Frazer: The Last Onslaught on Detroit*, Princeton, Princeton, N.J., 1975.

Langworth, Richard M., *The Milestone Car Number Seventeen*, Dragonwyck, Hopewell, N.J., Autumn 1976.

Langworth, Richard M., "1951–1955 Kaiser: The Memorable Generation," *Collectible Automobile*, vol. 1, no. 6, p. 22, March 1985.

Mishne, Patricia P., "A Passion for Perfection," *Manufacturing Engineering*, Nov. 1988.

Moody's Industrial Manual, 1915, 1920, 1922, 1924, 1926, 1928, 1929, 1930, 1933, 1935, 1937, 1938, 1939, 1942, 1946, 1948, 1952, 1953, 1954, 1955, 1958, 1961, 1964, 1968, 1972, 1975, 1977, 1978, 1979, 1980, 1981, 1982, 1983, 1984, 1985, 1986.

Naul, G. Marshall, and R. Perry Zavitz, *The Specification Book for U.S. Cars 1930–1969*, Motorbooks International, Osceola, Wis., 1980.

Schnaars, Steven P., *Megamistakes: Forecasting and the Myth of Rapid Technological Change*, Free Press, New York, 1989.

Smith, Philip H., *Wheels within Wheels: A Short History of American Motor Car Manufacturing*, Funk & Wagnalls, New York, 1968.

Wards Automotive Yearbook, 1977, 1985.

White, Lawrence, J., *The Automobile Industry Since 1945*, Harvard University Press, Cambridge, Mass., 1971

Chapter 8

Abernathy, William J., Kim B. Clark, and Alan M. Kantrow, *Industrial Renaissance: Producing a Competitive Future for America*, Basic Books, New York, 1983.

Automobile Manufacturers Association, *Automobiles of America*, Wayne State, Detroit, 1968.

Automotive Quarterly Editors and Princeton Institute for Historic Research, *General Motors: The First 75 Years of Transportation Products*, Automotive Quarterly, Princeton, N.J., 1983.

Bowers, Q. David, *Early American Car Advertisements*, Bonanza, New York, 1966.

Brown, Arch, "1948–1954 Hudson: Step Up to a Step Down," *Collectible Automobile*, vol. 3, no. 1, pp. 50–70, June 1986.

Chandler, Alfred D, *Giant Enterprise: Ford, General Motors and the Automobile Industry*, Harcourt Brace, New York, 1964.

Chilton's Automotive Multi-Guide Spring 1931, Chilton Book Company, Radnor, Pa., 1970.

Conde, John A., *The Cars That Hudson Built*, Arnold Porter Publishing, Keego Harbor, Mich., 1980.

Crabb, Richard, *Birth of a Giant: The Men and Incidents that Gave America the Motorcar*, Chilton, New York, 1969.

Cray, Ed, *Chrome Colossus: General Motors and Its Times*, McGraw-Hill, New York, 1980.

Dykes, A. L., *Dyke's Automotive and Gasoline Engine Encyclopedia*, A. L. Dyke, St. Louis, 1946.

Edwards, Charles E., *Dynamics of the United States Automobile Industry*, University of South Carolina Press, Columbia, S.C., 1965.

Feigenbaum, Armand V., *Total Quality Control*, McGraw-Hill, New York, 1983.

Fink, James J., *The Car Culture*, MIT Press, Cambridge, Mass., 1975.

Forbes, Bertie Charles, *Automotive Giants of America*, Books for Libraries Press, New York, 1972.

Hendry, Maurice D., "Hudson, The Car Named for Jackson's Wife's Uncle," *Automotive Quarterly*, vol. IX, no. 4, Summer 1971.

Homans, James E., *Self Propelled Vehicles: A Practical Treatise on the Theory, Construction, Operation, Care and Management of All Forms of Automobiles*, Theo. Audel, New York, 1906.

Jardim, Anne, "The First Henry Ford," #9-373-308, Harvard Business School, Boston, 1973.

Juran, J. M., and Frank M. Gryna, Jr., *Quality Planning and Analysis: From Product Development through Use*, McGraw-Hill, New York, 1980.

Kennedy, E. D., *The Automobile Industry: The Coming of Age of Capitalism's Favorite Child*, Reynal & Hitchcock, New York, 1941.

Kimes, B. R., and Henry Austin Clark, Jr., *The Standard Catalog of American Cars 1805–1942*, Krause, Iola, Wis., 1985.

Langworth, Richard M., *The Milestone Car Number Seventeen*, Dragonwyck, Hopewell, N.J., Autumn 1976.

Leland, Mrs. Wilfred C., and Minnie Dubbs Millbrook, *Master of Precision— Henry M. Leland*, Wayne State, Detroit, 1966.

May, George S., *A Most Unique Machine: The Michigan Origins of the American Automobile Industry*, William B. Eerdmans, Grand Rapids, Mich., 1975.

Mayborn, Mitch, and Ted W. Mayborn, *Hudson: An Historical Account of the Hudson, Essex, and Terraplane Automobiles*, Highland Enterprises, Dallas, 1975.

Moody's Industrial Manual, ·1915, 1920, 1922, 1924, 1926, 1928, 1929, 1930, 1933, 1935, 1937, 1938, 1939, 1942, 1946, 1948, 1952, 1953, 1954, 1955, 1958, 1961, 1964, 1968, 1972, 1975, 1977, 1978, 1979, 1980, 1981, 1982, 1983, 1984, 1985, 1986.

Nevins, Allan, *Ford: The Times, the Man, the Company*, Scribner, New York, 1954.

Norwood, Edwin P., *Ford: Men and Methods*, Doubleday, Doran, Garden City, N.Y., 1931.

Pound, Arthur, *The Turning Wheel; The Story of General Motors through Twenty-five Years*, Doubleday, Doran, Garden City, N.Y., 1934.

Rae, John B., *The American Automobile: A Brief History*, University of Chicago Press, Chicago, 1965.

Rae, John B., *The American Automobile Industry*, G. K. Hall, Boston: 1984.

Roberts, Peter, *The History of the Automobile*, Exeter, New York, 1984.

Sears, Stephen W., *The Automobile in America*, American Heritage, New York, 1977.

Seltzer, Lawrence, *The Financial History of the North American Automobile Industry*, Boston, Houghton Mifflin, 1928.

Slappey, Sterling G., *Pioneers of American Business*, Grosset & Dunlap, New York, 1970.

Sloan, Alfred B., Jr., *My Years with General Motors*, Doubleday, Garden City, N.Y., 1964.

Smith, Philip H., *Wheels within Wheels; A Short History of American Motor Car Manufacturing*, Funk & Wagnalls, New York, 1968.

Weisberger, Bernard A., *The Dream Maker: William C. Durant Founder of General Motors*, Little Brown, Boston, 1979.

White, Lawrence, J., *The Automobile Industry Since 1945*, Harvard University Press, Cambridge, Mass., 1971.

Chapter 9

Abodaher, David, *Iacocca: America's Most Dynamic Businessman*, Kensington, New York, 1985.

Edwards, Charles E., *Dynamics of the United States Automobile Industry*, University of South Carolina Press, Columbia, S.C., 1965.

Hambrick, D.C., and C. Schecter, "Turnaround Strategies for Mature Industrial Product Businesses," *Journal of Business Strategy*, Fall 1980.

Iacocca, Lee, and William Novack, *Iacocca: An Autobiography*, Bantam, New York, 1984.

Ingrassia, Paul, and Bradley A. Stertz, "Mea Culpa, With Chrysler Ailing, Lee Iacocca Concedes Mistakes in Managing," *The Wall Street Journal*, p. 1, Sept. 17, 1985.

Langworth, Richard M., and Jan P. Nordbye, *The Complete History of Chrysler Corporation 1924–1985*, Publications International, Skokie, Ill., 1985.

Mechanical Engineering, "Chrysler's Automated Convalescence," vol. 109, no. 7, pp. 55–59, July 1987.

Moody's Industrial Manual, 1915, 1920, 1922, 1924, 1926, 1928, 1929, 1930, 1933, 1935, 1937, 1938, 1939, 1942, 1946, 1948, 1952, 1953, 1954, 1955, 1958, 1961, 1964, 1968, 1972, 1975, 1977, 1978, 1979, 1980, 1981, 1982, 1983, 1984, 1985, 1986.

Reich, Robert B., and John D. Donahue, *New Deals: The Chrysler Revival and the American System*, Times Books, New York, 1985.

Wards Automotive Yearbook, 1977, 1985.

White, Lawrence, J., *The Automobile Industry Since 1945*, Harvard University Press, Cambridge, Mass., 1971.

Zimmerman, Frederick M., "Turnaround—A Painful Learning Process," *Long Range Planning*, vol. 19, no. 4, August 1986.

Chapter 10

Abernathy, William J., Kim B. Clark, and Alan M. Kantrow, *Industrial Renaissance: Producing a Competitive Future for America*, Basic Books, New York, 1983.

Abodaher, David, *Iacocca: America's Most Dynamic Businessman*, Kensington, New York, 1985.

Allis-Chalmers Corporation, *1985 Annual Report*, Allis-Chalmers Corporation, Milwaukee, Wis., 1986.

Allis-Chalmers Corporation, *1984 Annual Report*, Allis-Chalmers Corporation, Milwaukee, Wis., 1985.

Allis-Chalmers Corporation, *1986 Form 10-K*, Allis-Chalmers Corporation, Milwaukee, Wis., 1986.

Allis-Chalmers Corporation, *1985 Form 10-K*, Allis-Chalmers Corporation, Milwaukee, Wis., 1986.

Allis-Chalmers Corporation, *1984 Form 10-K*, Allis-Chalmers Corporation, Milwaukee, Wis., 1986.

Allis-Chalmers Corporation, *News Release #105-87*, Allis-Chalmers Corporation, Milwaukee, Wis., 1987.

Allis-Chalmers Corporation, *News Release #106-87*, Allis-Chalmers Corporation, Milwaukee, Wis., 1987.

Allis-Chalmers Corporation, *News Release #116-87*, Allis-Chalmers Corporation, Milwaukee, Wis., 1987.

Argenti, John, *Corporate Collapse: Causes and Symptoms*, Wiley, New York, 1976.

Bhattacharyya, S. K., "Allis-Chalmers Manufacturing Company." (B) #9-170-024, Harvard Business School, Boston, 1969.

Chilton's Automotive Multi-Guide Spring 1931, Chilton, Radnor, Pa., 1970.

Chrysler, Walter P., *Life of an American Workman*, Dodd, Mead, New York, 1937.

Coleman, Richard N., and Keith W. Burnaham, "Milestones in the Application of Power to Agricultural Machines," *An Historical Perspective of Farm Machinery*, Society of Automotive Engineers, Milwaukee, Wis., 1980.

Crabb, Richard, *Birth of a Giant: The Men and Incidents That Gave America the Motorcar*, Chilton, New York, 1969.

Dykes, A. L., *Dyke's Automotive and Gasoline Engine Encyclopedia*, A. L. Dyke, St. Louis, 1946.

Fink, James J., *The Car Culture*, MIT Press, Cambridge, Mass., 1975.

Forbes, Bertie Charles, *Automotive Giants of America*, Books for Libraries Press, New York, 1972.

Gray, R. B., *The Agricultural Tractor: 1855–1950*, American Society of Agricultural Engineers, Saint Joseph, Mich., 1954.

Heasley, Jerry, *The Production Figure Book for U.S. Cars*, Motorbooks International, Osceola, Wis., 1977.

Hunt, R. Douglas, *American Farm Tools from Hand Power to Steam Power*, Sunflower University Press, Manhattan, Kan., 1985.

Huxley, Bill, *Allis-Chalmers: Agricultural Machinery*, Osprey, London, 1988.

Kennedy, E. D., *The Automobile Industry: The Coming of Age of Capitalism's Favorite Child*, Reynal & Hitchcock, New York, 1941.

Kimes, B. R., "Blueprints and Balance Sheets, The Company That Charlie Built," *Automobile Quarterly*, vol. XV, no. 2, Second quarter, 1977.

Kimes, B. R., and Henry Austin Clark, Jr., *The Standard Catalog of American Cars 1805–1942*, Krause, Iola, Wis., 1985.

Langworth, Richard M., and Jan P. Nordbye, *The Complete History of Chrysler Corporation 1924–1985*, Publications International, Skokie, Ill., 1985.

May, George S., *A Most Unique Machine: The Michigan Origins of the American Automobile Industry*, William B. Eerdmans, Grand Rapids, Mich., 1975.

Moody's Industrial Manual, 1915, 1920, 1922, 1924, 1926, 1928, 1929, 1930, 1933, 1935, 1937, 1938, 1939, 1942, 1946, 1948, 1952, 1953, 1954, 1955, 1958, 1961, 1964, 1968, 1972, 1975, 1977, 1978, 1979, 1980, 1981, 1982, 1983, 1984, 1985, 1986.

Nevins, Allan, *Ford: The Times, the Man, the Company*, Scribner, New York, 1954.

Peters, Thomas J., and Robert H. Waterman, *In Search of Excellence*, Harper, New York, 1982.

Peterson, Walter F., and C. Edward Weber, *An Industrial Heritage: Allis Chalmers Corporation*, Milwaukee County Historical Society, Milwaukee, Wis., 1978.

Pettigrew, Andrew W., *An Awakening Giant: Continuity and Change in Imperial Chemical Industries*, Basil Blackwell, New York, 1985.

Pfeffer, Jeffrey, *Power in Organizations*, Pittman, Boston, 1981.

Quinn, James Brian, *Strategies for Change: Logical Incrementalism*, Irwin, Homewood, Ill., 1980.

Rae, John B., *The American Automobile: A Brief History*, University of Chicago Press, Chicago, 1965.

Rae, John B., *The American Automobile Industry*, G. K. Hall, Boston, 1984.

Roberts, Peter, *The History of the Automobile*, Exeter, New York, 1984.

Sears, Stephen W., *The Automobile in America*, American Heritage, New York, 1977.

Seltzer, Lawrence, *The Financial History of the North American Automobile Industry,* Houghton Mifflin, Boston, 1928.

Slappey, Sterling G., *Pioneers of American Business,* Grosset & Dunlap, New York, 1970.

Smith, Philip H., *Wheels within Wheels; A Short History of American Motor Car Manufacturing,* Funk & Wagnalls, New York, 1968.

Society of Automotive Engineers, *An Historical Perspective of Farm Machinery,* SAE, Warrendale, Pa., 1980.

Steers, Richard M., and Lyman W. Porter, *Motivation and Work Behavior,* McGraw-Hill, New York, 1983.

Tichy, Noel M., *Managing Strategic Change: Technical, Political and Cultural Dynamics,* Wiley, New York, 1983.

U.S. Federal Trade Commission, *Report to the Seventy-Fourth Congress on the Agricultural Implement and Machinery Industry,* U.S. Government Printing Office, Washington, D.C., 1938.

U.S. Federal Trade Commission, *Report to the Seventy-Fourth Congress on the Motor Vehicle Industry,* U.S. Government Printing Office, Washington, D.C., 1938.

Chapter 11

Abernathy, William J., Kim B. Clark, and Alan M. Kantrow, *Industrial Renaissance: Producing a Competitive Future for America,* Basic Books, New York, 1983.

Allis-Chalmers Corporation, *1984 Annual Report,* Allis-Chalmers Corporation, Milwaukee, Wis., 1985.

Ansoff, I., *Corporate Strategy,* McGraw-Hill, New York, 1965.

Argenti, John, *Corporate Collapse: Causes and Symptoms,* Wiley, New York, 1976.

Automobile Manufacturers Association, *Automobiles of America,* Wayne State, Detroit, 1968.

Barnard, Chester, *The Functions of the Executive,* Harvard University Press, Cambridge, Mass., 1953, pp. 283–284.

Bibeault, Donald B., *Corporate Turnaround: How Managers Turn Losers into Winners,* McGraw-Hill, New York, 1982.

Bluestone, Barry, and Bennett Harrison, *The Deindustrialization of American Industry,* Basic Books, New York, 1982.

Brown, Arch, "Almost a Classic: 1932 Nash," *Special Interest Autos,* no. 66, Dec. 1981.

Cannon, William A., *Studebaker: The Complete Story,* TAB Books, Blue Ridge Summit, Pa., 1981.

Chilton's Automotive Multi-Guide Spring 1931, Chilton, Radnor, Pa., 1970.

Crabb, Richard, *Birth of a Giant: The Men and Incidents that Gave America the Motorcar,* Chilton, New York, 1969.

Craypo, Charles, "The Deindustrialization of a Factory Town: Plant Closings and Phasedowns in South Bend, Indiana, 1954–1983," in *Labor and Deindustrialization,* Donald Kennedy (ed.), Pennsylvania State University Department of Labor Studies, State College, Pa., 1984.

Dawes, Nathaniel T., *The Packard 1942–1962,* A. S. Barnes, New York, 1975.

Delbecq, Andre L., Andrew H. Van de Ven, and David H. Gustafson, *Group Techniques for Program Planning: A Guide to Nominal Group and Delphi Processes*, Greenbriar Press, Middleton, Wis., 1980.

Dykes, A. L., *Dyke's Automotive and Gasoline Engine Encyclopedia*, A. L. Dyke, St. Louis, 1946.

Edwards, Charles E., *Dynamics of the United States Automobile Industry*, University of South Carolina Press, Columbia, S.C., 1965.

Emerson, Harrington, "The First Principle — Clearly Defined Ideals," in *Classics in Management*, Harwood F. Merrill (ed.), American Management Associations, New York, 1960.

Erskine, Albert Russel, *History of the Studebaker Corporation*, The Studebaker Corporation, South Bend, Ind., 1924.

Erskine, Albert Russel, *History of the Studebaker Corporation*, The Studebaker Corporation, South Bend, Ind., 1918.

Fink, James J., *The Car Culture*, MIT Press, Cambridge, Mass., 1975.

Follett, Mary Parker, *Dynamic Administration*, Henry C. Metcalf and Lyndall Urwick (eds.), Harper, New York, 1941.

Forbes, Bertie Charles, *Automotive Giants of America*, Books for Libraries Press, New York, 1972.

Fortune, "Packard," January 1937. Reprinted in *Packard's International Motor Car Club*, vol. 18, no. 4, Winter 1981.

French, John R. P., and Bertram Raven, "The Bases of Social Power," *Studies in Social Power*, University of Michigan Press, Ann Arbor, Mich., 1959.

Hall, Asa E., and Richard M. Langworth, *The Studebaker Century: A National Heritage*, Hall & Langworth, South Bend, Ind., 1983.

Hall, William K., "Survival Strategies in a Hostile Environment," in *Survival Strategies for American Industry*, Wiley, New York, 1983.

Hambrick, D. C., and C. Schecter, "Turnaround Strategies for Mature Industrial Product Businesses," *Journal of Business Strategy*, Fall 1980.

Harbison, Frederick H., and Robert Dubin, *Patterns of Union-Management Relations: United Auto Workers*, (CIO, GENERAL MOTORS, STUDEBAKER), SRA, Chicago, 1947.

Hayes, Robert H., "Strategic Planning — Forward in Reverse," *Harvard Business Review*, Nov.–Dec. 1985.

Heasley, Jerry, *The Production Figure Book for U.S. Cars*, Motorbooks International, Osceola, Wis., 1977.

Kennedy, E. D., *The Automobile Industry: The Coming of Age of Capitalism's Favorite Child*, Reynal & Hitchcock, New York, 1941.

Kilmann, R. H. and I. I. Mitroff, "Qualitative versus Quantitative Analysis for Management Science: Different Forms of Psychological Types," *Interfaces*, vol. 6, no. 2, Feb. 1976.

Kimes, B. R., and Henry Austin Clark, Jr., *The Standard Catalog of American Cars 1805–1942*, Krause, Iola, Wis., 1985.

Kimes, B. R., and Richard M. Langworth, *Packard: A History of the Motor Car and the Company*, Princeton, Princeton, N.J., 1978.

Lindblom, Charles E., "The Science of Muddling Through," *Public Administration*, vol. 19, no. 2, 1959.

Mahoney, John Thomas, *The Story of George Romney: Builder, Salesman, Crusader,* Harper, New York, 1960.

March, James G., and Herbert A. Simon, *Organizations,* Wiley, New York, 1963.

May, George S., *A Most Unique Machine: The Michigan Origins of the American Automobile Industry,* William B. Eerdmans, Grand Rapids, Mich., 1975.

Mintzberg, Henry, "Patterns in Strategy Formulation," *Management Science,* vol. 24, no. 9, pp. 934–948, May 1978.

Moody's Industrial Manual, 1915, 1920, 1922, 1924, 1926, 1928, 1929, 1930, 1933, 1935, 1937, 1938, 1939, 1942, 1946, 1948, 1952, 1953, 1954, 1955, 1958, 1961, 1964, 1968, 1972, 1975, 1977, 1978, 1979, 1980, 1981, 1982, 1983, 1984, 1985, 1986.

Pettigrew, Andrew W., *An Awakening Giant: Continuity and Change in Imperial Chemical Industries,* Basil Blackwell, New York, 1985.

Pfeffer, Jeffrey, *Power in Organizations,* Pittman, Boston, 1981.

Quinn, James Brian, *Strategies for Change: Logical Incrementalism,* Irwin, Homewood, Ill., 1980.

Rae, John B., *The American Automobile Industry.* G. K. Hall, Boston, 1984.

Roberts, Peter, *The History of the Automobile,* Exeter, New York, 1984.

Schroeder, Otto A., *Packard: Ask the Man Who Owns One,* Post ERA Books, Arcaria, Calif., 1974.

Scott, Michael G. H., *Packard, The Complete Story,* TAB Books, Blue Ridge Summit, Pa., 1985.

Sears, Stephen W., *The Automobile in America,* American Heritage, New York, 1977.

Selznick, Philip, *Leadership in Administration: A Sociological Interpretation,* Harper, New York, 1957.

Smallzreid, Kathleen Ann, and Dorothy James Roberts, *More Than You Promise: A Business at Work in Society,* Harper, New York, 1942.

Smith, Philip H., *Wheels within Wheels; A Short History of American Motor Car Manufacturing,* Funk & Wagnalls, New York, 1968.

Tichy, Noel M., *Managing Strategic Change: Technical, Political and Cultural Dynamics,* Wiley, New York, 1983.

Tushman, Michael L., and Elaine Romanelli, "Organization Evolution: A Metamorphosis Model of Convergence and Reorientation," in *Research in Organization Behavior,* vol. 7, L. L. Cummings and Barry M. Staw (eds.), JAI Press, Greenwich, Conn., 1985.

U.S. Federal Trade Commission, *Report to the Seventy-Fourth Congress on the Motor Vehicle Industry,* U.S. Government Printing Office, Washington, D.C., 1938.

Van de Ven, Andrew H., "Problem Solving, Planning and Innovation. Part I. Test of the Program Planning Model," *Human Relations,* vol. 33, no. 10, 1980).

Van de Ven, Andrew H., "Problem Solving, Planning and Innovation. Part II. Speculations for Theory and Practice," *Human Relations,* vol. 33, no. 10, 1980.

Wards Automotive Yearbook, 1977, 1985.

White, Lawrence J., *The Automobile Industry Since 1945,* Harvard University Press, Cambridge, Mass., 1971.

Zimmerman, Frederick M., "Turnaround—A Painful Learning Process," *Long Range Planning,* Aug. 1986.

Chapter 12

Barnard, Chester I., *The Functions of the Executive,* Harvard University Press, Cambridge, Mass., 1968.

Barnard, Chester I., *Organization and Management,* Harvard University Press, Cambridge, Mass., 1948.

Behling, O., and F. A. Starke, "The Postulates of Expectancy Theory," *Academy of Management Journal,* vol. 16, pp. 373–388, 1973.

Broehl, Wayne G., Jr., *John Deere's Company,* Doubleday, New York, 1984.

Business Week, "The Hollow Corporation," no. 2935, March 3, 1986.

Chandler, Alfred D., *Strategy and Structure,* MIT Press, Cambridge, Mass., 1962.

Coleman, Richard N., and Keith W. Burnaham, "Milestones in the Application of Power to Agricultural Machines," *An Historical Perspective of Farm Machinery,* Society of Automotive Engineers, Milwaukee, Wis., 1980.

Cooper, Arnold C., and Dan Schendel, "Strategic Responses to Technological Threats," *Business Horizons,* Feb. 1976.

Dawes, Nathaniel T., *The Packard 1942–1962,* Baines, New York, 1975.

Emerson, Harrington, *The Twelve Principles of Efficiency,* Hive Publishing Company, Easton, Pa., 1976 (first printed in 1911).

Follett, Mary Parker, *Dynamic Administration,* Henry C. Metcalf and Lyndall Urwick (eds.), Harper, New York, 1941.

Fortune, "Deere & Co," Aug. 1936.

Fortune, "Packard," June 1937. Reprinted in *Packard's International Motor Car Club,* vol. 18, no. 4, Winter 1981.

Gantt, Henry L., *Industrial Leadership,* Yale University Press, New Haven, Conn., 1916.

Gantt, Henry L., "The Parting of the Ways," in *Classics in Management,* Harwood F. Merrill (ed.), American Management Associations, New York, 1960, pp. 151–160.

Gantt, Henry L., "Training Workmen in Habits of Industry and Cooperation," in *Classics in Management,* Harwood F. Merrill (ed.), American Management Associations, New York, 1960.

Gilbreth, Frank B., "Science in Management for the One Best Way to Do Work," in *Classics in Management,* Harwood F. Merrill (ed.), American Management Associations, New York, 1960.

Gilbreth, Lillian M., *The Psychology of Management,* Macmillan, New York, 1919.

Gray, R. B., *The Agricultural Tractor: 1855–1950,* American Society of Agricultural Engineers, Saint Joseph, Mich., 1954.

Hamner, W. Clay, "Reinforcement Theory and Contingency Management in Organizational Settings," in *Motivation and Work Behavior,* Richard M. Steers and Lyman W. Porter (eds.), McGraw-Hill, New York, 1983.

Hamner, W. Clay, Jerry Ross, and Barry M. Staw, "Motivation in Organizations: The Need for a New Direction," in *Motivation and Work Behavior*, Richard M. Steers and Lyman W. Porter (eds.), McGraw-Hill, New York, 1983.

Latham, Gary P., and Edwin A. Locke, "Goal Setting—A Motivational Technique That Works," *Organizational Dynamics*, pp. 68–80, Autumn 1979.

Locke, Edwin A., "The Ubiquity of the Technique of Goal Setting in Theories of and Approaches to Employee Motivation," *Academy of Management Review*, vol. 3, no. 3, pp. 594–601, July 1978.

Locke, E., D. B. Feren, V. M. McCaleb, K. N. Shaw, and A. T. Denny, "The Relative Effectiveness of Four Methods of Motivating Employee Performance," in *Changes in Working Life*, K. D. Duncan, D. Wallis, and M. M. Gruneberg (eds.), Wiley, Chichester, England, 1980.

Marsh, Barbara, *A Corporate Tragedy: The Agony of International Harvester Company*, Doubleday, Garden City, N.Y., 1985.

Miner, John B., *Theories of Organization Behavior*, Dryden, Hinsdale, Ill., 1980.

Moody's Industrial Manual, 1915, 1920, 1922, 1924, 1926, 1928, 1929, 1930, 1933, 1935, 1937, 1938, 1939, 1942, 1946, 1948, 1952, 1953, 1954, 1955, 1958, 1961, 1964, 1968, 1972, 1975, 1977, 1978, 1979, 1980, 1981, 1982, 1983, 1984, 1985, 1986.

Mooney, James D., and Alan C. Riley, *The Principles of Organization*, Harper, New York, 1939.

Naylor, James C., Robert D. Pritchard, Daniel R. Illgen, *A Theory of Behavior in Organizations*, Academic Press, New York, 1980.

Selznick, Philip, *Leadership in Administration: A Sociological Interpretation*, Harper & Row, New York, 1957.

Sheldon, Oliver, "A Professional Creed for Management," in *Classics In Management*, Merrill F. Harwood (ed.), American Management Association, New York, 1960.

Society of Automotive Engineers, *An Historical Perspective of Farm Machinery*, SAE, Warrendale, Pa., 1980.

Taylor, Frederick W., *Scientific Management*, Harper, New York, 1911, 1947.

Taylor, Frederick W., *Shop Management*, Harper, New York, 1919.

Trist, Eric, "Referent Organizations and the Development of Inter-Organizational Domains," *Human Relations*, vol. 36, no. 3, 1983.

U.S. Federal Trade Commission, *Report to the Seventy-Fourth Congress on the Agricultural Implement and Machinery Industry*, U.S. Government Printing Office, Washington, D.C., 1938.

Zimmerman, Frederick M, "Managing a Successful Turnaround," *Long Range Planning*, vol. 22, no. 3, June 1989.

Zimmerman, Frederick M., "Turnaround a Painful Learning Process," *Long Range Planning*, vol. 19, no. 4, Aug. 1986.

Chapter 13

Abernathy, William J., Kim B. Clark, and Alan M. Kantrow, *Industrial Renaissance: Producing a Competitive Future for America*, Basic Books, New York, 1983.

Abodaher, David, *Iacocca: America's Most Dynamic Businessman,* Kensington, New York, 1985.

Broehl, Wayne G., Jr., *John Deere's Company,* Doubleday, New York, 1984.

Chrysler, Walter P., *Life of an American Workman,* Dodd, Mead, New York, 1937.

Edwards, Charles E., *Dynamics of the United States Automobile Industry,* University of South Carolina Press, Columbia, S.C., 1965.

Emerson, Harrington, "The First Principle — Clearly Defined Ideals," in *Classics in Management,* Harwood F. Merrill (ed.), American Management Associations, New York, 1960.

Forbes, Bertie Charles, *Automotive Giants of America,* Books for Libraries Press, New York, 1972.

Fortune, "Packard," June 1937. Reprinted in *Packard's International Motor Car Club,* vol. 18, no. 4, Winter 1981.

Gilbreth, Lillian M., *The Psychology of Management,* Macmillan, New York, 1919.

Hall, William K., "Survival Strategies in a Hostile Environment," *Survival Strategies for American Industry,* Wiley, New York, 1983.

Hofer, C. W., "Turnaround Strategies," *Journal of Business Strategy,* Summer 1980.

Leland, Mrs. Wilfred C., and Minnie Dubbs Millbrook, *Master of Precision — Henry M. Leland,* Wayne State University Press, Detroit, 1966.

Miner, John B., *Theories of Organization Behavior,* The Dryden Press, Hinsdale, Ill., 1980.

Mooney, James D., and Alan C. Riley, *The Principles of Organization,* Harper, New York, 1939.

O'Niell, Hugh M., "Turnaround and Recovery: What Strategy Do You Need," *Long Range Planning,* vol. 19, no. 1, 1986.

O'Niell, Hugh M., *Turnaround Strategies in the Commercial Banking Industry,* UMI Research Press, Ann Arbor, Mich., 1981.

Porter, Michael E., *Competitive Strategy,* Free Press, New York, 1980.

Quinn, James Brian, *Strategies for Change: Logical Incrementalism,* Irwin, Homewood, Ill., 1980.

Schendel, D., and G. R. Patton, "Corporate Stagnation and Turnaround," *Journal of Economics and Business,* Summer 1976.

Schendel, D., G. R. Patton, and J. Riggs, "Corporate Turnaround Strategies: A Study of Profit Decline and Recovery," *Journal of General Management,* Spring 1976.

Taylor, Bernard, "Turnaround, Recovery and Growth: The Way through the Crises," *Journal of General Management,* Winter 1982/1983.

Taylor, Frederick W., *Scientific Management,* Harper, New York, 1911, 1947.

Tichy, Noel M., *Managing Strategic Change: Technical, Political and Cultural Dynamics,* Wiley, New York, 1983.

Tushman, Michael L., and Elaine Romanelli, "Organization Evolution: A Metamorphosis Model of Convergence and Reorientation," in *Research in Organization Behavior,* vol. 7, L. L. Cummings and Barry M. Staw (eds.), JAI Press, Greenwich, Conn., 1985.

Chapter 14

Edwards, Charles E., *Dynamics of the United States Automobile Industry*, University of South Carolina Press, Columbia, S.C., 1965.

Hayes, Robert H., and William J. Abernathy, "Managing Our Way to Economic Decline," *Harvard Business Review*, vol. 58, no.14, July–Aug. 1980.

Kettering, Charles F., An informal recording of Kettering's speech on the *100th Anniversary of the Birth of Thomas A. Edison*.

Marsh, Barbara, *A Corporate Tragedy: The Agony of International Harvester Company*, Doubleday, Garden City, N.Y., 1985.

Chapter 15

Argenti, John, *Corporate Collapse: Causes and Symptoms*, Wiley, New York, 1976.

Lawrence, Paul R., and Davis Dyer, *Renewing American Industry*, Free Press, New York, 1983.

Index

About the Author

Frederick M. Zimmerman is the director of graduate
programs in manufacturing systems engineering for the
University of St. Thomas in St. Paul, Minnesota. Prior to
joining St. Thomas full time in 1985, he spent more than 25
years in industry as an engineer, manager, vice president,
and president. In addition, he has managed several
turnarounds and served on the boards of directors of 10
corporations. Mr. Zimmerman earned his Ph.D. in
management from the University of Minnesota and has
written a number of articles for professional journals,
including *Long Range Planning* and *The Journal of
Applied Manufacturing Systems*.